THE ITALIAN ACHIEVEMENT

AN A-Z OF OVER 1000 'FIRSTS' ACHIEVED BY
ITALIANS IN ALMOST EVERY ASPECT OF LIFE
OVER THE LAST 1000 YEARS

Arturo barone was born in London in 1933 of Neapolitan parents, but from the age of six lived and studied in Rome where he took his first law degree. He married his wife, Laura, (who comes from Turin) in 1963. They have three children and five grandchildren. After his studies in Rome, he read law at the University of London and was called to the Bar in 1961. In 1967 he became a practising solicitor and made international law a speciality, including Italian law. Arturo Barone is also the author of *The Comfort of Sin* (1995) and *The Divorce Dilemma* (2000), under his pen-name James Goodall.

The Italian Achievement

AN A-Z OF OVER 1000 'FIRSTS'
ACHIEVED BY ITALIANS
IN ALMOST EVERY ASPECT OF LIFE
OVER THE LAST 1000 YEARS

FOURTH EDITION
[Previously published as 'Italians First!']

Arturo Barone

RENAISSANCE BOOKS
FOLKESTONE, KENT

THE ITALIAN ACHIEVEMENT
AN A-Z OF OVER 1000 'FIRSTS' ACHIEVED BY ITALIANS
IN ALMOST EVERY ASPECT OF LIFE OVER THE LAST 1000 YEARS
4th Edition [previously published as 'Italians First!'] published 2007

Original edition 1989 published as 'Italians First!' by
Paul Norbury Publications Ltd

Second Edition 1994 and Third Edition 1999 published as 'Italians First!' by
Renaissance Books

Renaissance Books is an imprint of
Global Books Ltd
PO Box 219, Folkestone, Kent CT20 2WP

© Arturo Barone 2007

ISBN 978-1-898823-55-1

British Library Cataloguing in Publication Data
A CIP catalogue entry for this book is available
from the British Library

Set in Garamond by Bookman, Slough, Berkshire
Printed in England by The Cromwell Press Ltd, Trowbridge, Wiltshire

CONTENTS

Section 8: Sport & Leisure

Section 9: Transport & Travel

PART II: REFLECTIONS ON ITALY AND THE ITALIANS

PREFACE

I am often asked whether I feel that, brilliant though Italian efforts have been since the year AD 1000, as I have tried to demonstrate, the rot has now set in and Italy, especially after the Second World War, has not been able to produce very much other than a succession of weak, incapable governments, made up of numerous parties with fanciful names.

I believe that to be an over-simplification. There is obviously much in present-day Italy which does not work well, or which is objectionable and unpleasant. I should like to single out a few factors which I consider significant.

Nobody can rejoice at the Americanization of the country and at the repetitive, puerile, abject and unnecessary use of Anglo-American words and expressions where there is a perfectly valid Italian equivalent. As Sir Francis Bacon reminds us, it is not we who manage words, it is words that control us: the importation and use of Anglo-American expressions impacts not only on the language and on some of the day-to-day customs of the Italians but, above all, on their psyche.

The employment by Italians of such language, mannerisms and even syntax – apart from representing a shameful betrayal of our cultural traditions – affects not only radio and television announcers, presenters and advertisers but also a number of newspapermen and, with very few exceptions, most politicians, two classes who, in my view at least, ought to know better. The result is a tragic combination of linguistic snobbery and historical irresponsibility.

The fashion – for that is what it is – can be traced back to 1945 when the Allies 'liberated' Italy. Probably the classic in this context (if not the first such word used) is 'sciusciá' – an invention by Neapolitan urchins to describe the small service of shoe-polishing (shoeshine) which they rendered to the troops in return for a few coins or a handful of cigarettes. For that, the poor must be forgiven, above all since they unwittingly showed some remnant of linguistic dignity by converting the English expression into something Italian both in sound and in appearance. Whereas present-day Italians cannot be forgiven, because they have swallowed the 'cultural import' pill hook, line and sinker.

Furthermore, whilst I appreciate that religion today, even in Italy, has less impact on the lives of ordinary people than it used to have, say, before the Second World War, I must nevertheless ask myself whether it is really necessary to give Italian children names like Max, Kevin, Shirley, Deborah, Christian, Tony,

Kim, Jenny, Joe, Suzy, Mandy, Hilary, etc. (there are more!), thus countering a long-established practice that children could only be baptized with the name of saints.

Even so, it has to be said that the Italians continue to be topical. Leaving aside their undoubted gastronomic and stylistic dominance, the mere fact that Italian words are chosen to publicize motor cars, fashions, or in forms of address, is indicative that the country has still not died. I could not help smiling when I learnt quite recently that in Tokyo, of all places, a district which is the hub of the activities of architects and builders is known as 'collezione'. . . .

Shortly before the present edition went to press my friend and editor, Paul Norbury, asked me whether I had cause to alter any of the (far too many . . .) highly personal judgements made by me ever since the first edition of 1989. Food for thought, perhaps; but having digested the concept, I say in all candour that I do not recoil from any of my observations or digressions; on the contrary, the intervening years have strengthened the beliefs that influenced them.

For the record, however, I must correct the following factual statements made by me in previous editions, as they can no longer be supported.

In the first place, whilst I had boasted (in the first edition) of the fact that 90% of Italians voted in general elections, I should point out that this figure has now reduced quite substantially to something between 65% and 70%. As democracy becomes much more acceptable, so do the Italians realize that their innate suspicion of politicians is more than justified; hence their increased scepticism and abstention from voting.

Second, influenced by my own background, I had placed great importance on the Italian family. The ongoing 'emancipation' of women and the introduction of divorce in Italy have, however, exacted their toll on the family. Italy's population is currently 58.5 million. In 2004, 260,000 marriages were registered, whereas figures published in October 2005 show that this had reduced to 250,000. Today, more people tend to cohabit either before they marry or without marrying at all; the word 'single' to describe a fashionable status is now in everyday use in Italy where two out of ten 'families' consist of single parents, 82% of whom are women.

The divorce rate – per 1,000 persons in the population – has grown in Italy from 0.3 in 1983 to 0.7 in 2005. Slowly rising compared to other countries, but inexorably (equivalent 2005 figures for the US and the UK are 4.0 and 2.7).

These facts alone are beginning to change the perception that Italians have always had of the family unit and, when compared to the Anglo-American and the German/Scandinavian world, it remains surprisingly strong. Its impact is being constantly eroded at the same time as the powers of the state (of surveillance, interference) continue to increase. (The current excuse, of course, is the threat of terrorism; real though such threat is, it is no more serious than in any other country.)

Nor should one underestimate the damaging effects on Italian society of the consumption of illegal drugs (cocaine in particular) as well as the rather unfortunate habit amongst youngsters of imbibing alcohol to excess from an early age. Statistics published in November 2005 claim that increasing numbers of Italian youngsters start taking (and abusing) strong alcoholic drinks at the age of eleven, and there are at least 800,000 under the age of sixteen already addicted to alcohol. It comes hardly as a surprise to learn from the same statistics that no less than seven million Italians could, by certain definitions, be termed alcoholics. Not a pretty picture; but not unusual in the Western world.

Despite all this, there is still hope, especially whilst our gastronomic excellence and style continue to be acknowledged. As I have mentioned in the text, Italy has seen off most of its invaders throughout more than 2,000 years of history; in fact, it has successfully gone on to educate them, in many more ways than anyone may wish to acknowledge. Whether it will be able to deal as effectively with exasperated feminism, political correctness and American influence remains to be seen.

ARTURO BARONE
Bovingdon, Summer 2006

NOTE ON THE NEW TITLE

Finally, I should like to add that, given that this is actually the fourth edition of *Italians First!* (first published in 1989), now containing over one thousand entries, I was persuaded by my editor to celebrate the fact with a name change – *The Italian Achievement* being a more suitable book title, he argued, for a sourcebook of such enhanced significance. I leave the reader to be the judge.

PREFACE TO THE THIRD EDITION

I am truly delighted that the third edition of *Italians First!* is now in print. The book first emerged (in hardback) in 1989. At that time my rather limited researches had identified some 400 'firsts'. With more work on my part, but above all with the assistance of readers from all parts of the world, the number of 'firsts' increased to over 500, and this, together with the growing interest in things Italian, prompted publication in 1994 of an updated paperback edition, abridged as to text, but containing a number of additional and rather notable new 'firsts', such as the fax machine, which had not been included in the original volume.

In the intervening four years, a further 300 'firsts' have come to light, with a particular emphasis on the Italian contribution in the field of medicine. See, for example, the anticipation by Professor Bizzozzero, at the end of the nineteenth century, of the correct diagnosis of gastric ulcers.

The significance of the Italian contributions in a variety of contexts, and not merely at an educational level, is now so great that the publishers felt that a more encyclopaedic approach should be adopted in the presentation of the present work. I am confident that the revised text and layout will please all those readers who, from time to time, have tried to, and obviously succeeded in remedying my deficiencies in research; above all, it will make a contribution to what appears to me to be an ever-growing worldwide interest about Italy and the Italians.

What struck me in particular over the past ten years is how topical Italians and their approach to life have become. I do not mean that people did not know that we made Ferrari motor cars or composed beautiful operas. It is now an indisputable fact that, wherever you look, the Italian impact is more and more noticeable. In the field of gastronomy, the reliance on pizza, pasta, and the innumerable varieties of coffee, combined with ingredients which could not possibly have been considered, even as early as twenty years ago, is very great indeed. Whether in England or indeed in the United States, Australia and Japan, in France or in Germany, or in South East Asia, it is difficult to conceive of family life where pizza, pasta, espresso and cappuccino do not figure to some degree, if not prominently.

Ironically, it is perhaps the success of the Italians at the gastronomic level that distracts attention from what we have achieved in many other spheres of life. I hope that this book redresses the balance. Obviously, there is nothing wrong in teaching the rest of the world how to eat well: quite the reverse. By improving people's diet, we are inevitably making them healthier, and therefore, in all likelihood, happier. As a consequence, at least in theory, their sex life ought to improve, and they might be able to prosper without any need for Viagra. But we have done a lot more than teaching people to eat well and be merry. Above all, it is the Italian approach to life and style which creates the particular aura which appeals to so many. I rest my case.

ARTURO BARONE

London, October 1998

ACKNOWLEDGEMENTS

To list all the people who have been of help to me in compiling this work would take too long, particularly given the substantial assistance that I have received in preparing the second and, above all, the third editions. They range from my schoolteachers, to whom I am indebted for a broad classical education, to Elio Nissim for his unfailing encouragement, to my elder son Franco for checking the various references, to my younger son Paolo for his work on the Index, and more recently, to H.E. The Italian Ambassador in London, Dr Paolo Galli, to Margherita Moscogiuri, and to Angelo Cipullo.

Of the writers who have gone before me, I should mention Luigi Barzini because, essentially, he put the Italians so to say on the literary map of the general reader in a particular manner and in inimitable style. His analysis of them is quite perceptive, although not always faultless.

I am almost equally indebted to Stendhal but for a completely different reason. He loved Italy and its inhabitants so much that his love has served to reassure me that we can't be all that bad, because if a Frenchman loves an Italian, then there must be more to the Italians than meets the eye. I have always subscribed to the view that on the whole the French don't really like the Italians; but then, neither do we like the French too much either. The greater affinity amongst the Mediterranean people as far as Italians are concerned lies with the Greeks and not with either the French or the Spanish. The common language bond with these last two peoples does not make up for many fundamental differences in temperament and outlook.

I owe a great deal to John Addington Symonds. His hymn of glory to the Italian Renaissance was a great boost for my ego; his occasional analyses of the Italian temperament are perfectly accurate. My debt to him is indeed notable.

My thanks go to Francesco Sperotto for reading the book in its entirety. It is due to him that the text has benefited from many improvements, clarifications, and some additional 'firsts'.

Furthermore, I must acknowledge an even greater debt to all my friends, particularly my English friends who have enabled me to put things in a better perspective.

Lastly, I am grateful to my family because they actually provoked me into putting pen to paper. But the views expressed by me are not necessarily shared by them. . .

INTRODUCTION
On (Re)Discovering Italy and the Italians

In the pages that follow, it is my intention to offer a totally different picture of the Italians from that which normally springs to mind. The popular stereotype projects an exceptionally pleasant and easy image of Italy and the Italians but inevitably it is rather superficial. I hasten to add, however, that it is not entirely the fault of other nationalities that such an image prevails; in my view, the Italians themselves have to carry a great deal of responsibility for it.

Yet the image is almost an inevitable one, as it emerges from attitudes, patterns of behaviour and way of life which in themselves are very easy. After all, who would expect the Italians to be a complicated people, capable of anything exceptional, when they have with so much ease and success provided the world with 'spaghetti', 'pizza', 'vino', 'la dolce vita', Ferrari motor cars, etc. All these things are so pleasant and so universally acceptable that the Italians themselves must, by definition, be a pleasant and likeable people; but they cannot be capable of anything very great. On the contrary, I believe the data that I have presented in my own 'mini encyclopaedia' of Italian 'firsts' will convince you beyond any doubt that the Italians are a great and remarkably inventive people. Not unlike the English.

Furthermore, I intend to demonstrate that the contribution made by Italians to world knowledge and well-being is very substantial indeed, if not unique. I am reluctant myself to qualify it by saying that it is the greatest in the world, or the second best, or whatever. I shall leave that judgement to you.

It is, of course, true that we all have a mental picture of other cultures. We associate different races with different results and outlooks to our own. Most of the time this process of association is inevitable because we all, to some extent, live by generalizations. But it is not always meaningful.

Let me give you an example. It is a commonly-held view that we associate the English with reserve, democracy and an empire. In my experience, however, English reserve evaporates under the influence of alcohol. At the moment, English democracy is under a certain amount of pressure and the empire, as everybody knows, has gone.

Incidentally, I should make the point straight away that, for the sake of simplicity, I refer throughout to 'England' and the 'English', meaning 'Britain' and the 'British'. This is imprecise, but convenient, since many foreigners also use the word 'England' indiscriminately. Any remark I make about England and its inhabitants, therefore, should be understood as including also the Scots, the Welsh and, to a lesser degree, the communities of Northern Ireland. Most people tend to associate the French with high fashion and first-class cuisine. It seems to me that very few people nowadays can afford the former and indeed, when it comes to it, Italian fashions at the moment, at least for the man in the street, are a great deal more popular than French fashions; and when it comes to the latter, you will find that the French learnt it from us. Indeed, anyone who frequents restaurants as a matter of course, knows only too well that, at least as far as London is concerned, Italian or even Chinese or other restaurants provide better food than the French.

I believe the man in the street will associate Germans with militarism and efficiency. A cynic would remark that, despite both of these traits, they managed to lose two world wars and it is conceivable that today the Japanese are proving themselves more efficient.

One could go on generalizing and the exercise would not be too productive, for there are absurdities in the patterns of behaviour of most people. But as regards the Italians, because of generalizations about them, I think it is fair to say that they are the most misunderstood people in Europe.

To an Englishman, for example, the typical Italian is a short, black-haired, romantic with a more or less lovely voice, who is either a gigoló, a waiter, an ice-cream vendor or a footballer, and goes around pinching girls' bottoms. The Italian woman is a large, pasta-eating person, with many 'bambinos', who slaves away in the kitchen.

Both pictures are a travesty of reality and lead to much misunderstanding. For example, contrary to popular belief, Italian men are anything but romantic; they do not pinch girls' bottoms, although they may caress them; present-day Italian families are anything but large; Italian women may or may not be fat, etc., etc.

It is a pity, of course, that the Italians should be so misunderstood for, as I have said, their contributions to civilization and the quality of life have been very great indeed. The most modern authority in this regard is Luigi Barzini whose book *The Italians*, published in 1964 is, to me at any rate, the most perceptive study of his fellow countrymen I have encountered so far. Let me quote from its introduction:

'One of the sources of confusion was the absurd discrepancy between the quantity and dazzling array of the inhabitants' achievements through many centuries and the mediocre quality of their national history. Italians have impressively filled Europe and most of the world with the fame of their larger-than-life-size famous men. Italian architects and masons built part of the Kremlin in Moscow and the Winter Palace in Leningrad; Italian artists have embellished the Capitol in Washington. They have strewn churches, princely palaces, and stately villas all over Catholic Europe, especially in Vienna, Madrid, Prague and Warsaw; their influence on architecture was felt almost everywhere else, exterior architecture, to be sure, designed to impress and please the onlooker more than to serve strictly practical purposes. They have filled South America with ornate and rhetorical monuments to the local heroes.

'Italy's smaller contributions to everyday life are so numerous as to go unnoticed. There would be no pistols but for the city of Pistoia; no savon in France but for the city of Savona; no faience anywhere but for the city of Faenza; no millinery but for the city of Milan; no blue jeans but for Genes, the city of Genoa, where the blue cotton cloth was first produced, and no Genoa jibs; no Neapolitan ice-cream, no Roman candles, no Venetian blinds, no Bologna sausages, no Parmesan cheese, no Leghorn hens. Italians have discovered America for the Americans; taught poetry, statesmanship, and the rules of trade to the English; military art to the Germans; cuisine to the French; acting and ballet dancing to the Russians; and music to everybody. If some day this world of ours should be turned into a cloud of radioactive dust in space, it will be by nuclear contrivances developed with the aid of Italian scientists.'

And I add:

'There would be no America but for Amerigo Vespucci who gave his name to it. No Ancona hens but for the town of Ancona where they originated. No 'apostle spoons' but for the practice of wealthy Venetians and Tuscans to offer as the ideal baptismal gift a spoon whose handle would bear the figure of the child's patron saint. No artichokes but for the Italian 'articiocco' (which we, in turn, got from the Spaniards – 'alcachofa' – who got it from the Arabs – 'al-kharshuf'). No ballet but for the Italian verb 'ballare'. No 'baloney', said to have originated, perhaps, as a mark of disapproval, because it was alleged that some Bologna sausages were made with the skin and other parts of donkeys. . . No bankrupt or bankruptcy but for the Italian 'banca rotta'. No 'banks' but for the Italian 'banco' or 'banca' meaning 'bench', early Italian bankers conducting their business on benches in the streets. No 'belladonna lily' but for the fact that Italian women of the Renaissance used belladonna as eye make-up. No Boscobel House in Shropshire for Charles II to hide after the Battle of Worcester, but for the Italian 'bosco bello' (fair wood). No 'buffoons' but for the Italian 'Buffone'. No burlesque but for the Italian 'burla'. No 'Caesar's salad' but for Cesare Cardini who first entered it in his Tijuana Restaurant called Caesar's Palace. No 'callabra', a card game, but for the Calabria region of Italy, where it originated in the early-nineteenth century. No 'campana' form to describe a particular shape of wine coolers, usually in silver with vine leaf decorations. No 'campanula' flowers, no 'campanology' (the study or ringing of bells) and no 'campanulate' shape but for the Italian 'campana' (bell). No 'cannons' but for the Italian word 'cannone' meaning a large bamboo. No cantaloup(e) melons but for the town of Cantalupo, near Rome, a papal villa, where they were first found. No carbines but for the carabin soldiers from Calabria. No carnivals anywhere in the world but for the Italian 'carnevale', originally 'carnelevare', i.e. going without meat throughout Lent. No 'Carrara' marble to describe a particular kind of marble, especially favoured by Michelangelo, but for the city of Carrara in Tuscany. No 'carousel' but for the Neopolitan word 'carusiello', meaning originally a ball of clay for games in the shape of a young boy's ('caruso') head. No 'cassino', another card game for two, three or four players, and no gambling 'casino' or 'casinò' but for the diminutive of the Italian noun 'casa'. No 'confetti' to toss over the bride and groom, but for the plural of the Italian word 'confetto', a sweet meat, traditionally a small candy thrown in Italy during carnivals.

No 'Cremona bolts', used in building and woodwork, but for the Italian town where they were first manufactured. No 'cremone' in France, the type of locking system used there on windows and doors, but for the city of Cremona, where they originated. No dantesque but for Dante, the great Italian poet. No Diocletian windows but for Palladio who revived their use in the sixteenth century.

No Fallopian tubes but for Fallopio who discovered them. No 'fetta' (or 'Feta') cheese but for the equivalent Italian noun adapted by the Greeks to describe an essential part of their well-known salads. No 'Florentines' pastries to enjoy at tea or coffee time but for the city of Florence where they originated. No florins but for Florence where they were first minted in 1252. No 'Florence fennel', the plant with a bulbous root tasting of anise, but for the city of the arts after which it is named. No 'francolin' birds (a kind of partridge) but for the Italian 'francolino'. No 'French Riviera' for many Brits to flock over to but for the Italian noun (which is also used to describe the coastline that runs from Ventimiglia to La Spezia). No 'fumaroles', the air vents on volcanoes which look so picturesque at a distance, but for the Italian noun 'fumarola'. No 'Fustanella' (the white skirt) for Greek menfolk and soldiers to wear but for the Italian 'Fustagno', the coarse cloth from which the fustanellas originated. No galvanometer but for Galvani who invented it. No garibaldi biscuits but for Garibaldi, the Italian national hero. No 'Garibaldi fish' off the coast of the Western USA but for the colour of Garibaldi's red shirts. No gazettes but for the Gazetta, in Italy a small coin and later a newspaper.

No 'Génoise', the two-, three- or four-tier house tiling typical of Provençal roofing, but for the city of Genoa, where they originated. No 'Genoa' cake but for the town that gave it its name. No 'ghetto' but for the name of the small Venetian island where Jews were relegated during an epidemic many centuries ago, the noun now being used generally in a number of languages. No 'girandole' to describe a particular kind of wall/over mantel mirror, or jewellery, etc. but for the Italian 'girandola' a word used to describe, amongst many other things, a catherine wheel and a toy windmill. No Imprest system for the handling of petty cash floats or government lending but for the Italian book-keeping practice and the verb for 'imprestare' from which the Anglo-American equivalents are derived. No 'italic' script but for the 'aldine' types of Italy's Aldo Manuzio, who invented them. No jacuzzi but for Candido Jacuzzi who invented it and gave his name to it. No jerusalem artichokes (which have nothing to do with Israel) but for a contraction from the Italian 'girasole' meaning sunflower (a plant of the sunflower family). No Justerini and Brooks ('JB Whisky') but for Giacomo Justerini of Bologna who founded the well-known firm of wine merchants in the early-eighteenth century. No 'Lazzaretto' to prevent contagion but for the Venetians who set up the first isolation unit in 1423. No 'Leghorn Straw', namely a died and bleached straw of an Italian variety of wheat, which gave its name to hats made from the particular fabric. No lens but for the Italian 'lenticchie' meaning lentils, as Italians used to call glass eye discs (they were, in fact, so referred to for more than 200 years). No Lipizzaner horses but for the town of Lipizza near Trieste. No Lombardy Poplars but for the region of Italy from whence they originate. No 'Lotto Carpets', pile rugs hand-woven in Turkey, but for the 'publicity' given to them through the frequent representations in many paintings by the sixteenth century Venetian, Lorenzo Lotto.

No 'macaroons' and no 'Macaroni Penguins' but for the Italian 'maccheroni'. No 'maccaronic' verses but for the ancient Italian 'maccarone' (nowadays 'maccherone', a type of pasta). No machiavellian thoughts but for Machiavelli, the founder of political science. No 'madrepore corals' but for the Italian 'madre pora'. No madrigals but for the Latin/Italian 'matricale'. No magenta colours but for the bloodshed of 1859 at the Battle of Magenta during the Second War for Italian Independence. No Maiolica but for the style that the Italians gave to a particular kind of ceramic decoration which they got from the Arabs through Mallorca (Majorca or Majolica). No 'malaria' but for the Italian 'bad air – mal aria'. No 'mantelletta' for Roman Catholic priests to wear but for the equivalent Italian noun. No mantuas but for the town of Mantova (Mantua) famous for its silks in the seventeenth and eighteenth centuries. No maraschino liqueur for fruit salads but for the marasca cherry, an Italian variety. No marconigram but for Marconi who discovered radio. No Marco Polo sheep but for the Italian traveller who gave them his name. No 'martini' cocktails for barmen and drinkers to enthuse over but for the firm of Martini & Rossi of Turin who made

Vermouth so popular. No marzipan sweets or cake toppings but for the 'marzapane' that came out of Sicily. No 'Milan faience' and no 'Milanese lace' but for Milan from whence it came. No 'millefiori glass' but for the equivalent Italian noun. No 'millinery' but for the city of Milan which in the eighteenth century was the major producer of bonnets and hats, so much so that all women's headware were classified under this heading (in fact, a 'Milaner' craftsman was turned (in English) into a milliner). No Morello cherries or jam but for 'morello' from 'moro' meaning dark. No Norma Major (the wife of the British Prime Minister) but for the Italian librettist Felice Romani, who plucked the name out of the air as the title for his libretto of Bellini's opera. No 'ocarina' the musical instrument, but for its creator, one Donati (q.v.) who called it thus because he thought it was in the shape of a goose's beak ('oca' meaning goose in Italian). No Padua red, especially for huntsmen's liveries, but for the city of Padova whence the colour derives its name, and no Padua roosters but for the city.

No Pall Mall but for the Italian game of 'palla maglia' (ball and mallet). No pants or pantaloons but for the 'commedia dell'arte' character Pantalone. No 'paparazzi' but for the photographer by the name of Paparazzo, who was one of the characters in Fellini's film 'La Dolce Vita'. No 'pasquinades' but for the statue of Pasquino in Rome, to which political and satirical messages were stuck. No Pozzolana Ash with which to produce hydraulic cement but for the town of Pozzuoli near Naples which gave it its name. No Punch but for Punchinello which was the Italian 'commedia dell'arte' mask. No 'Russian Salad' but for the Italian cooks of the Italian Riviera who actually created it for members of the Russian nobility who settled there, escaping revolution in their own country (the Russians themselves call it Italian salad!). No sardine but for Sardinia (or is it the other way round?). No 'scarlatina' but for the Italian adjective 'scarlatto' (scarlet).

No sequins but for the Italian 'zecchino', another small coin. No Serlian windows but for Sebastiano Serlio, who first designed them. No 'sienna', a special clay containing iron and manganese oxides, in common use for oil and watercolour paintings, but for the well-known city of Siena in Tuscany. No Solferino purplish-red dye, but for the Battle of Solferino in Italy, which occurred in 1859, the year when the dye was first discovered. No 'soutane', the gown worn by the Catholic Clergy, but for the Italian 'sottana'. No spaghetti but for the Italian noun 'spago', meaning string. No sybaritic behaviour but for the town of Sybaris in Calabria where it is said they really enjoyed themselves. No 'tarantella' but for the city of Taranto (or is it the tarantula?). No 'termagant women' but for the Italian 'triviganti' (a word no longer in the Italian dictionary). No 'Theydon Bois' in Essex but for the Italian family of 'de Bosco' who owned the castle there in the twelfth and thirteenth centuries. No 'Venice' turpentine, a compound used, particularly by sixteenth century Italian artists, to glaze pigments in their oil paintings and made up of the clear exudation of the pine larch, but for the city from which in former times it was exclusively exported and but for the Venice school of painters represented in particular by Titian. No 'veronal', a popular barbiturate, sometimes also known in the USA as barbital, but for the city of Verona in Italy which, apart from being the home town of Romeo and Juliet, is said to have inspired its discoverer. No volts but for Volta who discovered electricity. And no White's Club in St James's but for Francesco Bianchi who founded it (originally as 'White's Chocolate House') in 1693.'

Incidentally, it is interesting to note that the Italian language has contributed a large number of words to the English vocabulary. Italian literature has been read and cultivated in England since the time of Chaucer (fourteenth century) and the arts and artists of Italy exerted a great influence in England. Apart from those words which relate either to poetry, music, architecture, sculpture or painting, there are many others for which England is indebted to Italy. A short list is appended at the end of this book.

But let's go back to Barzini.

'The list of famous Italians is awe-inspiring. It is as well to record them here, as they will scarcely be mentioned in the rest of the book, written with the presumption that the reader is well acquainted with them. Here are some of the main ones: **THE SAINTS**: Saint Francis, Santa Caterina da Siena, San Bernardino da Siena, San Luigi Gonzaga, Saint Thomas of Aquino. **THE SINNERS**: The Borgia family (Spanish but acclimatized), Cellini, Caravaggio, Cagliostro, Casanova. **THE POLITICAL THINKERS**: Dante Alighieri, King Frederick of Hohenstaufen of the two Sicilies (born in Italy, the inventor of the 'balance of power'), Machiavelli, Guicciardini, Mazzini, Cavour. **THE MILITARY LEADERS**: Giovanni dalle Bande Nere, Raimondo Montecuccoli (who led Austrian armies), Napoleon, Garibaldi. **THE ADMIRALS**: Andrea Doria, Mocenigo, Morosini, Bragadin, Caracciolo. **THE SCIENTISTS**: Galileo Galilei, Leonardo da Vinci, Volta, Marconi, Fermi. **THE NAVIGATORS**: Columbus, Vespucci, the Cabots. **THE THINKERS**: Saint Thomas of Aquino, Campanella, Croce, Vico. **THE POETS**: Dante Alighieri, Boccaccio, Petrarch, Leopardi, Manzoni. **THE SCULPTORS**: Verrocchio, Donatello, Ghiberti, della Robbia, Cellini, Michelangelo, Bernini. **THE PAINTERS**: Giotto, Botticelli, Fra Angelico, Leonardo da Vinci, Piero della Francesca, Perugino, Michelangelo, Raphael, Titian, Tintoretto, Tiepolo, Modigliani. **THE MUSICIANS**: Palestrina, Pergolesi, Monteverdi, Vivaldi, Rossini, Verdi, Bellini, Donizetti, Puccini, Toscanini. These are, of course, the names of first magnitude. The second and third could easily fill a small city's telephone book.'

Having read Barzini's magnificent commentary, you may well have been left wondering whether what he says is true. Admittedly, some of the names he mentions you will surely have heard of before; but is it all possible? Can he be trusted? Or is he just being Machiavellian as are all Italians? Is he displaying our presumed so-called duplicity?

I must admit that after I had myself read what I have just transcribed it occurred to me that I should go and check out everything he said; and I did. I discovered that Barzini had actually understated the position and it struck me that his grandiloquence ought to be supported by facts.

It was at that point that I decided that I should put pen to paper. I did so for a combination of reasons, some selfish, some disinterested.

The first reason was that I reacted against Barzini's unsubstantiated generalizations much as I react against politicians who also indulge in generalizations (mainly false) without citing any authority to support their view.

There was a second reason. My three children were all born in England and despite the fact that their mother is also Italian, they are hardly aware of the real traditions of their parents' country. Do not misunderstand me; it is not that they are not aware, say, that Italian food is the best in the world. They know that only too well, because of their mother's cooking. Nor do they have any doubt that, when it comes to things of beauty, it is difficult to beat what comes out of Italy. In due course, as they grow older, they will realize that there is more to being Italian than just good food and good taste.

But apart from these things, and the fact that Italian opera is more enjoyable than any other, the cultural tradition of Italy is almost non-existent as far as they are concerned. And it occurred to me that this must be the position with any number of children of Italians, either born in England, America or Australia or wherever – expatriates, who, apart from their name, have little left of what is Italian.

This is not their fault, of course, because England and the New World have the great ability to absorb, to permeate and, inevitably, to corrupt national characteristics. There are a number of reasons why England in particular has so far succeeded in this process. The principal is that the English damp weather has a softening and sobering effect in all areas of life. But there is a second and much more important reason and it is that England offers what, for example, Italy lacks, namely a political tradition, a tradition of freedom and respectability and of obvious patriotism. All this is kept alive by public ceremony and impeccably executed parades, the sensible, elegant display of pomp and the superb orchestration of displays of national history, the National Anthem and an efficient and dutiful monarchy.

It therefore provides something which people cling to and, as far as the Italians are concerned, it offers an excellent substitute. Whatever traditions

Italians may have, they are of a cultural and certainly not of a political nature. For all these reasons the Italians have blended in with the English community quite well. I remember that in the early fifties the brick industry in Bedfordshire needed cheap labour. Thousands of Italian workers were imported from southern Italy. There was a great outcry locally. It was said that the morals of the community would be corrupted; that these Italians would turn into criminals; that they could not be trusted and so on. Strangely, the same remarks were made then (and I recall them well) which have been made over the past twenty years about other 'importations' into this country.

Fears for the well-being of the local women were very prominent. Fears for their virtue, and for their physical safety.

I also remember, almost with nostalgia, the names of the brick companies involved (The London Brick Company, The Marston Valley Brick Company; the latter no longer in existence). A lot of fuss about nothing. The workers blended in perfectly, and as far as I know, they now represent a substantial, law-abiding section of the Bedford community; I am not aware of any problems. They even have their own Radio Bedford. Just imagine!

The point I am trying to make is that by blending in so well with the environment of their 'adopted' country, very many of the new generation of Italians (who have gone into management, politics, medicine, the law, etc.) have forgotten the contributions that their mother country has made to man's technical and cultural progress – at least in the Western world. I thought some of them might welcome the opportunity to get hold of the facts. Having done so, they may well come to the conclusion that Italians are a lot better at some things than they are normally given credit for. Of course, some might comment that it is a pity Italy did not produce a Beethoven or a Shakespeare. Putting that line of argument to one side, it has to be said that, in general, Italy's sum total of creativity is fantastic and, happily, continues to be so.

But there was a third reason for writing this book. On 17 January 1986 *The Times* published a letter from one of its readers where, in congratulating the Italian government on the manner in which they had dealt with the outbreak of violence at Rome Airport earlier on, the author indirectly expressed the view that it was probably the first time that the Italians had ever got anything right. That letter made me angry. My pride was hurt, my dignity offended, my self-respect slighted. I asked myself: How dare he? Who does he think he is? What were his ancestors doing while mine were civilizing the world? Are his traditions, cultural or otherwise, such as to entitle him to proffer public criticism of a whole nation?

My anger subsided because it struck me that the fault was not his, but it was ours, the Italians', and that his reaction was totally understandable. It was the reaction of the ordinary Englishman for whom the Italians are not too important. As has been said, thank God for the Spaniards for, without them, the Italians would be the last people in Europe.

It is of little use to remind the man in the street of what Dr Johnson said about Italy and the Mediterranean. The man in the street in England does not read Boswell. The passage I have in mind occurs in Boswell's *Life of Johnson* (Thursday, 11 April 1776): 'A man who has not been in Italy is always conscious of an inferiority from his not having seen what it is expected a man should see . . . all our religion, almost all our law, almost all our arts, almost all that sets us above savages, has come to us from the shores of the Mediterranean.'

The normal reaction to Italians cannot be helped, because we have encouraged it. We Italians deserve the way in which others, especially the English and Americans, think of us. We seem to enjoy projecting and encouraging the projection of a wrong image. We make everything easy, we behave in a clownish fashion, we never take anything seriously, we have no sense of duty, we are corrupt; or so it is said.

Our language itself is misleading. I remember that when I was a student here, I had to support myself by teaching Italian, amongst other things, at evening classes. And one of my greatest difficulties lay in disabusing my students of the notion that Italian was an easy language. After all, how deceptively easy it sounds: '*Grazie*', '*prego*', '*buon giorno*', '*buonasera*'. Anybody can learn that, it is so easy; but it is hardly the truth.

Indeed, it is so especially easy that when people, particularly English-speaking people, make an attempt to utter it, they do not bother to get the pronunciation or the spelling right. They seem to be incapable of finding out how they should pronounce or write Italian. The very same people who would go to the trouble of looking up a French or German word in the dictionary blissfully embark upon Italian without consulting anyone. This attitude can be traced to the Victorian era, when Italian was considered as a light and frivolous language, the language of lovers and minor poets, and as such fit to be taught only to wealthy young girls so that they might perhaps gain more appreciation of music and opera.

Leaving aside the absurdity of pronouncing the name of a well-known, but not terribly good, Italian actress as Ghinay Laulaubreegheeday, it is fascinating for an Italian to note the absurdities that flow when Englishmen (Americans, Australians?) speak Italian. And I am not considering the uneducated or the ignorant.

Some years ago, I was listening to a programme on BBC Radio 3 where someone was discussing the relationship between Verdi and his librettist Boito. He kept referring to Bóito as Boìto. It was really painful for me; it was painful because, apart from the grammatical unlikelihood of having a diphthong with the accent on the second vowel, the only word I could at the time think of in

Italian with a comparable sound was '*guaîto*', which is the representation of the sound that an animal makes when it is kicked or hurt. It was an interesting association of ideas, for me at any rate, as I felt like kicking back myself. But there was an even more delightful nonsense shortly after, this time on television, when in the course of an interesting programme on crime in Italy, the presenter referred to the code of solidarity amongst criminals in Italy as 'Omêrta'. The combination of the soft English-style pronunciation of the dental consonant and the accent on the 'e' will no doubt strike Italian readers as entertaining. For those who do not know Italian, may I add that, as a result, instead of pronouncing the word 'Omertá' with an accent on the last syllable which Italians all understand as representing a noun of strength, meaning and passion, whatever view one forms of the criminal aspects of it, one heard the pronunciation of a word which closely approximates to the Italian word for excrement. A suitable connotation for those who do not have sufficient respect for other people to bother to pronounce their language correctly.

So what? you may well remark. Well, it is important. I do not like that any more than I like people who purport to sing Italian opera in Italian with a foreign accent. After all, would you like it if a very primitive, ignorant Italian with a horrible accent stood on stage declaiming 'Friends, Romans, countrymen, lend me your ears' in tones and an accent that were totally alien to you? Would you not consider him presumptuous?

Furthermore, if I cannot trust you to get such a simple thing as the pronunciation or spelling of a word correct, how can I trust you to get the all important facts correct? Carelessness in one is an inevitable concomitant of sloppiness in the other.

At this point you may well be wondering, what gives Arturo Barone the right to don the mantle of criticism and censure. Well, other than my legal training which helps in factual analysis, I have no particular right, of course, any more than anyone else does; but I think my background and experience provide some justification. I have been living in England for over forty years. My three children were born in England and I have inevitably made a very long study, in comparative terms, of the English (but not forgetting our New World cousins either) and the Italians. Lest you should be misled by some of my critical terms into believing that I do not like England, let me make my position perfectly clear straight away: I love England. I love it despite all its shortcomings. I love it despite the present mood of materialism, self-aggrandisement and aggression; I love it even despite the break-up of the middle class centre ground and of the erosion and sometimes disappearance of traditional values. I should add at this point that in all honesty I have to say that my 'long study' has been of the English – as opposed to the Welsh, Scots or the Irish. I therefore refer mostly to England throughout.

I love the English countryside. I can think of nothing more beautiful, and now sadly missed, than the hedgerows of England stretching over undulating landscapes, with the English elm vibrating in the wind. I had always compared that lovely tree to the Greek statue of the victory (Nike) of Samothrace which adorns one of the landings in the Louvre. I think the description of that statue – 'Clothed in Wind' – given by Gabriele D'Annunzio, one of the most successful of modern Italian poets, could happily be applied to the English elm. But I digress.

The reader should also know that I consider myself to be Italian by tradition and English (British) by custom. I see no contradiction whatsoever in this, any more than a Welshman or a Scot might. Most of us have two parents anyhow; why not two cultures?

This duality of feeling, which I am certain is common to all those like myself who, originating from one country, live in another, is not even, and seldom has an equilibrium. I live in England and not in Italy. Whilst I am in England, I complain about a number of things; when I am in Italy, I will not hear a word said against England.

This patriotic ambiguity, if one could term it that, may appear almost schizophrenic: but it is not so. It is probably a good thing, because it enables one to broaden one's mind through close contact with two societies and two cultures. To that extent, it is a source of spiritual and, sometimes, material satisfaction.

At this stage, therefore, I have to make two apologies and two points. One apology follows from what I have just said, namely, that in the course of setting out what I consider to be the achievements of the Italian people I shall lapse from time to time into some form of comment or comparison; I shall digress. I know that, according to Byron, (*'Beppo'* stanza L) 'digression is a sin that by degrees becomes exceeding tedious . . . and therefore may the reader too displease', but I should not be criticized too much for doing so because I hope at least that, by using this approach, I may be able to break up the monotony and the repetitiveness of those achievements.

The second thing for which I 'apologize' in advance is a certain pride and relish in what I have to say about Italian 'firsts'. But why apologize? The fact is I am proud of my Italian origins; I do not subscribe to the view that pride is a cardinal sin. Indeed, I firmly believe that it is one of the qualities that is missing in today's world and its absence causes very many of the problems with which we have to live. But that is another story. By the way, in a book of this kind, there is a tendency to repetition because in attempting to examine so many traits and characteristics from different aspects and points in time, my thoughts inevitably meet the same milestones or 'tributaries' of fact and information. I apologize in advance if this becomes tiresome to the reader

One final observation. In researching my subject I found a considerable scarcity of material, especially contemporary references, published in English. There are, of course, innumerable books on Italy, whether travel books or books on food and wine or art and architecture. The country itself has been dealt with quite extensively. But to my way of thinking, it has always been dealt with somewhat superficially and the Italians themselves have been avoided. It is difficult to say whether this was done because the writers felt, possibly with some degree of justification, that they preferred the country without the Italians, or whether because they took the view that we were not worthy of detailed analysis, or, as I surmise, because they reached the conclusion that we defy classification.

The more I pursue the topic the more I am convinced that the challenge of classification is the reason why so little has been published about the Italians as a people, as distinct from Italy as a nation. There is an elusiveness about us that can be troublesome. The moment you think you have understood what it is all about, something happens which causes you to ponder; you have developed a certain theory and immediately something crops up to destroy it.

As a result, there is really no *detailed* analysis of the Italians in the English language that I could find. There are two modern works, however – one by Luigi Barzini (from which I have already quoted) and the other by David Willey. They are totally different and indeed cannot be compared in any way.

Barzini, a writer of considerable experience, knows and understands the subject matter quite well, since presumably he knew and understood himself quite well. (He has since died.) His analysis of Italian temperament and character is excellent. For that, he has only himself to thank. But some of his conclusions are wrong. For example, he says that divorce would never be introduced into Italy; he was, regrettably, wholly mistaken about this.

For his historical analysis and perception I think he owes a great debt to John Addington Symonds, as he himself acknowledges. But even with him, the reasons why we are as we are seem to elude him. I think this is probably because he was essentially a journalist and he was not prepared to delve too deeply into the subject matter, although the historical background which he provides is extensive.

At the opposite end of the spectrum, David Willey is basically a reporter. He is content to tell us what features the Italians of today display. His book really is almost a television documentary; all the more so because the text is copiously interspersed with photographs. His is a reasonably accurate portrait, but it does not purport to represent an in-depth study.

I'm not ignoring the late Peter Nichols's *Italia, Italia*. But, he is more concerned with modern Italy – its politics, its economics, what makes it tick – than with the reasons why Italians are as they are in the historical sense. As a lover of Italy, he is worthy of my respect.

The only other modern contributor in this field is David Scott Fox whose book *Mediterranean Heritage*, first published in 1978, betrays his approach in its title. Although it is dedicated 'To Italy and Greece' – and I suggest that the order in which he puts the two countries, which is neither alphabetical nor historical, shows where his heart really is – most of what he says applies to Italy much more than to Greece. This is really inevitable, because the later Italian developments were more extensive and had a much more immediate and greater impact than those of Greece. And indeed, if one indulged in an analysis of his book page by page, one would find that the number of times Italy or the adjective 'Italian' is used is infinitely greater than that when Greece or 'Greek' are referred to.

Even so, if, as the cover records, his book is based on a lifetime's observation and enjoyment, then he must be reckoned amongst the many inspired Englishmen who, despite all our faults, have learnt to appreciate us.

The Scott Fox book was written long before two very recent contributions appeared on the scene. They are *Democracy Italian Style* by Joseph LaPalombara (Yale University Press 1988) and *Agnelli and the Network of Italian Power* by Alan Friedman (Harrap 1988).

The former considers the Italians purely as political creatures and is, overall, a flattering exercise as far as Italy is concerned; the latter is effectively a biography of the Chairman of Fiat and is on the whole less flattering of him, if not of the Italians.

But enough of the preliminaries. As regards the task ahead, I should advise the reader that I had to draw the line somewhere in deciding at which point to start. I took the view that the achievements of ancient Rome are so well documented they could be taken for granted. Thus, I have ignored Roman civilization completely even though Italians claim to be the successors of the Romans. By the way, it is interesting that the English themselves have claimed to be successors of the Romans at least in the sense that they applied the same political criteria when founding an empire and, as the Romans used to extend their nationality to all those whom they conquered, so did the British. Whether the Italians are the true successors of the Romans is a matter I shall return to later on.

So, for this reason, and because it seemed like a sensible departure point, I have started at the year AD 1000. Furthermore, some of the most reliable records commence round about the beginning of the second millennium. I should also advise the reader not to be surprised by the absence of many of the 'great' Italian names, such as Verdi. The reason is simple: he was great, but was not the first at what he did. Opera had existed before Verdi and, obviously, so had sculpture, painting and architecture, let alone poetry, before Michelangelo.

The first edition of this book appeared in 1989. At that time, I was concerned with 'educating' my children on their Italian background. Chauvinistically, the title was 'Italians First!', although it could just as easily have been 'Italian Firsts'. I dealt mostly with discoveries, first events and concepts which could be termed seminal: I recorded a mere 420 'firsts'. I went on to say that: 'The list does not purport to be exhaustive and I am quite certain that many others will be found by more zealous researchers than I.'

This is exactly what happened. The second edition contained over 500 inventions or discoveries and the third (1999) (thanks in part to my own efforts but mainly to those of my readers) recorded more than 800 'firsts'.

In the intervening years, I must confess, I allowed myself to meander amongst less important, though equally interesting, achievements. For this, I call on the reader's indulgence.

I can almost hear some of you thinking: 'So, what is all the fuss about? The only good things that Italians have discovered are pasta and America.' If you are thinking that, you are totally mistaken. The discoveries made by Italians are of enormous importance. If I took you now through a whole day, as I will in my Conclusion, you would find that if you wake up with an alarm and you go to bed listening to the radio, not only will you have started and ended the day with an Italian invention but throughout the day you will not have been able to live or move or even eat, yes, even eat, decently, but for the Italians!

You do not believe me? Then let me assure you that most statements of fact (not my digressions, of course) are backed up by an authoritative source. Wherever possible, for example, I have referred to the *Encyclopaedia Britannica*. All references to the *Encyclopaedia Britannica* are drawn from the 15th Edition. But there are other authorities and other encyclopaedias and texts that are also referred to.

For ease of reference, I have divided the factual entries into sections, set out alphabetically according to subject matter. Thus, if you are interested in finding out what discoveries Italians have made in, say physics, look, under the section 'Sciences' sub-heading 'Physics'. In this way, you do not have to read through the whole of any one section to check a possible entry.

Are you still in some doubt? Let us try one out. As I have already mentioned, French cooking stems from Italian cooking, although most people, it appears, believe that it was the other way round. Well, it was Italian cooking that was the turning point in the development of gastronomic excellence and Italy influenced France extensively. If you want to check this statement, look it up in the *Encyclopaedia Britannica* under the heading 'Gastronomy', Volume VII, page 940. (If necessary, go to the library and look it up!) I should like you to do so because I wish my readers to be convinced at the outset that whenever a statement of fact is made in the pages that follow then, unless I have myself qualified that fact, it is incontrovertible.

You may think that is a tall order. But as the saying goes, the proof of the pudding is in the eating. Go and check the heading 'Gastronomy'! And whilst we are on the subject of food, did you know that it was the Italians who invented the fork for use at table? Yes, I know, Italian eating habits are dreadful, all that spaghetti being twirled around, splashing one's clothes and dropping on to one's lap. Nevertheless, the modern dining fork was invented in Italy in the sixteenth century. It did not come into use in England until one hundred years later. I do not say this, the *Encyclopaedia Britannica* does and the reference is Volume IV page 230. Go on, look that up too!

Am I provoking you? I am not surprised. It is exactly what I intended to do. You will find in what follows a number of provocative statements based on provocative, established, but usually unacknowledged facts.

Let us make a start.

List of Authorities

References to the *Encyclopaedia Britannica* (15th Edition) are :
a) **Micropaedia.** References are expressed as follows: the letter followed by Block Roman numerals, followed by the page number. Thus, for example, R - IV - p. 278, followed by either the name of the inventor or the subject matter of the invention;
b) **Macropaedia.** References are expressed by two numerals, namely the volume and the page. Other authors or texts are quoted in full.

Reference to 'Treccani' are references to the *Encyclopaedia Treccani* 1931-4 edition.

References to 'Harwin' are references to the *Harwin's Chronology of Inventions Innovations and Discoveries* 1987 edition, where there are no pages but only references to years.

References to 'Carter' are to the *Dictionary of Inventions and Discoveries* edited by E. F. Carter published by F. Muller - 1966.

References to 'Bibliographical Dictionary of Scientists' are to the *Bibliographical Dictionary of Scientists* published by Pitman, 1969 edition.

References to Bruno are to *Science and Technology Firsts*, Leonard C Bruno, Gale Research, 1997.

References to Harris are to *Book of Firsts*, Melvin Harris, Michael O'Mara Books, 1994.

References to Frugoni are to *Books Banks and Buttons*, Chiara Frugoni, Columbia University Press, 2003.

References to Panati are to *Browsers Book of Beginnings*, Charles Panati, Penguin Books, New York 1984.

References to Charles Panati are to *Panati's Extraordinary Origins of Everyday Things*, Charles Panati, Harper & Row Publishers Inc, New York, 1987.

References to Charles Panati 3 are to *Sacred Origins of Profound Things*, Charles Panati, Penguin Books, New York. 1996.

SECTION 1: Arts

Ballet and Dance

5 - p. 452 (dancing - da Piacenza)
2 - p. 647/8 (dancing - Belgioioso)
2 - p. 649 - R - X - p. 431 (dancing)
R - I - P. 373 (dancing Vigano Angiolini)
R - I - P. 765 (dancing Gastoldi)
R - X p. 412 (dancing Vestris)
2 - p. 650 (Blasis)
R - II - p. 664 (Cecchetti)
R - VI p. 124 (Legnani)

Caricatures

R - IV - p. 523 (Ghezzi)

Erotic Literature

Boccaccio – the Decameron
Johm Addington Symonds – *Renaissance Italy*, Vol. 5 - p. 103 (Cinzio)

Literary Criticism

10 - p. 1038 (Valla)
R - II - p. 621 (Castelvetro)

Music and Musical Instruments

R - IV - p. 785 (D'Arezzo)
R - VI - p. 22 (Landini)
4 - p. 448 (Frottola)
14 - p. 60 (Griffori)
10 - p. 440 (harpsichord)
Treccani - Vol. I - p. 729 (bassoon)

R - X - p. 449 (first violin)
10 - p. 442 (spinets)
17 - p. 7 (Gabrieli) and Treccani Vol. XXXII
p. 134
R - VI - p. 201 (Rinuccini)
R - I - p. 134 (Agazzari)
R - VII - p. 563 (oratorio)
R - IV - p. 316 (Frescobaldi)
13 - p. 645 (Monteverdi)
Harwin 1617 (Sonata)
4 - p. 23 (Rossi)
10 - p. 442 (Cristofori)
R - IX - p. 597 (Stradivari)
R - II - p. 150 (Bonporti)
R - VI - p. 289 (Locatelli)
R - IV - p. 54 (Farinelli)
R - IV - p. 455 (Geminiani)
R - IX - p. 832 (Tartini)
R - X - p. 84 (Traetta)
Carter 128 (mechanical piano)
12 - p. 692 (Leoncavallo)
6 - p. 673 (Russolo)
Harwin 1981 (Di Giugno)

Opera Houses

The *Concise Oxford Dictionary of Opera* (Ro-senthal-Warrack OUP 1964) (San Cassiano Opera House).

Painting and History of Art

Carter 126 (perspective)
R - II - p. 486
R - II - p. 486 (P. Uccello) Campagnola
R - X - p. 363 (Vasari)
12 - p. 98 (Michelangelo)
R - I - p. 753 (Baldinucci)
R - IV - p. 523 (Ghezzi)
R - VII - p. 18 (Morelli)
R - VI - p. 626 (Marinetti)

Philosophy

Carter 27 (Bruno)
R - IX - p. 870 (Telesio)

Pottery

T Wilson – *Ceramic Art of the Italian Renaissance* – British Museum Publications 1987 (Piccolpasso and ornamentation)

Theatre and Acting

1 - p. 60 and 12 - p. 212 (acting)
4 - pp. 984 and 987 (Commedia dell'Arte)
17 - p. 537 (Urbino stage)
18 - p. 223 (Ruzzante)
4 - p. 983 (theatrical contract)
17 - pp. 537 and 553 (Serlio)
17 - p. 537 and 18 - p. 243 (Palladio)
17 - p. 537 (Salviati)
17 - p. 537 (Sabbatini)
17 - p. 541 (Vigarani)
3 - p. 909 (Bernini)
R - X - p. 337 (Valentino)

SECTION 2: Civic Life

Harwin 1432 (Brunelleschi)
10 - p. 811 (Alberti)
13 - p. 933 (Palladio)
F. E. Halliday - *Cultural History of England* (Thames and Hudson) - p. 148 (Palladio)
R - VIII - p. 859 (San Gimignano) and Treccani XXX p. 654
R - IX - p. 263 (skyscrapers)

Amenities

John Addington Symonds - *Renaissance in Italy* - Vol. 3 - p. 42 (jetty)
John Addington Symonds - *Renaissance in Italy* - Vol. 3 - p. 42 (aqueduct)
John Addington Symonds - *Renaissance in Italy* - Vol. 3 - p. 42 (Venice)
John Addington Symonds - *Renaissance in Italy* - Vol. 3 - p. 42 (flags)
4 - p. 744 (horology)
Montanelli - Gervaso - :'*Italia dei Comuni* - p. 174 (chimney breast)
Treccani - XIII - p. 141 (clock)
Carter 186 (water chlorination)

Botanical Gardens and Botany

7 - p. 902, 3 - p. 64 and 4 - p. 685 (botanical gardens)
Biographical Dictionary of Scientists (Cesalpino)
2. - p. 1020 and 3 - p. 66 (Malpighi)
Biographical Dictionary of Scientists (P. Alpini)

Clubs

Algernon Bourke - *History of White's* - pp. 11-13 (White's Club)

Festivals

Thomas Ashby - *Some Italian Scenes and Festivals* - Methuen 1929 p. 8

Funerals

R - II - p. 1 (funerals)
Treccani - XXX p. 378 - (Sabbioneta)

Heraldry

8 - p. 796 (Bartolo da Sessoferrato)

Libraries

10 - p. 857 (Montecassino – library)
10 - p. 858 (Florence library)
10 - p. 860 (Panizzi)

Pedestrianization

Go there and see for yourself

Records and Archives

R - II - p. 436 (Caffaro di Caschifellone)

The Church in England

R - VI - p. 27 (Lanfranc)
R - I - p. 401 (Anselmo)

SECTION 3: Communications

Calligraphy

R - IV - p. 232 (Poggio)
R - I - p. 415 (Niccoli)

Cryptology Cryptography and Cryptanalysis

5 - p. 333 (de Lavinde)
Harwin 1411 ('Pasini' cipher) 5 - p. 332 (Simonetta)

Dictionaries

5 - p. 714 (Calepino's dictionary)

Newspapers

R - IV - p. 444 and 15 - p. 236 (newspapers)

Paperbacks

R - VI - p. 585 and 15 - p. 225 (Manuzio – paperbacks and imprint)

Photography

14 - p. 328 and Treccani VI - p. 132 (photography) Treccani XXVII - p. 951 (Porro)

Postal Systems

14 - p. 884 (post)

Printing

Harwin 1477 (maps)
R - V - p. 468 and R - VI - p. 585 (Griffo)
R - VII - p. 918 (Petrucci)
R - II - p. 113 (Bodoni)
Rizzatti (Ed. Vallardi) Gl' Italiani e il Bel Paese (*La Cultura Scientifica*) p. 201 and 208 (Milan 1915) - (paper factories) *Biographical Dictionary of Scientists* (Pitman 1969) (Aselli's book)
2 - p. 885 (Della Valle)

Scientific Societies

2 - p. 1020 (scientific societies)

Signalling

18 - p. 67 (Cardano)
18 - p. 68 (Volta)

Telephones

Colonnetti - *Grandi Primati Italiani* (Meucci)
Colonnetti - *Grandi Primati Italiani* (Marzi)

Traditional Tales

R - IX - p. 600 (Straparola)
John Addington Symonds - *Renaissance in Italy* - Vol. 5, p. 103 (Machiavelli)

SECTION 4: Economics, Law and Social Sciences

Anthropology

R - X - p. 418 (Vico)

Archaelogy

R - I - p. 963 and 1 - p. 1078 (Belzoni) R - III - p. 329 (Pizzicolli)

Banking and Book-keeping

3 - p. 37 (Pacioli)
John Addington Symonds - *Renaissance in Italy* - 1875 edition, Vol 1, p. 193 (Bardi-Peruzzi)
Montanelli - Gervaso - *L'Italia dei Comuni* - p. 169 (Letter of Credit)
Treccani - XXX - pp. 655/6 (Banco di San Giorgio)
16 - p. 449 (stock exchange)

Criminal Associations

R - VI - p. 478 (Mafia)

Criminology

R - I - p. 916 (Beccaria)
Salvatorelli - *Sommario di Storia D'Italia* p. 385 (Leopold II)

Economics

R - IV - p. 470 (Genovesi)
R - IV - p. 386 (Galiani)

Insurance

Edler de Roover (as quoted in text) - (marine insurance)
Edler de Roover (as quoted in text) - (insurance policy)
Treccani - XXXIII - p. 1035 (Tonti)

Law

R - VI - p. 26 (Lanfranc)
R - X - p. 321 (Vacario)
R - I - p. 702 (Azzone)
4 - p. 988 (law merchant)
4 - p. 988 and R - II - p. 20 (Bill of Exchange)
Calasso - Medio Evo del Diritto - Vol. 1 (Eleonora)
4 - p. 988 (company law)
4 - p. 988 (bankruptcy)
13 - p. 1071 (patents)
1 - p. 955 (military law)
R - IV - p. 472 (Gentili)
Montanelli - Gervaso – L'Italia dei Comuni - p. 293 (law of the sea)
Treccani - XXX - pp. 655/6 (cheques)

Statistics

R - X - p. 438 (Villani)

Time and Motion Studies

R - II - p. 320 (time and motion studies)

SECTION 5: Lifestyle

Aesthetics

1 - p. 154 (Croce)
Carter 131 (plastic noses)

Clocks and Watches

Treccani XIII - p. 141 (clock)
Allix - 'Carriage Clocks' - p. 5 (horology)
Harwin 1335 (automatic striking clock)
Harwin 1704 (jewelled watch)

Contraception

2 - p. 1067 (condoms)

Education

6 - p. 337 and R - II - p. 131 (Bologna)
R - VII - p. 757 (Paris)
R - VII - p. 898 (Perugia)
John Addington Symonds - *Renaissance in Italy* - Vol. 2 - p. 84 (Vicenza)
John Addington Symonds - *Renaissance in Italy* - Vol. 2 - p. 84 (Arezzo)
R - VII - p. 670 (Padova)
R - VII - p. 190 (Naples and Salerno)
John Addington Symonds - *Renaissance in Italy* - Vol. 2 - p. 84 (Vercelli)
John Addington Symonds - *Renaissance in Italy* - Vol. 2 - p. 85 (Ferrara)
John Addington Symonds - *Renaissance in Italy* - Vol. 2 - p. 86 (Florence)

John Addington Symonds - *Renaissance in Italy*
- Vol. 2 - p. 86 (Pavia)
6 - p. 344 (Vergerio)
R - I - p. 848 and 6 - p. 344 (Barizza)
John Addington Symonds - *Renaissance in Italy*
- Vol. 4 - p. 172 (Alberti)
R - VI - p. 1020 (Montessori)
6 - p. 780 (Bandini)
6 - p. 785 (Zara)

Fabrics and Fashions

F. Boucher – A History of Costume in the
West (Thames and Hudson)
R - V - p. 467 (lace)
18 - p. 171 (textiles)
Harwin 1854 (Bonelli-loom)

Cosmetics

R. Corson – *Fashions in make-up*, – Peter Owen,
London 1974 - p. 103 (cosmetics)

Food and Drink

7 - p. 940 (cooking)
R - IV - p. 230 (fork)
Biographical Dictionary of Scientists (P. Alpini)
Harwin 1946 (espresso machine)
Harwin 1800 (pasta)
Carter 8 (alcohol distillation)
R - V - p. 276 (Ice-cream)
Harwin 1896 (Ice-cream cones)

Gemstones

7 - p. 978 (Peruzzi)
Carter 46 (crystals)

Glass

8 - p. 184 (colourless glass)

Etiquette

R - II - p. 622 (B. Castiglione)
R - II - p. 604 (Della Casa)
Montanelli - Gervaso - *L'Italia dei Comuni* - p.
192 (handkerchief)
H. V. Morton - *A Traveller in Southern Italy* - p.
362 (eau de cologne)
R - IV - p. 151 (Firenzuola on women's
beauty)
Carter 179 (umbrella)

Spectacles (Eye Glasses)

R - IV - p. 16 (Spina)

SECTION 6: Politics and War

Bureaucracy

John Addington Symonds - *Renaissance in Italy*
- Vol. 1, p. 74 (bureaucracy)

Diplomacy

R - IV - p. 472 (Gentili)
R - IV - p. 473 (Gentili) R - I - p. 984
(Bentivoglio)

Political Power

17 - p. 609/610 (Machiavelli)
8 - p. 465 (Guicciardini)
R - VII - p. 41 (Mosca)
Garzanti - *Enciclopedia Europea* 1978 Ed. Vol.
VII, p. 333 (Mattei)

Trade Unions

Salvatorelli - *Sommario di Storia d'Italia* p. 125
(trade unions)

Treaties

Index to British Treaties - HMSO - Vol. 2 - p.
4 (treaties)

War

Harwin 1326 (cannons)
8 - p. 489 (Colleoni - gun-train)
R - VIII - p. 6 (pistols)
R - III - p. 7 (Colleoni)
R - IX - p. 831 (Tartaglia)
Treccani - Vol. XXXIV - p. 1031 (D'Avalos)
Biographical Dictionary of Scientists (Ramelli)
Carter 8 - (air gun)
Treccani - Vol. II - p. 409 (Alfonso D'Este)
Treccani - Vol. IX - p. 545 (Cavalli)
R - VII - p. 361 (Sobrero)
William Percy Jolly - *Marconi* - Constable -
London 1972

SECTION 7: Sciences

Astronomy

Harwin 1364 (astronomical clock)
11 - p. 520 (Fontana)
11 - p. 520 (F. Cassini)
11 - p. 917 (Schiaparelli)
R - II - p. 615 (G. D. Cassini)
R - I - p. 1048 (Bianchini)
R - VII - p. 985 (Piazzi)
R - III - p. 618 (Donati)
R - IX - p. 15 (Secchi)
R - VIII - p. 957 (Schiaparelli)

Atom Bombs

11 - p. 800 (Fermi)
R - IV - p. 102 (Fermi) R - VII - p. 280 (Fermi)

Autopsies

11 - p. 813 (post-mortems)
2 - p. 536 (autopsies)

Barometer

11 - p. 780 and R - X - p. 56 (Torricelli)

Biology

11 - p. 210 (Aselli)
2 - p. 1026 and R - II - p. 164 (Borelli)
11 - p. 831 and 12 - p. 109 (Redi)
R - VIII - p. 461 (Redi)
11 - p. 831 (Bassi)
R - VI - p. 19 (Lancisi)
2 - p. 1024 and R - I - p. 313 (Amici)
R - IV - p. 615 (Golgi)
R - VII - p. 244 (Negri)
R - VIII - p. 112 (Pontecorvo)

Chemistry

Carter 119 (nitric acid)
Carter 76 (gold wire)
Carter 56 (silver coins gilding by Brugnatelli)
2 - p. 333 and 13 - p. 334 (Avogadro)
R - VIII - p. 809 (Piria)
R - IX - p. 45 (Selmi)
2 - p. 333 (Cannizzaro)
Carter 82 (helium gas)
R - VII - p. 220 (polypropylene)

Contagious Diseases

12 - p. 109 (syphilis and theory of contagious diseases)

Geology

R - I - p. 497 (stratigraphy)

Geometry

7 - p. 1113 (Saccheri)
7 - p. 1091 (Torricelli) 7 - p. 1090 (Grandi)

Hydraulics

11 - p. 780 and R - X - p. 56 (hydraulics)
R - IV - p. 783 (Guglielmini)
R - IV - p. 328 (Frisi)

Longevity

Treccani - Vol. XI - p. 416 (longevity)

Mathematics

13 - p. 349 and 10 - p. 818 (Fibonacci)
10 - p. 811 (Pacioli)
11 - p. 677 (Brunelleschi)
11 - p. 642 (Del Ferro)
R - IX - p. 831 (Tartaglia)
R - IV - p. 106 (Ferrari)
11 - p. 662 and 7 - p. 858 (Tartaglia, Ferrari, Cardano)
R - II - p. 655 and 11 - p. 643 and 1 - p. 740 (Cavalieri)
11 - p. 643 (Torricelli)
R - II - p. 701 (Ceva)
Biographical Dictionary of Scientists (Mengoli)
7 - p. 1113 (Saccheri)
5 - p. 738 (Riccati)
R - V - p. 991 (La Grange)
R - VIII - p. 711 (Ruffini)
R - I - p. 1034 (Betti)
R - III - p. 233 (Cremona)
11 - p. 630 (Beltramini)
R - VIII - p. 563 (Ricci)
R - VII - p. 819 (Peano)
1 - p. 740 (Cesaro)
1 - p. 758 (Volterra)
11 - p. 637 (Zermelo)
1 - p. 796 (Levi-Civita)
1 - p. 764 (Tonelli, Cesari, Digiorgi)

Medicine

11 - p. 828 and R - VIII - p. 808 (Salerno)
11 - p. 813 (post-mortems)
R - VIII - p. 809 (Saliceto)
2 - p. 536 (Liucci) *Biographical Dictionary of Scientists* (Eustachio)
R - III - p. 15 (Colombo)
Treccani - XXI - p. 707 (VD)
Treccani - XXXIV - p. 1013 (Varolio)
R - IV - p. 40 (Falloppio) and 2 - p. 1067
R - I - p. 573 (Aselli)
2 - p. 1022 and Treccani Vol. XXVIII - p. 972 (Redi)
1 - p. 956 (Bellini)
R - VIII - p. 886 (Santorio)
Readers' Digest Universal Dictionary p. 932 (Malpighi and microscope use)
2 - p. 1020 and 3 - p. 55 (Malpighi)
11 - p. 829 (Malpighi and blood)
Treccani XXIX - p. 488 (transfusions)
15 - p. 748 and 5 - p. 1121 (Valsalva)
11 - p. 831 (Ramazzini)
11 - p. 830 and 2 - p. 536 (Morgagni)
10 - p. 900 and a2 - p. 112 (Spallanzani)
Carter 21 - (blood pressure)
Treccani XXV - p. 880 (Pacinian corpuscles)
R - VIII - p. 711 (Ruffini)
Treccani - XV - p. 609 (ear)
5 - p. 1133 (Corti)
Treccani - p. 681 (pneumothorax)
Harwin 1896 (sphygmomanometer)
Harwin 1937 (electro-convulsive therapy)

Metallurgy

11 - p. 1063 and Treccani IV p. 706 (Biringuccio)

Nobel Prizes

Nobel Foundation

Physics

Carter 29 (cam)
Carter 137 (jet propulsion)
Carter 137 (Di Giorgio)
Carter 77 (centrifugal governor)
Carter 143 (rainbow theory)
Treccani XXVII - p. 951 (Fabrizzi)
10 - p. 924 (Leonardo) - diving
10 - p. 929 (Leonardo) - light propagation
11 - p. 232 (Leonardo) - screw machine
11 - p. 236 (Leonardo) - gears
11 - p. 249 (Leonardo) - bearings
11 - p. 780 (Leonardo) - fluid flow engineering
12 - p. 55 (Leonardo) - Hygrometer
12 - p. 511 (Leonardo) - 'camera oscura'
17 - p. 747 (Leonardo) - underwater exploration
18 - p. 766 (Leonardo) - water turbine
Codex Atlanticus Folio 276 (Leonardo) flying machine
French Institute - Manuscript B, Folio 83 (Leonardo) - photometry
French Institute - Manuscript C, Folio 22 (Leonardo)
Harwin 1488 (crossbow gun)
Montanelli-Gervaso *L'Italia della Controriforma* - p. 388 (repeater gun)
Montanelli-Gervaso *L'Italia della Contriroforma* - p. 388 (parachute)
James Mc Donald - Worldly Wise (Constable 1984) - p. 215 (bicycles)
Carter 149 - (rope making machine)
Carter 3 - (retractable undercarriage)
Carter 27 - (explosive bullets)
Carter 165 - (submarine)
Carter 171 - (tensile testing machine)
Carter 152 - (handsaw for marble)
Carter 78 - (grinders)
7 - p. 851 (Galileo)
18 - pp. 97 and 415 (Galileo)
7 - p. 851 (Galileo)
7 - p. 852 (Galileo)
10 - p. 350 (Galileo)
11 - p. 520 (Galileo)
11 - p. 762 (Galileo)
11 - p. 830 (Galileo)
R - IV - p. 388 and 14 - p. 387 (Galileo)
16 - p. 273 (Galileo)
7 - p. 852 (Galileo)
6 - p. 849 (Galileo)
7 - p. 868 (Galileo)
17 - p. 799 (Galileo)
12 - p. 55 (Galileo)
18 - p. 321 (Galileo)
Carter 51 - (dredger)
Carter 31 - (cardan joint)
Carter 74 - (gimbal suspension)
Carter 107 - (light refraction theory)
Harwin 1616 (thermometer)
8 - p. 702 (Ferdinand II)
R - X - p. 56 (Torricelli)
R - X - p. 476 (Borelli and Viviani)

6 - p. 646 (Grimaldi)
R - II - p. 487 (Campani)
7 - p. 382 (Delana)
7 - p. 859 (Galvani)
R - VII - p. 985 (Piazzi)
2 - p. 1034 (Beccaria)
R - IX - p. 15 (Secchi)
Treccani - XXII - p. 819 (Melloni)
Treccani - XXXV - p. 392 (and)
Harwin 1824 (wine press)
Colonnetti - *Grandi Primati Italiani* (Barsanti
and Matteucci) and Carter 16
Colonnetti - *Grandi Primati Italiani* (Pacinotti)
and Treccani 1934 Ed. Vol. XVII
Treccani Vol. XXIX - p. 328 (Righi)
Colonnetti - *Grandi Primati Italiani* (Ferraris)
Carter 133 (electricity generation)
Carter 105 (lamp bulbs vacuum)
Carter 68 (arc electric steel furnace)
Carter 28 (oil-filled electric cable)
Colonnetti - *Grandi Primati Italiani* (Marconi)
Carter 2 (aerial)
Harwin 1937 (Segre)

SECTION 8: Sport and Leisure

Animals

4 - p. 635 (Franconi - circus diameter)
R - IV - p. 278 (lion-taming)

Bowling

3 - p. 86 ('bocce')

Fencing

7 - p. 224 (fencing)
7 - p. 225 (fencing)

Gaming and Gambling

7 - p. 868 and II - p. 557 (Probability Theory)
3 - p. 901 (playing cards)
11 - p. 114 (the Florence 'lotto')

Gardens and Horticulture

7 - pp. 893/4 (parterres)
Treccani - X - p. 853 (gardening book)
Treccani - XXXI - p. 452 and Harwin 1545

(conservatory)
Treccani - XI - p. 840 (De Crescenzi)
Harwin 1877 (viticulture)

Horse-Riding

15 - p. 836 (Grisone)
15 - p. 836 (Pignatelli)
15 - p. 836 (Caprilli)

Magic

R - VII - p. 1016 (Pinetti)

Mountain-Climbing

Garzanti - *Enciclopedia Europea* 1978 Ed. Vol.
1, p. 314 (Rotario D'Asti)
Rheinhold Messner's exploits are modern and
well known

Boating

2 - p. 1157 (boat race)
John Addington Symonds - *Renaissance in Italy*
- Vol. 1, p. 31 (compass)
16 - p. 158 (sails)
P. Riccardi - *Biblioteca Matematica Italiana* -
Modena 1873 (eight-point compass)
Treccani - XI - p. 840 (Crescenzio's compass)
Treccani - XI - p. 840 (detailed 'portolan'
chart)

SECTION 9: Transport and Travel

America

Common knowledge (Colombo's discovery of
America and Vespucci's naming of it)

Canada

R - II - p. 423 (Caboto)

Canals

3 - p. 753 (Naviglio Canal)

Flying

Treccani - XVIII - p. 257 (flying Guidotti)
Carter 16 (balloon night flight)

Carter 7 (jet plane)

Hydrofoil/Ships and Biplanes

R - V - p. 240 (hydroflois)
Harwin 1905 (hydrofoil biplane)

Map-Making

Treccani - XXIV - p. 329 (maps)

Motor Vehicles

2 - p. 764 (battery)
11 - p. 311 (Romagnosi)
Colonnetti - *Grandi Primati Italiani* - p. 57 (Pacinotti)
R - VIII - p. 1 (Pirelli)
R - X - p. 391 and 11 - p. 780 (Venturi)
R - I - p. 674 (autostrada)

Railways and Steam Engines

R - VII - p. 129 (Dellaporta)
Carter 104 (magic lantern)
Carter 85 (incubators)
Carter 89 (kite)

Carter 169 (electric telegraph)
Carter 133 (telescope)

River Nile

R - IV - p. 511 (Gessi)

Ships and Navigation

10 - p. 952 ('Lanterna' at Genoa)
11 - p. 179 (Cascariolo)

Travel and Exploration

R - VIII - p. 91 (Polo)
11 - p. 472 and R - VIII - p. 141 (portolans)
R - X - p. 474 (Vivaldi)
R - VII - p. 833 (Pegolotti)
Christopher Columbus
R - X - p. 410 (Vespucci)
R - II - p. 423 (Caboto)
R - VI - p. 623 (Marignolli)
R - X - p. 404 (Verrazzano)
R - X - p. 338 (Valignano)
R - VIII - p. 563 (Ricci) 11 - pp. 345/351 and 15 - pp. 616/1014

PART I

ENCYCLOPAEDIA

OF

ITALIAN

FIRSTS

1. ARTS

BALLET & DANCE

The word 'ballet' is taken from the Italian word 'balletto' stemming from the verb *ballare* meaning to dance. During my researches I was surprised to find that the Italian contribution to ballet is quite substantial.

I had always looked upon the ballet as a Russian development, but I was wrong. As Barzini said, it was the Italians who taught dancing to the Russians.

In case you think this statement rash, look at the facts.

1   In 1400, Domenico da PIA-CENZA wrote the first book on the dances of Europe. It was written, as was then customary, in the Latin language and it was called De Arte Saltandi Et Choreas Ducendi.

2   The first ballet was produced by Baltazarini Di BELGIOIOSO. It is not clear whether he did so in Tortona in Italy in 1489, or in France in 1581.

Let us not worry too much, however, about the dates; according to the *Encyclopaedia Britannica*, he did so.

3   At about the same time, Gasparo ANGIOLINI (born in Naples) was the first to integrate dance music and plot.

4   The first book purporting to teach ballet and published by a professional dancing master was *Il*

Ballarino (1581) by Fabritio CARO-SO.

5   In 1591, the term 'balletto' was used for the first time by Giovanni GASTOLDI.

6   In 1747, Gaetano VESTRIS (born in Florence) established himself as the first male ballet dancer. In his day he was referred to as the 'god of the dance'.

He was, in fact, incredibly well-known. In James Boswell's *Life of Johnson* (aetat 72, Friday 30 March 1781) his friends take Dr Johnson to task asking him to verify the accuracy of a ludicrous paragraph in a newspaper to the effect that he, Dr Johnson, was taking dancing lessons from Vestris

7   It was Salvatore VIGANÓ (born in Naples) who really established dramatic ballet in Milan in 1809.

It was of him that Stendhal ('Rome Naples and Florence') wrote: 'the finest tragedy that Shakespeare ever wrote can scarcely move me half as much as a ballet by Viganó . . . he is a genius whose art will die with him.' (see p. 90 of the 1959 John Calder edition, translated by Richard Coe.)

8   In 1820, Carlo BLASIS (born in Naples) codified the techniques of classical ballet.

9   In 1887, Enrico CECCHET-TI (born in Rome) developed his

method of training for dancers which is still widely used throughout the world and is known as **Cecchetti's Method.**

Cecchetti had gone to the United States when he was very young. He appeared aged five with the Ronzani Troupe at New York's Broadway Theatre and, thereafter, toured the country with them. However, the tour was a failure and Cecchetti returned to Italy. He would not visit the United States again for another fifty-six years; however, when he did he returned as the world's leading ballet master, with a famous student of his, Anna Pavlova.

But even before Cecchetti established his method of training, the great dancing tradition had found its best nineteenth-century exponent of the Romantic style in the person of Marie Taglioni, whose debut in Vienna in 1822 was as notable as that of our next character. Taglioni was among the first to dance on tiptoes. Ten years later, in *La Sylphide*, she displayed leaps, arabesques and, above all, a style of dress which has continued almost to this day.

In 1893, Pierina LEGNANI established her virtuoso ballet technique which formed the basis for the Russian School of Ballet.

She did so in a rather flamboyant fashion when she made her debut in Saint Petersburg. She executed a series of thirty-two fouettées, a technical feat never before seen on stage.

The Russian audience was ecstatic. Her positioning was so true to the vertical that she is said not to have moved one inch from the spot on which such brilliant execution occurred. It was left to her and to the Italian ballet corps to salvage Tchaikovsky's *Swan Lake*, which had not received a good press the first time it was performed by Russian dancers.

CARICATURES

10   In 1665, architect and sculptor Gian Lorenzo BERNINI (born in Naples) re-established the idea of caricature into France.

11   According to the *Encyclopaedia Britannica*, the first official caricaturist was Pier Leone GHEZZI (born in Rome), who established himself in 1700.

Britannica seems to wander a little when it comes to caricature. For example, you will find that *Britannica* also attributes caricature to Bernini, whereas Scott Fox in his book *Mediterranean Heritage* attributes it to Annibale Carracci, who was born at least 200 years before Ghezzi.

I shall opt for Leonardo da Vinci as the true Italian originator of caricature, as some of the drawings in the Louvre (and there are many) show. However, according to Harwin's *Chronology of Inventions, Innovations and Discoveries*, there is an even earlier attribution: this publication ascribes it to Buffalmacco Buonamico De Cristofaro in 1330, a painter of the earlier Florentine School, with a great reputation as a practical joker. He drew comic figures and put labels to their mouths with sentences.

Whichever way you look at it, it does not really matter, because Ghezzi, Bernini, Carracci, Leonardo and Buffalmacco were all Italians.

It is a matter of choice as to who deserves the accolade but it is an historical fact that caricature portraits became exceptionally popular with English visitors who went to Italy on their Grand Tour. As a result, the English developed the Italian caricature into a satirical and political weapon (see Hogarth); and that tradition is maintained to this day (see the television programme 'Spitting Image').

CINEMA

12 DELLAPORTA, that immensely versatile sixteenth-century scientist mentioned in numerous places elsewhere in this book, invented the Magic Lantern projector.

13 Italians pioneered the composition of music especially for films, a practice that became more widespread in the late twenties. It is recorded that the first film composer was Romolo BACCHIONI, who produced the score for two 1906 films by Cines. The first American film score was not to be seen until at least ten years later.

14 The first wide screen process known as 'panoramico alberini' was developed as early as 1914 by Filoteo ALBERINI. He had to wait ten years to see it applied when Guazzoni's *Il Sacco di Roma* was released.

And whilst we are on the subject of films, I cannot help mentioning the contribution of Gabriele D'Annunzio who, in 1913, started work on the film 'Cabiria'. It was on the occasion of the production of 'Cabiria' that the cine-camera on wheels was first used. The importance and originality of the film lay in the grandeur of its proportions and cast of thousands; it became a pioneering example of epic screen production (it lasted an unprecedented three hours). (I am quoting J. Woodhouse in his 1998 biography of D'Annunzio at p. 268.)

15 In 1918, the first film star was created, namely Rodolfo VALENTI-NO (born at Castellaneta, in Apulia).

A product of the US film industry publicity machine, Valentino died young (aged thirty-one) of peritonitis, allegedly said to have been caused during a fist fight with John Wannamaker II over a woman.

I trust the reader will forgive me if at this stage I record that, in January 2006, the Roman cinema studios of 'Cinecitta' celebrated their seventieth anniversary.

EROTIC LITERATURE

There is nothing new about pornography, as anyone who has visited Pompeii and seen the mosaics there well knows. However, the firsts that follow are in fact masterpieces of literature and not pornography. Only part of Cinzio's book can be said to be capable of being considered pornographic in my opinion and none of Boccaccio's *Decameron* can.

There are two ways in which the Italians can be said to lead the field in the sphere of erotic literature.

16 In the early fourteenth century, Giovanni BOCCACCIO (born in Paris, the illegitimate son of an Italian father and a French mother) who followed closely on Dante and Petrarca, wrote the *Decameron*, which is a masterpiece of earthy, bawdy, funny prose, written in a quiet, understated manner.

The chapters on putting the devil where he belongs, namely in hell, and on cleaning vats of wine whilst one's wife looks on, have a sauciness and a style which our present-day purveyors of cheap pornographic rubbish will never be able to imitate, let alone understand.

Boccaccio had great influence worldwide on writers of short stories who came after him; but as far as England is concerned, his influence went beyond the style of short-story writing, since his themes were utilized in a number of different contexts, both in poetry and prose. The 'locale' was changed, and the style differed; the descriptions were adapted to the language and to the taste of the reader; but most English writers found something in him that could be put to use in their work. From Dryden to Hazlitt, Shelley to Scott, Keats to Landor, Milman to Lloyd, Byron to Coleridge, Tennyson to George Eliot, Boccaccio's *Decameron* was topical in nineteenth-century England five hundred years after it was written.

Indeed, Boccaccio's stories have a particular charm. His characters are real people, taken from all social classes, masters or slaves of their senses and their passions. Woman is no angel for Boccaccio, but she, too, is quite real. Not fragrant, but vibrant. In fact, Boccaccio's women are quite modern and you could argue that he himself was a pioneer of sex equality.

Surprising though this may sound to Americans or British, in the field of equality the Italians got there first as well. Let me give you an example.

In his seventh novel of the sixth day, when a woman caught in adultery has to defend herself to avoid death, the following 'cri de coeur' is recorded (my own free translation):

'Laws should be of universal application and made with the concurrence of those who are subject to them; but this does not happen, because (this law) only affects poor women . . . ; but apart from any other consideration, not only did a woman never consent to such a law, but no woman was ever consulted about it. Therefore, it is a bad law. . . .'

By the way, the all-male 'jury' acquitted her! But they did so on a different ground, I think, and I shall not spoil your fun by revealing it to you in case you have not read the book.

17 **Boccaccio's espousal of the cause of women ante-dates that of the first 'feminist' writer, Christine DE PISAN, by over 100 years.**

Ardent feminists should also be reminded that in 1772 there was published *Lana Caprina* or 'Letters from a Licanthrope' which was written by Casanova. This item of information will certainly not make such women happy because, on the whole, women of any kind do not like Casanova. The reason is that he gave women everything but never his inner being: and all women want to possess the inner man. On the other hand, compared to Don Juan, he was modest in his performances because he boasts only of having possessed about 200 women or, as some authorities have worked out, an average of about twelve encounters every year.

Modern authors appear to be agreed that Mozart took Casanova as his model for the character 'Don Giovanni'. This belief is based on the following facts:
1. Both were Venetians
2. Both appear to have the same kind of personality
3. Casanova was a friend of Mozart's librettist Da Ponte
4. Both were Freemasons.

But I digress: Casanova, it could be argued, is a very authoritative feminist. For example, he argues that woman has an independence of mind of her own which is unrelated to the functions of her sex and he continues to display his appreciation for them, not only on the physical but also on the intellectual level: a flattering judgement by a born flatterer.

The 'courtesans' of the fifteenth and

sixteenth centuries, in particular, who flourished in Italy were high-class whores who often distinguished themselves through their love of the arts and knowledge of literature. Even here we have a first.

18 It is said that IMPERIA, a prostitute who lived in Rome astride the end of the fifteenth and the beginning of the sixteenth centuries, was the first woman of her ilk to whom the term 'courtesan' was applied.

She was incredibly well known and much liked by both the humbler folk and by the aristocracy. When she died, she was buried in the Church of St Gregory on Mount Celio and the following inscription appeared on her tomb:

Imperia, cortesana Romana, quae digna tanto nomine ('Imperia, a Roman courtesan, well worthy of that title.')

Modern tourists would be hard put to find this writing, because it has faded away with the passage of time. The tomb itself is still there in the atrium of the Church of St Gregory on Mount Celio but the priests who served there were already so bored and annoyed with the existence of Imperia's tomb since it had become a place of pilgrimage, especially for the humanists of the sixteenth and seventeenth centuries, that, probably out of spite, they removed her body from the tomb and replaced it with one of their brethren. Even today, the odd German, armed with his 'Baedeker', turns up at St Gregory's and asks to see the tomb of Imperia.

A digression is called for at this stage. Obviously, not even a fervent and conceited Italian like myself would claim that the Italians invented prostitution. The oldest profession has appeared at the beginning, if not at the heart, of all

cultures regardless of colour or race. Even the Bible gives us the prostitute Rahab, the only person to survive the fall of Jericho. Most civilizations have known it. In Ancient Greece the lawgiver Solon (himself a homosexual) had his reasons for setting up a cheap 'twopenny' brothel called 'dikterion'. But just as Imperia showed how the function of selling sexual favours could be elevated, so the Italians were able in certain respects during the Renaissance to provide some style to compensate for the inherent vulgarity of the prostitute. The reader who is interested in pursuing the subject is referred to in the numerous books written on prostitution, and more recently, to 'The Comfort of Sin – Prostitutes and Prostitution in the 90s' by Richard Goodall, Renaissance Books, Folkestone, 1995, from which it is apparent that the Italian courtesans in the Renaissance were no mere harlots, displaying style and conversational skills, both in Rome and in Venice, of a very high standard. We have recorded one; Tullia was another and Faustina was immortalized when Michelangelo wrote a verse epitaph for her in which he praised her beauty, although he regretted that she was putting it to bad use.

Nevertheless, in the same way as the Italians taught the French the finer points of high-class cooking (v. Gastronomy) so they exported to France in the fifteenth and sixteenth centuries the concept of the high-class 'tart'. The authority for this statement, as well as for the first that will shortly be recorded, is Jacques Rossiaud, a French Professor at the University of Lyon, in his book 'Prostitution in the Middle Ages'.

Italian cities decided to institutionalize the openly but casually and offensively distributed, inevitable prostitution activities.

The first recorded officially recognized and funded brothel ('Prostibulum Publicum') was established in Italy in or about the year 1350, at Lucca. It was followed about ten years later by the larger one set up in Venice and known as Il Castelletto. The Lucca brothel was set up in a group of houses in the parish of San Matteo di Rialto, owned by two titled families, Venier and Morosini (others followed in Florence in 1403 and at Siena in 1421). It competes for priority with the private house at Tarascon, in South West France, for which a reference exists, dated 1374. Later French 'houses' were opened in 1424 at Sisteron and at Cavaillon in 1430.

Some six and a half centuries later, in an endeavour to compensate for years of hypocritical inactivity, the British Government announced on 15 January 2006 that it would make legal brothels where 'up to three girls' would dispense sexual favours (no longer to be called 'prostitutes', of course, the dictates of political correctness prevailing upon etymology).

No comment. . .

19   In 1566, Giraldi CINZIO (born in Ferrara) wrote his 110 Novelle.

The first ten deal exclusively with the manners of Italian prostitutes and are a clear attempt to attract the vulgar reader; but they are nevertheless very stylishly written.

Interestingly, although Italians can boast of two firsts under this heading, there is a great lack of erotic literature in Italian apart from some romantic/epic writings in the sixteenth century (Ariosto and Tasso in particular).

Pornography is practically unknown in the Italian literary field. There is only one modern exception, *D'Annunzio*.

If I discount Ovid's *Ars Amandi* because of its antiquity, I find that Italian literature is conspicuously lacking not only in any material of the kind that could be classed as pornographic but especially in any writing that is even remotely connected with amatory functions or techniques. Apart from the studies of prostitutes in the sixteenth century by Pietro Aretino (see his *Ragionamenti* published in Venice in 1534), and Lorenzo Veniero in *La Prostituta Errante*, and in the nineteenth century by Lombroso, Mantegazza and others mainly in connection with their criminality, there are no major works in the Italian language concerning the subject of sexuality.

It is almost as though there were a reluctance on the part of the Italians to discuss sex in the abstract. It is interesting to note that until the late 1950s, the word 'sesso' (sex) in Italian merely identified in current usage the physical connotations of men and women. The translation to a synonym of 'sexuality' or, even worse, of sexual activity or the act itself, was the result of American influence. One may discuss in Italian the sex of the angels, but one does not 'have sex'. Even in English the word is abused as a matter of semantics.

Italian men may discuss a particular woman or an activity: never sex as a concept. If one feels sexuality, one has no need to discuss its theory.

LITERARY CRITICISM

20   In 1498, Lorenzo VALLA (born in Rome) proved the forgery of the donation of Constantine. He also happens to have translated Aristotle's poetics into Latin.

21   1570, saw the establishment of the first literary critic in the

person of Lodovico CASTELVE-
TRO (born in Modena).

Our criticism, however, is not confined to
literature. The Italians are constantly
criticizing. They criticize their neighbours,
their friends, their nation, other peoples,
but never themselves.

We have a very highly developed
critical sense that knows no social,
political or religious barrier; but we seem
quite incapable of turning it inwards. To
this extent, we are continuing the Roman
tradition. We hardly need reminding of
Horace's satire, which in laughter re-
proaches customs (*Castigat ridendo mores*).

We are also in this sense continuing the
other Roman tradition of the Fescennine
Verses that, round about the middle of
the first century BC, became so offensive
that they had to be banned. I still
remember from my school days how
Horace puts it: *Donec iam saevus apertam in
rabiem coepit verti et per honestas ire domos
impune minax*, which roughly translated
means that the jocular dialogues which
were already offensive became vicious
and more open and affected even
reputable homes. An early version of
Private Eye!

But, as I have said, I am not sure how
good we are at self-criticism. If we were
better at it, we might be more willing to
make allowances for others: we would
then find it somewhat easier to remedy
one of our major faults namely, our utter
inability to pull together as a nation.

Whilst I am in the mood for self-
criticism, may I draw to the reader's
attention another two faults of Italy as a
nation. First, our lack of civic sense, said
repeatedly by many to stem from the fact
that we have only been a nation since the
First World War; in my view, however, to
be ascribed to our exasperated individuality.

Second, our hopelessness at public
relations, especially at State level (a friend
of mine, a senior Italian government
official, years ago described them as
'rubbish relations'). By that I do not
mean that individual household name
industries cannot publicize their wares,
but simply wish to draw attention to what
I find quite extraordinary, namely our
inability, if not unwillingness, as a nation,
to show off what we have been and what
we have done. (I'll make an exception for
myself, of course. . .)

I state unhesitatingly that if any of
those countries which I can only describe
as having, or having had, imperialistic
frames of mind (Great Britain, the United
States, France, Germany) had or could
claim to have achieved or produced one
hundredth part of what the Italians have
done, the rest of the world would never
hear the last of it.

MUSIC & MUSICAL
INSTRUMENTS

In the list that follows there will be names
you know and names you think are
'missing'; there will also be names, no
doubt, that you have never heard before.
As I said earlier, this should not be
considered unusual. For example, Puccini
may have been the initiator of a particular
melodic line, but he discovered nothing.
Opera and music pre-existed him.

The names that follow are the names
of people who were, each in their own
way, the first in their fields; alternatively,
the events that are recorded occurred in
Italy for the first time ever.

22   In 1028, Guido D'AREZZO
established the Western system of
notation based on eight notes in an

octave which is still used extensively throughout the Western world despite attempts by Schoenberg and others to upstage it with a twelve-note system. D'Arezzo is said to have produced his system while in the Benedictine Abbey at Pomposa, on the Adriatic.

To him we owe even the abbreviations for the seven notes which, apart from 'doh' which he had initially called 'ut' (as it remains in France) and 'si', which was added at the end of the fifteenth century, are still known today as 're mi fa sol la', the first two letters of a Latin verse in a hymn praising St John.

23   In 1490, the 'frottola' came into existence as the predecessor of the madrigal.

24   In 1492, whilst Christopher Columbus was travelling to the Indies, Franchino GRIFFORI first described tuned glasses.

25   Temperament is, of course, of great interest to musicians. The reader with a musical bent might like to know that the first mention of temperament is owed to Franchino GRIFFORI, who wrote the treatise *Practica Musica* (see *Britannica*, Vol. 18, p. 742).

26   Around the year 1500, the first thin-cased harpsichord construction was achieved in Italy.

27   In 1501, in Venice, Ottaviano PETRUCCI printed the first music to show staves, notes and words together.

28   The first (printed) book dealing entirely with music is the *Theoricum Opus Musicae* by musical theorist Franchinus GAFURIUS (1451-1522). It was printed in Naples in 1480 by Francesco di Dino.

Although devoted entirely to music, it contains no printed musical examples, but rather has spaces left for the notes to be inserted by hand. (Bruno)

29   AFRANIO (of Pavia) was a Canon at the cathedral in Ferrara and is said to have invented the bassoon. He is certainly given as the inventor of the bassoon in the year 1500 in the *Harwin Chronology of Inventions, Innovations and Discoveries*. But according to Treccani, whatever he did invent it was not the same instrument as the modern bassoon.

30   During the Renaissance, the violin evolved in Italy.

31   In the sixteenth and seventeenth centuries, the first virginals and spinets were built in Italy.

32   In the middle of the sixteenth century, Andrea GABRIELI, born in Venice in 1520, established the procedures that were later to result in the Sonata and dedicated extensive attention to the question of orchestration.

33   Together with his nephew, Andrea, Giovanni GABRIELI, believed to have been born in Venice in 1556, set up the systems of performing music, both in St Mark's Church and elsewhere which, relying on different positions in the auditorium both for instrumental players and, above all, for singers and chorus, laid down the foundation upon which the modern orchestra was built.

34   Giovanni GABRIELI was also the first to specify the use of particular instruments for portions of a musical composition, and also to consider the position of sections

of players. It was left to his compatriot Claudio Monteverdi to standardize the principles of orchestration.

35 Temperament has just been mentioned. In the middle of the sixteenth century another Italian, Luca MARENZIO, was the first to rely on the existence of lutes, tuned in equal temperament, to experiment in chromaticism (see *Britannica*, Vol. 18, p. 743).

The sixteenth century also saw the establishment – in 1563 – of the 'Camerata dei Bardi' (otherwise known as 'Camerata Fiorentina'), a sort of meeting-place or club for those who, dissatisfied with the musical trends of the period, decided to add music of their own to established literary works, especially madrigals, or even to lyrics of their own. They are often referred to as the founding fathers of opera and they paved the way for Monteverdi.

The Camerata counted amongst its members Vasari, the court painter Bronzino and the sculptor Bartolomeo Ammannati. One of its first tasks was the organizing, in the year following its foundation, of the funeral of Michelangelo. (John Hale, *The Civilization of Europe and the Renaissance*, Harper Collins, 1993, p. 408).

36 In 1597, Ottavio RINUCCINI (born in Florence) wrote his *Dafne*, thus becoming the first musician to use a libretto.

Rinuccini's libretto – if such it may be termed, because essentially it was merely a simple text prepared by a poet – allowed Jacopo Peri to develop for the first time what became known as 'opera'. Opera is a useful abbreviation of the Italian expression 'opera in musica', namely an exercise that has been set to music; the end of the sixteenth century represented a period where Italy's primacy in the field was asserted with Peri, Cavaliere and Monteverdi laying the foundations of this particular style of music.

37 In 1600, Agostini AGAZZARI (born in Siena) wrote the earliest known musical instruction book.

38 The oratorio originated in Italy. The earliest surviving oratorio was written by Emilio del CAVALIERE in 1600.

The oratorio was originally a musical entertainment mixed with religious education and evolved around the middle of the sixteenth century. Saint Filippo Neri instituted it in the oratory of the Roman Catholic Church which takes its name from him and which is still in existence.

39 In 1607, Girolamo FRESCOBALDI (born in Ferrara) established himself as the first master of organ composition.

40 In 1607, Claudio MONTEVERDI (born in Cremona) had his opera *Orfeo* first performed in Mantova. He had started his musical career some twenty years earlier and from about the year 1587, he can to all intents and purposes be considered the founder of modern music.

41 In 1617, Biagio MARINI (Brescia) wrote the first sonata for solo violin.

42 In 1622, Salomone ROSSI wrote the first specification of instruments for dance sets.

43 In 1634, Francesco LANDINI established the cadence that bears his name.

44 Tomaso ALBINONI (born in Venice in 1671) was the first composer to write concerti for solo violin.

45 In the seventeenth century, the Sordellina, a kind of musette, was invented in Naples (not to be confused with the sordino, the contrivance for damping or muting wind, string and percussion instruments.)

46 In 1698 Bartolomeo CRISTOFORI (born in Padova) constructed the first pianoforte.

What Cristofori did was to combine the qualities of the clavichord and the harpsichord into a single instrument. The clavichord would produce numerous shades of sound, but it was not a powerful instrument; the harpsichord had a bigger sound, but did not lend itself to crescendos or diminuendos. Hence his brilliant synthesis.

47 The Italian composer Alessandro GRANDI, who died in 1630, was the first to use the word 'cantata' in the modern sense. He was an assistant to Monteverdi at St Mark's in Venice and, as Britannica records: 'His "cantatas" are the precursors of the ground bass songs of Henry Purcell, the voice varying the melody over a repeated bass.'

48 Around the year 1700, the modern violin was first manufactured in Italy. Its principal makers were Gasparo da SALOÒ, Andrea AMATI and Giovanni Paolo MAGGINI. A few years later they were joined by the maker of the Rolls Royce of violins, namely Antonio STRADIVARIO (born in Cremona).

(Cremona in its time was well known for its musical instruments and there are still fifty violin makers at work there even today.)

STRADIVARIO

Stradivario's violins are world famous for their tone, power and beauty. For over 200 years, violin makers have been trying to reproduce the same features that make a Stradivarius unique, but so far without success.

Indeed, despite all the technical resources at our disposal, we do not even know whether such features are due to the varnish used, to the especially high mineral content of the wood, to a combination of both, to a special film of 'pozzolana' ash, just to a special knack he had, or whether it is the combination, as it in fact is claimed for his Cremonese violin, of Balkan maple wood and a similar wood from the Val di Fiemme.

Recently, Joseph Nagyvary, a Professor of Biochemistry and Biophysics in Texas, has suggested that the benefit of the violins constructed by Stradivario and his successors was derived from spruce wood that was stored in the sea, which created minute holes in the wood that improved the sound, by providing extra richness and unique resonance. Even so, he was unique, as were his instruments.

Stradivario also manufactured cellos, violas, lutes, mandolins, guitars and bows. His output was enormous: it is claimed that he manufactured between 700 and 1500 instruments.

When he died in 1737, aged ninety-three, he was universally acclaimed as the successor of Amati; he was also the richest man in Cremona. He certainly lived life to the full, in a city full of life. He had two wives each of whom had five children.

Stradivario had started his apprenticeship quite early, so that by the time he was eighteen he was already in the workshop of his master, Nicolò Amati. Even in his lifetime, people were conscious of his greatness. The world's most famous scientist, at the time, Galileo, himself the son of a musician, called Stradivario's instruments 'incomparable'. Most interesting of all, perhaps, is the fact that he made his greatest and most successful instruments during his seventies.

49 Stradivario also devised the violin bridge in modern form and the proportions of the violins which he manufactured set the standard which has prevailed to this day: his patterns have been followed by all subsequent manufacturers of stringed instruments, particularly cellos.

I have already remarked on our inability to explain away the success, in tonal terms, of what he produced. But apart from tone, the instruments that he made were unique because they were exceptionally strong, and yet light, resonant, without being harsh, and of outstanding patination. The Stradivari sound has been variously described as warm, glowing, rich, deep; it is not so strong as that of a Guarneri, and yet it is more vital: it is almost as though his instruments are living things and gain from the association with the human being who plays them.

To all intents and purposes his instruments are his heirs, and, as far as one can tell, all those that have survived are in excellent condition. Most of them are dated and many of them have names; for example, the Rawlins guitar, the Cristiani, Tuscan and Davidoff cellos, the Hellier, Tuscan and Archinto violas, the Emiliani, Tuscan, Cathédrale, Amatise, Soil, Reyner, Francescatti, Kreutzer, Marie Hall, Gibson, Cremonese and Parke violins. Each has its own history and personality, style and sound. They are all members of a unique family of exceptional vitality and continuity. For over 300 years Stradivar-

io's techniques have given the world the joy of the sounds of his instruments. Cristofori produced the piano, Stradivario developed the violin: how much delight and pleasure have these two names provided for future generations. Pleasure for the performers as well as for the audiences.

It is no small claim to lay, that one has been able to give pleasure; others may have fared better in different fields but when it comes to style and pleasure (whether of the table, of the arts or particularly of music) the Italians' claim is paramount: it would appear that the Almighty has endowed Italy with the ability to make people happy.

One final consideration: with such a plethora of first-class instruments available, it must have been comparatively easy for Stradivario's esteemed contemporary, Antonio Vivaldi, to write his music, especially *The Four Seasons*. (Vivaldi was the son of a barber.)

50 In 1712, Francesco Antonio BONPORTI (born in Trento) wrote his *Invenzioni* for the harpsichord. Of significance is the fact that Bach (JS) got his ideas from Bonporti.

51 In 1721, Pietro LOCATELLI (born in Bergamo) anticipated Paganini by being the first virtuoso violinist and bravura performer.

52 In 1721, Carlo BROSCHI, otherwise known as Farinelli, established himself as the most celebrated castrato singer ever.

He was Neapolitan, like Caruso, and he was at least as famous as the latter. He was the best known 'soprano' of his generation and sang in most places in Europe. He spent a long time at the Spanish Court and had an outstanding success in London. Being to all intents and purposes a 'primadonna', it is recorded that he behaved exactly like one.

He was jealous of his reputation as a singer and whenever he was on stage with anyone whose voice might compete with his, to ensure that in the high notes they did not out-perform him, he would either tread on the toes of the other singers or actually pinch their thighs in order to upset their vocal balance. He had been preceded by another 'castrato', Niccoló Grimaldi, otherwise known as 'Nicolini', who however did not quite achieve the same notoriety as Farinelli. Other 'male' singers taking female roles in the eighteenth century were Giovanni Carestini and Giacinto Conti Gizziello, amongst many.

53 Giovanni Battista SAMMAR-TINI (born in Milan early in the eighteenth century) an organist and initially a composer of sacred music, was the first to compose a four-movement symphony in 1734. Haydn's *First Symphony* is dated 1759.

54 SAMMARTINI took the stringed quartets, which had become quite fashionable by then and added a number of other instruments, namely the horn, the oboe, the clarinet, the trumpet and the flute.

55 SAMMARTINI was also amongst the first, if not the first, to compose symphonies for concert performance, taking as a starting point the overtures that were common in Italian opera.

He was a very prolific composer. Varying estimates have been given of his works, ranging from 2,000 to 3,000, but of these only some three or four are extant. He influenced all his contemporaries and some of his successors.

56 SAMMARTINI was the first to use the 'mordente' and syncopation. Gluck studied with him from 1737 to 1741.

57 It can also be said, without fear of contradiction, that SAMMARTINI was the first true composer of symphonic music. Burney describes the instrumental score of Sammartini as 'marvellous', since it ensures that none of the orchestral performers ever stay idle, the violins in particular being given no respite ever from playing

Fetis records the anecdote according to which the German composer, Mysilweczech, was attending a concert in Milan when, for the first time, he heard performances of the 'old symphonies' of Sammartini and exclaimed: 'I have found the father of Haydn's style.'

Sammartini's elder brother Giuseppe, born like him in Milan, settled in London where he died after having entered the service of the Prince of Wales. He was so closely associated with the capital that he became known as 'the Londoner'.

(The authorities for the above are:
(a) *Britannica*, R VIII, p. 832
(b) A Colombani, *Le Nove Sinfonie di Beethoven*, Bocca, Milan, 1947, pp. 15-19).

58 In 1740, Francesco GEMINIANI (born in Lucca) wrote the first published violin method.

59 In 1750, Giuseppe TARTINI (born in Padova) discovered the so-called 'difference tone' or 'resultant tone'. This has the effect that a note emitted a third sound. (Tartini was famous for the short violin piece known as the 'Devil's Trill', the result, so it was said, of his having made a pact with the devil that he would be the greatest violinist ever. Curiously enough, the foremost virtuoso of the following century,

Nicoló PAGANINI, took it up as one of his own show pieces.)

60   In 1758, Tommaso TRAET-TA (born at Bitonto) started operatic reform. His works were accompanied by the orchestra, the chorus as well as the ballet sequences, and were all brought more closely into the action and integrated, thus anticipating Gluck and future operatic developments.

61   The first mechanical piano was invented towards the end of the eighteenth century by Nicoló FRABRIS.

62   Around the same time, Muzio CLEMENTI invented a self-performing piano.

Clementi, whom all piano students know because of his Sonatas, primarily, was also well known on the London scene. Although born in Rome in 1752, he was still in his teens when Sir Peter Beckford invited him to stay in England where Clementi made his home, becoming quite anglicized.

He substantially improved the new keyboard and pedalling system set up in 1770 by Americus Backer and subsequently refined by Broadwood and Longman and even set up a pianoforte factory.

He was a virtuoso who, in 1790, retired and dedicated himself to teaching. One of his most famous pupils was John Field but above all, he should be remembered for having founded in 1813 together with Cramer, Viotti and Salomon, the Royal Philharmonic society.

Amongst his other pupils may be mentioned Czerny, Moscheles, Cramer and Bertini.

63   The first opera star, as that term is understood nowadays, was Adelina PATTI. Although she was

born in Madrid in 1843 of Italian parents, she went to the USA as a child and started appearing in concerts in New York City from the age of seven; in 1859 she made her operatic debut there in *Lucia di Lammermoor.* She was only sixteen: what was subsequently termed the 'reign of Patti' had begun.

During the following forty-six years, or perhaps more correctly until 1906 when she retired from professional singing, she created quite a furore. Her voice was not only one of the greatest, but the evenness of production and the purity of sound were considered as unique at the time as her extravagances, for which she became a legend, both in America and in Europe. She would travel through the United States in a private railroad car, which is said to have cost $60,000, her earnings during three seasons from 1882 to 1885 reaching the fabulous sum of $450,000.

When she was scheduled to appear in a city people used to get into line for tickets as early as the night before (see G. Schiavo *Four Centuries of Italian-American History,* Centre for Migration Studies, New York, 1992, p. 190). In keeping with her stardom, she married three times, divorcing her first two husbands.

64   In 1859, Giuseppe DONATI created a musical instrument known as an 'ocarina' – an elaboration of traditional Italian carnival whistles in either clay or metal. The instrument was to gain professional popularity, especially in the USA in the 1930s. We know that he came from Budrio, a small town associated with the production of musical instruments.

65   In the nineteenth century, the accordion was invented by Paolo SOPRANI. His firm still exists nowadays manufacturing probably

the best accordions in the world as well as other musical instruments (e.g. small pianos).

66   The first song specifically written for recording was, according to its label, 'Mattinata' by Ruggero LEONCAVALLO, being played for the first time on 8 April 1904 with Caruso singing and the composer accompanying him at the piano.

67   CARUSO was the first singer ever to sell more than one million gramophone records.

68   In 1913, Luigi RUSSOLO experimented with electronic music, thereby anticipating synthesized music.

69   In 1981, Giuseppe di GIUGNO built the first super-computerized musical instrument. Di Giugno's musical instrument is a far cry from the melodies of the eighteenth and nineteenth centuries.

The impact on the world of Italian opera is too well known to be rehearsed by me. The impact of the works written by Monteverdi and Cherubini, as forerunners of a musical style, is equally great. But sometimes the influence of opera occurs where it is least expected. It may, or may not, surprise you to know that Italian opera generally, and the music of Cherubini in particular, exercised a very great and formative influence upon Chopin. In his book *Chopin* (Dent, London, 1947), Arthur Hedley (p. 59) considers that the debt Chopin owes to Italian opera in general is 'enormous'.

It is worth noting that the British National Anthem was composed by Giovanni Battista Lulli, who was born in Florence in 1632. He spent most of his life in France, however, where he gallicized his Italian name when he took up

French citizenship. It was part of a commission which he received to mark the inauguration by Louis XIV of the Maison St Cyr, a young lady's college.

ITALY AND THE BAGPIPES

The impact on music which has already been referred to above (suffice it to recall that at the time of Haydn's London successes it was calculated that there were in London itself at least sixty-three Italian opera composers) was not confined to England.

It may come as a surprise to Scottish readers that 'piobaireachd', the classical music of the bagpipes, may be an Italian importation. It is a matter of record that the development of this particular form of musical art in Scotland and its extension to many other countries is due in the main to the musical genius of one family, the MacCrimmons.

Much has been written about this family, which is first recorded in Skye in the 1500s, and who became known as the leading composers and players of bagpipe music.

Although the debt owed to the MacCrimmon family is widely acknowledged, their origins are clouded in mist and the most that can be said (see p. 162 in *The Companion to Gaelic Scotland*, Basil Blackwell Limited, Oxford, 1983), is, (1) according to the Scots, they came over from Harris, (2) to the Irish, they emigrated to Glendale from Ireland, and (3) to other more objective observers and historians, they were Italians. Unbelievable though it sounds, it has been claimed that the founder of the MacCrimmon line was a Protestant musician from Cremona who was escaping from the clutches of the Catholic Inquisition. There is no doubt, according to the authority cited above, that some at least of the later MacCrimmons believed that the founder member of their family was in fact an Italian from Cremona.

This is less surprising than it sounds. The surname prefix 'Mac' is the Gaelic (both Scottish and Irish) for 'son'. The conversion of 'Cremona' into initially Crimona (the English always pronounce the Italian 'e' as 'i'), and the later transformation into something more British than the Italian of the kind that we have seen elsewhere in this book (see for example Corsini into **Curzon** and Rucellai into **Russell**) is by no means unusual, and could almost be considered a natural development. Indeed, in Gaelic MacCrimmen becomes MacCruimmen or MacCrummen.

But leaving aside such linguistic refinements, it should be noted that the Highland bagpipe with its two tenor drones and a bass drone is not that far removed from the rather unique 'zampogna', so that there is no reason why it should not have been possible for an Italian in Scotland to replicate the 'zampogna' of his own country.

Nor should it be thought that Scotland is far removed from Italy. Italians have always had a great interest in Scotland. Suffice it to recall the Ossianic Poems and the Scottish epics were translated as early as 1763 by the Italian Abbé Melchiorre Cesarotti.

The principal objection to the tradition that the MacCrimmons were originally Italians who settled in Scotland, is that 'zampogna' originates and is used mainly in southern Italy (Abruzzo, Campania, Calabria, and to a lesser degree, Sicily). The use of bagpipes in northern Italy is less common, although the French were quite fond of them and used them extensively, especially at the time of Lully. So it is possible that Italians from northern parts of Italy, like Cremona, could have learnt about the bagpipes from the French.

All this is speculative, of course, because there appear to be no extant records to deal with this aspect of the matter. But the fact remains that members of the MacCrimmon family believed that their ancestor was Italian.

*   *   *

One final point. Evidence has emerged (October 1997) that the music of the eighteenth century composer Pasquale Anfossi, who came originally from Liguria, but spent a good part of his life in Naples, was copied by Mozart in the last section of his great *Requiem Mass*. (It has also been suggested that there are similarities to Anfossi's work in *Don Giovanni, The Magic Flute* and *The Marriage of Figaro*.)

Mozart's *Requiem Mass* was left unfinished and was completed by his pupil Sussmayr, who is said to have utilized the themes created by Anfossi. Maybe. It is worth noting that Anfossi in his lifetime was probably better known than Mozart. Whether there was actual copying and technical plagiarism, or whether Mozart developed the tune himself, having heard Anfossi's work, must be a matter of conjecture.

A further statistical datum is that from 1675 to the end of the century, no fewer than eighty-three Italian composers, mainly of opera, lived in London, Italian opera paving the way for Handel's triumphs.

70   Now possibly a more controversial 'first'. The founder and creator of jazz was an Italian from the USA, Domenico (otherwise 'Nick') LA ROCCA. He founded the 'original Dixieland jazz band'. In his autobiography, Louis Armstrong has this to say about La Rocca and

his band: 'Only four years before I learnt to play the trumpet . . . the first great jazz orchestra was formed in New Orleans by a cornet player named Domenic James La Rocca.'

I say controversially firstly, because it is conceivable that La Rocca did not actually create jazz, but elaborated existing tunes; and secondly, because he was a citizen of the USA. Nevertheless, he was undoubtedly the first to record jazz music on 26 February 1917, courtesy of Victor 'Talking Machine' Coy. The band's repertoire numbers (*Livery Stable Blues* and what was later called the *Original Dixieland One-Step*) were the first jazz phonograph records to be issued. (See *The Story of the Original Dixieland Jazz Band* by H.O. Brunn, Louisiana State University Press, 1960.)

PAINTING & HISTORY OF ART

In this field, the contribution of the Italians is so great that it would take volumes to record it. Since, however, I am concerned only with 'firsts', the task is somewhat easier.

71   Perspective drawing was first studied by Paolo UCCELLO in the fifteenth century.

72   In sculpture, DONATELLO, (born in Florence in 1386) one of the greatest of all Renaissance artists, was the first to highlight the personality of the individual in his sculptures. He looked upon the human body which he was re-creating 'as a self-activating, functional organism', whose human personality he represented with confidence in his own work and that of the individual, whose shape he was sculpting.

73   He was also the first to develop the 'schiacciato' technique of lower relief in order to gain greater fluidity and, in his sculpture of 'David', to exhibit the first free-standing nude of the Renaissance and, indeed, the first nude statue since Graeco-Roman days (*Britannica* Vol. III p. 618). It was also the first free-standing bronze statue.

74   In 1390, Cennino CENNINI in his book *Il Libro dell'Arte* wrote the first 'how to do it' book for artists, a sort of do-it-yourself guide. In it, he anticipated to some extent the work of Alberti because he actually included a section on 'the proportions which a perfectly formed man's body should possess'. A male chauvinist, one might consider, since he ignored the proportions of a woman's body; but conscious of the criticism he explained it away on the basis that: 'the proportions of a woman. . . . are not exact multiples of one another in the way men's are'.

No comment.

75   Domenico CAMPAGNOLA (born at Padova) was the first print maker in 1500.

76   At the same time his brother Giulio CAMPAGNOLA anticipated by more than 200 years the stipple engraving technique.

77   The first art school of the modern world is attributed to Lorenzo de'MEDICI, who set it up in 1488.

I have added the qualification 'of the modern world' because there seems to be little evidence that there were any organized art schools before this time. The Greek sculptors Scopas, Praxiteles and Lysippus have come down to us as great, but we know nothing of whether there were properly set up schools around them. In search of further glory to enable him to qualify for the title given to him in his lifetime of 'Il Magnifico' (The Magnificent), Lorenzo set up courses for artists. Aside from his patronage of Botticelli, he is noteworthy for having allowed the twelve-year old Michelangelo to grow up together with his own seven children whilst the future master was learning his trade.

78 Sofonisba ANGUISSOLA, born at Cremona in 1528, was the first recorded woman painter who achieved any kind of recognition as well as to work on commission.

She was already reasonably well established by the middle of the sixteenth century in an artistic world where woman's form may have reigned supreme in the paintings of Anguissola's contemporaries, but not women's abilities in the artistic sphere. She was well known at the court of Philip II of Spain for her portraits, was twice married, and as a well-established woman of ninety-six years of age Anthony van Dyke drew a portrait of her in Palermo. Her style was influenced considerably by that of Raffaello and Parmigianino.

I nearly forgot!. . .

79 Giotta da BONDONE who died in 1337 (there is some doubt as to his precise date of birth) was the first great painter of the 'modern' era. He was the first to depict the naturalness of postures and facial expressions and, above all, to achieve depth in his pictures by his two-dimensional representation of figures and objects.

80 In 1550, Giorgio VASARI (born in Arezzo) became the first art historian.

He was himself a painter of repute. He painted the scene of the final judgment on the ceiling of the dome of Florence Cathedral.

His 'Lives' of Italian architects, painters and sculptors provides biographies and anecdotes for all the artists who had gone before him, as well as for his contemporaries. Despite a fertile imagination, his eminently legible account represents compulsory and enjoyable reading for anyone interested in the artists of the Italian Renaissance.

He shows that those whom he describes were well aware of their uniqueness in society and he confirms the high quality of the cultural climate of Renaissance Italy.

The information, facts, gossip that he provided and the judgements he formulated are of fundamental importance for any student of Renaissance art. Anticipating, to some extent, the extensive data I shall be providing about Leonardo, and purely as an aside, I should like to record at this stage what Vasari has to say about him. He is at pains to point out that on top of all his virtues, Leonardo had 'a beauty of body never sufficiently extolled'.

The only fault that Vasari could find with Leonardo was his restlessness or rather the restlessness of his imagination, his constant desire to acquire knowledge in all possible fields, to explore the workings of the least significant things, almost to amuse himself in doing so. As a result, given the nature of his temperament and the constraints of time, Leonardo – always according to Vasari – had a tendency to start things and never finish them. (Just imagine if he had had the time to bring to conclusion what he started and then. . .)

His work (full title *Lives of the Most Eminent Painters, Sculptures and Architects*) was started in the 1540s and was published for the first time in 1550. An expanded and revised edition appeared in 1568.

The town (Arezzo) where he was born in 1511 is about seventy-five-odd kilometres south east of Florence in the valley of the River Arno. The Florentine influence on him therefore is exceptionally marked.

He knew many of the artists whose work he described, but apart from that, he was in a very good position to understand their character because he himself was a very busy and reasonably competent painter of whom it can be said that, although he did not have the genius of some of the others whose work he recorded for posterity, he did produce an exceptional number of colourful works, particularly in Florence.

His success, apart from being a contemporary of artists whose fame exceeded his own, lies in his exceptional powers of observation and his skill in describing what he saw.

It is mainly to Vasari (as well as to Condivi and Giannotti) that we owe the wealth of information about the life of the greatest Italian artist, Michelangelo (born 1475, died 1564, the year in which Shakespeare was born). He is one of the great names of world culture; a painter, architect, sculptor, poet and humanist. Indeed, it has been said that to him are to be traced the Italian Renaissance, the Northern Reformation and the Baroque. There is no doubt that his contemporaries knew that he was a great man and that he would outlive his age. Also, to him we owe what is probably the first

recorded forgery in sculpture.

81   In 1495, MICHELANGELO executed a sculptured 'Sleeping Cupid' which is now lost, with the aim of passing it off as an antique. As such, it was resold to a high dignitary of the Roman Catholic Church who genuinely believed it to be an object of antiquity. When Michelangelo realized what had happened, he offered to reimburse the money that he had originally received for it.

Michelangelo had displayed such copying abilities especially in painting, from a very early age, when he was apprenticed to Domenico Ghirlandaio for he had then copied a printed sheet by the German, Martin Schongauer, so accurately in terms of colours, forms and tints that in this instance as well as in many others, when the copies were compared with the originals, they were wholly indistinguishable.

We owe this information to Giorgio Vasari who dedicates some time to the question of Michelangelo's copying ability.

82   Sandro BOTTICELLI (1445-1510) has been described as the first botanical painter of modern times. One is referred to his famous painting known as 'La Primavera' (Spring) which is to be seen in the Uffizi Gallery in Florence.
The painting was the first to contain a number of plants (specifically, more than thirty) with descriptions of beautiful garlands and accurately drawn flowers.

83   The Italian painter and architect believed by all to be the principal heir of Raphael, Giulio ROMANO (real name Giulio PIPPI) is said to be the initiator of the Mannerist style. *Britannica* records his 'Palazzo del Te', on the outskirts

of Mantua, begun in 1525 and built and decorated by him and his pupils, as one of the first and greatest examples of Mannerist architecture.

84   The first formal academy of art was founded in Florence in 1563. It was called the 'Accademia delle Arti e Disegno' (v. *Britannica*, Vol. 9, p. 1112), and became known later as the 'Accademia di Belle Arti'. Similar academies were founded in Perugia in 1573 and in Rome (as the 'Accademia di San Luca') in 1577. Its first president was Federico Zuccaro.

Another Italian painter of the female sex who is receiving belated recognition as one of the very first women painters is Artemisia GENTILESCHI. She was involved in a rather complicated rape trial in Rome in 1612 and that interfered with her career. In 1639 she was invited to come over to England by Charles I, who was an obsessive collector of Italian art. Her father was also a well-known painter of the Italian baroque school (*Britannica*, Vol. IV, p. 472).

85   In 1696, Filippo BALDI-NUCCI (born in Florence) was the first art historian to make full use of original documents.
I distinguish between him and Vasari because Vasari relied mainly on gossip and did not document himself quite so scientifically as Baldinucci.
He was also the first to realize the importance of drawings in the study of paintings; the great collection of drawings in the Uffizi Palace in Florence is the result of his efforts.

Nor were Anguissola and Gentileschi the only women painters of significance. Just over a century later Rosalba CAR-RIERA (born in Venice in 1675) became exceptionally well known and established her own 'school' which by the beginning of the eighteenth century was very well frequented by members of the European nobility. Her portraits of the beautiful women of Venice are quite valuable even today.

86   In exceptional recognition of her fame, she was the first woman to be admitted in 1720 to the Academy of Painting in Paris. Sadly, she lost her sight a long time before her death in 1757.

(The authority for the foregoing statements is to be found in Treccani, Volume 3, p. 351 and Volume 9, p. 157.

87   In 1880, Giovanni MORELLI (born in Verona) established the so-called 'Morellian method'. His was a system of direct study which formed the basis for subsequent art criticism and relied on the evidence of the work of art itself. Bernard Berenson was his principal follower.

88   In 1909, Filippo Tommaso MARINETTI (born in Egypt) established Futurism.

It is well known that Marinetti published his first manifesto on the front page of the French magazine *Le Figaro* on 20 February 1909. Of course, French at the time was a language in fairly common use but it is a fact that Futurism was born in Milan where Marinetti, despite having been born himself in Alexandria in Egypt, had been living for a few years. Indeed, he wrote: 'Even though I was born in Egypt I am tied to the forest of Milan chimney-pots and to its old duomo.'
He had a keen feeling for public relations. He once stood above a square in Venice, in his very early days, dropping copies of his manifesto onto the crowd below.

PHILOSOPHY

89 In or about the year 1535, Giordano BRUNO (born in Nola) was the first to represent the universe as infinite. His ideas were 'picked up' by Galileo, Kepler and William Gilbert and he anticipated many concepts developed later on by Darwin, Huxley and Vogt.

Bruno was a convert to Calvinism and arrived in London in 1583 from Paris. He was hoping to get a professorship at Oxford but was too outspoken, going so far as to describe England as 'an island of barbarians', echoing the feelings that a number of Italians at that time had about this country for quite a while.

I believe that Giordano Bruno is grossly underrated in the Anglo-American world. The reason cannot be that the Inquisition charged him with heresy in 1592 and he always refused to recant, with the result that he was burnt alive at the stake. Perhaps it is because his comments on London society (he spent a little time in England) were on the whole fairly negative; I cannot tell, but his view of the universe propounded nearly five centuries ago is increasingly being endorsed by modern science. Maybe he was wrong when he suggested that there may be life on other worlds around us: but his intuition and his interpretation of the universe are unique and have, in fact, been described as 'truly revolutionary'.

90 In 1565, Bernardino TELESIO (born in Cosenza) was the first philosopher and natural scientist to adopt empirical criteria, to object to the practice of making generalizations without providing concrete data, as had been done by a number of the Greek philosophers, especially Aristotle, and to move over to the evidence of the senses rather than of primary theoretical concepts. In so doing he was anticipating both Sir Francis Bacon, who called him 'The first of the moderns', and his two compatriots, Campanella and Bruno (both from the south of Italy) as well as Thomas Hobbes.

None of the above-mentioned Italian philosophers can truly be termed great. In his *History of Western Philosophy* Bertrand Russell does not mention any of them. This is understandable in respect of Bruno, who was most unpopular in England when he stayed there; it may be understandable also for another reason, namely that not all Bruno's works have been translated into English. I wonder whether Bertrand Russell read Italian?

But to ignore not only him but also Campanella and above all, Telesio, seems stretching italophobia somewhat too far. Indeed, it is also interesting to observe that the only Italian 'philosopher' whom Russell records, (apart from St Thomas Aquinas, St Augustine and Galileo), is the political philosopher Machiavelli. No criticism of that, but one wonders what the rationale was that caused him to omit Bruno, Campanella and Telesio and to include, for example, Byron.

That the Italians have not made a greater contribution to philosophy is somewhat surprising. Philosophizing seems to suit us. There is also a contemplative element in some of our thinking that, especially in the south of Italy, must be derived from the Arabs directly. Nevertheless, there is an explanation.

On the whole, Italians are realists. As they themselves defy categorization, they abhor classification and systematization. They are only interested in practical solutions: their resourcefulness dictates this.

In a strange way – and I know that by saying this I shall contradict all that the English (and probably most of the rest of the Western world) have ever believed about the Italians – we are doers rather than thinkers.

This is why Italians have never really been too interested in philosophy. Philosophy, or love of knowledge, is by definition a theoretical science. It teaches us to make an effort to understand what goes on around us, what are the causes of our thinking and of our behaviour, what is the reason for our existence, whether God exists, etc. Although it may have practical applications, it is not in any sense a practical science.

When it comes to the reality of life, one needs a concrete approach; one needs a concrete science that will enable us to improve our lot, to learn new techniques, new methods, in substance, to change the world about us.

And in this, as becomes more apparent under the entries for 'Physics', Italians have been leaders. The practical importance of science was recognized by Leonardo, Galileo and many others. True, for Leonardo, more in connection with war than with everyday life; true for both him and Galileo because both of them had to justify their existence to their paymasters. But even so, this shows that scientists/philosophers like Galileo and artists/scientists like Leonardo had, like other Italians, their feet firmly on the ground.

The same practical approach also explains the Italians' lack of patriotism. The great Italian hero is not Mazzini. I know that we are all taught at school that his contribution to Italian political emancipation and to the repulsion of the Austrian yoke is great. But his thoroughly honourable, stirring cries of 'God and country', 'thought and action now and forever', never really meant very much to the Italians even when they were first uttered. The Italian revolutionary movement, as all historians have observed – in common with most revolutionary movements – was inspired by a small group of intellectuals. We have never been able fully to understand Mazzini's austerity and his capacity for suffering, nor I suppose, cynically, his appeal to thought.

The Italian national hero is Garibaldi. He donned a red shirt and, in defiance of authority, with little official support, if any, and with even less apparent chance of success, he went to free the kingdom of the two Sicilies. There was adventure, there was resourcefulness, there was the 'locus classicus' of the Italian way of doing things, 'alla garibaldina'; for what that really means is, without necessarily thinking the matter out, impulsively, relying on one's heart and one's instinct.

I do not mean to sound critical. Reliance on one's heart and instinct is, to me at any rate, the greatest virtue in life: 'rationality' be damned!

The use of language is significant. Italians pray to emulate the behaviour of Garibaldi; nobody ever suggests that they should do things 'alla mazziniana'. If and insofar as we refer to Mazzini at all as representative of a particular style or manner, we do so when considering his beard and sideboards, but certainly not his spirit.

In the final analysis, all I am doing here is drawing a distinction between theory and practice, between Mazzini and Garibaldi. Ultimately, those who have things have even less need to broadcast the fact. Those who know things do not go around clamouring about their knowledge.

Be that as it may, it must be admitted

that in philosophy we have not contributed much. Perhaps it is because in essence we prefer not to be rational.

POETRY

91 **The sonnet was created in the thirteenth century by Jacopo da LENTINI.**

POTTERY

92 **Italians were the first to apply to the Islamic achievement of tin-glazed earthenware ornamentation additional colours and the painting of figures and scenes.**

This resulted in the 'istoriato'-type of pottery more especially known as maiolica (or majorica, from Majorca whence the first importations may have come).

Dates and places in this connection seem uncertain. The most that can be said with any degree of accuracy is that the first Islamic earthenware was imported into Italy around the year 1200, probably from North Africa.

It took the Italians almost three centuries to evolve a style which became unique. According to records, the 'istoriato' style started about 1515 in central Italy. The main centres of pottery were Faenza, Urbino, Deruta, Castel Durante, Orvieto, Gubbio and Caffaggiolo. The potters of Caffaggiolo were outstanding. 'Between 1500 and 1530, Stefano and Piero Di Filippo produced some of the most striking maiolica painted anywhere'. (Timothy Wilson, *Ceramic Art of the Italian Renaissance*, p. 86).

93 **Italians also developed the**

'sgraffio', namely the technique of incised slipware.

Italian maiolica was exported from the end of the fifteenth century to the rest of Europe. With it, Italy exported also its master craftsmen who travelled to France, Spain and the Low Countries, as well as to the rest of Central Europe, and played a leading role in the establishment of local traditions.

In 1567, they were established in Norwich and from there moved to London, firstly to Aldgate and then to Southwark.

94 **The first English pottery factories were set up by Italians. London delftware was extensively copied from maiolica.**

It is correct to say that 'wherever a national tin-glaze tradition exists, it can be traced back to sixteenth-century Italian immigrants' (*London Delftware* by Frank Britton, Jonathan Horne, 1986).

95 **In 1557, Cipriano PICCOLPASSO (born in Castel Durante) wrote the first treatise on the art of pottery. He then published his 'Three books of the Potter's Art'.**

THEATRE & ACTING

96/8 **Gian Giorgio TRISSINO (born Vicenza 1478, died Rome 1550) is well known to students of Italian literature as a philologist, a dramatist and a major contributor to the 'consolidation' of the Italian language.**
 To him we owe three firsts:
  1. **He turned away entirely from religious inspiration to Greek models (he was also a follower of the Roman playwright Plautus).**

2. More importantly, he was the first to set out the dramatic unities of action and time.

3. Finally, he was of fundamental importance for Italian dramatic works because he set out for the first time what was to become the standard poetic form in Italy by making extensive use of blank verse ('verso sciolto').

Trissino deserves mention also in a somewhat different context. It was he who discovered a young man by the name of Andrea Di Pietro Della Gondola who was working as a mason at one of his villas. Trissino gave him the kind of education that allowed him to become one of the most important architects the world has ever known, namely Andrea Palladio (q.v.).

The work he did, appreciating the Tuscan idiom, and ennobling the Italian language, is all too often forgotten, even by the Italians themselves.

99 In 1513, the first three-dimensional structures were erected on stage in Urbino.

100 In 1520, Angelo BEOLCO, otherwise known as RUZZANTE (born in Padova), organized one of the earliest professional troupes.

101 To Beolco's company we owe another first, namely the first theatrical contract with its members which listed the discipline which he had set up, the organization of the troupe and the rights and duties of the members. It was a novelty at the time, although in later years it became common practice.

102 In 1537, Sebastiano SERLIO (born in Bologna) published a work that concentrated on the practical stage of the sixteenth century. He

included lighting effects in his analysis which resulted in the most influential architectural treatise at the time and which has, in fact, passed into theatrical tradition. I should also mention at this stage that his work was also well known and admired, as well as studied, by Andrea Palladio (q.v.).

Henry VIII is credited with having adopted for the first time, in the early part of the sixteenth century, the Italian habit of dressing up in disguise after a dinner-party. This was a development clearly copied from Italy and known as a 'mask' or 'masque' and followed from the elaboration of stage effects and complicated scenery of the kind that Inigo Jones was to adopt and reinterpret for the English taste (see Allardyce Nicol: *The development of the Theatre* pub. 1927).

103 Acting can be said to have started in Italy with the Commedia dell'Arte in 1545. The Commedia dell'Arte lasted well into the eighteenth century.

104 The Commedia dell'Arte became famous throughout Europe and was the first troupe to 'go on tour'.

Italian Companies, and there were a number, went to Germany, France, Spain and England where, with greater or lesser success, they influenced the theatre developments of the countries they visited.

'Commedia dell'Arte' means both a professional, and an artisan performance. The term was initially used with some degree of contempt by the more knowledgeable Italian theatre members simply because no script was used: the 'Commedia dell'Arte' was improvised. There were no parts to learn and, when the actors went on the stage, they trusted their own judgement and ability to create a show, simply because the four essential characters were familiar to their audiences. There was 'Pantalone' (pantaloon), an old man, usually a bachelor or a widower, the 'Doctor' in his black hat who, in trying to show his knowledge and wisdom, usually spoke nonsense; and the two 'zanies', a noun taken from the Italian 'zanni', which is a bergamasque . . . . . corruption of Giovanni (John). These were Arlecchino and Brighella, the former usually in a tight-fitting suit with his mate Brighella, all four wearing masks and speaking Venetian dialect.

Already in 1570 the Austrian and German courts had resident 'Commedia dell'Arte' actors; in 1577, one of the 'Commedia dell'Arte' companies settled in London, a most important event since, as a result, Shakespeare was introduced to the clowns and the fools of the 'Commedia', which he was then able to employ so successfully in his plays.

The path of the 'Commedia dell'Arte' was followed into the next century, so much so that as early as 1645 one was established in Paris under the well-known actor Tiberio Fiorillo; another important occurrence, this time for the French, since Molière learnt much from the Italian actors, essentially how to construct his plays, but more particularly by borrowing characters.

As regards the theatrical disciplines of mime and pantomime, the Commedia dell'Arte still continues to influence England to this day.

105   The Christmas pantomime originated in Italy. Pantomime was already known to ancient Rome but in 1530 it was introduced into Italy as a 'modern' invention by Ruzzante.

106   The first modern style theatre

ever built was the Teatro Olimpico at Vicenza, commenced by Palladio in 1580 and completed by Scamozzi in 1583.

From 1605 to 1640, Inigo Jones applied in England all he had learnt about the theatre in Italy between 1596 and 1604.

107   In 1750, the first Italian scene designers were imported into England. From that moment onwards, Italian theatre design, architecture and scenery extended to France, Spain, Germany, Austria and Russia.

So much for the architecture and design of theatres. As regards the theatrical art itself, the only notable contribution I can recall in recent times by an Italian is that of Pirandello – the founder in effect of the modern theatre – who can be said to have exercised considerable influence upon some English writers, especially Harold Pinter.

108   In 1628, the first permanent proscenium was built at the Teatro Farnese in Rome (a temporary one had been built fifty years earlier by Francesco SALVIATI)

109   In 1638, Nicola SABBATINI (born in Pesaro) wrote the first manual for constructing theatrical scenes and machines and was the first to describe systems for shifting scenes about the stage.

110   In 1641, Giacomo TORELLI established what was known as the chariot-and-pole system of scene changing, an invention which was soon adopted by every European country, except England and Holland, and which became the standard method of shifting scenery until the end of the nineteenth century. (*Britannica*, Vol. XVII, p. 537).

111 In 1660, Gaspare **VIGARANI** built, in Paris, the **Salle des Machines**, the world's largest theatre, for the wedding of Louis XIV to Maria Theresa, daughter of Philip IV of Spain.

112 Towards the middle of the seventeenth century, Tiberio **FIORILLO** (1608-94), an Italian actor who frequently appeared at the Palais Royale with Molière, created the comic servant Scaramouche. He had previously become famous in the character of a braggart captain called Scaramucci, his technique consisting essentially of a form of mime, relying more on novel and expressive movements than on his voice.

113 While not strictly coming under this category the first designer of catafalques, in 1722, was Giuseppe Galli **BIBIENA** (born in Parma). He was one of seven members of a family of artists who did all sorts of things, including designing scenery for plays and ballets.

Apart from the actual catafalques, funerals in Italy are quite a spectacle. I should like to believe that if a deceased gets a very grand funeral indeed, it is because he was dearly loved and will be sadly missed. But, I am not so sure. Because of the Italian fondness for form, I think a funeral in Italy is very often the equivalent in death of the English

debutante ball. Those involved are very keen to out-do one another.

In southern Italy, the tradition is probably stronger. It finds its origins in the Roman 'Preficae' who were paid to go and cry and pull their hair at a funeral.

Funerals aside, the Bibiena brothers were surely the greatest scenographers ever. They dabbled in everything that gave colour or created effects.

One of their best exercises is to be found in the Chapel of the Sacred Heart at Sabbioneta. There, when you look upwards, you see the sky. Well, you believe you do; but in actual fact, the Bibiena brothers painted it on the dome of the chapel so successfully that the first impression is totally deceptive.

The illumination in the same church is also a great feat, considering that it was carried out over 250 years ago.

The general public no doubt associates the town of Parma with 'prosciutto di Parma' and 'Parmigiano' cheese but it should not be forgotten that Parma has been a centre of art and not merely of good food. For example, the dome of its cathedral decorated with Correggio's paintings is a small masterpiece.

Its Teatro Farnese was in its time the largest theatre in Europe, a marvel of the age, noted both for the steep layout of its seating as well as for having the first moveable stage.

114 The Farnese Art Gallery was the first open to the general public.

2. CIVIC LIFE

AMENITIES

The misconception still exists in some parts of the world of Italy being a poor agricultural country with little civic history; true, the land of art and beautiful things, of wine, women and song, but not much more.

The reader should be reminded that Italy's tradition as a country of cities goes back to the Roman era. It was at that time that the foundations were laid for the development of the major Italian cities, which continued to expand during the Middle Ages.

It was during the Renaissance that Italian architects and scientists spent time on the organization and the shape of the city, practical or ideal, thus laying the foundations of modern urban development.

The towers at San Gimignano (discussed under 'Skyscrapers') represented the first type of development typical of Italy, namely, houses set high above the remainder of the place; there are other examples in Florence.

Gradually, the houses became lower in height, often set within city boundary walls (a beautiful example is Lucca, symbol of an Italian view of life which saw the urban development as fairly distinct from the surrounding area) and, much later on, the kind of palaces that are to be found in many parts of Italy and especially along the Venice canals.

It is fundamental, however, to remember that the central square of the Italian city represented its heart and is where the principal statues and monuments were established. In that way, it became a feature of Italian social life, which also either mimics or gave rise to, depending on one's point of view, the theatrical aspect of Italian life. Put differently, the square was the theatre of Italian cities. That is where everything happened: government, executions, major events, marriages, and what John Ruskin described as the 'ephemeral' architecture, namely the little market, the stalls (typical of many Italian cities even to this day).

Probably the best-known example of a square in an Italian city representing a theatre is to be found in Siena, where it is quite clear that the stage is the centre part of the square in front of the Mangia Tower and the remainder represents the stalls.

But it is worth observing too at this point that a typical example or urban design dating back to the sixteenth century is to be found in the northern Italian town of Palmanova.

The town was built by the Venetians in 1593 in order to protect the eastern boundaries of the principality from possible invasions by either the Austrians or the Turks. The town has a wall perimeter in the shape of a nine-pointed star, incorporating at its heart a polygon with nine sides from which the streets radiate to the remainder of the town.

The advanced stage of civic amenities of Italian cities was remarked upon from very early days.

Less known perhaps are the observations of Stendhal on his journey in Italy

(*Rome, Naples and Florence, Journey in Italy from Milan to Reggio Calabria*). Travelling through Milan, on 5 December 1816, he observes the workmen building a new road: 'They commenced with excavating, in the middle of the road, a drain four feet deep, into which ended the pipes, which from the height of the roofs carried down rainwater to the road.

Since the front of the houses are made of bricks, often those pipes are hidden in the wall. Once the drain is completed, the street itself is paved over with four strips of granite and three of cobbles. . . . . so that you see two granite pavements three feet wide by the side of the houses and two strips of granite next to them, so that the wheels of the carriages do not suffer too much. The remainder of the road is paved with small pointed cobbles.

The carriages themselves never leave the two strips of granite and pedestrians remain on the pavements; therefore, accidents are very rare indeed.

The two strips of granite destined for the wheels of the carriages rest on two small brick walls four feet high, which form the underground sewer beneath the street. Every hundred steps there is a bored stone, which allows drops of water which have fallen on the cobbles to be conveyed to the drain. This is how the streets of Milan are the most comfortable in the world, without mud. In this country they have, for a very long time, been concerned about what is "useful to the humble citizen".'

115   In 1276, the city of Genoa started the construction of its harbour jetty consisting of two docks; this was a gigantic feat of engineering for those days and a world first in terms of size and scale.

116   In 1295, Genoa built the first aqueduct of the modern era.

117   By 1300, Venice had consolidated its base on sea and mud.

118   By 1300, the streets and squares of most towns in Italy were paved by flagstones. The streets of London and Paris at that time were still unpaved and muddy. Indeed, it is a fact that many side streets in St James's, London, were not even paved until about the middle of the nineteenth century.

119   Even earlier than that, in 1179, Milan had built the world's first canal.

120   In 1335, the first public striking clock was made and erected in Milan. It was placed on the bell tower of the nearby church of San Gottardo by Azzone Visconti.

Towards the end of the seventeenth century, the first public bathhouses were established in London, contributing to improved hygiene at least among the better off. They were known as 'bagnios', a misspelling of the Italian word '*bagno*', since they were copied from Italy. They soon became places of corruption and vice, some of them, if not most, acting as high-class brothels.

The city of Venice, its impact and some of its history will be mentioned again later on. Under this heading, I merely wish to record the fact that Venice was well ahead of its times because the first Dogal ordinance to prescribe compulsory street lighting at night goes back to 1128.

As early as 1699, the Republic of Lucca 'had enacted a decree directing citizens to burn all objects remaining after the death of a person suffering from phthisis' (tuberculosis) (*The White Death – A History of Tuberculosis*, Thomas Dormandy, the Hambledon Press, London, 1999, p. 53).

At the same time, physicians were ordered to notify the appearance of the disease to the authorities without delay. Over the next hundred years, most Italian states followed suit, thus endorsing concern for the possibility of the transmission of diseases from dead bodies either to those who had carried out post mortems or to their patients; such concern was very marked in Italy but not at all in other European countries.

121   In the eighteenth century, Venice undertook the first construction of sea walls to be built in marble and stone that protect the town (the 'murazzi').

Conceived initially in 1716, they were completed in 1782, work having started about thirty-seven years previously at an enormous cost. The walls were badly needed because the previous defences were of wood and had to be constantly replaced, apart from the fact that they were not very efficient.

The 'murazzi' are nearly twenty feet high and over a foot thick at the base, built of marble and stone. They are a great feat of engineering and of effort, the crowning glory, in building terms, of the Venetian era. To this day, they continue to perform the function for which they were undertaken. The 'Queen of the Sea' became extinguished as a power when Napoleon invaded Italy in 1797: but the stones linger on as a memorial to Venetian determination, resourcefulness and wealth.

122   By the eighteenth century, Milan could boast cornices and balconies that jutted out from the walls of buildings to protect passersby from the rain, as well as the first tin-plate guttering, which was collected in surface water drains. Its

streets were paved with granite stones and were always kept clean.

123/4   In 1785, for the first time, Milan streets had a name shown on a tablet at the beginning of the street. This was an initiative of Count Wilzeck who at the time was the Austrian plenipotentiary. At the same time he insisted that all houses should be numbered and that oil lamps should be positioned at all street corners.

The first *public* museum was inaugurated on 18 January 1471 in Rome. It is the museum of the Capitol which resulted from the gift that Pope Sixtus IV made to the people of Rome of all the works of art in the Vatican that had been collected over the centuries relating to the capital itself.

One of the best known items is The Wolf, symbol of Rome. It was constructed in bronze in the fifth century before Christ. We are used to seeing the wolf feeding the twins, Romulus and Remus, but in fact the original had no twins: they were added in the fifteenth century, in all likelihood by Pollaiolo.

I hope the reader will forgive me for listing another 'first' under this heading. I do so, to some extent, with tongue in cheek but the contributions to civic amenities which have been listed so far are really so substantial that it may not come amiss to mention the fact that we owe to an Italian the first proposal of town planning.

125   In 1552, Anton Francesco DONI published his book 'The Worlds'. He was not a town planner, rather in this context a satirist. He was mocking what John Hale (*The Civilization of Europe in the Renaissance*, Harper Collins, 1993, p. 417) calls 'the ruthless planning zeal of the Utopians'.

He described how the city should be laid out. It should be circular, symmetrical, with a hundred streets radiating out from a central piazza, each street devoted to a single craft, and with all hot food to be fetched from communal kitchens. All citizens should be equal in wealth and live in uniform houses, identically and simply furnished, be dressed in identical clothing, whose colour would denote the decades of their age.

He went much further than town planning concepts because he dealt with the principles that would inform the perfect city. He did not stop at the city: each segment of countryside beyond the walls was to be dedicated to the cultivation of a specific crop; marriage would be abolished, promiscuity permitted, sick or deformed children killed, the remainder being looked after by the State.

I do not know whether Doni was serious or not, but his compatriot Tomaso Campanella (died in Paris 1639) certainly meant it when, in his *La Cittá del Sole*, published in 1602, he stated certain principles of socialist philosophy and policy. Campanella's ideal commonwealth was to be governed by men enlightened by reason and everything was to be designed to contribute to the good of the community as a whole. Individuals did not count for much. Private property would be abolished, undue wealth and poverty would be non-existent, and the State would ensure that nobody had more or less than he needed.

Campanella wrote the book when he was a prisoner of the Spanish Inquisition and tempered the severity of his philosophical beliefs by writing lyric poems and madrigals at the same time. How ingenious can Italians be . . .?

In 1732, Jean-Jacques Rosseau, who spent some time in Turin, made his first visit to Paris and, by comparison with 'the beauty of the streets, the symmetry and alignment of the houses', which he had noticed in Turin, he was struck by the 'dirty, stinking little streets, ugly black houses, a general air of squalor and poverty, beggars, carters, menders of clothes, sellers of herb drinks and old hats', which he found as he entered Paris (*The Confessions*, Penguin classics, p. 155).

Illumination of public buildings was also fairly well developed in Italy at an early date. Certainly by the beginning of the nineteenth century, the technique of using reflectors was well established. In one of his 'Letters to his Parents' – 24 June 1845 – Ruskin records a celebration at the Ponte Vecchio in Florence where apart from 'the arches of the bridges all lighted around and the innumerable boats gliding about with lamps', he found the illumination of the cathedral dome and of the Palazzo Vecchio 'very noble because of the use by the locals of lamps with strong reflectors to throw the light on the walls'.

But long before that, Goethe (*Italian Journey*, 30 June 1787) had remarked on the spectacular illuminations in Rome to celebrate the feast of Saints Peter and Paul. It was, says Goethe, 'like a scene from fairyland'; the spectacle of St Peter's colonnade and dome outlined in fire prompted him to suggest 'that nothing like it could be seen anywhere else in the world'. The brilliance of the lighting was so great that 'the moonlight was eclipsed'.

126   The process of water chlorination on a large scale – effectively to stem an epidemic of typhoid – was first used at Pola in 1896.

127   The first open-air swimming pool was established in the early years of the twentieth century at Venice Lido.

128 Siena was the first city to create a traffic-free pedestrians-only area in the centre of the city. The central square (the Piazza del Campo) and adjacent streets were closed to traffic in July 1965. The local authority order to that effect came into force after the Palio of that year was run.

As far as Rome is concerned, what are known as the Seven Sectors of its 'historical centre' were all closed to motor traffic in 1973 and 1974.

A number of other Italian cities have adopted the principle of closing the 'historical' centres to all but essential traffic. The classic example is the delightful town of Lucca, which has gone so far as to ensure that only bicycles and mopeds, apart from the most necessary motor cars, are allowed through its ancient streets.

129 It is San Gimignano in Tuscany, not New York, which boasts the first skyscrapers in the world.

Known as 'tower houses', they were built in about 1200 when San Gimignano came under the dominance of the Etruscan town Volterra. San Gimignano itself is of Etruscan origin.

According to extant records, about seventy-six of these towers were built, but only thirteen remain standing today. They were quite a feature at the time as each of the owners vied with the other to build a taller and more impressive residence. They were so famous that the town became known as San Gimignano 'of the beautiful towers'.

Indeed, there were complaints of overcrowding of buildings right up to the fourteenth century when the town passed within the sphere of influence of Florence.

The towers (some of which are over 175 feet high) rise well above the rooftops, and stand out against the sky as sentinels, almost as though they were endeavouring to protect the architecture of the place and its historical heritage.

130 The first brick hearth with a chimney breast and flue was constructed in Venice in 1227.

131 From a very early date, the principal Italian cities took steps to control buildings. It is recorded that the first building bye-law was passed by the Municipality of Siena in 1295; it related to the size and construction of windows.

Art and architecture flourished in Russia during the fifteenth century and it is a matter of record that in 1472 Ivan III got married and travelled to Italy with his spouse on several occasions. There they met many Italian artists, but particularly architects and craftsmen who were invited back to Russia. This is not the place to record the extensive relations between Russia and Italian craftsmen, which can be said to have started in 1476 when Fioravanti was asked to come to St Petersburg and rebuild the cathedral where all Russian sovereigns were crowned until the 1917 revolution. Others who came at the same time were Solari in 1491, Caresono in 1494 and De Montagnana in 1505. They set the tone of what was to become known as the Russian baroque.

When Peter the Great became sovereign, he decided that St Petersburg should be turned into one of the world's major cities which he rebuilt. For this purpose he invited Italian architects and engineers to contribute, one of whom was D. Trezzini who built Peter's Summer Palace, and rebuilt his Winter one. He was followed by G. Fontana, N. Marchetti, B.C. and B.F. Rastrelli, S. Torelli, G.

Quarenghi, C. Rossi, V.V. Rastrelli, C. Rinaldi, V. Brenna, G. Quadrelli, C. Rossi and L. Rusca. Their mark is indelibly stamped not only on the Winter Palace and similar buildings but also on a number of summer palaces, churches, institutes and many other buildings which make St Petersburg such a delightful city, both from an architectural and cultural point of view and which have allowed not only the Russians but a number of tourists to refer to that city as the 'Venice of the North'.

132   In 1432, Filippo BRUNEL-LESCHI (born in Florence) developed the concept of the negative side thrust and designed and built the dome on the Florence Duomo.

The first unsupported structure of this size ever built in 'modern times', weighed some 37,000 tons and required a total of some forty million herringbone-type bricks to create the famous octagonal dome.

The secret of how this was done has been revealed only in recent times, namely, that the bricks were laid in herringbone fashion.

He was fortunate in being able to enjoy the patronage of Cosimo de'Medici. The dome was completed in 1436.

133   Brunelleschi was also the first engineer in the world to devise what is known as a reverse gear. He had to cater for the inability of the oxen that were used to lift building materials to the top of the scaffolding, to move backwards. The reverse gear enabled the weights to be shifted up and down.

Brunelleschi is referred to elsewhere in this book in connection with time and motion studies, trade unions, etc. but it is to his credit that he was exceptionally concerned about the safety of the men working for him. He went so far as to ensure that sufficient water was added to their wine rations to dilute the alcoholic content, for obvious safety reasons.

134   In 1437, Leon Battista ALBERTI (born in Florence) gave the first pinhole demonstration of the perspective view. He systematized the plan and layout of houses.

135/6   ALBERTI also pioneered the designing of houses in particular locations, with special reference to the physical features of the surrounding landscape, particularly gardens.

In a book published in 1435, by the title *De Pictura* (on picture making), he provided the first *written* explanation of the rules of perspective.

137/8   In 1485, ALBERTI wrote the first textbook ever on architecture. It was written in Latin and it was called *De Re Aedificatoria*.

He was also the discoverer in this connection of a screen, which has become known as the Alberti Veil, which allowed a painter to get the correct perspective for drawings. What the painter does is to use a grid in front of the object he intends to draw and, in order to give the illusion of depth, he shortens the lines which project away from the onlooker, a technique which became very popular with successive Italian painters in the Renaissance.

Alberti was responsible for the Tempio Malatestiano at Rimini and the façade of Santa Maria Novella in Florence. He was a man of many parts: one of the earlier Italian humanists, a lawyer, a mathematician, a cartographer and an educator. (In this last capacity he is referred to later on.) He was also one of the first developers of ciphers, (see 'Cryptography').

The technique of showing artistic

representational elements on the outside of plastered houses (e.g. traditional designs of game birds or trees and animals or sometimes, even more unusual representations) originated in the scratchwork ('stucco', 'duro' and 'sgraffito') façades of Renaissance Italy and arrived in England with the plasterers which Henry VIII obtained from Italy in order that they might work on his royal palace, Nonsuch in Surrey, in about 1538.

The local English plasterers had to adapt the more refined 'stucco'-type finish to local materials, thus giving rise to what became established as the technique of 'pargeting'.

Whilst it is true to say that examples of pargeting have been found in places as far apart as Cumbria and Devon, it is in East Anglia, and especially in Essex, that the greatest quantity is to be found and it is there that the pargeting technique reached its heyday in the seventeenth century with stick-work and comb-work, uses of wet plaster and its borrowings from carvings, Jacobean panelling, joinery and internal plasterwork.

Finally, I must record that Alberti also anticipated the modern explorers' activities on sea bottoms when in 1446, utilizing breathing apparatus and underwater masks as well as inflatable bladders invented by Francesco di Giorgio, he raised part of the hull of one of Caligula's ships from the bottom of Lake Nemi, near Rome.

139   Sabbioneta is the first example of a new town, although it was never inhabited.

One of the first Gonzagas, Vespasiano, in about 1562, pursued one of his many whims whereby he would establish a new town in the province of Mantova that would be a Rome in miniature.

He demolished the existing hamlet and over a period of about thirty years he had erected in its place two palaces, a church, a theatre, a library, a mint and a small printing works.

Vespasiano Gonzaga was an odd character: he could not bear his wife's adultery, and killed her; at the same time he showed extreme tolerance to Jews. In fact, he entrusted the printing works to Jews and encouraged them to come and settle in Sabbioneta.

The place, however, was never quite fully lived in because, before he could complete it, Vespasiano Gonzaga died in 1591. He himself is buried in the Church of the Incoronata and his funeral monument is a life-size statue of himself which is probably the only true-to-life edifice in the whole town. The buildings terminate suddenly in fields of corn and the whole affair has qualities almost of a mirage. There is a metaphysical character to the place which, as has been said, reminds one of a De Chirico painting.

Before the countryside took over, about two centuries later, the Bibiena brothers complemented the work that Vespasiano set out to achieve. But even though the ducal palace is now open to the public, one derives an uncertain feeling from visiting this 'new town' which is both new and old at the same time.

Vespasiano engaged SCAMOZZI to build a small Court theatre at Sabbioneta in 1588. It is still standing, and although the furniture has gone, it shows the grandeur of its conception and of the architectural concepts of Sebastiano SERLIO whose ideas Scamozzi applied. It has a novel design in that it consists of a single amphitheatre behind a shallow raked-open platform and a horseshoe-shaped bank of seating; a design that was to influence Inigo Jones extensively and paved the way for the Teatro Farnese which would be built about thirty years later at Parma, only twenty kilometres away.

140 In 1570, Andrea **PALLADIO** (born in Padua) published his four books 'On Architecture' which were translated into sixteen languages. His style was easily assimilated in England and influenced all subsequent English architects including Sir Christopher Wren. There is still an extant copy of Palladio's work signed by Lord Burlington and dated by him 1728.

He was born Andrea Di Pietro della Gondola, but became known as Andrea Palladio thanks to his patron Giangiorgio Trissino (q.v.) who chose it as a reminder of a character in one of Trissino's literary works.

His *Quattro libri dell'architettura* were also read and annotated by Inigo Jones when he accompanied the second Earl of Arundel on a tour of Italy.

The effects can be seen in everything Inigo Jones did, from the Palladian bridge at Wilton to the house at Burghley.

Indeed, it can be said that the English country house would not exist but for Palladio and the influence of Italian architecture throughout the world, stemming from Palladio's style, is too well known to need detailed restatement here. Suffice it to say, however, that the earliest example of Palladian influence is to be found at Houghton House, London, built between 1712 and 1726 as a residence for Robert Walpole. The influence of Italy there is all-pervasive; in the outline, in the stucco ceilings, in William Kent's work. It was Lord Burlington who had spotted Kent's potential and had taken him on a tour of Italy; when Kent came back, he profitably and stylishly applied to the English environment all he had learnt in Italy.

One more example: Dashwood House at West Wycombe, the home of Sir Francis Dashwood, the founder of the Dilettanti Society, continued the Palladian and Italianate tradition particularly in its double loggia, a rarity in England.

Sir Francis Dashwood was himself somewhat of an exception because he was a merchant and not a nobleman by birth. But he appreciated fine things: Dashwood House is Italian both in thought and effectuation. Nor should this be surprising to accept in any event, because since the time of Elizabeth I the English had had a love affair with Roman architecture generally: to superimpose on it, or to blend it with, Palladian influences, came very naturally. Just as the English ruling class could be compared to that of Rome, so its taste and appreciation of things Italian was a mark of refinement; just as Rome had defeated the Gauls, so had England subdued the French.

This is apparent if one visits Syon House in Isleworth, Middlesex, where Robert Adam gave the Dukes of Northumberland what one could describe, if one may be forgiven the pun, as a home from Rome.

From England, the Palladian style was exported to the Empire. It lent itself, imposing as it is and easy to assimilate, to the embassies, residences of High Commissions, palaces, mansions, etc. which were erected wherever British rule extended. It is a solid, reliable style: it pleased the rulers, enhanced their status in the eyes of the local population and added to their power and majesty.

The Victorians were particularly enamoured of it as it suited the great power of England at that time with territories throughout the world. Furthermore, Queen Victoria's personal style in architecture was somewhat Italianate, as witness her Isle of Wight residence, Osborne House.

It is built in the manner of an Italian seaside villa, with a 'campanile'-type tower.

Indeed, if one just saw a photo of it, one would probably want to place it somewhere along the shores of the Riviera.

I can do no better than to transcribe at this stage, the concluding paragraph in *Britannica* (1970 edition) on Palladio:

> The qualities that made Palladio so influential are varied: he designed prototypes that came to be accepted as the ultimate solution in each case; his palazzo type was imitated all over Europe [and I add, also in the United States]; his church designs of intersecting temple fronts remained the most popular solution for the classical church and he was the first to systematize the plan of a house and to consistently use the temple front as a portico (probably his most imitated feature).

141 In 1584, Andrea **PALLADIO** built the Teatro Olimpico at Vicenza. This still survives as one of the first and most typical expressions of the architectural style of the period. It is the oldest surviving theatre in Europe.

142 We owe to **PALLADIO** the invention of the arched device known as a 'serliana'. Such a device had the advantage of lightening the piers, reducing the span of the arch by almost 50% and to adjust the dimensions of the side beams to fit the varying dimensions of the bay (*The Perfect House*, Witold Rybczynski, ed. Scribner, p. 71).

143 Venice can boast of the first public opera house in the world. This is the Teatro San Cassiano which opened in 1637 with a performance of the opera Andromeda by Mannelli.

San Cassiano continued in use until the beginning of the nineteenth century. Among the city's other opera houses were the Teatro Ss. Giovanni e Paolo and the Teatro San Moise. Its most famous opera house, however, was the Teatro La Fenice which was opened in 1792.

144 The first arcaded walkway was erected in Bologna between 1674 and 1739. It is the portico that runs from Porta Zaragoza to the Church of San Luca on the Colle della Guardia. It is 3.5 kilometres long and consists of 666 arches.

All the citizens of Bologna are said to have contributed to its construction in some way or other, whether by working or providing money, and it was used by pilgrims who used to climb up, sometimes on their knees. It is said that watersellers and others were available under these arcades to provide help and refreshments to the pilgrims.

The number 666 is the biblical sign of the beast (*Bible*, Revelations, Chapter 13). The beast has been interpreted as the Anti-Christ.

Not obviously a first in the sense in which this book understands the concept, but it is worth noting at this stage that Bologna has more porticoes than any other city in the world. There are thirty-five kilometres of them and they represent one of the most successful solutions to the problem of separating the pedestrian from the motor car.

One can walk round practically the whole of the city under cover and only come across the motor car at the inevitable road intersections.

There is an historical justification for this development which is totally unrelated to motor vehicles. The usage of porticoes is derived from the centuries-old tradition of building the upper floors protruding above the ground floor. A similar trend can be found in other countries, for example in the Tudor buildings of England.

Most of the cities of northern Italy had, from a very early date, established a sort of city centre with arcades or colonnades or, effectively, covered areas where people could carry on business without interference from the weather. One of the major differences in city architecture between the north and the south of Italy is in fact to be found in these arcaded or colonnaded passageways.

For example, Torino (Turin) has a total of 18 kilometres of covered walkways, of which 12.5 are continuous and connected, thus representing the longest 'pedestrian way' in the world. The first two kilometres of them, from the Royal Palace to Piazza Vittorio, was set up by Victor Emanuel I of Savoy, who wanted to be able to walk around part of the city adjacent to the Royal Palace regardless of weather conditions.

Like the rest of Torino, their beauty and elegance is understated. And whilst I am in Turin, already back in 1730 what was then known as Via Dora Grossa, now Via Garibaldi, had pavements which were raised above the level of the actual street itself, (For authority v. *Torino – Citta' Di Primati* by Pier Luigi Capra, publ. Graphot 2001).

145 **Milan provided another first when, a hundred and seventeen years ago, the Galleria Vittorio Emanuele II was opened, followed twenty years later by the Gallery Umberto I in Naples. It is a glass-roofed area of streets with shops, offices, cafes and restaurants, which was to be copied throughout the world, particularly in North America. There, these covered areas are known as 'malls' and I am informed that there are more than 25,000 of them.**

I discount for present purposes Cavendish's Burlington Arcade in London (1819) and the Arcade in Providence, Rhode Island (1828) which were on a totally different scale and followed different principles. The architectural validity and the spaciousness of the Milan Galleria were, in my view, a true 'first'.

My American readers might like to know that the suburban shopping malls developed in the 1940s, 50s and 60s in the USA were due to another Italian, Edward J. De Bartolo, the son of an Italian immigrant.

146 **The first scientific society known as the Academy of the Lynx (Accademia dei Lincei) was founded in Rome around 1603.**

The Academy was exceptionally popular in its time especially thanks to the efforts of one of its 'Presidents', Cassiano Dal Pozzo, a humanist who had a very rich collection of antiquities and who, amongst other things, was secretary to Cardinal Barberini. Dal Pozzo is probably better known for being the mentor of the French painter Poussin, who was very strongly influenced, as some of his paintings clearly show, by the Roman archaeological tradition.

It was Cassianno Dal Pozzo who contributed to scientific advances by organizing a collection by every known artist of the time (Poussin only contributed once) of drawings of every thing the natural world had to offer. The collection, known as the 'Museo Cartaceo' ('the paper museum') contained a total of 15,000 drawings and water colours, a great part of which were bought up by George III in 1762 and are now housed at Windsor. They cover practically everything which was available for drawing at the time and range from a double-headed melon to Roman cutlery.

One of these drawings represents the mitral valve and is further referred to in connection with Leonardo Da Vinci.

Galileo contributed an instrument to it which the German entomologist Faber was later to name 'microscope'; and all other European Societies followed the Italian example.

England's 'Royal Society' united a number of smaller associations and was incorporated by Royal charter in 1662.

The Italian connection with The Royal Society is interesting and for those who wish to pursue it, there is a lecture on the topic by Mary Boas. In 1667, Count Ubaldini became its first Italian member, followed by Malpighi in 1668, G.D. Cassini in 1672 and Viviani, Toricelli's colleague, in 1696.

That same year saw the election of Bonfigliolo, a colleague of Malpighi. Between 1662, when it was founded, and the end of the seventeenth century, no less than ten Italians were admitted; to date, there have been around ninety.

The eighteenth century saw a spate of admissions. To record them all would be too cumbersome but the following might be of interest: Scipione Maffei, a tragic poet, was admitted in 1736, the same year in which he received a degree at Oxford; also admitted in 1736 was Francesco Algarotti, a friend of Lady Montagu, who had written a book, explaining Newton's principles 'for the ladies'; in 1782 the Society celebrated a visit by Alessandro Volta, the discoverer of electricity, who gave a lecture on his 'condenser', received a gold medal, met Priestley and Watt and is said to have enjoyed himself immensely, despite the rainy weather. He was made a fellow in 1791.

The Italian connection with The Royal Society is even greater than might first appear. For example, the first item on the first page of the first issue of the Society's *Philosophical Transactions* dated 'Munday, March 6th 1664/1665' is headed: 'An Accompt of the Improvement of Optick Glaffes at Rome'.

This first article in an unbroken tradition of publications by The Royal Society, spanning more than three centuries, records the improvements made by Giuseppe Campani to Galileo's telescope by the use of special tooling and recorded in his paper 'Ragguaglio di Nuove Osservazioni'.

147 **The first cruise ship, the *Francis I*, was built in 1833 by the King of the two Sicilies, Ferdinand II.**

148 **The first *public* elevator connecting Piedigrotta to Via Manzoni in Naples was inaugurated in 1885.**

ITALIANS & CLUBS

Generally speaking, Italians are often envious of the English, or the British as the case may be. Some of them envy them their monarchy and their history, others their Empire and their traditions; some are appreciative of the Mother of Parliaments, others wish they could enjoy the same civic sense and efficient bureaucracy. But all are united in envying the British their clubs: these are something that the Italian has never had.

It is true that in Italy one has the Club Nautico, or the Round Table, or some other association; but there are few, not quite so exclusive nor quite so welcoming as in Britain. In Italy, the English word 'club' is used to describe them, thus showing where they originate, but it is pronounced 'klab'. The reason for the comparative scarcity of clubs in Italy is that, on the whole, Italians are not what Dr Johnson called 'clubable' men (the *Concise Oxford Dictionary* prefers 'clubbable'), nor do they in any sense adopt the view of Addison that clubs are 'a natural offshoot of men's gregarious nature'.

It all follows from the fact that Italians are much less gregarious than the English. Real club life could only exist in its inception and conception in England and not elsewhere.

We are taught that historically English clubs followed from the coffee houses that became established in the seventeenth century. But there were reasons why clubs became established in England to the extent and in the manner which has lasted until the present day. These reasons included the desire to be together with people of the same class and taste, as an outlet for conversation, as a place to drink at any time of day, as an escape from the female sex, for the reassurance provided from the continued presence of people from the same school and background whom one knows and trusts, the haven of tranquillity thus established, the ability to use smoking and billiard rooms (today, of course, it is snooker), the need to belong to a group for company or support, a genuine liking for one's fellow men, a sense of loyalty, the camaraderie of sport and, where appropriate, the political affiliations that distinguish White's from Brooks's or the identification with particular strata of society like the Athenaeum or the Garrick.

All these are perfectly proper and sensible reasons why English club life became established as a male preserve. Clubs not only provided meeting places where views on society and on politics could be voiced privately, and exchanged freely, they also ensured conformity: conformity both of dress and of thought. Of course, there were leaders of dress, like Brummel, and leaders of thought like Pitt. But the dilution of individual traits was great and the blackballing system was such as to ensure that nobody was admitted who, because of his schooling, background, family connections and attitude, would not make a jolly good fellow and not become one of the boys.

Thus clubs represented one of the major sources of strength of English society: namely, its ability to provide uniformity, to absorb and permeate, to bind together, to reinforce patriotic feeling and unity and, where necessary, to Anglicize.

The requirement that individuals should conform to English manners, thought and attire, if not to Shakespeare's language, is manifested in the subtle but inexorable prescription that if strangers do not Anglicize their names – as Francesco Bianco did when he became Francis White – they should at least change the Christian name to an English one. Thus, Giovanni Florio was called John Florio, Giuseppe Bonomi (architect 1739-1808) becomes Joseph Bonomi, Antonio Genesio Maria Panizzi becomes Sir Anthony Panizzi, Giovanni Caboto is turned into John Cabot and more recently, Giovanni Battista Barbirolli becomes Sir John Barbirolli, Carlo Forte is first Sir Charles Forte and then Lord Forte, Paolo Girolami (Chairman of Glaxo plc) becomes Sir Paul Girolami. Examples abound.

John Florio apart, the fashion could almost be said to have been started by Dr Johnson, who entitled his history of the Italian friar as that of Paul Sarpi instead of Paolo Sarpi.

The only example of an Italian who was made 'Sir' and did not change his name is Francesco Paolo Tosti, the well-known musician and teacher, who was knighted in 1908.

But in the case of males-only clubs, I think that Italians would find them boring. I for one can think of nothing more dreadful than having lunch or dinner or even a chat surrounded only by tailored suits. I suppose an Italian would prefer to see the warm face of a woman who displays an attractive smile and is well dressed: that is for most of us a pleasant experience. It should not be believed for a moment that such a view is solely the result of a normal sexual inclination: on the contrary, it is purely a form of aesthetic appreciation. After all, is it not the case that women dress largely to impress other women?

Be that as it may, the Italians do envy the English their clubs. More than once, I have been asked by Italian visitors whether they could be taken to a truly English club. I am also aware of the pride with which some Italians – and I know more than one – make known their membership of White's or Brooks's, and so on. As far as they are concerned, it is, they believe, proof of their respectability and acceptance in British society since they are admitted to the 'sancta sanctorum'.

Whilst this reaction is understandable, I would suggest that it is totally misconceived in today's world. Most clubs are now run by committees whose assessment of candidates is on the whole reasonably superficial: provided there is a suitable introduction with adequate bank and other references, it is unlikely that an otherwise respectable member of the community would be turned away: gone are the days of blackballing, in most instances.

Present-day reality is that clubs have ceased to be havens of tranquillity where members, all of the same social strata, all of the same scholastic background, all of equal traditions, attire and taste, could meet in peace to discuss the political and social events of the day.

But what, you may ask at this stage, has all this to do with the Italians?

Let me tell you.

149 The first English club, White's, was founded by an Italian, Francesco BIANCO.

This fact is recorded in the first *History of White's*. Compiled by the Honourable Algernon Bourke of 39 St James's Street, London in 1892, this limited edition publication in two volumes (with betting book from 1743-1878 and a list of members from 1736-1892) was published by Waterlow & Sons Limited of London Wall. The document provides a full history of White's Club from its inception as the Chocolate House founded by Francis White.

Let me quote an extract from p. 13:

'At the enlarged premises, White carried on the business of the Chocolate House until his death in 1711. He was buried in February of that year in St James's Church in Piccadilly and his Will shows that he was a man of some property.

This document, executed in 1708, begins in the impressive manner usual in Wills at that time and states that the Testator is "weak and infirm in body but in sound disposing mind and memory (thanks be given to Almighty God for the same)". From it we learn that White left four children, minors, and a widow, Elizabeth, but that the rest of his connections were settled in Italy. Thus there are legacies to his sister, Angela Maria, wife of Tomaso Casanova of Verona, and to "my aunt, Nicoletta Tomasi", also settled at Verona. *It is possible that White himself was an Italian or of Italian extraction.* It is not unusual for foreigners settled in England to assume an English form of their patronymic. White may have been some Bianco and Bianchi . . .'

The author goes on to say that White probably decided to take advantage of the reputation which one or two countries had established in England for their cooking.

I think the author is being unnecessarily cautious. It is *possible* that White came from Outer Mongolia, or Transylvania. As Euripides put it, it is possible that what we call death is in effect life and what we call life is really death. But given the foregoing statements that the author himself makes, it is obvious that White was an Italian: if he had come from Outer Mongolia or elsewhere his sister would not be called Angela Maria nor would his aunt be called Nicoletta Tomasi, nor would they all be living in Genoa or in Verona.

One wonders whether the psychological reluctance of the Honourable Algernon Bourke to acknowledge that White was Italian induced him into what I consider a Freudian slip, namely the use of the adjective 'possible' instead of 'probable' when he should have used in reality no qualification at all.

It is well established that Francis White was in fact Francesco Bianco or Bianchi, who was born in Verona (the home town of his sister and aunt) and who had decided to make a success in this country at a time when the drinking of coffee was spreading. (See *Royal St James's* by E.J. Burford, Robert Hale, London 1988, p. 131, as well as *White's – 1693 to 1950* by Percy Colson, Heinemann, London, 1951, p. 16.)

In his will, White refers to himself as 'Gentleman', that is to say, a man of means, and his estate must have been substantial, judging from the size of the legacies. (For those who wish to know more, a copy of his will is obtainable from the Public Records Office, London.)

He was probably the first of many Italians to make a good living in England out of catering to the general public.

There is no doubt that club life in England began with the establishment of White's, a London institution which antedates the Bank of England by one year, since White's Chocolate House was founded in 1693. White's Club soon developed into a gambling den where huge sums of money were ventured, mainly at faro. For example, on 21 February 1775, Sir John Bland lost £230,000 at one point (though he recovered most of it). (See *Selected Letters of Horace Walpole*, edited by W.S. Lewis, Yale University Press, 1973, p. 61.)

Who would have imagined that the oldest and probably most respected club in London, from which most others took their cue, was founded by an Italian? But then, facts which elicit amazement, astonishment and disbelief is the recurring theme of this book!

150   The first commercially-operated incinerators for crematoria came into use at Padova on 10 March 1869, when a woman's body was cremated. The furnace was designed by Luigi Brunetti (see *Book of Firsts – the Invention and Origin of Nearly Everything*, Michael O'Mara Books, 1994, p. 234).

151   The world's first *public* crematorium opened in Milan in 1875, its first funeral being that of Albert Keller who designed it.

152   As a result of Benjamin Franklin's invention, the Venetian Republic was the first state to introduce lightning rods throughout the area under its control.

FESTIVALS

Festivals abound in Italy. Religious or historical, whether processions or pageants, they are very numerous indeed and are especially prominent during the summer months (especially the 'Palio' at Siena) when the weather allows greater scope to imagination and to movement. Leaving aside opera performances, trade fairs and other music festivals (e.g. Spoleto, Ravello and so on), what one could term the 'traditional events' in Italy taking place throughout the year, number no less than forty.

I should like to mention a few which the reader might find interesting before coming on to what I consider is an unusual first under this heading.

At Nola (near Naples), the patron saint San Paolino is celebrated by a procession of the 'gigli', tall heavy structures which are meant to represent lilies and by the firing from the church steeple of 3000-odd bangers which drop multi-coloured streamers on the crowd below, the predominant colours being yellow and red, which coat the streets.

The celebration known as 'A Sciuta' at Palazzolo Acreide in Sicily, a mixture of Christian and Pagan rites, allows the locals to display a religious, almost hysterical kind of fervour which perhaps owes something to the Arab influence that is so noticeable throughout Sicily.

Even in a comparatively small island halfway between Rome and Naples, Ponza, the celebrations in favour of the patron San Silverio engage the population and all the tourists on a scale more suited to a large city.

The procession of the Madonna called 'La Bruna' at Matera in southern Italy has very marked medieval pageant overtones, with the broadcast music ranging from Beethoven to Strauss and ending in the destruction of the impressive float, an event harking back to Saracen times.

On an inevitably larger scale, because of the numbers involved, is the festival of Santa Rosalia at Palermo. The event is meant to celebrate the recovery from the plague that had been brought to the city by Saracen pirates and is almost a display of collective hysteria, endorsing the veneration felt by the people of the city for their patron saint, familiarly and affectionately known as 'Santuzza', the small or gentle saint. The people of Palermo claim that the fireworks display that ends the festival is the longest in duration of the world.

Venice too celebrates the saving of the city from the plague as a result of the prayers to Christ the Redeemer ('Il Redentore') in whose favour the well-known church by the same name was erected on the island of Giudecca. Nowadays, a temporary bridge is constructed on the occasion of the festival to join the Giudecca to the city of Venice so that the inhabitants of the city can cross over for church functions, the event being marked by open air wining and dining and a display of fireworks which is said to compete with that of Palermo.

I should not forget to mention the 'candles' at Gubbio, the 'machine of Santa Rosa' at Viterbo, the Festival, spreading over three nights and three days, of Santa Rosalia at Catania, and possibly less well known, the masked 'Jews' of San Fratello (Messina).

So much for titbits of information that may be of interest to the reader. Now on to the unusual first.

153 It is said that, in 1625, Benedetto DREI, head gardener of the Vatican flower garden, first invented mosaic patterns in fresh flowers.

Drei's example was followed in many parts of Italy, and abroad: the Italian classic in this respect is the 'infiorata' at Genzano, celebrated on the feast of Corpus Christi. There, flowers, instead of being thrown at a procession, are elaborately laid out on the surface of the street through which the procession is to pass. Acacias, brooms, roses, poppies, with evergreens like box and laurel, are picked the night before and laid out early next morning in sections of the street, each arranged by a different group. The sections then blend into a unit, for all to admire until the procession itself destroys the whole pattern.

Similar deckings of streets with flowers occur in many parts of Italy. (See Thomas Ashby, *Some Italian Scenes and Festivals*.)

154 It is claimed that the first Christmas crib of the Christian world was that at Assisi.

One of the most vivid memories of the many years of my youth spent in Rome was the making at home of a small crib. I used to crumple brown packing paper, apply brown and green waterpaint to it unevenly and lay it out on a flat surface. Those were the mountains. Small pieces of wood went to make up the stable, cotton wool replaced the snow, and pebbles represented the paths on which shepherd figurines of all kinds were placed strategically, if not artistically.

Lighting was provided by 0.5 watt bulbs operating off a transformer; in a corner there was a fire (red paper taken off sweets covering a bulb to create a glow) and baby Jesus was in the manger with Mary and Joseph, the ox and the donkey. The three kings were kept in reserve until Boxing Day when they began to make their appearance about as far away removed from the stable. Memories. . . . .

After the arrival of the Allied Forces, in 1945, the Italian custom of a Christmas crib gradually gave way to the Christmas Tree and the day of the Epiphany (6 January) slowly began to lose some of its significance since Christmas presents were located under the tree and were opened on the morning of 25 December.

I was reminded of all of this when I had to record the fact that the first crib is said to have been created by Saint Francis of Assisi in 1223 in the Chapel of St Lucia. The location was a cave in the small village of Greccio in the province of Rieti (in the Lazio) and the scene was made up by living persons and real animals. The tradition of living cribs has lasted in Italy because they abound in the Christmas festivities season in many regions, but more especially in Sicily.

155 The first international film festival was held in Venice in 1932.

INSIGNIA & MEDALS

156 In the fourteenth century, the international lawyer Bartolo da SASSOFERRATO was the first to write about heraldry.

I must say that I found this 'first' somewhat surprising and slightly inconsistent with the commonly-held views about the history of chivalry.

I had always associated heraldry much more with England and France than with Italy; but it is clear beyond any doubt the Bartolo da Sassoferrato was the first who actually studied it in depth.

In his famous treatise *De insignis et armis*, written in either 1350 or 1356, he propounded the view that anyone can assume a coat of arms at will as long as it has not already been adopted by another. A similar situation arose quite normally in the use of seals.

Sassoferrato is a very small town not far from Ancona, which is one of the major ports on the Adriatic. It produced Bartolo but it was also the birth-place of the well-known painter Gian Battista

Salvi, otherwise known as 'Il Sassoferrato' who gave his name to a whole school of painters of pictures of the Madonna and Child of a particularly gentle, pleasant image.

Incidentally, his name in not mentioned in the edition of *Britannica* with which we are dealing either under 'Salvi' or under 'Sassoferrato'.

Not strictly part of the present heading, one should consider the matter of national flags.

It would appear that they originated in China, travelled westwards until they arrived in the Middle East and were taken up by the Romans when they in turn reached there. There is evidence to show that flags were not unknown in Italy about 500 BC but, ultimately, it was the Roman 'Vexillum' which is the true forerunner of the modern flag. This was a tactical distinguishing mark to enable one detachment of a legion to be recognized as from another. The Romans, however, were not the only ones to use flags. In the ninth century, they were used in western Asia and there is some evidence that the grandsons of Mohammed had triangular fringed flags flowing from vertical staffs.

The famous raven flag of the Vikings appeared in 878, surrounded by stories of magical properties and mysteries. Whilst it is true that in their inception the flags were banners or insignia of individuals, gradually the use of the personal or regimental or tribal flag was replaced by that of a national one. The first of such national flags appeared in the Mediterranean when the city state of Genoa adopted the cross of St George as the flag of their state. This was said to occur in the twelfth century.

St George appears to have become the patron saint of England in the year 1277 and, accordingly, it has been suggested that the British 'bought' the cross of St George from the Genoese and developed it into the red ensign.

Interestingly, the mottoes which appear normally on seals, if not written in English, are more usually expressed in Latin and less frequently in French (although I have seen one motto written in Greek. . . . .).

Italian expressions do not appear that often but the reader might be interested in a few which I was able to pick out of 'The General Armory' by Sir Bertrand Burke, London Harrison 1884.
1. 'Che Sara Sara' – Russell Family
2. 'Chi la fa l'aspetti' – count Mazzinghi
3. 'Chi dura Vince' – Spiers (a Glaswegian)
4. 'Ció che dio Vuole, io voglio' – Baron Dormer
5. 'Fatti Maschi, Parole Femine' – Lord Baltimore
6. 'Chi non Risica non Rosica' – Judge Bennett

Mottoes 1 and 6 are further referred to in the text.

As regards 5, I have to record, with considerable surprise, the fact that the particular statement is to be found in the State Seal of Maryland, USA. It was no doubt taken from the coat of arms of Baron Calvert, Lord Baltimore, who named the province after his wife Mary.

The Seal shows the following wording: 'Fatti Maschii, Parole Femine' (*sic*). The translation provided in the USA for these four Italian words (Manly Deeds, Womanly Words) is somewhat more benevolent than the original Tuscan, whose slant is sexist.

157   **Whilst on a visit to England as part of the retinue of the Emperor Philip II, the Italian medallist Jacopo da TREZZO produced the first classically-inspired image of a reigning monarch when he depicted Mary Tudor.**

'His influence on the medallists he met on further tours with or on minor diplomatic missions on behalf of Philip took the tradition he had derived from Pisanello, Matteo de Pasti and other Italian medallists of the fifteenth century, to Flanders and to France where even the greatest medallist of his day, Guillaume du Pré, derived inspiration from Jacopo's work' (see John Hale, op.cit. p.309).

158 **Although some Roman medallions of bronze and other metals have survived, it is the generally accepted view that the art of the medallist began with Antonio PISANELLO (born Pisa 1395) a medallist and painter. The start of the medallist's art is said to be the medal that Pisanello struck of John Paleologus in 1438, in bronze.**

It was the first of a series of fine portraits which Pisanello engraved on medals resulting from his extensive study, not only of the art of painting but, more particularly, of Greek and Roman numismatic portraits.

All the persons depicted are shown in profile, an approach which is reflected in various paintings.

159 **Italian medallists were responsible for a number of innovations brought to the art. For example, the architect Bramante developed during the papacy of Julius II (1503-1513) a press for leaden seals which allowed the engraver to do away with the technique of hammering to create impressions.**

The Florentines are believed to have been the first to make use of Coats of Arms to decorate reception or banqueting halls. In the 'Palazzo del Bargello' in Florence (built in the sixteenth century) the walls are lined by the badges of the

various mayors 'podestá') who had been in office.

This anticipates a practice which soon became quite common, especially in England.

I recall in this connection that, when dining in Lincoln's Inn Hall, I noticed that amongst the badges of the Judges lining the wooden panelled walls there is one dating to 1929. It is the badge of a County Court Judge, Judge Bennett, having an Italian flavour since it reads 'chi non risica, non rosica' (which freely translated, and eliminating the machiavellian overtones, could be said to read 'nothing ventured, nothing gained'. . . . .)

Benvenuto Cellini was well known a century later for the same work and another Italian name prominent in the field – a traveller through Europe, especially to France and to Flanders – is Matteo de Pasti. More recently (eighteenth century), Pistrucci (referred elsewhere in this book) also became quite well known. (See *Britannica*, VI, p. 742).

160 **The inventor of tincture, according to the book *Tessarae Gentilitia*, printed in Rome in 1638, was the Jesuit, Silvester PETRA SANCTA.**

Tincture, the reader should be reminded, is an inclusive term for the metals, colours and furs in a coat-of-arms. The mode of representation of the tincture by lines was an invention which is attributed to the said Silvester Petra Sancta.

PARKS & GARDENS

We shall not embark upon any discussion of whether Dr Johnson was right when on Monday, 4 June 1781, he enquired rhetorically whether every garden was not in fact a botanical garden. Suffice it to say that . . .

161   In 1543 and 1545, respectively, the first two botanical gardens in the Western world were both established at Padova (the one established in Oxford followed in 1621). It was at the Padova Botanical Garden that the first lilac trees (1568), sunflowers (1568) and potatoes (1590) were grown in Italy, though not originating there. We owe the second botanical garden to an Italian physician called Francesco Bonafede.

162   The first national park of the world was established in Italy in 1821. It was the Parco Nazionale del Gran Paradiso.

Thereafter George Catlin, of the United States of America, developed the philosophy of the national park and paved the way for the formation in 1872 of the Yellowstone National Park. Others followed all over the world.

RECORDS & ARCHIVES

163   In or about the year 1110, Caffaro di CASCHIFELLONE (born in Genova) wrote the chronicles of both the first Crusade and twelfth-century Genoa. In 1152, he presented his work to his home city who decreed that it should be kept in public archives. His annals and chronicles were the first recorded history of a township.

164   In 1300, Giovanni VILLANI (born in Florence) published his history of Florence. It is a study of all that happened in Florence, and to the Florentines, what they manufactured, what money they spent and

how they did so. He was one of the first historians and chroniclers and the first one to look at history from the standpoint of economics and statistics. Villani anticipated Holinshed and Stow by two centuries.

According to Villani, in the early fourteenth century Florence was a thriving, wealthy city.

It had 110 churches and countless workshops producing many products and tens of thousands of rolls of wool. Its population was literate, attended schools, was cared for in numerous hospitals, fed itself well and drank much wine. It was politically active, though the two main parties (the Guelphs and the Ghibellines) were constantly at each other's throats.

(THE) CHURCH IN ENGLAND

A somewhat unusual heading, but it is a fact that the Church in England owes its structure and its first Archbishop of Canterbury to two Italians, namely Anselmo of Aosta and Lanfranc of Pavia.

165   In 1070, an Italian cleric, LANFRANC (born in Pavia in 1005), was appointed (rather than consecrated) the first Norman Archbishop of Canterbury. He reformed, reorganized and systematized the English Church, assisting William The Conqueror in maintaining his fullest possible independence from Rome.

166   In 1093, ANSELMO, later a saint (born in Aosta in 1033), followed Lanfranc as Archbishop of Canterbury. He was the founder of scholasticism and the originator of the ontological argument for the existence of God.

Lanfranc had moved from Pavia to France to teach Roman law and there he became head of the Benedictine Monastery at Bec in Normandy. William chose him as adviser and he became the first Norman Archbishop of Canterbury. Norman, in the sense that he followed William the Conqueror; but he was Italian. He was a very good organizer.

167   LANFRANC was the first to state that the Archbishop of Canterbury prevailed over all the other Bishops in England, a supremacy which is maintained to this day.

His most important task, however, seems to me to have been to ensure that whatever directives the then Pope Gregory VII issued (Gregory VII was a great reforming Pope) should be diluted before they were applied in England, assuming they were going to be applied at all, a matter as to which Lanfranc had his own opinions.

Anselmo, who succeeded Lanfranc at Canterbury, as he had followed him at Bec, was not a lawyer but a theologian and philosopher. He was a great thinker and came into conflict with William the Second, though he came to terms with his successor, Henry, whose daughter he married off to the King of Scotland, quite usefully and intelligently.

I was taught at school that St Anselmo of Aosta was a philosopher but I never realized that he and Lanfranc had played such a big part in England's history.

From far away Italy, they brought the knowledge of Roman and canon law, as well as up-to-date theology and philosophy.

They were not looked upon as foreigners but as Normans, they were fully absorbed into the system and were amongst the first Italians to become Anglicized.

Anselm, in particular, was a political churchman, who felt no compunction in bending the rules of the Church for reasons of State. For example, he caused Edgar's daughter, Edith – when she married Henry I – to change her name to Mathilda, a more Norman name, and he conveniently disregarded the fact that she was a nun. Dynastic reasons had to prevail.

But Lanfranc and Anselm were not quite the first, for they had been preceded in their posts by Augustine of Canterbury, a Roman Benedictine prior, who was consecrated first Archbishop of Canterbury in the year 598.

I have not spent too long on him for, as you will recall, I am only dealing with events after the year 1000. Even so, it is useful to remind ourselves that the first Archbishop if Canterbury, the founder of the Christian Church in England was an Italian. (*Britannica*, Volume I, p. 649) and the founder of the greatest of the religious orders, St Benedict, was also an Italian.

3. COMMUNICATIONS

BOOKS & PUBLICATIONS

It has to be said that Allen Lane with his Penguin books was not the originator of paperbacks. In his field, too, the Italians laid the foundation stone even though the building did not start until some 300 years later.

168 **In 1490, Aldo MANUZIO (born in Bassiano) was the first to produce printed editions of Greek and Latin classics.**

169 **According to Edward Hutton (Pietro ARETINO *The Scourge of Princes*, Constable, London, 1922), Italy can claim the first journalist. The first, not only in the sense that Aretino's letters, pamphlets and squibs are representative of the approach of newspaper men in the centuries that followed, but also because he antedates the existence of newspapers themselves. He was born in 1492 and the bulk of his writing was produced long before the Venetian Gazette (see below) ever came into existence.**

There is a widely-held view that Pietro Aretino was a pornographer, a philanderer, and someone who did nothing but criticize the prominent representatives of the society in which he lived. On his grave it is related that it was written:

Qui giace l'Aretino poeta tosco,
Che disse mal d'ognun, fuor che di cristo
Scusandosi col dir, non lo conosco

which I freely translate as follows:

Here lies Aretino
A writer from Tuscany
Who is excused from ill-
speaking of God
And from committing blasphemy
On the grounds that he had
never met him

However, that is clearly unfair. His pamphlets and the learned squibs, which were distributed in Mantua, Venice and especially in Rome by being pinned to the statue of Pasquin to be found at a corner of Piazza Navona there (and from which the English word Pasquinade is derived), bear witness to his extraordinary literary ability and journalistic expertise.

170 **The first encyclopaedia ever to be compiled is ascribed to Domenico BANDINI in the fifteenth century.**

However, this is controverted by Norman Davis (*Europe – A History*, Oxford University Press, p. 445) where he says that the book of universal knowledge or Catholicon, namely an encyclopaedia, had first been compiled by the Genoese writer, Giovanni BALDO in the thirteenth century.

POLIDORO VIRGILIO (better known in England as Polydore Vergil, because he became a naturalized British subject and often referred to as de Castelo) was born in Urbino in the latter half of the fifteenth century and educated at the University of Bologna.

171 VERGIL first became known to the literary world by the publication of a collection of proverbs, known as *Proverbiorum Libellus*, printed in Venice in 1498, which was gathered chiefly from Latin writers and dedicated to the then Duke of Urbino, Guido Ubaldo. This was clearly the first printed collection of proverbs.

Erasmus claimed the same priority for his *Adagia*, which upset Vergil, who complained about the matter. Erasmus stated that he did not know of Vergil's work, Vergil believed him and they became good friends.

172 Leonardo BRUNI (1379-1444), a well-known humanist, wrote the *History of the Florentine People*. The twelve books were published in the year of his death and represent the first modern work of history.

173 In 1499, VERGIL published a second work, another first, namely his treatise *De Inventoribus Rerum*, the first publication of its kind, consisting of a collection of inventors. It was a treatise that contained several things which the Inquisition disliked so that it never got an 'Imprimatur' until Gregory XIII caused it to be printed in Rome in 1576, after it had been purged of all those passages of which the Catholic Church did not approve. It was translated then into several European languages.

It gave Vergil much notoriety, as can be gathered from the fact that, soon after it was published, he was appointed Chamberlain to Pope Alexander VI, by whom round about 1501 he was sent to England as collector of the tax then known as 'Peter's pence'. Here we know that he was recommended to Henry VII, and he made friends with Sir Thomas More and Latimer, amongst others, on whose recommendation in 1510 he became a naturalized British subject.

He was then asked to write a history of England, but for that he became quite unpopular and vilified, known as the *Cronica Polidori*. It was said that he should not be believed because he was a foreigner (an Italian) and 'in our matters merely a guest'. His major sin seems to have been that he considered Geoffrey of Monmouth's History a mixture of fact and fable, and as such, unreliable.

I suppose the truth is that other historians were envious that, as a foreigner, he should have been asked by King Henry VII to write a history of England and the fact that it took poor Vergil twelve years to write it, in the first place, was completely discounted by his critics.

As a matter of record, however, before Polydore Vergil's 'History' was officially presented to King Henry VIII, twenty-eight years had elapsed. Apart from the fact that it is a history of England, Vergil's *Cronica* is a first in the sense that its writer had the audacity to criticize and challenge established facts and, above all, decide what weight should be attached to the statements of his predecessors.

174 MANUZIO was also the first to issue 'pocket editions' of Latin texts in 'octavo'. These Aldine editions, the first of their kind, started in 1501 and were widely copied.

175/6 To the same MANUZIO we also owe two firsts:
1. He set out for the first time the rules of punctuation as we use it nowadays.
2. He introduced the question mark symbol. It is reported that what he did was to take the Latin

noun 'quaestio' (meaning question), convert it into the abbreviation 'qo', which the copyist of the time then transformed into an 'o' below and a 'q' above. The 'q' became a scrawl and the 'o' was turned into a dot: and that is how we got our question mark.

177 In 1502, Ambrogio CALEPINO (born in Caleppio) compiled the first dictionary.

Calepino's dictionary was so popular that at the time, and for many years thereafter, the word 'calepin' in English was used as a synonym for dictionary.

The noun 'calepino' is still in use in the Italian language as meaning a diary or notebook. (In French, 'calepin'.)

178 In 1550, Gianfranco STRAPAROLA (born in Caravaggio) published the first known collection of traditional tales under the title *Le Piacevoli Notti.*

Some of Straparola's material was used by Shakespeare and Molière and his tales were dipped into by all and sundry. However, he was not entirely innocent of plagiarism himself because he had borrowed a considerable number of ideas from Boccaccio.

At about the same time, MACHIAVELLI was also writing novels and developing ideas similar to those of Straparola. Both the ideas of Machiavelli and Straparola were also borrowed by John Wilson, John Dekker and Ben Johnson, as well as Shakespeare and Molière.

There is a long standing argument that the original stories on which 'modern' fairy tales are based had less pleasant endings; that, for example, once she woke up, Sleeping Beauty did not live happily ever after with her Prince but was first raped and then abandoned; similarly, that Little Red Riding Hood was in fact torn to pieces by the wolf.

When the Frenchman Charles Perrault (born Paris in 1628) started writing the fairy stories for which he became famous, publishing in 1697 *Tales of Times Past,* he did none other but collate oral traditions which had changed the endings of most of the stories to what we know today.

I certainly have no intention of minimizing his contribution to children's tales; I suppose I should recall that it is said that Perrault was unaware of Basile's book. This must remain a matter of debate since Straparola's book had already been published in France during Perrault's lifetime. But it is worth putting the record straight on one or two aspects of it, given my aim to 'rehabilitate' Italy's contributions in most fields.

For example, the opening story in his book is 'The Sleeping Beauty in the Wood'. This is by no means an original work because the first written version of the tale was published in Italy in 1636 by Giovanni Battista Basile (born in Naples 1575) in his collection called *Pentamerone* or, more correctly *Cunto De Li Cunti* ('The Tale of Tales'), in Neapolitan. Basile was a Neapolitan who changed the story around from what had been traditionally handed down.

All the children learn about Cinderella, the original of which seems to have appeared for the first time in China about the ninth century, a different version from that produced again in his *Pentamerone* by the said Basile under the title 'Il Gatto' ('The Hearth Cat'). His Cinderella (named Zezolla) is fairly topical by modern standards; he makes her a victim of child abuse. Zezolla is anything but pleasant since she breaks her wicked stepmother's neck.

Another of his characters is Zoza, a form of transvestite; his 'Percuonto' was imitated in poetry by Christopher Martin Wieland but, more importantly, his 'Cagliuso' was copied by Perrault in his 'Puss in Boots' when he described it as 'Le Chat Botté'. Perrault's originality must be questioned here since the story was already well narrated in 1553.

Important though Basile is, he owes a great debt to the said Giovan Francesco (alternatively, Gianfrancesco or Gianfranco) Straparola whose contribution dates back to the sixteenth century.

Little is known of Straparola's personal life which remains clouded in mystery. All that one can gather from his style is that he was not an exceptionally learned writer and possibly less genial than his successor Basile; but he had a fair amount of imagination.

His book contains seventy-five short stories told, as in the *Decameron*, on successive nights by a party of men and women relaxing in the air on the Island of 'Murano' (opposite Venice). According to *Britannica*, Vol. IX, p. 600: 'It introduced into European literature twenty folk tales among them "Beauty and the Beast" and "Puss in Boots".'

A more recent development is Italo Calvino's collection of Italian Traditional Tales published in 1956. There are 200 of them and they echo many themes of 400 years ago.

179 'Pace', 'The World Association of Newspapers' (WAN), which in March 2005 celebrated the alleged 400th anniversary of the birth of the first newspaper relying on a discovery in the town archives of Strasbourg and associating with the Gutenberg Museum in Mainz, Germany. The first newspaper was published in Venice in 1563 in order to provide the Venetians with news of the war with Turkey. It thus anticipated the *English Mercury* by twenty-five years exactly.

To Venice, we owe the word 'gazette' derived from the local 'Avviso' or port news sheets, which were also called gazettes because they cost a few cents, the then current coin which was known in Venetian dialect as 'gazeta'.

Incidentally, the oldest Italian newspaper, the *Gazzetta di Parma*, first published in 1735, is still being issued. But it is not the oldest continuously published paper in the world: that record belongs to the *Ordinari Post Tijdender*, a Swedish newspaper first published in 1645, which however became an official bulletin in the 1970s.

180 **The first public library was opened in Florence in the year 1571, though set up in 1481.**

The library was built by Michelangelo, and housed the rich collection of books and texts of Lorenzo the Magnificent; it is still in existence today, known as the Biblioteca Medicea-Laurenziana. It is quite a masterpiece of design, forty-six metres long, ten metres wide, with eighty-eight 'reading compartments'.

There is however an earlier attribution namely, that the first public library was set up in Florence in 1441 (see John Man, *The Gutenberg Revolution*, Review Headline Book Publishing, 2002, p. 89).

The oldest public library in England was founded in 1612 and is to be found in the Great Hall of Lambeth Palace. It is the library of the Archbishops of Canterbury and arose out of a bequest made two years earlier by Archbishop Bancroft.

181 **In 1581, Vincenzo CERVIO wrote a manual which could be termed the first book on carving**

meat. In about 2,000 words he explains how to carve a pheasant and, in double that quantity, how to do the same for a peacock.

182 And now onto a first which is not technically such, because way back in 45 BC Julius Caesar had already created the calendar: but his Julian calendar contained a number of errors and these were put right when in 1582 Ugo BONCOMPAGNI, namely Pope Gregory XIII, promulgated what became known as the Gregorian Calendar.

Obviously, he did not do the work himself: he relied on a Neapolitan astronomer and physician by the name of Luigi Ghiraldi and a German mathematician (also a Jesuit priest) called Christopher Clavius (born Christoph Clau). Nevertheless, this was the first calendar of the modern era and to that extent I am appropriating it to Italy. . . . .

183 Antonio (afterwards Sir Anthony) PANIZZI, who began work at the British Museum in 1831, and was its principal librarian from 1856 to 1866, revolutionized library administration by evolving a complete code of rules for cataloguing books and by understanding the potential of libraries in the modern community as instruments of research and study.

To quote *Britannica* (volume 10 p. 860): 'His ideas have dominated library thought in the field of scholarly, or as they are now called research, libraries up to the present day, and may have achieved their major expression so far in the Library of Congress in Washington D.C.'

184 The first Grammar of the Italian language for the English-speaking people was published in London in 1578 under the title 'Primi Frutti'. Its author was Giovanni FLORIO, better known to the English-speaking people as John Florio, who is better known for another first, the English-Italian dictionary.

The Grammar was not very extensive; the only copy left to be found in the British Museum lacks its frontispiece and consists of ninety-nine short pages embodying basic grammar rules and forty-four 'dialogues'. Florio was the principal exponent of Italian Humanism in sixteenth-century England and his works, generally, but particularly the dialogues in the Grammar, are believed to have influenced Shakespeare quite extensively.

Florio's impact on Shakespeare is perhaps worthy of a little more attention, also because from time to time Italians come up with the wholly mistaken idea that Shakespeare was, in fact, one of their own. I believe that this is part of the 'bad press' that the origins of Shakespeare have had especially in the Anglo-American world, possibly because his output is so immense and brilliant.

Far from me to express any view on the accuracy of the various theories about Shakespeare; there are those who maintain that he wrote none of his works, the true author being Sir Francis Bacon, Lord Chancellor for Queen Elizabeth I (a popular view in the USA); others, especially Americans, claim that it was Christopher Marlowe who did most of the work and maybe even Edward De Vere, 17th Earl of Oxford.

Theories come and theories go but one fact cannot be disputed, namely the Italian influence on Shakespeare's work which I would unhesitatingly describe as striking. *The Sonnets, Venus & Adonis, The Rape of Lucretia* and his happiest and most charming works (*The Two Gentlemen of Verona, Love's Labour Lost, All's Well that*

End's Well, The Merchant of Venice, Romeo & Juliet, As You Like It, The Taming of the Shrew, A Midsummer Night's Dream, as well the historical pieces) all have an Italian flavour and inspiration which is, to some extent, troublesome. By the canons of his time Shakespeare is said not to have been too learned, never to have travelled outside England (as far as anybody can tell) and not being too brilliant in his knowledge of the Italian language, which was not always accurate.

John Florio is recorded as arriving in London in 1576. As an anti-Catholic he was fortunate to gain the protection of the Earl of Leicester and to publish in 1578 the text already referred to, by the title *First Fruites*.

Some years later he published his *Second Fruites*, in 1591, the number of words recorded reaching 46,000.

His *World of Wordes* ('dedicated to the Honourable Earl of Southampton'), representing an erudite Anglo-Italian dictionary, was quite a success being reprinted in 1611 and remaining a model throughout the seventeenth century.

He is known to have met Shakespeare, although it would appear that the two did not get on, so much so that a Shakespearean Scholar, Arthur Acheson, has striven to show that the character of Sir John Falstaff was created by Shakespeare in parody of the hated John Florio himself. When the Earl of Leicester died, Florio was able to get on with those who succeeded him in power and gained the protection of the Earl of Essex, the Earl of Southampton and the Countess of Bedford. An Italian author (Carlo Maria Franzero) in a book in Italian by the title *John Florio in London in Shakespeare's Time* (published in Parma by Guanda in 1969) – to whose work I am particularly indebted – has suggested that it was Florio himself that prompted Shakespeare

to rely so much on Italian culture. He supports this theory by referring to numerous expressions which appear in Florio's *Second Fruites* which became very popular at the time it was published, also because it contained a number of Italian proverbs and sayings.

Franzero claims that it is evident from some of these sayings of Florio's that Shakespeare was influenced by them.

I shall mention a few to give the flavour, if I can put it that way, of the argument (my own free translation):

1. A woman made me and a woman ruined me; a woman gave me birth and a woman has defeated me.

2. Women are the purgatory of your purse, the paradise of your body, but hell to your soul.

3. The pulling power of a single hair of a beautiful woman is greater than that of a hundred pair of oxen.

4. Women are saints in church, angels in the street, devils in their homes, sirens at the window, magpies on their doorstep and goats in their gardens.

This somewhat chauvinistic last statement is lifted almost in its entirety by Shakespeare when in *Othello*, Act I Scene II, he says: 'Women: pictures out of doors, bells in your parlours, wild cats in your kitchens, saints in your injuries, devils being offended, players in your housewifery and housewives in your beds' . . . . . 'You rise to play and go to bed to work.'

This last connection I make myself but Franzero claims that the expression 'Love's Labours Lost', the title of one of Shakespeare's works, is a translation of Florio's own 'Fatiche d'Amore Perdute', which he uses for the first time in *First Fruites*.

But, even leaving aside any scholastic approach to the subject matter, no one can deny the Italian influence on Shakespeare whether emanating from Florio or from other sources.

186 The first printed book on earthquakes is attributed to Filippo BEROALDO, who wrote it in the second half of the fifteenth century. It is a short work by the title of *De Terremotu et Pestilentia* which, as its title conveys, deals not only with earthquakes but also the plague.

186 First notice of 'errata' in a printed book appears in an edition of Juvenal's *Enarrationes Satirarum Juvenalis* printed by Gabriele di PIETRO of Venice in 1478. Di Pietro lists the mistakes contained in the book in two, two-column pages and apologizes for the carelessness of a workman.

The author John Man, whom I have already mentioned above in connection with public libraries, records in the same work (pp. 230-231) that: 'by 1480, Italy far outdid Germany in the number of printing centres. . . . . Venice was the printing capital, not simply of Italy, but of all Europe, with 150 presses.'

187 The first copper-plate engravings to be printed as an integral part of a book appeared in 1477 in the book *Monte Santo de Dio* by Antonio BETTINI (1396-1487) bishop of Foligno. The printer is Niccoló de Lorenzo. Copper-plate engravings did not come into general use until the end of the sixteenth century. (Bruno)

188 The painter Piero della FRANCESCA wrote in 1478 his *De Prospectiva Pingendi*, the first treatise on perspective; in it he describes a method by which one can graphically depict three dimensional objects. He gave substance to his studies in his well-known paintings, improving on the work of Leon

Battista Alberti (q.v.) and relying on the mathematical work on perspective carried out by Fillippo Brunelleschi (q.v.). (Bruno)

189/90 Camillo LEONARDI wrote two books which, each in their own way, were firsts.

In his *Speculum Lapidum* he discusses stones and identifies as their essential features density, hardness, porosity and weight.

In his second book, *De Mineralibus*, published in 1505, he is the first to classify minerals according to their physical characteristics.

191 In 1460, Giovanni BALBI (also known as Johannes Balbus) published his book *The Catholicon*. This is an encyclopaedic work and it represents the first 'large non-religious book to be printed' to come into being. It was probably printed by Gutenberg. (Bruno)

192 The first book on dyeing fibres and fabrics was the *Plictho dell'arte de'Tintori* published by Giovanni Ventura Rosetti in 1540. (Bruno)

193 The first book on oceanography was published in 1725 by Luigi Ferdinando MARSIGLI (1658-1730) – *Histoire Physique de la Mer.*

194 *Yellow Pages* throughout the world were anticipated way back in 1789 by Giuseppe ASTOLFI, who published a practical guide identifying traders and professional people of the same kind, all operating in the cities of Milan and Mantova, as well as in the surrounding area.

195 Bandini's encyclopaedia did not have an index. The first compiler of an index for encyclopaedias was Antonio ZARA in 1614.

196 The Italian, Pietro della

VALLE, was the first to secure in Damascus, in 1616, the *Samaritan Pentateuch*, thus making known in the West that text of the Bible for the first time (*Britannica*, Vol. 2, p. 885).

197   Between 1770 and 1842, Niccolo' BETTONI from Milan was the first modern publisher to issue popular editions actually equivalent to present-day paperbacks.

CALLIGRAPHY

198   In 1430, POGGIO was the first to establish a formal miniscule type of script.

199   In 1437, Niccolò NICCOLI (born in Florence) invented the type of writing known as 'antico corsivo', a forerunner of the Italic script.

These inventions are very much in keeping with the Italian fondness for form. Indeed, this fondness is one of our basic failings.

It is quite a respectable approach to life. Even Dante, at one stage in his *Divine Comedy*, complains not so much about what was done but of the manner in which it was done to him ('*E il modo ancor m'offende*').

The Italians' fondness for form, however, is not entirely negative. It has resulted in the acquisition of an aesthetic appreciation for things, particularly those things with which we have a close association, as it were. This trait is a distinguishing feature of Italy. Things may be empty inside, but they always look pretty outside. For example, Italian medieval armour was the most handsome then manufactured, and acknowledged to be so by many writers, but not the most

resistant. In modern times, some Italian motor cars have beautiful lines but sometimes rust away quickly.

The examples are numerous. I shall not labour the point too much, for it hurts sometimes to have to acknowledge one's failings. But this is the reason why Italians are so fond of clothes and on the whole take very great care about their appearance, men and women alike. This may not be such a bad thing after all; as Byron puts it (*Don Juan*, Canto XIII stanza XXVIII) '. . . and to be well drest will very often supersede the rest'.

200   **The Italians and the Typewriter**

The idea of mechanizing writing has been around for some time. It is said that towards the end of the first Millennium the Chinese had already created certain terracotta seals representing ideograms, in the form of somewhat moveable characters.

In the Middle Ages, the process of xilography allowed the reproduction of images, and the printing of playing cards.

As most schoolchildren know, it was left to Gutenberg to construct individual metal moveable characters which allowed printing to proceed.

Leonardo himself provides a representation of some sort of printing press (Codex Atlanticus) and we have already recorded elsewhere in this book the contribution to printing of Aldo Manuzio and G.B. Bodoni.

All these interventions, however, were fairly piecemeal, and it was apparent that what was required was a more efficient and fast way of allowing the printed thought to be recorded. The typewriter was clamouring to be invented.

When we come to the paternity for the invention, however, we find certain difficulties. The Italians claim that already at the beginning of the sixteenth century, one Rampazzetti had created a form of 'tactile writing' consisting of a series of wooden dice representing letters in relief mounted on a metal bar. The French have recorded that towards the beginning of the seventeenth century, Leroy, clockmaker to Louis XIV, appears to have invented a kind of machine with letters operated by levers.

It was left to the Englishman, Henry Mill, in 1714, to invent and patent a sort of typewriter which enabled the blind to express their thoughts.

Most Anglo-American writers, however, agree that it was an Italian called Pellegrino Turri who, in 1808, invented a kind of typing machine which he donated to a noblewoman by the name of Countess Carolina di Fivizzano, with whom he was passionately in love and whom he wanted to encourage to write to him. She was blind and he expected that he would thus make her job easier; it is recorded that she was much appreciative of the machine and that the two continued corresponding over a number of years (see the *ITN Book of Firsts*, Michael O'Mara Books Limited, London, 1994).

We do not really know how the machine worked, and can only presume that some type of carbon paper was used. There is no doubt that the Italian archives in the town of Reggio Emilia contain letters which it is claimed were typed by the Countess on Turri's typewriter.

Turri was followed by Pietro Conti da Cilavegna, who, in 1823, invented a 'tachytype' which it is believed the American Burth had in mind when he created his 'typograph', both of them influencing the Frenchman Progin, who invented the 'plume kryptographique'. These are all important-sounding names, but it is clear that at least as at the middle of the nineteenth century, people preferred to display their handwriting than to rely on machines which were still in their infancy.

There are no extant specimens of the machine invented by Turri, whereas, in 1855, a lawyer from Novara by the name of Giuseppe Ravizza, applied for and obtained a patent for his 'cembalo scrivano'. The Italians themselves tend to discount Turri's invention and consider that the true creator of the modern typewriter was in fact Ravizza. To give but one example, in the town of Livorno there is a street bearing his name, and on the relevant tablet he is given as the inventor of the typewriter.

The first model was completed by him in 1846 and exhibited in Novara in 1856, where it was awarded a silver medal. The machine itself has disappeared but drawings have remained, from which we can see how it worked. Practically at the same time, in the USA, Sholes patented in 1868 his own typewriter. That specimen and the 'cembalo scrivano' are very similar in technical specification. One cannot say whether, when Sholes got his patent in 1868, he was aware of what Ravizza had done, but this is probable because a model of Ravizza's typewriter was present at the London exhibition in 1857. Nevertheless, one cannot, and we do not say, that Sholes copied Ravizza. All we record is that Turri and Ravizza were clearly the first modern inventors and those who are interested can actually see a specimen of Ravizza's typewriter at the Leonardo da Vinci National Museum of Science and Technology in Milan.

CRYPTOGRAPHY

Ciphers were known to all ancient people; the Greeks and the Romans used them extensively.

Modern cryptography, however, was born in Italy. By the thirteenth century the Papal State had already begun using ciphered correspondence. The 'Fibonacci' system which was set up in 1202 is now used in all ciphers (see 'Mathematics'). It is amazing to consider that even today espionage depends on a form of arithmetic first evolved by an Italian over nine centuries ago. (If you are in any doubt, see *Spycatcher*, Viking, 1987 edition, p. 179.)

201 **In 1379, Gabriele de LA-VINDE (born in Parma) published the world's first manual on cryptography.**

Lavinde's manual is still available in the Vatican archives. It is fairly elementary by today's standards.

202 **In 1411, Luigi PASINI (born in Venice) established his own cipher.**

Refinement came in 1470 with the publication by Leon Battista ALBERTI of his book *Trattati in cifra*, which was followed in 1563 by Giovanni Battista della PORTA's own treatise on the same subject.

203 **In 1474, Cicco SIMONETTA set down for the first time rules of crypto-analytic procedure.**

204 **Girolamo CARDANO, referred to elsewhere in this book, was also the inventor of what became known as a cardan grille, a device containing numbers, which was used as a matrix to decipher hidden messages. It was used quite extensively in Elizabethan times, especially by Sir Francis Walsingham's spies.**

PHOTOGRAPHY

205 **In the fifteenth century, Leonardo da VINCI first set out the principle of a 'camera oscura', thus laying the foundation for the much later development of photography.**

The Italian contribution to photography, however, is much greater than some readers might imagine and the debt that Niepce and Daguerre owe to Italy is substantial.

But even leaving aside the question of photography, the said principle proved its worth in many spheres. For example, it is suggested that the painter Vermeer used it extensively in his paintings.

206 **In 1568, Domenico Daniele BARBARO (born in Venice) in his book *Pratica della Perspettiva* makes the first mention of the application of the lens to the Camera Oscura elaborated by Leonardo about a century earlier.**

The same concept was restated in 1585 by G.B. Benedetti and in 1589 by G.B. Dellaporta.

The chemical aspects of photography, if I may use that expression, had already been mentioned in tentative form by Aristotle.

But the Italian contribution goes further than the 'camera oscura'.

207 **There is said to be an earlier attribution. 'First published treatment of the camera obscura is made by Cesare CESARIANO, student of Italian artist Leonardo da Vinci (1452-1519), who published his master's observations of this phenomenon. During the Renaissance, experimenters used a dark room or chamber ("camera obscura" in Ita-**

lian) to "experiment" with this phenomenon in which a small hole in the wall of a dark room produces an inverted image (of the view outside the room) on the wall opposite the hole. The camera obscura becomes the direct ancestor of the modern photographic camera.' (Bruno)

208 Ignazio **PORRO** (born at Pinerolo) was the inventor of numerous optical instruments (e.g. stereogonic telescopes). He revised a number of existing theodolites.

209 **PORRO** was a pioneer in the application of photography to topography and, in effect, the creator of aerial photography.

210 **PORRO** also set down the metrophotographic criteria, and invented the photogoniometer which were later respectively applied and modified by Kappe.

211 **PORRO**, however, is principally known nowadays as the inventor of the Porro prism, an essential device in optical instruments, particularly in binoculars and telescopes.

By 1854, Porro had finalized most of his inventions, which had to wait until the First World War before they were developed and applied commercially.

212 The first to succeed in making photographic records of radiations given off by different substances which were capable of reproduction was Guido **CREMONESE** (see *Guido Cremonese e Raggi della Vita Fotografati* Rome 1930, as recorded in *The Secret of Life* by Georges Lakhovsky, London William Heineman, 1939, p. 12).

POSTAL SYSTEMS

What we have today we owe originally to the Romans, whose public system of communication known as the 'Cursus Publicus' lasted well into the Middle Ages.

The Italian postal system itself was only established in 1862 but it is a fact that:

213 **In the thirteenth century, the Mercantile Corporations of Genoa and Siena provided postal links at fairs which were held from time to time.**

Since the early fifteenth century, Italian merchants, both bankers and traders, who came to London had operated a system of deliveries for letters to and from England which during the reign of Elizabeth I, became known as the 'Merchant Strangers Post'. The Italians who ran this service owned establishments in all the main European cities and, initially at any rate, had practically a monopoly at a time when no official postal system was available to the English public.

The Italians used their own terminology (for example, 'pp' – *'posta pagata'* = postage paid; 'pq' – *'per questa'* = payment made for this; and many others) and made their own charges (the *'scudo'* being a common tariff).

One of the most important Italian families in this field were the 'Corsini'. Over the years, they were variously referred to as 'Cushen' and later as 'Cursen'. Thus, they were the forerunners of the Curzons and thereby gave their name to Curzon Street in Mayfair, London.

PRINTING

214 The first manufacturing establishments for producing paper were established in the twelfth century at Fabriano.

This is not to say that the idea was an Italian one; they got it from the Arabs who in turn got it from the Chinese. What Italians did first, however, was to proceed to produce paper on what one might call an industrial scale.

215 The first large-scale paper factory was established in Bologna in the year 1200.

It was operated by machinery which was activated by water, a novelty for the period.

216 At the same factory at Fabriano in 1286, they first used watermarks for paper identification.

There seems to be some doubt as to the precise date when watermarks first became established in Fabriano. The representation of the city by the letter 1F' has been stated to have occurred even earlier than 1286, more specifically in or about the year 1250 (see *Europe – a History* by Norman Davis, Oxford University Press, 1996, p. 350).

It is a pity that the invention of moveable characters is due to Gutenberg for otherwise Italy could boast quite a few firsts under this heading.

217 In 1472, in Milan Filippo di LAVAGNA printed the first book in Greek type.

218 In 1475, in Reggio Calabria the first book in Hebrew was printed.

219 The first map was printed in Bologna in 1477. This was originally drawn by Ptolemy and included an outline of Britain.

The Italian contribution to printing which occurred during the Renaissance was very substantial. What became known as the humanistic hand (a round neat hand) was introduced at that time in Florence mainly for literary productions, whilst a more cursive style was used for everyday life. These styles developed into two main varieties, namely the Venetian miniscule, which is nowadays known as 'italics' and the Roman type used predominantly in Northern Italy in the printing presses, from the end of the fifteenth to the beginning of the sixteenth centuries. From Italy the technique spread to Holland, Germany, France and Spain and reached England in about 1518.

The more classical Roman character was adopted for the 'Majuscules' and this type of writing, along with the Roman miniscule and the Italic, spread all over the world. Both were adopted in England in the sixteenth century (see *Britannica*, Vol. 3, p. 657).

Printing became very common in Italy in the fifteenth century. By 1480, Venice was the printing capital of Europe and is said to have had in operation more than 150 presses.

220 In 1501, Francesco GRIFFO (born in Bologna) designed the first italic typeface used in printing: a far-reaching innovation,

221 Also in 1501, Ottaviano dei PETRUCCI (born in Fossombrone) became the first printer of polyphonic music from moveable type.

222 Six years later in 1507, he published the first book of lute music.

223   The earliest designer of modern typefaces, of which he is credited with many, was Giambattista BODONI (1740-1813, born in Saluzzo). The typeface still in use today continues to bear his name.

224   The first book in Arabic was printed in Fano in 1514.

225   Gaspare ASELLI's description – made some time in 1627 and published posthumously – of the lymphatic system represents the first medical work to contain coloured 'illustrations'.

RADIO

226   In 1897, Guglielmo MARCONI (born in Bologna) registered his patent number 12039.

Marconi had started work quite young but after his experiments at Pontecchio he, like many Italians, found that he would be more appreciated abroad. Acting probably at the suggestion of his teacher Righi, and certainly that of his mother, a Scotswoman from Ayr, he came over to England and established the historic radio station at Poldhu in Cornwall.

227   On the 12 December 1901, at 12.30 USA time at Poldhu, MARCONI transmitted the world's first signals to St John's in Newfoundland, Canada. He was twenty-seven years old.

228   MARCONI also invented the directional aerial.

229   Other MARCONI contributions include the discovery of short waves.

230   The applications of MARCONI's principle, above all to its uses in war – especially Radar which he anticipated in 1934 and 1935 (W.P. Jolly, *Marconi*, Constable, 1972, p. 266), are recorded elsewhere.

It can fairly be said that it was Marconi who laid the foundations upon which the whole system of modern communications was built.

'Marconigrams' became quite popular but their inventor had started working on radio waves at a very early age. By the time he was twenty-one he had already invented the 'coherer' which would play such an important function in picking up the signals that were transmitted from Cornwall.

His study of electromagnetic waves discovered by Hertz not too many decades previously was fairly extensive and the only doubt that remained in his mind was whether the signals would be able to overcome the curvature of the earth.

In 1909, he deservedly received the Nobel Prize for Physics.

The usefulness and importance of his invention was acknowledged immediately but the general public first saw it at work in 1912 when the *Titanic* sank and the signals that its radio operator had transmitted were able to reach the *Carpathia*.

231   The first radio transmission from an aircraft occurred in 1928, when G. BELLANCA and C. SABELLI were attempting the first non-stop flight from America to Rome in what was then the largest single-winged aircraft of the day, the *Roma*. The plane lost three cylinders and was forced to turn back but not before the first radio transmission was despatched by them to Marconi in London.

SIGNALLING

Church bells, of course, have long been used for signalling.

232 We owe, probably to a fifth-century Italian bishop, **PAULINUS OF NOLA** in Campania (only a short distance from Naples), the introduction of church bells. Both 'Nola' and 'Campana' are the Latin names for bell. From the latter we have derived the words 'campanile' and 'campanology'.

233 In 1551, Girolamo **CARDANO** (born in Pavia) was the first to use torches to spell out letters.

Cardano will subsequently be referred to in a number of instances. He was a man of great versatility apart from the fact that it is said he was a lunatic all his life.

His contemporaries called him 'the greatest of men and the most foolish of children' and he himself in his autobiography (*De Vita Propria*, Chapter 45) describes himself as 'a stammerer, impotent, with little memory or knowledge, having suffered since childhood from hypno-fantastic hallucinations'. He was undoubtedly a megalomaniac but some of his intuitions have stood the test of time.

Cardano worked out a system using five torches that were placed on towers for spelling out letters of the alphabet.

Possibly out of context, Cardano is also the inventor of what has become known as metoposcopy, namely the interpretation of facial wrinkles, especially those on the forehead, to determine a person's character. How scientific this kind of exercise is must, of course, remain a matter of opinion.

234 In 1777, Alessandro **VOLTA** (born in Como), inventor of the voltaic pile, proposed iron wire signalling lines from Como to Milan.

TELEGRAPH & FAX

235 To Giambattista **DELLAPORTA** we owe in practice the first electric telegraph.

236 In 1558, DELLAPORTA devised a compass needle telegraph known as the 'sympathetic telegraph'.

237 Alessandro **VOLTA**, with many other inventions to his credit, appears to have anticipated the electric telegraph. In April 1777, he had written a letter to his colleague, Barletta, from which it is clear that he had divined the use of what was to be an electric telegraph. It was, of course, left to others to give practical form to Volta's intuition.

238 The Telefax machine, now an indispensable tool of modern communications, was invented by Giovanni **CASELLI**, a versatile scientist with many firsts listed elsewhere.

Understandably, it was not the same kind of machine in use today. Caselli (who was a priest) called it a 'pantelegrafo' – a machine of his invention which relied on synchronous transmission of electrical impulses. The technique had been considered earlier by the Englishmen Bain and Blackweir who had not been so successful as Caselli who made his first transmission in 1856. He then offered his invention to Foucault, who passed it in to Froment, who presented it to the French

Academy of Sciences a hundred years later in 1858.

It is a matter of record that on 22 January 1860, through the use of this machine, the composer Rossini was able to transmit the score of a recent piece of music. As a result, in 1865, a telecopier service was inaugurated between Paris and Amiens, Paris and Marseilles, with a similar service between London and Liverpool in 1863.

The machine, however, was much slower than the telegraph which was fashionable at the time and also cost a great deal more. When war broke out between France and Prussia, in 1871, the service ceased, and even though Napoleon III had become quite interested in the potential of the 'pantelegraph', it was never revived.

A fascinating entry, I'm sure you will agree. The authority for this invention is the 1978 edition, Vol. 21, p. 331, of *Dizionario Biografico Degli Italiani*.

239   The reader might also like to know that the sign that is now associated with e-mail and which for hundreds of years has meant in the English Language, 'at a price of' (subsequently abbreviated as 'at', and more commonly '@') was an Italian creation.

According to the authoritative *Enciclopedia Treccani*, (and its contributor Professor Giorgio Stabile) the sign '@' first came into use in a Venetian commercial document of 1536. Italian merchants used it as an abbreviation for amphora, the two-handled jug of the Greeks and the Romans.

The amphora was used for centuries as a unit both of weight and of volume, and was known as such to the Arabs. In a Spanish-Latin dictionary of 1492, the word 'arroba' is translated as amphora, which is evidence of the fact that it was known both to the Latin and to the Arab world. To this day, the symbol '@' is known to the Spaniards as 'arroba'.

TELEPHONES

240   In 1871, Antonio MEUCCI (born in Florence) applied for a patent for what became the telephone. The application of Alexander Graham Bell was lodged in 1876 and Edison's carbon refinement is dated 1877.

There was litigation in the American Supreme Court between Meucci and Bell and there is no doubt that, from the strictly legalistic point of view, Bell was entitled to succeed because the provisional patent granted to Meucci had expired in 1873. But Meucci got there at least five years before.

Indeed, it goes further than that because the first demonstration by Meucci of his 'teletrofono' was given in New York in 1860, which was sixteen years before Bell, who at one time had shared a laboratory with Meucci, gave a public demonstration of his own.

Meucci's discovery that electrical impulses could cause sound to travel through copper wire had occurred in the early 1830s.

If he had been less honest, temperamental and naïve, his paternity of the invention would have been recognized much sooner.

A brilliant, honest, inventive, stubborn man, his was a difficult life, led for the most part in poverty, saddened by the loss at birth of his only child and the sickness (rheumatoid arthritis) of his ever-loving wife.

It has been suggested that he was effectively cheated out of his invention.

Belated recognition for him came on the 11 June 2002, when the House of Representatives of the United States passed, rather exceptionally, a resolution acknowledging that he was in fact the inventor of the telephone.

The significance of Meucci's name in the mention of the telephone was celebrated by the Italian Republic on 28 May 2003 in public ceremonies and by the issue of a postage stamp.

It is sad that Meucci should have been neglected for so long. Even as late as 1994, he and his invention were described as 'shadowy' (by Melvin Harris in *The Book of Firsts*, Michael O'Mara Books Ltd, London, 1994, p. 107. . .). No doubt that author may wish to revise his view of Meucci in future editions now that even the Americans have acknowledged his priority.

241 **In 1886, Giovan Battista MARZI (born in Rome) installed and operated for three years an automatic telephone exchange (ten lines) in the Vatican city. Although the number of users was very limited, this was the world's first system of automatic selection. It ceased working in 1890 but nevertheless it anticipated the automatic exchange at Laporte, USA, by six years.**

242 **The inventor of the Algorithm, which forms the basis of the whole of the GSM telephonic network, is Andrea VITERBI.**

4. ECONOMICS, LAW & SOCIAL SCIENCES

ANTHROPOLOGY

243   The word itself, clearly derived from the Greek, is an Italian creation. We owe it to Galeazzo Flavio **CAPELLA**, secretary to the Duke of Milan, who in 1533 published in Venice a book by the title *Anthropology*.

244   The forerunner of anthropology (and ethnology) was Giambattista **VICO**.

Vico was born and died in Naples and had no formal education. He was also one of the first philosophers of history and evolved the theory of historical cycles by analysing the various phases of civilization and making comparisons between them and the history of the earlier Greek and Roman civilizations. He was hampered by the limited knowledge available in 1720-21 when he wrote his '*Scienza Nuova*'. Two centuries later, Oswald Spengler, a German historian and philosopher, was able to operate over a much broader spectrum than Vico.

Like all Neapolitans, he was extremely independent in outlook. He did not get on well with his contemporaries, rather like the earlier philosopher Giordano Bruno who was born in the same area.

Vico's work was practically ignored by scholars for over one hundred years. His outspoken radicalism did not help much either and caused problems with the

Church. His biography is one of the saddest ever for a man of genius. He died suffering from dementia.

His work was almost unknown in England until Coleridge became interested in it in 1824. The first known (English) translation of *Scienza Nuova* was published in 1834.

ARCHAEOLOGY

245   Italians can boast the first archaeologist on record: Ciriaco de **PIZZICOLLI**, known to the English as Cyriacus of Ancona, where he was born. He is considered the father of classical archaeology.

De Pizzicolli was a merchant who travelled extensively and who in the first quarter of the fifteenth century summarized his travels in southern Italy, Greece and Egypt in his 'Commentaries'. There, he records inscriptions on monuments, makes drawings of them and annotates the artefacts which he either found or collected. All later archaeologists and classicists owe him a great debt.

246   The first fully documented tomb-robber (would you believe!) was Giovanni Battista **BELZONI**. He was born in Padova in 1778, the son of a barber. He started out in life as a circus showman, playing at fairs and fairgrounds as a pantomime giant and as a conjurer. He later

became an irrigation engineer.

His first discovery dates back to 27 July 1816 when, at the request of the local British Consul, Henry Salt, he found the heads of Memnon and Rameses; but his career as a tomb-robber can be said to have started on 16 October 1817 when, on the instructions of the British Museum, he discovered the tomb of Seti The First.

Seti's tomb is as long as St Paul's Cathedral in London and can probably be termed Belzoni's greatest discovery, so much so that, in acknowledgment of that fact, it was renamed 'Belzoni's Tomb'.

He had local competition from a Frenchman (with an obviously Italian name) Bernardino Drovetti: they were in fact arch-enemies.

After that, Belzoni stole the obelisk from Philae (only to have it taken away from him at gunpoint by the French) and provided more than two dozen principal Egyptian antiquities for the British Museum.

Indeed, most of what is best in the Egyptian Galleries of the British Museum (the young Memnon, the Pharoah's queen from Abu Simbel, the figures of Sekhmet, the head of Thothnes The Third and the statues of Rameses The First) were all stolen from Egypt by Belzoni.

He can be said to have laid the foundations of the English School of Egyptology; he certainly established a world-wide interest in Egyptology which has lasted to this day.

He was a typical larger-than-life Italian character who died young (in 1823) and whose work, if one can put it that way, is extensively described in Stanley Mayes's book *The Great Belzoni* (Puttman, London, 1959).

He was throughout his life much concerned about plagiarism. But Belzoni was not to be defeated: he carved his name in permanent fashion on anything he found and wherever he went.

You will be reminded of him if you visit the Sir John Soane Museum in London, for on display there is the Sarcophagus of Seti The First which Belzoni obtained for Sir John Soane, a patron of the arts, who is said to have been so delighted with it that as soon as it was installed in his house he gave a party for all his friends to celebrate the event; the party lasting three days. We were in 1817, approximately 3,317 years after the burial of the Pharaoh.

A few years before Belzoni had embarked upon his plundering, another Italian, Gian Battista Lusieri – an illustrator and painter – had been employed by Lord Elgin to take possession of the metopes from the Parthenon, then under the control of the Turks.

The task was handled much more carelessly by Lusieri than by Belzoni and history has still to decide whether Lord Elgin was a lover of Greece and its antiquities, who only acted out of the best possible motives, or whether, in taking possession of what clearly did not belong either to him or Britain, he was abusing his position as His Majesty's Ambassador and displaying the well-known acquisitiveness of the English in the artistic field, putting it into practice with the help of an Italian.

If, as appears to be the case, taking possession of the Elgin Marbles in 1801 was the result of bribery of the local Turkish officials (at that time, Greece was under Turkish occupation) there is little doubt that when the committee of the House of Commons in 1868 awarded Lord Elgin the sum of £35,000 for his efforts by almost the narrowest possible majority (eighty-two votes in favour, eighty votes against) they were swayed by considerations more of an acquisitive than an historical and artistic nature.

This is not an unusual approach to antiquities by the British, or the Americans for that matter.

BANKING & BOOK-KEEPING

As you will see from the extent of this entry, Italian interest in this field has traditionally been very high indeed.

247 Double-entry bookkeeping is an Italian invention and is believed to have first appeared in 1314. (See also fact 255.)

248 The first operational bank providing facilities for its customers was the Bank of San Giorgio, founded in Genoa in 1149.

The Bank of San Giorgio was the result of eighteen Genoese citizens of substance lending to the Genoa Municipality the sum of 1300 Genoese lire for a period of fifteen years. This money was needed by the local government to pay for the expenses of its wars against Almeria and Tortosa in the previous two years.

The loan itself was secured by the assignment of certain income from indirect taxation and the concept was applied again in 1150 for similar purposes.

249 The Bank of Venice established the first letter of credit in 1171.

250 Florence is believed to have been the first city to mint a gold coin – the florin – in 1252. (See Ruskin, *Mornings in Florence*, p. 56).

The florin was so called because it bore a floral design. So says Ruskin. *Britannica*, however, disagrees by stating that it was Frederick II of Sicily who, in 1231, struck the first gold coins of commercial importance to be seen in Western Christendom since the failure of the old imperial Roman coinage in the eighth century. His example was soon followed in Venice and Florence.

The 'Fiorino D'Oro' was made of solid gold. It contained fifty-four grains of it, a content which did not vary. For this reason it was of great advantage to trade throughout Europe and could be termed the 'dollar' of the thirteenth/fourteenth centuries.

The Italians have left another permanent mark on England in matters of credit. The emblem outside a pawnbroker's shop is no more than the reproduction of the Medici crest, consisting of the famous '*palle*' which, on a totally different background, enclose the gorgeous ceilings of the cathedral of Pisa. (The Medicis in turn borrowed the design from old representations of St Nicholas of Bari who to this day is considered the Patron Saint of Moneylenders.)

Long before Britain acquired its American debt, it had the Florentine debt. I do not know what happened to the former but it appears that the latter was not repaid. (L. Salvatorelli, *Sommario della Storia d'Italia*, p. 212.)

It is also worth recalling that the design for the gold sovereign with the St George and Dragon was by the Roman artist Benedetto Pistrucci who also designed the half-crown, the shilling and the sixpence coins. He was Chief Engraver to The Royal Mint and to him we owe also the Waterloo Medal and the Coronation Medal of George IV.

251 The Bank of San Giorgio was

dramatically extended in the thirteenth century when shares were issued to those who were lending money to the bank, who thus became the first shareholders in a banking institution.

252 The first Stock Exchange was established towards the end of the fourteenth century in Bruges (Belgium) by members of the della BORSA family.

These were merchants who moved from Venice to the Low Countries and owned a building in the main square of the town where traders from northern Europe met to negotiate deals and to fix the price of government bonds, currency exchanges, etc. Other Italian merchants, especially Genoese and Florentines, followed suit and took up residence in the same square astride the end of the fourteenth and the beginning of the fifteenth century: round about 1460, they moved to Antwerp. In the meantime, the family changed its name to van der Bourse.

About a century later in 1535, Gresham took the idea from the Antwerp Bourse to build the Royal Exchange. Other such exchanges soon followed in Toulouse, Hamburg, Bremen and Lubeck.

The classic modern example was built in the early part of the seventeenth century in Amsterdam. It was a major development with a dealing hall that would accommodate 4,500 people and where the first official sales and auctions of goods and shares took place. (*Britannica*, vol. 16, p. 445.)

253 In the early part of the fifteenth century, the Bank of San Giorgio began issuing 'notes' which represented in total or in part the equivalent money deposits it held on behalf of its customers. These notes were the forerunner of the present-day bank cheque.

254 Private account services were started by the Bank of San Giorgio in 1407.

The Bank of San Giorgio itself increased its power steadily over the centuries and extended its activities to all the Genoese colonies, especially to Cyprus and to the bases on the Black Sea, as well as to Corsica. The colonial structure of the Bank of San Giorgio was taken as a model by the British Government when it set up its East India Company.

The reader should be reminded that one of the consequences of Henry VIII's schism resulting with his disagreement with the Papacy, as regards the alleged nullity of his marriage with Katherine of Aragon, was that, although the religious bond between England and Italy was seriously affected, England's increasing wealth gave rise to a major interest on the part of the Italians. One cannot say that there was an invasion by Italian bankers, but there was certainly an extensive penetration of England by artists, artisans, businessmen and, especially, bankers.

I have already mentioned some names. One can add that the Frescobaldi and the Bonvisi were as influential during the reign of Henry VIII as the Ridolfi and the Pallavicini were to be under Elizabeth I. In particular, Orazio Pallavicini has gone down in history because of his epitaph which reads:

'Here lies Horatio Pallavezene
Who robbed the Pope to lend
     the Queen'.

He had initially come over to England as a representative of the Holy See to obtain payment of taxes which the Roman Church was claiming. Whilst here, he converted to Protestantism and with the funds he had received on behalf of the Pope, opened a bank which was so successful that, at a certain moment in time, the Queen herself owed him £30,000. His religious conversion was matched by his political adherence, for he went so far as to provide funds to equip a ship to fight against the Spaniards.

As Lawrence Stone has put it (*An Elizabethan, Sir Horatio Palavicino*, Clarendon Press, Oxford, 1956), Palavicino was the next but last of a long line of Italian financiers who, for 400 years, had served the English crown. His activities, his successes and even his failures were only possible in the Elizabethan age.

255 In about 1450, Luca PACIOLI (born at Borgo San Lorenzo) wrote the first bookkeeping manual.

Luca Pacioli was a Franciscan friar who wrote the *Summa de Arithmetica Geometria Proportioni et Proportionalitá* referred to elsewhere in this book.

It is worth underlining the fact that this publication is regarded as the text that signalled the commencement of the history of accountancy. He is not credited by me with the invention of double-entry bookkeeping because the Italians had already established it way back in the early thirteenth century, but one can say unhesitatingly that he was the father of all accountants. He was not a businessman, but he was a true mathematician, who spent his life as a university lecturer and was, in fact, appointed court mathematician by Lodovico Sforza, the Duke of Milan.

The reader should bear in mind in this context that the Sforza Court of the period was a focus for the arts and sciences. Luca Pacioli found himself working alongside Leonardo and Bramante. It has, in fact, been suggested that

Pacioli may have helped Leonardo with calculations of angles of perspective for 'The Last Supper'.

The pre-eminence of Pacioli was acknowledged by the Institute of Chartered Accountants of England and Wales in an exhibition which ran from 25 February to 27 May 1994.

It is, however, the Italian bankers of the Middle Ages who deserve most credit.

The best known example of the influence of Italian bankers in England is the fact that Lombard Street is so called. Lombards were Italian merchants who originated not just from Lombardy in Italy but also from many other cities as well – principally from Florence who, thanks to the support of the Popes and the impetus given to trade by the crusades, formed a sort of 'establishment' for their time, inasmuch as they had a monopoly over money. Not unexpectedly, Florentine bankers were exceptionally rich. It has been estimated that the gross national product of England in the year 1350 was less than that of the city of Florence on its own.

The Florentine names are quite well known: Medici, Ridolfi, Guidotti, Bardi and Peruzzi (there were many others, of course). They started establishing themselves in England towards the end of the twelfth century. To call them bankers, at least at this stage, may be a nonsense since, initially, they were essentially only money-lenders. In the third story of the second day in Boccaccio's *Decameron* – written between 1348 and 1353 – there is an early reference to the three children of Messer Tedaldo who came to London, rented a small house there and began his money-lending business.

The Medici family in particular were exceptionally powerful and it is thanks to their patronage that some of the greatest works of art could be created in Florence (for example, the Dome of the Cathedral, Donatello's David, etc.); but their activities were not confined to Italy nor merely to money-lending since the Medici 'bank' had branches in Barcelona, Bruges and Cairo. They were gradually closed down as the fortunes of the Medici fell apart mainly, though not exclusively, because of somewhat careless lending. A classic example of this was the loan, never repaid, made to Edward IV of England.

Towards the middle of the fourteenth century at least, Bardi and Peruzzi had a monopoly of customs and excise, minting money and exacting taxes. (They were 'kicked out' in 1456 but recalled in 1459.) It is recorded that the Bardi family had a lease on premises in Lombard Street as early as 1318.

The words *sterling* and *shilling* come from the Italian '*sterlino*' and '*scellino*' and, as every schoolboy knows, the abbreviation '£.s.d.' stands for *Lire, Soldi* and *Denari*.

But there are a few more names such as 'bank' and 'bankrupt' which come from '*banca*' and '*bancarotta*', 'fee' that comes from '*fio*' and even on all English bank notes and the wording 'Bank of England and Comp. A' appears to be taken from the Italian '*compagnia*' rather than company.

The importance of the Italian bankers in London is also evidenced by the fact that when Sir Philip Sidney, probably the most Italianate Englishman of his time, went to Venice in 1573, he had with him a letter of credit from Vetturelli, a famous Italian banker in London. They were major establishments. The firm of Peruzzi, for example, included more than a dozen other families interested in banking, and had offices in Naples, Bruges, Tunis and elsewhere.

A similar family business were the Frescobaldi, whose representative sat on Edward II's Council.

On what is said to be the negative side of the Lombard's performance, it should be recorded that Sir Edward Coke, in his 'Institutes', accuses them of having brought the practice of homosexuality that was to become entrenched in England, as elsewhere. He based his view on the fact that the word 'buggery' comes from the Italian '*buggerare*'. This is a judgement made without considering the facts fully because it ignores the etymology of the word. Whilst it is certainly a fact that the word '*buggerare*' found its way into English, French and Spanish, it should be pointed out that in turn it originated in the Italian description of the 'Bulgarian' heretics who later became the Milanese patarines, the object of much criticism in the eleventh and twelfth centuries. Of them it was said that they were the worst possible kind of people who indulged in a number of anti-Christian and strange practices, including sodomy.

Perhaps Sir Edward was being xenophobic; perhaps he was right; who knows.

Perhaps one is being unkind: since the Cathars were firstly generally known as Bougres, which I take to be a corruption of Bulgars, but secondly and, more particularly, they were known to practise strict sexual celibacy, it was easy perhaps to accuse them of sodomy.

The two bankers Bardi and Peruzzi together lent King Edward III more than 1,365,000 golden florins; which must be one of the biggest loans then ever floated, since it corresponds to more the £500 million today.

Many of the English modern commercial financial terms owe their origin to Italy (see 'Law').

The wealth of the Florence of the Middle Ages, and of the Renaissance, cannot in all likelihood be compared with that of the Italian Republic, although it should not be forgotten that, on 1 January 1998, Italy – much to everyone's surprise – ranked as the fifth industrialized country of the world. It is a long time since gold coins were minted in Italy!

256   The first pawn brokers' shops (known as 'monti di pietá') were established in Perugia in 1462 by two Franciscan Friars, Bernardino Da FELTRE and Barnaba Da TERNI, whose aim was to see that a reasonable rate of interest was charged but, above all, that 'economic transactions were taken out of the hands of the "infidel" Jewish lenders'. (Frugoni)

Not strictly a first, obviously, but a small matter to be recorded for the benefit of my American readers.

The Bank of America, the largest bank in the USA, was established in 1904 in San Francisco by Amedeo Pietro Giannini who was also responsible for innovating the system of branch banking.

Originally called the Bank of Italy, it changed its name in 1928 to Bank of America.

Giannini was more than just a banker, he was also an enterprising personality who financed the Golden Gate Bridge as well as the fledgling American film industry. Amongst those projects that he backed were Cecile B. DeMille's 'Ten Commandments' and Disney's 'Snow White'.

In 1932, another 'American', Frank Capra (who was born in Sicily in 1897) made a film about Giannini's life by the title 'American Madness'.

257   In 1982, Italy established another first when it issued its 500 lire coin. This was the first time in history that a coin emerged made up of two metals; the inner part, a mixture of bronze and aluminium (suitably named 'bronzital') and the outer rim made of cupro-nickel (an alloy of copper, steel, aluminium and nickel), now reflected in one and two Euro coins.

It was nominated the most beautiful coin of 1982. The mixture was patented by Nicola Ielpo for the Italian Mint.

The Italian Republic offered its patent to other European states, all of whom gratefully accepted, apart from France, who decided to do its own thing. One appreciates the typical French cussedness, of course, but as with cooking, referred to elsewhere, the idea was ours, no matter how others developed it.

Had it not been for the fact that the borders of the German state were wrongly defined, the new L.1000 Italian coin issued in 1997, which reversed the idea with 'bronzital' on the outside and cupro-nickel on the inside, would otherwise have competed for the accolade of the most perfect coin in the world.

258   The concept of originality was maintained when, in 1998, Italy became the first European country to mint the new Euro currency.

CRIME & CRIMINOLOGY

259   The first criminal association of the Western world became known in Sicily about the year 1000. It was established as an 'onorata società' but is now known as the 'Mafia'.

According to Migliorini's dictionary of the Italian language, the *mafia* is 'a secret organization of people who help one another to make illicit gains, acts of violence and other things forbidden by the law'. If we then look at the etymological dictionary of the Italian language by Battisti Alessi, we find that perhaps the word comes from the Arab '*mahja*', meaning boastfulness. Of course, nobody knows for certain, but I for one am very unhappy about this attribution because if there is something that a true mafia man will never boast about, it is that he is a mafia man.

I am reassured in this approach by other authors who make the point that the etymology is different and that the word 'mafia' comes from the Arab '*maha*', which describes the stone caves where the original mafia men met to plan their deeds or misdeeds.

After the third edition of this book was published my attention was drawn to another possible origin of the word 'mafia' which, however, I have been totally unable to verify and which I mention solely for record purposes: namely, that whilst the Bourbons reigned over the Kingdom of the Two Sicilies, the Italian equivalent of freemasonry, namely the 'Massoneria', operated also as a semi-illegal organization. In old style printing, the letter 'f' often represents the letter 's', so that one had the noun 'maffia', that is to say another way of conveying the idea of freemasonry. This theory is said to be supported by the fact that, for example, in Calabria the word 'mafia' is pronounced with a double 'f'. Who knows?

But whatever may be said about its etymology, we have to take into account the fact that 'mafia' is a comparatively new word: it appears it was practically unknown in Italy until 1862 when it was given prominence in a theatrical work by Rizzatto bearing the title 'I Mafiusi di la Vicaria' which described both the deeds and the mentality which distinguished the mafia in existence at the time.

Today, however, the word 'mafia' has ceased to be distinctive. In the same way that we now use the generic word 'hoover' to describe the carpet-cleaning equipment that originally was manufactured by Hoover, we now use the word 'mafia' to describe criminal organizations, whether Italian or not. It is, of course, correct that it was the Italians who established mafia as *the* criminal organization; but nowadays, the word has ceased to have any particularly distinctive connotation that identifies it with Italy.

If the word 'mafia' is a little over a hundred years old, the concept is indeed ancient. Before the word came into existence, the people and the activities that the noun 'mafia' now embraces were referred to as the '*onorata società*' (the respected/respectable society). There is no doubt that, historically, these two words were used to describe those Robin-Hood-type characters who, in a feudal Sicily ruled by cruel barons or distant landlords, acted as just men to redress wrongs.

It is impossible to understand what went on without realizing that we are dealing with a desperately poor island, invaded at varying times by Normans, Arabs, Moslems, Spaniards, Austrians, with great landed estates, where the Bourbons ruled indiscriminately and where the feudal mentality took a hold stronger than in any other part of Italy: a hold which to this day has not been entirely severed.

There were no police, no independent judiciary and, in most cases, no courts of any description: the recourse to other means of obtaining justice or of avenging an injury was therefore inevitable. Those men who had either the ability or the power or the sense of justice to act as such avengers formed the first kind of organization to which the said label of '*onorata società*' was applied in circumstances of which we know little, if anything. There was thus established the kind of mentality and feeling which arose from ancient concepts of chivalry, a great sense of hospitality, the instinctive tendency to assist the weak and to uphold basic concepts of justice, a marked sense of honour in the context of self-respect, even consideration, of a very odd kind, for women, and pride in one's word and one's masculinity.

This way of thinking creates bonds of association and of friendship which are very difficult to break. It ensures that secrets are kept and debts paid. These bonds are described by the noun '*omertà*'. '*Omertà*' is an interesting noun because it is derived from '*omineità*', which is another way of expressing manhood and masculinity and which is associated with pride.

I am only drawing attention to the derivation of '*omertà*' because it highlights the male-dominated kind of society which has prevailed over the centuries in Italy. The mafia is obviously a man-oriented society: I have never heard of a woman as a member of the mafia.

The mentality that has developed over 900 years is with us to this day. What I shall call mafia attitudes still prevail in Sicily and will not be easy to eradicate. By mafia attitudes I mean disrespect, if not contempt, for constituted authority, the need to protect oneself and one's family at all costs, a sense of honour and pride, absolute solidarity towards one's supporters and friends, and gratitude for those who have done a good turn to oneself or one's family. Not all these traits are negative; what is negative is their employment towards totally different ends from those for which they were established; and above all, the abuse of such leanings for the purpose of financial gain.

What we have today is a totally different kind of mafia, it is Mafia with a capital M; and dictionary entries reflect the concept, for they list both names.

It is Mafia with a capital M that is the mafia of money and not of dignity; the Mafia of profit and not of right; the Mafia of organized crime and not of concerted opposition to a repressive regime; the Mafia of dishonour and not of honour.

260/1 In 1764, Cesare BECCARIA (born in Milan) published his book *Dei Delitti e Delle Pene* (translated into English as *Crimes and Punishments*) which was the first critical study of the criminal law and represented the first systematic statement of the principles that ought to govern criminal punishment.

He proceeded from purely utilitarian principles, propounded a radical reform of both the criminal law and criminal procedure and argued that the purpose of punishment was not retribution but social defence. Torture ought to be abolished and, for practical purposes, he was the first criminologist to advocate the abolition of capital punishment.

He was then only twenty-six years of age. He also wrote books on economics and he was a keen student of agriculture.

In the years 1768 to 1770, he delivered certain lectures in Milan on economic principles in which he anticipated the thoughts of both Adam Smith and Malthus.

262 Following Beccaria, the Grand Duke of Tuscany, LEOPOLD II, was the first of the European princes to abolish the death penalty and torture.

Feminists may like to be reminded that the first movement to protect woman from the dire consequences imposed by the law in matters of infanticide originated in Italy.

263 In **1888, G. BALESTRINI** published in Turin his book *Aborto Infanticidio ed Esposizione d'Infante* in which he argued for the first time that the death penalty should be removed from abortion.

His book has been described by Havelock Ellis as 'a very able and learned book, inspired by large ideas and a humanitarian spirit' (see Havelock Ellis *Studies in the Psychology of Sex*, Heinemann, London 1906, Volume VI, p. 608).

264 The father of anthropometric criminology was Cesare LOMBROSO (born in Verona 1836).

This claim can be made without hesitation, even though before him, Lauvergne, who was a prison surgeon at Toulon in France, had made plaster casts of his patients' heads, to demonstrate 'degenerate' features of the skull.

Lombroso is a greatly underrated and misunderstood scientist. He started his career as an army doctor, and later was appointed medical supervisor of a lunatic asylum in the Marche, at Pesaro.

He convinced himself that it was more important to study the criminal than to consider the crime, and by so doing he can be said to have laid the foundations of modern criminology.

His approach quite clearly predisposed him to relate criminal behaviour to distinct criminal types, which could be identified by anthropometric measurements. In 1876, he published his great work *L'Uomo Delinquente*, which was based on a study of about 7,000 criminals, whom he considered to display particularly nasty, primitive and inferior instincts of an animalistic type.

He laid great, though not exclusive, stress on physiognomy, and identified particular physical features in killers, rapists, thieves, arsonists and others with a criminal disposition.

Because of this, he was ridiculed and maligned, especially in the Anglo-American world of criminology, which concentrated upon the measuring instruments adopted by Lombroso and his successors (such as for example Anfossi, who invented the craniograph) discounting completely the first plank of Lombroso's thinking, namely that, in most cases, certain types of criminality were congenital. In other words, some men are born criminals.

In fact, Lombroso and, after him, his colleague, Ferrero, when they published *La Donna Delinquente* in 1893, argued that biological factors were most important in determining whether a woman would become a prostitute. In other words, they maintained, as others have done after them (see Richard Goodall *The Comfort of Sin*, Renaissance Books, Folkestone, 1995, pp. 54/55 et passim) that the only explanation of prostitution as a social phenomenon is that some women are actually born prostitutes.

The view of Lombroso (and Ferrero) that prostitution is only the feminine sign of criminality, was not so criticized as his views on male criminality, which were termed fatuous. However, recent studies (see *American Journal of Human Genetics*, June 1993) appear to indicate that there is a defective gene in criminals which is inherited and which results in aggressive and sometimes violent behaviour. In other words, there is a specific genetic mutation for some men which, by producing a build-up of natural chemical messengers in the brain, leads them to overreact in an aggressive way, coincidentally with a tendency to develop learning difficulties. The technical explanation is that '. . . the inherited predisposition to aggressiveness is the result of a mutation in the mono-amine oxidase A gene'.

It would appear that modern science is vindicating Lombroso. And in any event, those who treated his contribution to criminology so dismissively, were not only short-sighted, but also unfair. 'He was a man of great scientific integrity, continually revising his ideas to take account of new information from others working in the new field of criminology' (see *The Encyclopaedia of Forensic Science* by Brian Lane, Headline Book Publishing, 1992, p. 161).

Towards the end of his professional life, Lombroso was appointed successively Professor of Medical Jurisprudence and Professor of Psychiatry at the University of Turin. A much maligned man, clearly a century or more ahead of his times. It will be clear that this writer at least does not agree with the statement made by *Britannica* (Vol. VI, p. 308) that his views are now largely discredited.

It should be added that it has been suggested that some of the very first scientific drawings made by Della Porta, whose inventions have been itemized elsewhere, were intended to describe the physiognomy of criminals and to that extent to anticipate the work of Lombroso.

To Lombroso, we owe the creation of what has become known as the science of anthropometry, namely the study of the human body measurements for use in anthropological classification and comparison.

265   More recently, Alfredo IAN-NARELLI has added another first to the fingerprint technique through the use of the ear in the identification of criminals.

He is the only one to have researched the matter in detail, highlighting the fact that the ear presents very marked individual morphological features and is a part of the body that is little subject to change, growing very slowly.

He has proved that no two ear lobes are identical, although certain similar characteristics are to be found in children of the same parents (see *Encyclopaedia of Forensic Science*, Headline Books, 1993, p. 249).

ECONOMICS

266   The fashionable 'Euro' was anticipated way back in 1582 by Gasparo SCARUFFI. In a book he wrote about currency and the proportions of gold to silver, he had, in fact, used for the first time the word 'Euro' to identify a European single currency which the various states could agree upon. He maintained that each state would be free to have its own type of currency provided the national coins had the same shape, composition, weight and value of those of other states.

267   In 1750, Ferdinando GALIA-NI (born at Chieti), an economist who spent most of his life in Naples and who wrote both in French and in Italian, wrote a treaty on money (*Della Moneta*) which anticipated much later work; it was amongst the first analyses of utility and scarcity.

He took as his starting point Locke's 'Considerations on the lowering of interest and raising the value of money'.

268   In 1754, Antonio GENOVESI (born at Castiglione), a philosopher and economist, as well as an admirer of Leibniz, was the first to occupy the first European chair of 'Commerce and Mechanics', that is to say

political economy, that had been founded by Bartolomeo Intieri.

He wrote his *Lezioni di commercio* in 1765 which was the first Italian work on the subject of commerce.

Genovesi advocated the free circulation of goods, especially corn and, as *Britannica* puts it, his mercantilist view of economics is distinguished by a brilliant analysis of demand, by his high valuation of labour and by his efforts to reconcile free competition with protectionist policies.

In 1848, whilst his father was there in exile, Vilfredo Pareto, was born in Paris. But as soon as the family could, they returned to Italy, more particularly to Turin where Pareto made a career as an economist and sociologist, known first for his theory on elitist interaction. He was one of the first to apply mathematical principles to economic analysis. For example, he argued that the distribution of wealth was not random, but followed consistent patterns throughout history and could be verified over a period of time in the development of different countries.

269 **The principal reason why PARETO is recorded here, however, is because in 1906, in his *Manuale d'Economia Politica*, he introduced as an analytical instrument of economics his so-called 'curves of indifference'. These were neglected and despised until they were revived in the 1930s. (See *Britannica*, VII, p. 754)**

His name is associated with the Pareto Efficiency and the Pareto Index (a measure of the inequality in income distribution).

More importantly, perhaps, he became well-known for his observation that in Italy 20% of the population owned 80% of the property, a statement later generalized as the Pareto Principle and incorporated into the concept of the Pareto Distribution. Its accuracy, however, has not gone unchallenged.

INSURANCE

NOTE: This entry should be read in conjunction with the entry on Law which follows.

The Italian contribution in this field is considerable; but to understand it one must first look at the historical backcloth against which it was developed.

The fourth Crusade took place at the beginning of the thirteenth century. Venice was the principal city to benefit from this, but Genoa and Florence also expanded considerably in the process. Italy was ideally located to serve as a trading post between the kingdoms of north-west Europe and those of the east. Italian merchants widened the scope of their activities and in so doing looked afresh at relationships such as companies, partnerships and insurance, that were already known both to Greece and Rome. This was the time, however, when a rather fundamental refinement was made to the basic contractual precedents established by the Romans.

The details can be found in Enrico Bensa's *Il Contratto di Assicurazione nel Medio Evo*, written in 1884; Bensa was a Genoese lawyer. Although this is the principal work, it is not the only one. It is clear, however, that:

270 **The first policy of Marine Insurance for which a premium was paid came into being in Florence about 1319 to 1320. (F. Edler & Roover, 'Early examples of Marine Insurance' in *Journal of Economic History*, Vol. V, p. 178).**

It had been preceded, before the end of the thirteenth century, by the practice in Palermo where a form of loan was established under which the Lender became the shipowner and the Borrower the shipper of goods and the loan itself was repayable on safe arrival. Some authors have looked upon these Sicilian loans as a precedent which is even earlier than the Florentine one previously recorded. Palermo itself was not a principal port at the time – nor, indeed, had it ever been one – but it is to that city that we have to trace the following:

271 **The first genuine Policy of Insurance, drawn in contract form as such, of which there is an extant record, was executed there on 13 March 1350.**

This policy covered against all risks wheat being carried from Sicily to Tunisia and the premium was about 18 per cent of the value of the cargo (op. cit. p. 183).

Indeed, it is fair to say that some of the wording used in the policies drawn up in Italy at this time, particularly one drawn up in Florence in 1397, were up to the standard of the sixteenth-century marine insurance policies that were adopted in London.

Florence itself, though not on the sea, seems to have been fairly prominent in the field of insurance because, on 28 January 1523, it codified its ordinances covering insurance practices and, as has been observed, (see GOW, 'Marine Insurance') the perils enumerated in the Lloyds Policy are listed 'in the same order as in the Florentine Policy of 1523'.

The practice of marine insurance which was thus established by the Italian merchants of the fourteenth century reached the towns of the Hanseatic League. But its journey to London was fairly direct because it was imported into

England by the Italian merchants, or Lombards, who resided here.

It is also worth noting that the earliest policies upon which actions were brought in the Admiralty Court (as far as records go) are in Italian. The first one is dated 20 September 1547. This is not the place to embark upon any discussion as to what the Italian wording and hand of these policies proves. Suffice it to record the fact, and to remind the reader that the word 'policy' comes from the Italian 'polizza'.

272 **Lorenzo TONTI (born in Naples), in 1630, established during his lifetime the concept of what was known as a 'tontine annuity' which he initially proposed to Cardinal Mazazin of France. The concept was followed up both there and in England and forms the basis of life insurance.**

LAW

The traditional Italian 'disrespect' for law does not arise from any dislike of the law as a concept but rather from an intolerance of authority. It stems from the instinct that exists in every Italian that one should always be very cynical and very critical of authority. It is, in a strange sense, a form of safeguard for the individual which is more appropriate to an ancient democracy, such as we find in Britain, than to Italy where the democratic process really only began in 1948. But I do not think that this attitude has ultimately anything to do with democracy.

The Italians have taken democracy to heart and even though it is not working quite so well as it should, because it is fairly new, deep down most Italians would like it to succeed; and by Italian standards, it is succeeding. It is neither a British- nor an American-type democracy, nor could it ever be: the country is too different. But one should not underrate its solidity. To look at it from either a British or American standpoint is wrong: political concepts do not transplant easily. Suffice it to say at this stage that in both local and general elections in Italy in excess of 90 per cent (much less in recent years) of the voting population cast a vote. That may tell something about the Italian democratic process, if by democracy we mean that all people should exercise their right to vote.

What the Italian objects to is the panoply of law enforcement. There is an Italian saying – *Varata la legge, trovato l'inganno* – which, roughly translated, means that no sooner is a new law passed than one can drive a coach and horses through it. This saying reflects the attitude to which I have been referring.

However, in order to understand the Italians, one must always remember the fact that they were invaded throughout their history. To ensure their survival, therefore, they had to develop techniques for dealing with their invaders. Or put another way, they had to try and be more resourceful and craftier than their overlords. In the present context, I shall ignore the resourcefulness and concentrate on the craftiness.

It is almost a universal fact in Italy that people instinctively want to outdo others. There is no nastiness in this, for it is a spontaneous reaction which arises from centuries of experience. But the fact remains that the average Italian is always trying to be clever. There is a well-established expression, *fare il furbo*, which can be translated roughly (not literally, of course) as 'I'll show you'. The Italian shows the tax collector how clever he is

by not paying his taxes. Since he is not allowed to distinguish between tax avoidance and tax evasion, as the legal system does not recognize the right of the citizen so to order his affairs as to minimize the impact of taxation, the Italian keeps two sets of books. The same approach is reflected in the strenuous efforts made by most Italians to negotiate reductions in the price of anything; whether it be at the market for the price of potatoes or in the shop for that of a dress, one must always try and get a 'special' discount. The special discount relates to the particular ability of the negotiator who will 'show' the sales person that he is better at it than others and therefore will get a greater reduction. The same principle applies again in the network of friends that one establishes, a sort of benevolent '*camarilla*', the sole purpose of which is to outdo someone else.

I am exaggerating, of course: there are plenty of Italians who pay taxes, who keep only one set of books, who walk into a shop and pay the asking price without murmur, who are not concerned with scoring point off their opponents, who would think twice before being clever at the expense of their neighbours. But the basic mentality and the framework that give rise to that mentality is ever present – hovering, as it were, in the background.

It is an incredibly time-consuming exercise and an absurd waste of resources that could be harnessed to better and, indeed, more profitable pursuits.

In Italy, everybody is watching everybody else; the state police watches the military police and vice versa; the managers watch their staff and vice versa; the politicians watch the voters and vice versa. And so on.

That this somewhat negative attitude has also some advantages cannot be denied: but it is an unfortunate fact that very often, because of this approach, the Italian cannot see the wood for the trees, he becomes over-sensitive about certain situations and therefore takes hasty decisions from which he later may have to withdraw, and is incapable of adopting long-term views.

Be that as it may, there is undoubtedly a sense in which the approach of the Italian to law is ambivalent. He wishes to be respectful of it and deep down he knows that he should; but it gives him pleasure to try and wriggle out of it. It is almost a game. It is in fact one of the national pastimes. It is almost a necessity, and all in Italy succumb to it, even foreigners who live there.

But people should not be too misled by what they hear said about the attitude that the Italian has towards law by what they see on television in connection with the trials of the Red Brigades, the Mafia and so on. This ambivalent attitude does not apply to more serious crimes and in any event the Italian system of law is on the whole no more objectionable than any other.

Indeed, Italian substantive law is no worse, and in many respects is better, than many other systems of law. It is Italian procedural law which leaves much to be desired and which causes the absurdities and inordinate delays which are so much publicized and which are taken by the ignorant viewer or reader as representative of the Italian judicial system as a whole. They are representative only in the sense that nobody in Italy has so far had the courage to reform dramatically the legal system and to modernize and improve the codes of civil and criminal procedure.

It is regrettably true, as Wendell Holmes has said, that it is in the interstices of civil procedure that justice is to be found. He is quite right. And to that extent, justice is not found very easily in Italy.

But that is a different matter from saying, as I heard not long ago, that Italians have a hypocritical attitude when it comes to law. I contest this. It is no more hypocritical than any attitude which distinguishes between tax avoidance and tax evasion. In my view this is pure sophistry.

An example of logical inconsistency in English law could be found in the earlier divorce laws. It was then authoritatively stated, to justify the concept of the matrimonial offence, that the courts had to strike a balance between 'the binding sanctity of marriage' and the 'considerations of public policy which made it necessary to recognize the fact that two human beings could no longer live together'. What utter nonsense. Repeating an observation of Sir James Fitzjames Stephen – a marriage is either holy and binding forever; or man-made, holy or otherwise, and determinable at will. It is illogical to look at it in any other manner. It must be said, however, that nowadays Italians can no longer complain of such false, Byzantine thinking as I have just mentioned, since they, too, have introduced divorce. There is progress for you.

273 **One of the four maritime republics, that is to say Amalfi (Genoa, Pisa and Venice were the others), set up the first code of maritime law by its Statutes of Amalfi about the year 1000. All the statutes that followed, firstly in Italy and later on in other countries, are derived from the Amalfi Statutes.**

Barcelona's 'Libro del Consulado del Mar', often claimed to be the first medieval maritime code, was compiled in the thirteenth century.

274 In 1070, LANFRANC of Pavia brought Roman law to Britain. As noted earlier, he was a trusted counsellor to William the Conqueror, apart from being the first Norman Archbishop of Canterbury.

But Lanfranc's contribution to English law and legal development went well beyond his official functions as a churchman. Before coming to England, he had been a lawyer in his home town, Pavia, in Lombardy (see 'The Church in England'). Incidentally, the laws of Lombardy were well known at the time inasmuch as they were more progressive than Roman law which had become somewhat fossilized.

Lanfranc was a well known advocate who taught law and forensic techniques to many Normans (clerics and otherwise).

He contributed to Latin becoming the official language not only of the Church but also of the law because the Normans, who had not long taken over, did not yet speak English.

It is to Lanfranc's activities as a lawyer that we owe one of the first recorded English cases, for he took proceedings against Archbishop Odo, who is referred to in the Bayeux tapestry, for the return of Church properties which Odo had appropriated.

That case lasted three days, a record for the time, and Lanfranc was successful. His success increased his already substantial reputation but it also contributed to the establishment of two precedents. Firstly, Lanfranc can be seen as the first barrister on record in England; secondly, he confirmed the position of clergymen as lawyers at the time when there was not a legal profession as such in the country.

It is a sad fact that, as far as I could ascertain, many Anglo-American lawyers do not know of Lanfranc's contribution and, unless they have made a careful study of Holdsworth or Maitland, they are certainly not aware of the fact that, in the twelfth century, Italian lawyers successfully practised as barristers in England. Two examples, Vacario and Irnerio, are referred to elsewhere. But there were others, such as Master Ambrose who, with Vacario, defended Richard de Anestey in his long trial (it lasted five years). It is believed that, despite his origin, Peter de Mileto was Italian as well.

I find it amusing to reflect on the debt that the English Bar owes Italy; and the more so since, judging by the average barrister's normal behaviour towards, and appreciation for, things Italian, members of the Bar are blissfully unaware of such debt. (Solicitors have often maintained that members of the Bar are blissfully unaware of many other facts as well . . ., but that is certainly a different story.)

The primacy of medieval Italy in matters of law, and particularly of ecclesiastical law, was well acknowledged from a very early date. For example, it is recorded that during the period 1146 to 1148, Archbishop Thomas á Becket went to Bologna to study under Gratian, who was at that time the oracle on ecclesiastical law.

275 In 1146, VACARIO (in English, Vacarius or Vicarius) (born somewhere in Lombardia) was the first teacher of Roman law in England.

A little earlier, in about 1100, Irnerio had advised Henry V in his fight with the Church of Rome.

276 In 1230, AZZONE (born in Bologna) was the first to write systematic 'summae' of Roman law and most of Bracton's writing is derived from him.

(I pause at this stage to remind the

reader that if he really wants to pursue the question of the debt that the English common law owes to Roman law he should read Buckland's textbook *Roman Law and Common Law*.)

The Italian influence on English law is very substantial indeed. In 1275, for example, Francesco Accursio, a teacher at the University of Bologna, was invited to come and teach law at Oxford University, after he had assisted Edward I in codifying parts of English law. Oxford and Bologna cooperated quite closely; indeed, under the patronage of the Duke of Gloucester, brother of Henry V, there was established in Oxford, a nucleus of English Professors of Law, who profited substantially from their visits to Bologna, Padua, Florence and Ferrara. It is a matter of record that, throughout the period up to the seventeenth century, Oxford University remained very closely connected to the centres of culture and learning in Italy, in addition to matters of law. The main sources of English mercantile trade law are to be found in the trade customs of the Northern Italian cities of the twelfth century.

Commercial law in Italy at that time was fairly extensive. For example, there was a statute of the City of Como dated 1219 (valid until abolished by Napoleon in 1800) which dealt with defaulting debtors. It dealt with them in a somewhat unusual and possibly Italian way because it provided that whenever a debtor defaulted he, dressed solely in a nightshirt, had to publicly beat his backside three or four times on the stone of shame which was set up in a public place. The Latin, for those who enjoy this sort of thing, is quite expressive: *Concusserit seu crolaverit super lapidem broleti cumarum in camixia tantum et ter vel quater dederit de cullo super lapidem publice.*

(I am providing this information more as an item of amusement than of fact but it is recorded in a charming book called *Guida alla Lombardia Misteriosa* published by Sugar Editore, pp. 132/33.)

277 **In the thirteenth century, the first bill of exchange was created in Lombardy by the Lombard bankers.**

I have already touched upon the Lombard bankers who gave their name to Lombard Street. But the bill of exchange was a most significant development and to this same period we must trace its endorsement and discounting as well as the establishment of bankruptcy concepts.

The Bill of Exchange became common usage for Italian merchants who travelled through and opened businesses all over Europe. Its use spread and it became standard in form. We have an example dated 12 February 1399 in the so-called Datini Archive. This collection of over 150,000 letters, 500 account ledgers, 400 insurance policies and 300 deeds of partnership records the activities of Francesco Datini, a typical Italian merchant, who had businesses in Avignon, Barcelona, Valencia, Majorca and Ibiza, as well as in Pisa, Genoa and in his home town, Prato, from where he ran a truly multinational operation (his specialization was in the wool trade and he bought fleeces direct from producers in Spain and the Balearic Islands, as well as in England).

It was thanks to the creation of the Bill of Exchange that money and credit moved around Europe very freely indeed.

It would be stretching Italian pride too far to record Francesco Datini as the first capitalist, but there is no doubt that from the fourteenth century onwards the Italian merchants became inordinately rich. We have already mentioned some of the names under the heading 'Banking and Book-Keeping'. They were the predecessors of the Fuggers, the Rothschilds and the Neckers.

Norman Davis (op. cit. p. 443) records that Francesco Datini's ledgers were found in a pile of sacks under the stairs of his house in Prato. His motto was written inside each ledger: 'In the name of God and of profit' ('*In nome di Dio e dell'interesse*').

278   The first codification of administrative law after that of the Romans was provided in 1230 by the Kingdom of Naples (Peter Robb, *Midnight in Sicily*, Panther Books, 1996, p. 113).

279   Venice had always had a monopoly in the production of clear glass (q.v.) and it was the first to impose penalties (lawyers would call them restrictive covenants) on those working in the glass factories to ensure that they did not take production secrets abroad. The relevant ordinance goes back to 1291.

280   The year 1365 saw the first recorded woman judge in Europe, ELEONORA OF ARBOREA, who published a code for Sardinia originally drafted by her father Mariano, another judge, and known as the '*Carta de logu de Arborea*'.

This was the result of the attempts of the King of Spain Alfonso of Aragon (known as the Magnanimous) who wanted to put the administration of the island on a more formal footing.

Apart from its legal aspect, the Latin text of 1395 provides a first mention of wine in Sardinia by laying down cultivation rules banning badly managed vineyards. . . . .

Eleonora was renowned for her love of falconry and one of the first recorded falcons, the 'falcon eleonorae', is named after her.

281   Company law is also traceable to the northern Italian cities. The '**compagnia**' and the '**comenda**' anticipated modern concepts of partnership and limited liability companies.

282   Also in the fourteenth century, the Italians invented bankruptcy (the word itself reminds one of 'breaking the Bank'!) as a method of safeguarding the rights of the creditors of a merchant who had failed.

283   In 1421, the first known patent was granted by the Republic of Florence.

284   The first known ordinance relating to patents was issued in Venice in 1474.

285   In 1563, Pierino BELLI (born in Alba) published his book *De re militari et de bello, the first manual of military law.*

Belli also dealt with the rules of conducting war. He is considered one of the founders of international law, though he never acquired the fame of Gentili.

286   In 1588, Alberico GENTILI (born in San Ginesio) wrote his *De Jure Belli*, the first known treatise on international law, as well as his *De Legationibus* (see 'Diplomacy').

Nearly a century later in 1625, Hugo Grotius, who is often credited, erroneously, with being the father of international law, wrote his *De Jure Belli ac Pacis* (the attentive reader will no doubt appreciate the similarity in the title. . . . .) which clearly reveals his indebtedness to the work of Gentili.

Gentili was consulted by the English government when the Spanish ambassador was found to be involved in a conspiracy against Elizabeth I; indeed, his second work was written to consolidate the advice that he had tendered. He was a friend of John Florio and enjoyed the protection of Sir Francis Walsingham.

> **287**   I cannot provide an authority, but from my reading I have a record of the fact that in the twelfth century Frederick II of Sicily established the first European system of land registration by creating a '*catasto*' (land registry).

Land registration, however, was also well known to most of the Italian Communes which had each established their own local registries. These were clearly inefficient and the concern that prompted them was certainly not a guarantee of title, but the more precise and extensive collection of taxes.

Gradually, however, a certain degree of sophistication was reached. It is recorded that in 1428, for example, the city of Florence could boast of five land registries, subdivided into ones for the city, the country, the district, the nobility and, lastly, for aliens.

> **288**   Italians were the first to use the concept of a commercial lien.

Although I could find no legal authority to support this, indirect evidence of it can be gleaned from Boccaccio's *Decameron* (Day 8, Story 10) where it is clear that we are dealing with goods stored in a warehouse, a loan of 1,000 gold florins and security for it in the shape of a lien recorded with the customs authorities.

It may be useful to remind ourselves that we were still in the fourteenth century. (A civil lien was already known to Roman law.) And where an agent

guarantees, at least in part if not wholly, that a customer whom he introduces to his principal will in fact pay, thus becoming a '*del credere*' agent, English law adopts almost in its entirety the Italian wording of the '*star del credere*', thus underlining even further the debt owed to Italy.

Finally, although the Common Law developed upon novel and native lines, freeing itself from subservience to Roman law was not easy particularly when it came to terminology. As Maitland has observed: 'How shall one write a simple sentence about law without using some such word as debt, contract, heir, trespass, pay, money, court, judge, jury. But all these words have come to us from the French. . .' And, I add: yes, through French but via Rome!

Indeed, the reliance, both substantive and terminological, of English law upon Latin is fundamental, though taken for granted. The following words, all representing essential concepts, derive directly from Latin:

Alibi, attest, attestation, bail, calumny, camera, challenge, court, contest, culprit, dictum, entail, equity, evidence, indenture, intestacy, intestate, judge, judgement, judicature, judicial, judicious, jury, jurisdiction, jurisprudence, libel, moratorium, onus, perjury, posse, prejudice, right, slander, stipulation, subpoena, testament, testator, verdict.

> **289**   The first law on copyright was enacted in Venice in 1544.

TIME-AND-MOTION STUDIES

I am sure that the Egyptians would never have built the pyramids without firm discipline over workers and slaves and without some careful calculation of how long it took to carry out each function. But, there is no evidence of any control ever having been exercised over artists and craftsmen – as distinguished from mere manual workers – to get them to conform to predetermined work procedures and schedules. This, on the other hand, was done in Italy.

290 Filippo BRUNELLESCHI (see 'Architecture') in 1424 laid down detailed times and systems of work for his masons engaged in the construction of the Duomo at Florence. Brunelleschi, therefore, was the first to carry out proper time-and-motion studies anticipating Frederick Taylor by 450 years.

Brunelleschi even went so far as to control and time each single act of shovelling. As a result, his craftsmen did not like either him or his new methods of building any more than they liked his systems of control. Consequently, in that same year they downed tools and, four years later, twenty-five of them were sacked: Brunelleschi always meant business.

He was so thorough in his approach that to avoid workers climbing up and down the ladders during the construction of the Dome of Florence Cathedral, he arranged for toilet facilities to be placed in the dome itself. This anticipates, by about five centuries, the modern building practice of having men's toilet facilities and canteens moved up the building in order to save many man hours by the workers travelling up and down in the lifts.

He also insisted that his workmen should take their lunch break whilst remaining on the scaffolding.

5. LIFESTYLE

AESTHETICS

We know that some kind of primitive 'plastic surgery' existed long before the next fact to which I shall come. In India for example, in olden days, adultery was punished by cutting off the noses of those found guilty of it, and replacements are said to have been found relying on leaves; but the notion is fairly vague.

The Greeks and the Romans took an interest in some kind of rehabilitation in aesthetic terms of those injured in war.

But the first reliable record of artificial noses goes to an Italian.

291   In 1553, Gaspare TAGLIA-COZZO was the first to make artificial noses, thus establishing himself as the forerunner of a very popular development in the modern world, namely plastic surgery. He was much criticized during his lifetime and maligned by his colleagues as well as by the Church, especially because he is said to have used in his work skin taken from other members of the human race. He was rehabilitated after his death.

292   Aesthetics (or the study of beauty) as an art was founded in 1903 by Benedetto CROCE (born in Pescasseroli). In his *Estetica*, Croce establishes the link between intuition and expression. Jenkins and Dewey followed on.

CLOCKS & WATCHES

It is almost a contradiction in terms to say the Italians have made any contribution to time-keeping because on the whole, as far as Italians are concerned, time does not exist. Their lack of punctuality is proverbial.

It is not discourtesy; it is not lack of consideration; it is not even poverty in the sense that one may not possess a time-keeping piece. I have never known what it is and I should welcome hearing from anybody who could explain it.

It is far too easy to say that the influence of the Spaniards in southern Italy, coupled with that of the weather, makes people indolent, if not lazy; since they cannot move fast, they will always arrive late. But I find that a rather facile explanation because in my experience this lack of punctuality is to be found all over Italy. The position is better, of course, in the north, in the sense that people are more punctual there. But the reason why they are more punctual has nothing directly to do with the weather, rather with their approach to business. People in business have a different value of time and do not wish to squander it.

It goes deeper. I believe it is to be found in the basic individualism and consequently disregard which the average Italian has for the activities of others. This disregard, coupled with the fact that Italians on the whole resent discipline and object to authority of any kind, has resulted in Italians being considered highly individualistic persons. (They certainly are in many senses but in many others they also like to conform.) In fact, Italians have always been most impressed by the precision and punctuality of the English. Nothing but extraordinary praise is lavished by all the Italians I know upon the ability of the English to organize Royal events or parades or military tattoos, etc. The Italian would like to be able to do it, but he cannot. It is interesting that one of the events about which the Fascist regime boasted almost above any other was that Mussolini had made the trains run on time in Italy. In fact, this was considered a much more important and significant result than even the elimination of malaria from the Pontine Marshes.

In lavishing such praise upon their ruler for twenty-two years the Italians were acknowledging that he succeeded in getting them to do something which was almost contrary to their nature, namely to be punctual.

Elsewhere, I have already recorded the fact that the first public clock was erected in Milan in 1335 and the first astronomical clock in 1364.

293 In the early part of the fourteenth century, Jacopo de DONDI (probably born in Cremona) created the first clock moved by weights. He was a member of the same family as Giovanni de DONDI (see 'Astronomy'). The whole family was renowned for its clock-making and commonly referred to as '*Dondi dell'orologio*'.

It should not be forgotten that Dante mentions a clock in his Divine Comedy (in the *Paradiso*) and it would appear that there are records of clocks existing in London's St Pauls and in Milan as early as 1309 but, nevertheless, ...

294 Horology was born in northern Italy. Already early spring clocks existed there in 1482. Italian horology influenced the world but, after 1500, was eclipsed first by Germany and then by France.

For the record, however, I am reminded (Frugoni) that there was in the cathedral at Strasbourg a clock installed in 1354, being later, in 1789, transferred to the local museum when it ceased working. The clocks in the cathedrals at Salisbury and Wells still exist and appear to be in working order despite having been installed respectively in 1386 and 1392.

295 Leonardo was the first to illustrate and describe in 1490 a fusee for clocks, although fusees were known since about 1405.

We owe the first grandfather clock, as we know it today, to an English clockmaker named William Clement, who is said to have produced in 1670 a type of pendulum clock with a glass front.

It is also a fact that the Dutch astronomer and physician Christian Huygens was the first to apply the pendulum to a clock in 1656.

But Huygens got his idea from Galileo Galilei who, in 1582, 'noted that pendulums, then employed by physicians for taking a patient's pulse, presented a principle that might be applicable for keeping time'.

Galileo worked on the principle and tried to perfect the clock but it was left to Huygens to give practical effect to his ideas.

296 Filippo BRUNELLESCHI, the architect (q.v.), was also an engineer of some ability. He designed the first clock which is said to have included an alarm bell. Unfortunately, no evidence survives of this rather clever device. (Frank de Prager, *Brunelleschi's Clock Physics*, 10 (1963), pp. 203, 216)

297   The first automaton clock was set up in 1351 on a tower of the cathedral at Orvieto. It was called 'Maurizio' and it is still known by that name. (Frugoni)

298   In 1704, the first jewelled watch was designed by Niccolo' FACIO.

CONTRACEPTION

The modern methods of contraception, all prompted by the feminist priority that woman rather than man should be in control of the birth-giving function – thus, it is commonly believed, becoming at long last emancipated from her slavery to man – have greatly contributed to the spread of sexually-transmitted diseases. This was apparent even before the AIDS scare. It can hardly be a coincidence that at the same time crimes of violence against women and young girls have increased dramatically.

There must be a moral somewhere in this situation: perhaps one should not divorce the function of procreation from that of pleasure; perhaps, at the very moment that the parties determine that the act of intercourse should have as its primary aim their mutual enjoyment rather than the essential, natural life-giving finality for which it was developed, the act itself ceases to be of any real significance by eliminating the risk of pregnancy and by transforming the woman from the cradle of humanity she has always been to a receptacle of dubious enjoyment for multifarious partners; perhaps, at that very same moment, man

ceases to consider woman as the potential mother of his children and looks upon her in the same way as he would an object or tool by which he can more efficiently pander to his pleasures; perhaps Marie Stopes did not, after all, quite understand the consequences of her insistence that woman should be mistress over her own body; perhaps we are none of us masters of our bodies anyhow, but mere tools in the hands of nature; perhaps society will one day determine that women should decide once and for all whether to be givers of pleasure or fountains of life, classing them, helping them, taxing them and treating them accordingly. To do so would certainly make relationships between the sexes clearer.

But I digress – again!

Let me get to the fact that I wish to record. I shall not say that methods of birth control were invented by an Italian because it is not the case. The oldest recorded medical recipes to prevent conception are to be found in Egyptian papyri. Ancient Greece and Rome, as well as Islam, were well aware of contraceptive techniques. But it is to an Italian that we owe the invention of the condom.

299   At some time in the sixteenth century, Gabriele FALLOPPIO (born in Modena) designed a medicated linen sheath for use by the man. (See 'Medicine'.)

In 1564, Falloppio published in Padova his book *De Morbo Gallico* where the use of sheaths made in Italy of fine linen, and later of isinglass and the caecum intestine of the lamb, was recorded (V. Havelock Ellis *Sex in Relation to Society* – 1921 Edition, p. 599). Casanova, according to his memoirs, used Falloppio's condoms about a century later. Not too successfully, though, for Casanova – if his memoirs are to be believed – had nine bouts of venereal disease of some sort or other; but they did not seem to trouble him unduly. He appeared to look on them more as a war-veteran would his battle scars.

Casanova himself was exceptionally interested in contraception well apart from occultism, alchemy, preaching and gambling. In his memoirs, he claims that he relied on the use of a golf ball some 18 mm in diameter, which was to be inserted in the vagina before intercourse took place. It is not clear from his memoirs whether in fact it was an effective barrier to impregnation but there is no doubt that Casanova seemed to be exceptionally pleased with the purchase because he went on using this particular item for some fifteen years.

In this, he was clearly a forerunner of certain modern thinking. This great lover of the eighteenth century proceeded from the premise that the establishment of a mechanical barrier between sperm and the ovum was an effective method of contraception and found its clearest manifestation in the nineteenth/twentieth century development of the contraceptive cap. On the other hand, his was not a new idea since attempts to block the entry of the sperm have been known to humanity certainly for more than a thousand years. Many forms of primitive contraceptive techniques rely in fact on this particular principle.

Returning to Falloppio, he not only described a particular kind of linen sheath, he also gave very clear instructions as to its use. The British Museum Library contains one of the earliest editions of his *De Morbo Gallico*. I offer below the following extract, translated by me from the Latin, from p. 52 thereof:

'Therefore every time (a man) has intercourse he should, if possible, wash his genitals or wipe them with a cloth;

afterwards, he should have a small linen cloth made to fit over the glans which he should then put upon the glans drawing it forward over the prepuce. Although not essential, it would be useful to moisten it with saliva or with a good lotion.

I myself have experimented this in hundreds, nay thousands of men, and as God is my witness none of them caught any infection.'

'*Cave Luem*', my biology teacher used to say, which roughly translated means 'Watch out for syphilis.' Nowadays, I suppose we would say 'Seek some aid to prevent AIDS.' Nothing changes really.

300   Giacomo CASANOVA, referred to elsewhere, is credited with the *modern* idea of a 'cervical cap' (Charles Panati). I put it this way because it is well-known that ever since the sixth century BC physicians had been working on numerous ideas for cap-like devices to be inserted over the opening of the cervix (e.g. pomegranates). Casanova is said to have 'presented his mistresses with partially squeezed lemon halves'. The lemon shell acted as a physical barrier and its juice as an acidic spermicide, so that one could claim that we owe to him rather than to Wilhelm Mensinga, a Dutch anatomist and physician, what is popularly known as the 'Dutch Cap'.

May I add that I am old enough to recall the days when brothels existed in Italy (we closed them down in or about 1954, following the example of France that, first amongst Western countries, had closed them down in 1946).

Feminists had campaigned for the dignity of woman. I consider that such dignity is more debased nowadays by newspapers, TV and magazine photography than it ever was in the days when a particular kind of behaviour was catered for and controlled.

I am sure that there was very much less venereal disease in Italy in the days when brothels were run in supervised form by the State, than there is in the last decade of the twentieth century, when contraception of the more progressive and liberated kind has become freely available to all.

Finally, I cannot resist the temptation of mentioning one thought that recurs as a result of contraception and it is this: I wonder how southern Italians now manage when they go looking for a wife. Let me explain.

It has long been an established practice in southern Italy that what was called a woman's honour was of fundamental importance. People killed for it and people searched for it long after it ceased to be a normal commodity.

The average southern Italian would not as a rule marry a girl who did not reach the marital chamber inviolate. He must have wondered at the custom reported by Marco Polo about the Tibetans, namely, that in that country no-one would marry a virgin on the principle that a wife is worth nothing if she has not had intercourse with other men: there, the more she has known, the more appreciated she is. But perhaps southern Italians have not read *Il Milione* because the search for virginity is a well-established feature of their mentality (or rather, was) and is the result of a number of causes and traditions, some practical, some religious, of which the following may serve as examples.

The principal reason, I believe, is that the male looked upon a woman as a chattel. Not for nothing we have in Italy the saying 'choose your wife from the same places where you choose your oxen'. The equation of women with a thing is perfectly clear. An interesting analogy is to be found in the purchase of cars: on the whole – and I appreciate that this is a generalization of the type that I have tried to avoid – Italians have not, until very recently, been inclined to buy second-hand motor cars. They prefer them new, in the same way as they prefer their woman to be new.

The second reason is the basic selfishness of the Italian male. Selfishness perhaps is too harsh a term: I suppose he feels the defloration of his wife provides the same sensation as the climbing of Everest for the first time. Nobody was there before him.

This is an understandable reaction, no matter how unpopular it may be with feminists.

The next reason is possibly a rationalization of an instinct, but it is that a woman who has not had previous sexual experiences is less capable of analysing the sexual ability or otherwise of her partner. This not only makes it easier for the man because his performance is subject to less stringent standards and criticisms, but it also provides greater peace of mind for the woman since she cannot miss what she has never had; and to that extent it may, although it need not, even strengthen the marital bond.

There is also the question of hygiene. This is now widely discussed throughout the world but it has always been very much at the forefront of people's minds in Italy, especially in the south. Apart from syphilis, which is inherited, I think I am right in saying that until the advent of AIDS, there were no other sexually-transmitted diseases that could be passed on by a woman who had not previously had intercourse with other men.

These are some of the reasons: there may be others. But, I have little doubt that all of them have contributed to the creation of a culture which has imposed virginity. A culture which has drawn a very clear dividing line between the woman who will be the mother of one's children and the woman who will merely provide a sexual diversion; a culture that recognized, until after the Second World War, that human frailty had to be catered for by a particular type of woman in a particular type of establishment: hence the comparative success of the brothel in Italy. A culture that has attributed to the Italian mother an importance which has resulted in her being venerated well beyond any limit imposed by her own limitations as one. And this type of culture has been reflected in Italian art and literature generally. The distinction between sacred and profane love is an often repeated motif which proceeds from a clear-cut assessment of humanity and its weaknesses. As has been observed so many times, the Italian has a tendency to put motherhood on a pedestal.

I feel sorry for the southern Italian male. I heard it said recently by one of them that the gospel should now be adapted to say that it easier for a camel to go through the eye of a needle than for a virgin to be found in Italy at the altar. Which brings to mind the joke about the Sicilian boy who, just after the marriage ceremony and before departing with his bride for their honeymoon, is seen by his male friends busily painting a particular part of his anatomy with green paint. When asked by them what he is doing, he replies in all seriousness: 'If she looks even mildly surprised, I shall kill her.'

COSMETICS

There is nothing novel in make-up as far as the Italians are concerned. The art of painting the human face is lost in the dawn of history and can be traced back to the Egyptians and Assyrians.

Taking our starting point, however, as the year 1000, it can be said that already in the eleventh century in Italy make-up was worn extensively by women of all classes. The upper class used bright pink, the lower classes used a less expensive reddish colour.

In thirteenth-century Tuscany, eye make-up was common among upper-class women. The upper lids were lined black and shadowed in either brown, grey, blue-green or violet.

301 **Giambattista Della PORTA was the first to provide a recipe for a powder that could be used not only for cleansing the face but also for caring for the teeth. It was made by mixing flowers and herbs with clay and white wine and then burning the resultant concoction to obtain a paste.**

A versatile man, Della Porta, referred elsewhere in this book. In 1558, he wrote 'Natural Magic' in which he investigated those forces in nature that one could not see or touch or identify scientifically. He picked up an idea that had already been mooted by Girolamo Cardano (also referred elsewhere in this book), who in 1551 had also written a book on natural magic in which, amongst other things, he reviewed the attraction of necromancy.

His total literary output consisted of more than thirty books, including an agricultural encyclopaedia (*Villae*, 1583-92) where he gave the first recipe for ice cream.

Somewhat out of context, I record that he was also the first person to suggest the use of the lamp to illuminate his camera obscura, as well as the creator of the first home movie, which was ancillary to his 'darkened chamber'. By means of a lamp he was able to provide images of many people famous at the time.

These were extremely popular and it can be said without any fear of contradiction that his invention of the camera obscura explains why so many realistic pictures of Kings, Queens, Knights, etc. appear in Tudor England.

302 Caterina de MEDICI (see also under 'Gastronomy') is credited with having spread the art of face-painting from Italy into France when she insisted on its use at the court of her French husband.

Some products were known by the name of the place where they were manufactured. For example, there was Venetian Talc (or chalk) for use as present-day Talcum powder and for powdering wigs; and Venetian Ceruse (or rouge for the face).

The art of creating perfumes goes back a long way in history. Nobody can claim that the Italians were first in developing perfumes because that would not be true (although see also 'Etiquette'). But there is certainly one additional first connected with perfumes, and that is a literary one.

303 In 1548, the Florentine Agnolo FIRENZUOLA, a monk (who had received dispensation from his vows), and a man of letters, wrote the book *Dialogo Della Bellezza Delle Donne*, a discourse on the beauty of women.

In it he provides for the first time full descriptions of what he considered to be the ideal Renaissance Beauty and he establishes himself as the first writer of a manual on beauty. According to him, the classic Tuscan gentlewoman had a white face, fair hair, ebony eyebrows and thin, short eyelashes.

Her eyes were carefully painted, her ears were touched up in the colour of pomegranate seeds and her cheeks had a slight vermilion paint applied but, as he says, not too much. Rouge was used discreetly, particularly on the mouth; the intention was not to make the mouth too sensual a part of the body. It was left to Casanova to describe in rather more sensual terms the need for women to apply lipstick liberally to heighten men's desires.

The Medici tradition in Florence encouraged the arts but also fashion styles; men of the period, as appears from a well-known painting by Bronzino, were known to pluck their eyebrows in the feminine manner.

Finally, the Medici family were great supporters of the perfumery industry. With funds advanced by the Medicis the Dominican monks of Santa Maria Novella established in 1508 what was to become one of the most celebrated perfumeries in Europe. Their '*spezieria*' was located in the cloisters of the church, where rooms were open to the public each containing different products, some of which were made from plants and herbs grown in the garden annexed to the church itself. It must have been almost an inconsistent sight to see the monks as apothecaries.

CYCLING

304 In the early 1940s, Tullio CAMPAGNOLO (born in Vicenza), an ardent cyclist, realized that climbing hills would become much simpler if the drive could be fitted with derailleurs. Although bicycles at the time had two speeds, in order to change gears the rider would have to dismount and fiddle about

with the wheel. Rather like a change of tyres in Grand Prix performances, the ability of cyclists at the time was rated on the basis of the speed with which they could do just that. In 1940, tired of this particular struggle, Campagnolo invented the dual-rod shifter, or cable activator, followed by the roubaix which combined the quick-release and chain mover into a single lever. This was subsequently improved in 1951. The system, repeatedly refined over the years, spread quickly, especially on racing cycles, and is still much in use today.

305   The first officially recognized cycle race took place in 1870. It was run from Florence to Pistoia, a distance of 27 km.

EDUCATION

Nobody can accuse us of not having been at the forefront in the establishment of educational institutions even though, ironically, we may have failed to educate ourselves properly. For example, no matter where they were founded, all universities stem from the colleges of students and teachers that became established in Italy at the beginning of the eleventh century. That is to say, long before any other country ever thought of the concept of 'education'.

306   There is no doubt that the first true university in the world was that of Bologna.

According to the Italians, and to Volume R-X, p. 1004 of *Britannica*, it was founded in the year 1000. But *Britannica* seems to be in some doubt about it because in Volume 6, p. 337 and in Volume R-I, p. 131, it claims that Bologna University was founded in the year 1158. But I do not suppose this matters very much.

Paris University was founded twenty-two years later, in 1180. There then followed the University of Perugia which was founded in 1200. This was closely followed by the University of Vicenza which was founded in 1204. Cambridge came next in 1209, the University of Arezzo in 1215, Padova in 1222, and Oxford, finally, in 1229.

Padova is interesting because, contrary to some of the other Italian universities, it soon became known for its very liberal tradition ('*patavina libertas*'). For example, Protestants were unmolested there and the only other city in Italy which at that time was so liberal, at least as regards religious thinking, was Venice (which, however, did not have a university until much later).

The University of Naples and that of Salerno were both founded in 1224, Vercelli in 1228, Ferrara in 1264, Florence in 1321 and Pavia in 1362.

I must not ignore Scotland and Ireland and I should add that the University of St Andrews was founded in 1412 and that of Dublin in 1591, as can be verified under the same reference as for Cambridge and Oxford.

(There is a great deal to be said about the first medical school at Salerno but that is provided under 'Medicine'.)

307   In his book *Midnight in Sicily* (Panther Books, 1996, p. 113), Peter Robb records that the university founded at Naples in 1224 was in fact the first *state university*.

308   In 1400, Pietro Paolo VERGERIO wrote the first significant exclusively paedagogical treatise and contributed to the development

of humanism at Padua University.

He published in about 1402 his book 'On the Conduct of Honourable Men' where he remarked that although the body should be kept fit through physical exercise, the character of the child should be shaped to prepare him for a useful life in society. Accordingly, he should learn grammar to make his speech acceptable and his writing fluent, history to decide how to behave, poetry in order to be virtuous, and moral philosophy because in that way he would be an upright citizen. Admittedly, he was under some kind of job compulsion to write such a treatise, because he was tutor to the son of the ruler of Padua, the town in which he lived. Even so, not a bad effort for something written nearly 600 years ago; and quite topical, if the 'illiteracy' of contemporary youth is to be believed.

309   One of the first acknowledged educators was Guarino BAR-ZIZZA.

310   'The first school inspired by humanistic principles was founded in 1423. . . . .' Thus, *Encyclopaedia Britannica* recording that Gianfrancesco I (1395-1444), a member of the well-known Gonzaga family of Mantua, established it through Vittorino da Feltre in one of his own family's villas near the town of Mantua.

Britannica continues: 'this school which outlived Vittorino by many years, was attended not only by the Gonzaga children but by many pupils from outside, rich and poor, foreign and Italian. . . . .'

311   In 1444, the architect Leon Battista ALBERTI published his *Trattato della Famiglia* which was the first manual of family life.

Alberti's book deals with marriage, marital harmony, the education of children, the economic resources of the group and the citizen's duties to his family and to the State. It is not good reading for exasperated feminists although I suppose even they would be prepared to make allowances for the fact that it was written over 500 years ago. He is clearly a misogynist but then, perhaps, so are, deep down, the Italians, even though they may not readily admit to it.

The first private children's nursery was set up in Turin in 1825. (For authority v. *Torino – Citta' Di Primati* by Pier Luigi Capra, publ. Graphot 2001.)

312   During the closing years of the nineteenth century and the first ten years of the present one, Maria MONTESSORI (born in Chiaravalle AN) founded the Montessori method of education which revolutionized teaching techniques.

The official date of the establishment of the Montessori method could be said to be 1907. The techniques she used are quite normal and familiar today, but at the time they were revolutionary and despite some of the strictures that certain American critics expressed about her (such as, for example, a reference to her system as 'an Italian modification of Froebelian methods', by Jenny B. Merrill in 1909), there is no doubt that the influence of her work was very great and can still be experienced in every classroom throughout the world.

Her writings setting out her method were translated into twenty languages. She herself was a first of a different kind because in the summer of 1896 she became the first modern woman to graduate from a medical school in Italy.

313   The *regular* use of the surname or family name, with the

consequent major implications both in the structure of society and its administration, is credited to the Venetian Republic around about the year 1100.

ETIQUETTE

314   In the year 1513, Baldassarre CASTIGLIONE (born in Casatico MN) wrote *Il Cortegiano*. It was a book that was to have an enormous impact upon England. It was the first on court manners but it also dealt with the relationship between the courtesan and the prince and it was used by young members of the English establishment until the days of Edward VII as their bible on manners.

Thus states the *Encyclopaedia Britannica* more or less paraphrased by me. But the contribution of Baldassarre Castiglione goes beyond that since his book was not only an etiquette manual but was taken by all concerned as an aid to social climbing.

He had visited England when Henry VIII had made the Duke of Urbino (the town in which Castiglione lived) a knight of the most noble order of the Garter. One wonders whether he could ever realize when he was here, what impact he was going to have.

Henry VIII knew Italian and spoke it and was very keen to maintain close contacts with the Italian Courts of the Renaissance. Apart from his disagreements in religious and political matters, he seems to have got on quite well with the Italians. His son Edward had an Italian riding master and Elizabeth was taught Italian at an early age; it was an Italian, Polidoro Virgilio, who wrote a history of England for him and was rewarded by

being made Archdeacon of Wells Cathedral. It is suggested that his *Anglicae Historiae* were absorbed in Holinshed's *Chronicles* and as such contributed quite a lot of material to Shakespeare who relied upon the latter publication.

The book's popularity in England was due to the translation made of it by Thomas Hoby, published in 1561 after he had gone on the 'Grand Tour'.

He gave it the title *Courtyer* and, giving credit where it is due, his style was a great contribution to the success of Castiglione's text.

But there is no doubt that at this particular time there were many Italians in London, whether artists or craftsmen, secretaries or Court musicians, writers, doctors and even lawyers. As we shall see later, at or about the same time as Castiglione's *Il Cortegiano* appeared, there was published Machiavelli's *The Prince* and in the same general period there was started the course of training for English gentlemen, or otherwise, namely the Grand Tour to Italy. It did not start initially as so grand a tour as it became later in the eighteenth century but the Italian universities were well known; and it was part of the curriculum of good breeding that English gentlemen should spend a few terms at one of them, thus acquiring the polish and refinement for which Italy was in those days held in the highest esteem.

That in so doing they should acquire also the bad manners of the Italians is not surprising; it is impossible to copy only the good without being tainted by the bad of any culture. The ideas and morals that some of these English gentlemen brought back provoked scandal to the extent that the English adopted the saying which originated in Italy and not in England, namely that 'The Italianate Englishman is the devil incarnate.' I am sure that that is an exaggeration; I suppose all it shows is that it is a mistake to ape others. (Lord Burghley said that in Italy young men would learn nothing but pride, blasphemy and atheism.)

Certainly, however, by the time Roger Ascham wrote his book *The Schoolmaster* (Constable, 1935) Baldassarre Castiglione was only too well known.

Ascham wrote between 1563 and 1568. To show how much impact Castiglione had at the time, let me quote an excerpt from what Ascham has to say in *The Schoolmaster* about *Il Cortegiano*:

'Which book, diligently followed, but one year at home in England, would do a young man more good than three years travel abroad spent in Italy.' (p. 66)

Ascham faced a problem. He did not object to what Castiglione said, because all that Castiglione says is admirable. But he certainly did not like Italy.

Another example:

'Italy now is not that Italy that it was wont to be; and therefore now not so fit a place as some do count it for young men to fetch either wisdom or honesty from it' (p. 72).

I suppose the same is true even today. . .

On the other hand, this attitude of Ascham's is probably understandable because he hated popery and therefore he hated Italy. How he could possibly reach the conclusions he did about Italy as he had only spent nine days there (p. 83) escapes me.

The Schoolmaster is divided into 'books'. The first book deals with the bringing up of youth and the second with the ready eighty-six pages to vilify Italy but eighty pages to praise the Latin tongue, almost as though you could have one without the other.

But he certainly did not like Italy (p. 83):

'I was once in Italie my selfe; but I thank God, my abode there was but ix daes; and yet I sawe in that little tyme in one citie more liberti to sinne then euer I heard tell of in our noble citie of London in ix yeare.'

(I suggest that all this is rather unfair. Castiglione's men are paragons of virtue, or at least ought to be and his Renaissance gentlemen certainly knew how to treat a lady. In his book *Italian Renaissance*, John D. Clare quotes an extract from *The Courtyer* where one of his men, Giuliano Dei Medici, declares: 'all of us know that it is fitting for the courtier to have the greatest reverence for women. . . . a serious woman strengthened by virtue and insight, acts as a shield against the insolence and beastliness of arrogant men. . . . .')

Nor was he alone in criticizing the all-pervasive Italian influence on the England of the sixteenth century. One cannot help recalling that Shakespeare himself – who owed much to Italy – had to complain about the slavish acceptance of Italian culture. (See *Richard II*, Act 2, Scene 1, Line 21: (. . .proud Italy, whose manners still our tardy apish nation limps after in base imitation.') The fame of the Italian courtiers is recorded elsewhere by Shakespeare. For example, he says in *Cymbeline* (Act 1, Scene 1, Line 103): 'Your Italy contains none so accomplished a courtier to convince the honour of my mistress.'

The connection between Italian culture and the English nobility is even closer than the foregoing would indicate.

Well apart from the Italian influence on court manners and personal etiquette, if the reader could spare the time to visit the village of Thornhaugh (off the A5 not too far from Peterborough in Cambridgeshire) he would be well advised to enter the local church. It is normally locked, but the key can be obtained from one of the church-wardens who lives across the road. There is to be found in the church a monumental tomb of the Russell family which on its crest bears the motto of the Rucellai, a well-known Florentine family of noblemen and financiers. It is sculpted in the original Italian *'Che sara sara'* and it is clear to see how the Italian name through the years changed to Rucell, Rusell and then Russell. (Incidentally, the same motto was adopted by the Dukes of Bedford, and may be seen wherever they wished to leave their mark – for example, in their box adjacent to the royal one at Covent Garden Opera House. As well as in the ancestral home and vault in the village of Chenies in Buckingham-shire, where all members of the Russell family are buried and, when cremated, preserved in funerary urns, some of questionable style.)

Meanwhile, back in the seventeenth century, the Italian puppet theatre was beginning to take over in London. In 1662, *Pulcinella* made its London debut, and stayed to this day in the title of the magazine 'Punch' (until, that is, it ceased publication in 1992).

315 A little earlier, at the beginning of the seventeenth century, Silvio FIORILLO established himself as the first Pulcinella, the chief figure in the Punch & Judy puppet show at an earlier date called 'Punchinello', 'Policianello', 'Polichinelle', in addition to 'Pulcinella', this last name being crystallized in its use by the 'Commedia dell'Arte'.

316 In 1550, Giovanni della CASA (born in Mugello) wrote *Il Galateo*, the first etiquette manual.

This book became quite well known in England but it never acquired the popularity of nor did it have the same impact as *Il Cortegiano*.

317 The handkerchief was invented in Italy during the Renaissance.

318 The first skinheads of history are recorded in Venice, where some youngsters organized themselves into the 'Compagnia della Calza' (or 'the company of the hose') having fancy clothes but, above all, the habit of shaving half their heads and wearing a close fitting cap. Am I going too far to claim their activities as the first rebellious fashion statement by teenagers in history?. . . . .

319 The umbrella is recorded as having been in use in Italy as early as 1578 (Carter p.179). Its first mention in England occurs in a comedy by Ben Johnson in 1616.

320 Eau-de-Cologne was invented by Giovanni FARINA, a barber by trade. He was born in 1685 in southern Italy and in 1709 he settled in Cologne in Germany where he reproduced certain experiments that he had been carrying out in his home town of Reggio Calabria. He based the scent on the essence of bergamot, a citrus fruit which appears to grow successfully only in Calabria, in a restricted area between Cannitello and Roccella Ionica.

Up to about the 1950s, the essential oils of bergamot were indispensable for perfumes and they remain important, but only for the highest possible type of product; for the run-of-the-mill perfumes, nowadays we have synthetic scents.

Speaking of *perfumes*, a small item of gossip. The many English tourists who flock to Provence, that most Italian region of France, and almost unfailingly visit Grasse, would be surprised to find, when attending at one of the most famous 'parfumeries', Fragonard, that the establishment was founded in 1926 by an Italian called Costa. He chose the name fragonard by way of homage to the painter Jean-Honoré Fragonard, born in Grasse, himself having a connection with the industry since his father was a 'Gantier Parfumeur'. Indeed, the development after the First World War of the whole of the flower industry for perfumes in the area surrounding Grasse was promoted by Italian immigrant labour. Four generations later their nationality may have been consolidated as French, but their Italian names remain.

FABRICS & FASHIONS

321 **The textile industry was born in Sicily in 1130 (despite the fact that the first crepe textiles were manufactured in Bologna around the year AD 1000). Tuscany followed in 1226; by the middle of the sixteenth century Genoa and Venice had come to the forefront. Later, France took over as leading producer.**

322 **Buttons first appeared in Italy in the twelfth century. (Frugoni)**

323 **In 1339, the technique of Italian needlepoint lace was first applied in Venice. This 'punto in aria' was the springboard for the use of needlepoint around the world.**

Italian mastery of lace-making is exemplified by the skills found even today on the island of Burano near Venice, a compulsory stop for tourists. Incidentally, it is not widely known that during the eighteenth century numerous Venetian lace-makers established themselves in England, for instance, in Bedfordshire and in Dorset.

324 **Up to the seventeenth century, velvet was made exclusively in Italy.**

In the Middle Ages, imported Italian velvet was very popular in England for the making of clothes and shoes.

The interplay between Italy and France is historic. Throughout history, there have been a number of fields where Italy has started a fashion and France has taken it over, improved on it and subsequently established itself as master in that particular field. Such interplay is recorded by Shakespeare when he differentiates between the two countries in the *Merchant of Venice* (act 1, scene 2, line 80): 'He bought his doublet in Italy, his round hose in France.'

325 **The fashion designer first made his appearance in Italy in the early fifteenth century. This coincided with the development of the concept of ideal beauty and the increased importance of the qualities of the female body (more so than ever before). As Francois Boucher observed in his *A History of Costume in the West*, 'in all the Italian States men and women translated this search after formal beauty into costume, thus satisfying their taste for elegance, their passion for colour harmony and their aspirations towards a greater distinction'.**

One has only to look at Pisanello's paintings for confirmation of the foregoing statement.

Not only Pisanello, but also Pollaiolo and Jacopo Bellini created costume models and designed textile patterns. As a result, the role of Italy as a precursor of national costume is of vital importance; in all the Italian Courts, large or small, says Boucher, there was 'a studied pursuit of elegance and a taste for lavish costumes'.

Italians made the running. France then overtook them, as Italian influence declined, and as large numbers of Italian merchants and workers took up residence in Lyon, Paris and Tours. But as the 1980s have shown, Italian influence on the world of fashion is once again a force to be reckoned with, catering now for the masses as well as the gentry!

326 Costume textiles were first introduced in Lombardy towards the beginning of the fourteenth century.

The output of Italy in this field was enormous. Coloured hose, new mixtures of colours, new colours, new mixtures of silk, new linens, laces, fur trimmings, edgings, linings, satins, velvets, taffetas and damasks all became established in Italy, and from there spread to the rest of Europe. At about this time, woman (a subject we shall return to later) was glorified. Clothes were the concomitant of such glorification – the square cut neckline for women, for example, was an Italian creation, as was fancy headgear, like the Florentine toque. The influence on France was considerable.

With the Spanish domination established by Charles V, costumes became more severe: but the tradition was by then very marked and recorded for posterity in the paintings of Pisanello, Pollaiolo, Jacopo Bellini, Paolo Uccello, Masolino, Benozzo Gozzoli, Carpaccio, Ghirlandaio and Titian.

Italian clothes were as fashionable in the Renaissance as they are today. In his book *The Civilization of Europe in the Renaissance* (Harper Collins, p. 173) John Hale quotes a letter sent by Magdalena Paumgartner in 1591 from Nuremburg to her husband whilst he was on one of his business trips to Lucca, in which she begs him not to forget about her 'Italian coat –

one like the one Wilhelm Imhoff brought his wife from Venice. . .'

The letter makes perfectly clear the concept recorded under this heading.

327 In 1884, Gaetano BONELLI (born in Turin) invented the first electric loom.

His was an attempt to provide a cheaper machine than the Jacquard and was based on electromagnets.

FOOD & DRINK

In matters of food, the Italians are undisputed masters, and with the exception of the French and perhaps the Japanese, most other societies' approach to and appreciation of food is at best crass or inconsistent and at worst appalling.

Of course, I must hasten to add that there is absolutely no authority in the *Encyclopaedia Britannica* or in any other book that I am aware of to substantiate these two statements: they merely represent my opinion. This is not to say, however, they are not perfectly true!

Let me try to demonstrate, and, for the sake of argument, let me take the English and Americans first.

Until the Italians started educating them, the English and the Americans knew very little about good food. There are three principal reasons for this:
1. The appreciation of culinary expertise is part of a frame of mind and an approach to life which is associated with good wine and good living in a sunny clime and against the backcloth of our Latin civilization. The former does not exist in either England or the USA and the latter is usually to be found only around the Mediterranean

shores in combination with the former.

2. There is no tradition of cooking in either the British Isles or the USA. If ever there was, which I doubt, it has long ceased to exist.

3. Good cooking is a cultural and emotive fact, as well as a physical one. It is born, and it dies, within the family, and is a labour of love. It is taught by mothers to daughters and it represents the distillation of all the teachings and remarks by whomsoever spends most of her life in front of a stove. It is not learnt from a book any more than it is learnt by part-time mothers/wives. Cooking, like looking after a family, is a full-time occupation which cannot be left in the hands of anyone, male or female, who has already spent some eight or ten hours in an office or has been busy at some other job. People who get home in the evening after a full day at work are tired; they do not want to cook, though they might just want to eat.

If they have to prepare a meal, theirs is not a labour of love but of hasty necessity. They cut corners, they lose their critical sense, their touch, and, above all, their own appreciation for what they are doing.

Where the housekeeper is out at work there can be no real cuisine. Hence the ready-made, pre-packed, pre-cooked, pre-frozen so-called food which has no taste, no style and no freshness. It suits those who buy it, who end up by getting exactly what they deserve.

Inasmuch as the family (and extended family) has ceased to have any real significance in England and America (for the most part), there cannot possibly be any appreciation of good food there. The tragedy is that the family is being demolished in Italy as well; but that is a different story. However, when that happens, the consequences will be exactly the same: canned spaghetti and a couple of tablets!

I hold as an absolute fact that in all matters of food the Italians have given the lead.

I have watched with increasing amusement over the past ten to fifteen years the number of recipes for Italian food that have emerged on the back of pasta or cheese packets or elsewhere, which have all been copied direct from Italian cookery books. I can think of at least three so-called English authorities on cooking, the bulk of whose recipes – proffered not only as Italian recipes, but as their own advice – have been abstracted in their entirety from the leading Italian books on cooking by Pellegrino Artusi and Ada Boni.

The spread of Italian restaurants in England and America has obviously contributed to a greater appreciation of the fine things in life but the standard of Italian cooking outside Italy and particularly in England is not always constant.

In actual fact, it is not Italian cuisine that the Anglo-American public is being accustomed to, but a cuisine which has been adapted to suit national requirements and to make it more acceptable to the local palate.

Italian cafes, restaurants and other food establishments variously named, some abusive of the Italian language, have sprouted like mushrooms throughout the UK and the USA. They are usually opened by people whose only claim to Italian cooking is that they have an Italian name. (Sometimes they are not even opened by Italians!) They have no gastronomic education, and little taste. It is as though a butcher had determined that merely because he knew how to handle a knife he should become a surgeon. It is true that there are some surgeons who are butchers but I know of no butchers who are surgeons. By parity of reasoning I know of few Italians abroad who know anything about the real art of Italian cooking.

I feel very strongly about this aspect of the so-called cultural education that present-day Italians have been imparting, in matters of cooking, not only to the English and Americans but to the world at large. The standards of true Italian cooking are not being maintained abroad, save in very few cases.

It is difficult enough to maintain them in Italy where we have an appreciative and highly critical public; it is expecting too much that they should be maintained wherever the public is undiscerning. This is not to say that Italian food establishments abroad are not good, or do not offer value for money. They are, and they do, but they reflect falling standards and have had to adapt to local requirements and availability of produce. This is inevitable; in fact, it is a mark of Italian inventiveness that surprisingly good results are still achieved.

On the optimistic side, there is no doubt that the lead we have over all other nations, France included, is great. In fact, I believe it is so great that we have ample justification for being conceited in this context. I suppose we feel as Red Rum's jockey must have felt when he won the Grand National for the third time: supreme in the field.

It is difficult, however, to disabuse people of the notion that the French are better. The use of language is significant: the English refer to French cuisine, but to Italian cooking. The nuance is not great but is very significant. I still feel that the Italians have greater imagination with food. Suffice it to say that it is too easy to ascribe the reason to the Mediterranean climate. Spain and Greece enjoy the same climate as Italy, but food in the former is,

to put it mildly, barely adequate except in Cataluña and in the latter good cuisine is non-existent. What makes the food enjoyable in Spain and Greece is the sun and not the technique of those who prepare it.

In Italy, on the other hand, there is not only the sun but also a gastronomic tradition which goes back at least 400 years. In the Renaissance, Italian cooking was the turning point in the development of gastronomic excellence. Italy influenced France extensively.

328　It was Catherine de' MEDICI who was the first to bring Italian cooking to France when she married Henry II of Navarre and took with her a retinue of Italian cooks.

Italian supremacy has been established since that time and has continued uninterrupted. It is not so much a matter of Parmesan cheese, known in England since the fourteenth century, or Parma Ham, known since the seventeenth century, or indeed, Bologna sausages being the best in the world. (For the sausages, you will find the observation in Boswell's *Life of Dr Johnson* for Saturday, 9 May 1772.)

Catherine ensured that a number of novelties were introduced into French cuisine especially new vegetables such as artichokes and truffles, but is probably better known for her cooks' creation of the 'zabaione' namely whipped egg yolk with sugar and marsala wine.

She was very fond of food, so much so that, as she grew older, she put on weight and tried to shed some of it by dancing; partly to that end she imported Italian dancers, male and female, and can be credited for having introduced ballet as an art to the French court.

Certainly, she can claim the merit of having, through her retinue, laid the foundation for the popularity of French cuisine, at least in the sense that the locals moved from heavily sauced dishes to a more subtle and lighter approach to cooking. It was then, and it continues to be, despite the occasional aberration due to the desire of importing concepts from Asian and Pacific dishes, the merit of Italian gastronomy not to rely exclusively on heavy sauces but rather on the quality and purity of the ingredients used. In Italy, the flavour of a meat or a fish is enhanced without smothering it in sauces but instead almost exclusively relying on its own juices: a much lighter and healthier cuisine. . . . .

The tradition of good food was kept up by another member of the Medici family, Maria de'Medici, who married Henry IV of France, becoming known to the French as Marie de Médicis.

329 Alcohol was first distilled in Europe at the Salerno School of Medicine in the year 1000.

The American writer William Faulkner is said to have remarked that civilization begins with distillation.

I'm not sure whether he was right, even assuming he said it, but again, we were there. . . . .

330 Large-scale production of alcohol, however, is recorded for the first time at Modena in the thirteenth century.

The mention of alcohol brings to mind Italian wines.

331 The world's oldest officially defined wine-growing area is the Chianti region between Florence and Siena. It was established by Cosimo de' Medići, Grand-Duke of Tuscany (see *Florence and Tuscany,* Udine Magnus Edizioni, 1981).

This is not the place to embark upon a dissertation on genuineness and quality which would be entirely inappropriate in any event. Suffice it to say that the writer subscribes to the view – probably obvious, you might observe – that the supremacy that the Italians hold in matters of gastronomy is almost matched by a similar primacy in matters of alcoholic drinks. But be that as it may. There can be differences of opinion on the issue but what is incontestable is that the first known historical reference to a law that sets out the type of grapes to be used in wine relates to the white muscat grape. This variety is quite ancient and originated in the eastern Mediterranean. It was called *'apiciae'* by Cato and was referred to by both Columella and Pliny as *'apianae'* (both terms deriving from the appeal of its sweet aroma and from bees).

The white muscat grape is cultivated in many parts of the world, but nowhere more successfully than in Piedmont and it is there that we find the reference in 1511 to *'muscatellum'*. It occurs in a document known as the *'La Morra'* Statutes. *'La Morra'*, as some readers may know, is one of the many attractive villages scattered around the area where some of the best Italian wines are made.

The statute stipulates that anyone planting a new vineyard must cultivate the muscat grape in a ratio of 1:5 with other varieties. The effect of the *'La Morra'* statute, however, extended beyond Piedmont for it is recorded that in 1597 the Duke of Mantua requested cuttings of muscat vines from the vineyards of another Piedmontese village, Santo Stefano Belbo, for the Duke's estates.

Nor can we ignore the debt that the world owes to Italy when it comes to ice-cream. How many Anglo-American makers of ice-cream would not exist but for the recipes provided by Italians and the use of Italian names, for example 'Neapolitan',

'Tartufo', 'Cornetto' and 'Cassata'.

From the historical standpoint, however, the Italians themselves got there first only in the sense that they continued what the Romans or the Chinese had done. Water ices, in fact, were already known to the Romans.

If we listened to modern dieticians, then I am not sure to what extent we should be too proud of the next 'first', although one cannot deny that it has been a source of considerable enjoyment especially to those who can claim to have a sweet tooth.

332 **We owe to the Venetians the development of the first large scale sugar import trade. They started in the fourteenth century negotiating, usually on a barter base, with the Arabs and as a result they were also the first in giving an incredible impulse to the manufacturing of sweets.** (Charles Panati)

333 **The recipe for milk ices originates in the Far East. It was recorded by Marco POLO during one of his travels in China and was brought back to Europe by him.**

We are told that Charles I of England was particularly appreciative of the milk ices prepared by his Italian cook, Mireo, and it is claimed that his Italian wife, Enrichetta Maria Medici, and her said cook introduced ice-cream into Britain.

Leaving aside Mireo, the association of Italians with ice-cream comes naturally. And this must be based on the factual recognition that particular techniques of ice-cream making, especially from Naples and Sicily, have been the foundation of the later manufacture of ice-cream on an industrial scale.

There is something exceptionally sensual about ice-cream. It is addictive almost in the same way as smoking or drinking; but it does not have the same drugging effect. Indeed, it seems to me that the effect of tobacco is primarily chemical and only secondarily sensual; that of alcohol is primarily psychological and again only secondarily sensual. In the case of ice-cream, however, one's sense of taste determines the addiction.

It is interesting that poets and writers seem exceptionally fond of ice-cream. Both Goethe and Stendhal praised Italian ices; our own Leopardi waxed lyrical about Neapolitan sorbets. Whether Dickens liked it or not I am not sure, but in his *Pictures from Italy* he records the extent to which the locals partook of ice-cream practically the year round.

The identification, especially in Victorian England, of Italians with the selling of ice-cream is well known. Perhaps less well known is that fact that the Victorian ice-cream sellers were known as 'hokey pokey', an expression which is believed to be derived from the Italian '*ecco un poco*', meaning here's a little bit of something nice.

And how many other nations are indebted to us when it comes to food? One example only, namely salami: it was an Italian chestnut-vendor called Piazzoni who taught the Hungarians how to make salami. He is credited with founding their salami industry, which is now fairly substantial, in the year 1850. But our contribution goes beyond simple inventiveness; it goes deeper than the mere product. It is rather a question of the enjoyment that the Italian derives from his expertise in making something out of comparatively simple ingredients. This is the ability and the ingenuity of the Italians when it comes to food, and it is not shared by any other people I know except the Chinese.

Apart from any other consideration, this excellence is not limited to the taste of food, or to its presentation. It goes beyond that to its substance.

334   There is nothing new about the Italians' success with ice-cream. For example, by the sixteenth century, the Florentines were the first to discover the art of preserving ice and snow throughout the hottest summers by burying it in well-insulated pits. Visitors to the Boboli Gardens are shown one that is said to be such.

They used it more to keep white wine cool in hot summers and Elizabeth David has recorded (*Harvest of the Cold Months: the Social History of Ice and Ices,* London, Michael Joseph) how Montaigne, when visiting Florence in 1581, during a summer so hot as to astonish even the natives, remarked on how beautifully cool and delicious the wine that he was offered seemed to be. In fact, so surprisingly cool that he got a headache on the strength of it.

I observe in passing that the Italians at the time were well-versed in the art of storing ice for culinary use. I recall reading somewhere that 'the meanest person in Italy who rents a house has his vault or cellar for ice'.

335   The Italians claim that Bernardo BUONTALENTI, to whom we have already referred, was the inventor of the ice-cream.

Whilst accepting that the Chinese discovered the technique of cooling, if not freezing things, as far back as the eighth century BC, they argue that the ice-cream, as we understand it today, was created by Buontalenti in 1565, on the occasion of a banquet given by Cosimo, one of the Medici, to honour certain Spanish compatriots of his wife, Eleonora, who came from Toledo.

Given that Buontalenti had already displayed his talents (the surname itself means that he had good talents. . .) in the Villa at Pratolino, The Uffizi Gallery, the façade of Santa Trinita, the topography of Leghorn and Fort Belvedere, Cosimo is said to have asked him to do something else special. Bountalenti provided a cold cream of milk, zabaione, and fruit, which delighted the Spanish guests. Florence became an ice-cream factory and the very same Catherine de Medici asked Buontalenti to train a group of ice-cream makers whom she took to France with her.

There is no doubt, however, that the Italians did turn ice-cream making into an art. By 1650, ice-cream was commonly available for sale in Naples.

The people of Turin claimed that it was in 1884, at an ice-cream shop known as 'Pepino' in Piazza Carignano, that the first ice-lolly came into being which its inventor, Domenico Pepino, termed 'pinguino'. (For authority v. *Torino – Citta' Di Primati* by Pier Luigi Capra, publ. Graphot 2001.)

336   I should not wish to minimize in any sense the experience and significance of the French; but even here the Italians have left their mark. It is recorded that way back in 1335, Francesco SCACCHI wrote down the first recipe for making sparkling wine. Obviously, in much simplified form and without special corks, metal caps and wire, etc. for bottling.

337   In 1570, a doctor from Brescia, Girolamo CONFORTO, published a book by the title *Libellus De Vino Mordaci*. In it he discussed for the first time a technique for allowing wine to ferment in the bottle, thus anticipating by a few hundred years the French monk Dom Perignon.

338 The first cookery book of the 'modern' world was published in Venice in 1475. It was written by Bartolomeo SACCHI (born in Cremona in 1420, died in Rome sixty years later), sometimes known as '*il Platina*', and was an immediate success. It was reprinted a total of eleven times in the original Latin and was subsequently translated into French in 1548 and into German in 1530. No English translation appears to be available.

It is clearly a one-off enterprise in two senses: firstly, all the remaining publications of '*il Platina*' are of an historical nature and are connected with the Catholic Church's development and history, as well as that of the Popes. Secondly, whilst it ties up with the books on Roman cookery by Apicius, and whilst the author quotes fairly freely from the Latin authors who took an interest in the science of gastronomy (Columella, Varro and Pliny), it purports to be a book on the art of living. The title *De Honesta Voluptate et Valitudine*, which freely translated means 'on healthy enjoyment and fitness', was only in later years amplified to *De Arte Coquinaria* or *De Arte Coquendi* (The Art of Cooking).

The first chapter deals with choice of homes, exercise, play, sleep and even intercourse. The bulk of the book, however, consists of ten chapters, a total of ninety-three pages, and about 300 recipes. From cucumbers through medlars to fennel, from stag and bear meat, through hare to most varieties of birds, with an extensive analysis of herbs and nuts, from brassicas through peppers to mustard and marzipan, from baked eels through fried carrots to fried cheese, there is little that '*il Platina*' does not deal with. There are presented eight ways of preparing eggs, and he spends some time in explaining how to cook sturgeon and properly serve caviar. Shellfish, turtles and frogs are dealt with in detail, and there are a total of sixty-three recipes for fish.

The wine producers of Northern Italy may not be quite so fond of him as those from the centre and the south. He mentions, as best for his times, the wines of Sorrento, as well as Falerno, San Gimignano, Trebbiano and Piceno.

Clearly a forerunner.

He is also credited with writing a *History of the Popes*, an important source of information for historians. (*The Oxford Illustrated History of Medieval Europe*, Oxford University Press, 1988, p. 295)

339 The fork for dining was invented in Italy in the sixteenth century. It came into use in England about one hundred years later.

John Julius Norwich has taken me to task about the above statement. He claims that in the *Chronicles of John the Deacon*, it is already clear that the teodora Ducas, Greek wife of the Doge Domenico Silvio, as early as the year 1072 or thereabouts, was so refined and sybaritic in her approach to life that, as John the Deacon puts it, she did not 'deign to touch her food with her fingers but would command her eunuchs to cut it up into small pieces which she would impale on a certain golden instrument with two prongs and thus carry it to her mouth'. This may be, but it was what one may call a one-off. The practice of using a fork on a *daily* basis became established much later. Indeed, even after the Italians invented the four-pronged fork for dining, it took a very long time before it was accepted in general use. It is a fact that even 300 years ago a fork was looked upon as a curious item. It is also well known that in France, for instance, everyone used fingers until the seventeenth century.

Since the third edition of this work was published, my attention has been drawn to a work by Charles Panati (*Panati's Extraordinary Origins of Everyday Things*, Harper & Row Publishers Inc, New York, 1987) where he records that 'small forks for eating first appeared in eleventh century Tuscany', they being introduced nearly two centuries later into England by Thomas à Becket, Archbishop of Canterbury, where they remained as a curiosity until about the eighteenth century.

It must be admitted that there are conflicting statements about the dining fork. This is probably due to the fact that it must be an obvious thought that even primitive man would in all likelihood have used some kind of skewer to pick up his food, in the same manner as the Greeks used an implement with two tines which helped to carve meat more easily.

There is some evidence that by AD 600 something of the same type was in use at the courts of the Middle East but, in a sense, these were what I would term one-off situations.

It also has to be considered what exactly one means by 'dining fork'. Two prongs, three, or even four? Surely one cannot mean an instrument like a skewer which may have been around from time immemorial. When I attribute the invention to the Italians it is because it was due to them that the 'modern' version of the dining fork came into being and, above all, in general use.

340   It is interesting to note in this connection that the original versions of the dining fork were of either two or three prongs. It was a Neapolitan, Gennaro SPADACINI who, at the court of Ferdinand II of Naples, is credited with having manufactured the first four-pronged fork in 1700 with the specific aim of facilitating the eating of spaghetti.

Different nationalities adopted different approaches. It has been said that the French did not really like the idea of using the fork since they considered the practice an affectation. Indeed, the English themselves for quite a long time ridiculed it also on the ground of effeminacy. So much so that it is recorded that King Henry III was laughed at when he decided to introduce individual forks for use at table.

It was the Englishman Thomas Coryate, who is said to have brought back to England the first forks after his Italian travels. Travelling through Italy in 1611, he observed Italians using forks when eating and remarked that they were ultramodern, fastidious people. Not all people's fingers were clean in those days.

As an aside, I observe that he may also have remarked on the use of what we might term modern plates. By that I mean not the medieval bread trenchers made of either wood, pewter or even, for the better-off, silver or silver-gilt, but the flat modern plate in round form (the earlier trenchers were usually square). One can in fact see pictures of flat plates in a fresco at the Palazzo del Te in Mantua dating from about 1525. They appear to be made of metal and, in all likelihood, were not meant for invididual portions in the sense in which we understand them. It was only some eleven years later in 1536 that King Franćois I of France ordered a set of six plates (assiettes) to be made for use at court.

But back to the fork.

The film industry has regaled us with memories of the luxury and magnificence of the Court of Louis XIV and the great banquets at his palaces; but no one there used a fork and even in Venice itself, when people were served beside a knife and spoon with a fork to hold the meat to facilitate cutting, they were thought a little peculiar if they actually used it. It was only in the late seventeenth century that silver forks began to appear all over Italy and only by the end of the eighteenth century that the fork came into its own, as an ordinary item in general use.

341 It is commonly believed that meringues also originated in Italy, being first cooked by a chef called Gasparini in 1720.

342 Out of chronological order I should mention that Panati records that 'the criss-cross shaped pretzel was the creation in 603[!] of a medieval Italian monk from Northern Italy who awarded pretzels to children as an incentive for memorizing prayers. He derived the shape of his confection from the folded arms of children in prayer. That origin, as popular folklore has it, is supported by the original Latin and Italian words. . .'
In Latin, 'pretiole' means little gift, and in Italian 'bracciatelli' means small arms.

343 Luigi Alvise CORNARO (born in Venice) – one of the many members of the well-known Venetian Corner family – wrote in 1558 *Della Vita Sobria*, the first treatise on how to live to be one hundred years, as he thought he would. He died aged ninety-nine and wrote it when he was aged eighty-three.

By profession, Cornaro was an architect and was the first to import the Romantic Renaissance-style to northern Italy. It is likely that he knew and influenced Palladio.
But he also dabbled, with good results, in hydraulics, agriculture and land reclamation. Above all, however, he was best at building villas.
He maintained that the key to a long, healthy life is sobriety in everything, but particularly in food.

He was himself fortunate in more respects than one. He was successful, he had money, he lived well; he had two homes. The one where he spent most of his time he had designed himself and was very comfortable, cool in the summer and warm in the winter. He ate and drank exclusively products from his own land. It was easy for him to lead a healthy life. But well apart from the healthy life he led, he certainly displayed great will-power.
As he says: 'I have carefully avoided heat, cold and extraordinary fatigue, interruption of my usual hours of rest, excessive venery, making any stay in bad air and exposing myself to the wind and sun.' He limited himself to 12 oz of food a day.
His house was situated in the most beautiful quarter of the noble and learned city of Padova and was 'very convenient and handsome'. He also enjoyed many days' stay in his villa by the river Brenta. (The Brenta Canal – for a canal it is, more than a river – runs from Padova to Venice and on or by it are to be found some of Palladio's best works, from the Villas Cornaro and Capra to La Malcontenta and La Nazionale, some of over 4,000 villas that were built in that part of Italy at the very time that the Venetian Republic was declining.)
Cornaro's philosophy was that up to the age of fifty, one might allow oneself to deviate from the norm. But after fifty, our lives should in everything be governed by reason which teaches us that 'the consequences of gratifying our palate and our appetite are disease and death'.
Correct he might have been about the wisdom of self-restraint, particularly in food, but I believe he is important for a totally different reason. I think it can be fairly said that he anticipated the concept of food allergy. For example, he remarks that he had applied himself diligently to

discover what kinds of food suited him best. In so doing he found that mature wine upset him, but new wine did not, that pepper could properly be replaced by cinnamon and that different foods affected different people. Of course, he was not saying anything very new: 400 years before Christ, Hippocrates had mentioned the fact that there were certain people who showed intolerance for specific constituents of their physical environment. In Roman times, Lucretius, the author of *De Rerum Natura*, was the first to use wording the modern equivalent of which is 'One man's meat is another man's poison'.

It is a fact that before the word 'allergy' was invented, essentially in the nineteenth century, it had long been recognized that there were some of us who are made ill by eating, drinking, inhaling or sometimes even touching things which most others take in their stride.

A great number of twentieth-century theories have elaborated upon his intuition of food intolerance, more particularly when suggesting that the suitability of some foods to the digestive system and the general health of the individual may be determined by one's blood group.

344   CORNARO was the first modern writer who actually elaborates the concept of 'allergy' in the sense that he builds a whole philosophy of life or, perhaps more accurately, an entire way of living upon the fact that some foods suited him and others did not.

(It is interesting to note that the 1975 version of the 15th Edition of the *Encyclopaedia Britannica* only mentions him in passing as an architect at Volume III, p. 154 and at Volume XIII, p. 932. The 1978 version of the same edition does not mention him at all.)

He correctly anticipated by centuries the allegedly modern 'discovery' that, by imposing caloric restrictions, one can prolong life spans.

Morton records the fact that Cornaro has been called the 'Apostle of Senescence'.

345   In 1581, Vincenzo CERVIO published the first book containing detailed instructions on carving. He deals for example with how to carve pheasants or peacocks.

346   Since at least in the eyes of the Mediterranean people one cannot separate good food from good coffee, it should be recorded that it was the Venetians who introduced coffee to Europe. Coffee appears to have originated in Abyssinia and thence spread by the Arabs to the Balkans, Spain, India, North Africa and Turkey. The Venetian traders are credited with having been the first to introduce coffee to Italy round about the year 1615.

Coffee was already known to the Europeans by then.

347   In 1592, in Venice, Prospero ALPINI, a botanist at Padua University, published the first recorded description in the Western world of both the coffee plant and the drink in his treatise *The Plants of Egypt*.

Seven years prior to that publication, Gianfranco Morosini, who had been governor of Constantinople when it was part of the Venetian empire, had reported to the Venetian Senate on the Turkish habit of drinking coffee. In fact, it is believed that he was himself the first importer into Venice of coffee berries.

348   The first health cook book was written in 1614 by Giacomo CASTELVETRO, under the title 'A

Brief Account of the Fruit, Herbs and Vegetables of Italy'.

Castelvetro himself, with the help of the British Ambassador to Venice, escaped from the Inquisition in 1611. In 1613, he took up residence in England and earned a living as a teacher and a linguist. It is claimed that he was appalled by the amount of meat that the English consumed and he decided that they should be converted to a healthier diet, hence his said work which he dedicated to the Countess of Bedford.

It is interesting to note that his manuscript remained unpublished; two years after he composed it, Castelvetro died penniless in London. His book was published in England in 1989 by Viking and those who are interested in this forerunner of modern ideas of healthy eating can now read for themselves his little gems of advice.

A classic, which is commonplace in Italian culture anyhow, is the suggestion that you should peel figs before offering them to friends and do likewise to peaches before offering them to enemies. The underlying concept is that the skin of the fig is not so wholesome whereas that of a peach is. Modern science has, in fact, confirmed his belief: it is now maintained that, provided it is properly cleaned to wipe off most traces of the chemicals which are unfortunately used nowadays, the skin of the peach has highly nutritious qualities, whereas that of the fig can cause irritation to the bowel tract.

349 **Venice also claims another first, namely the establishment of the first coffee house in the Western world in 1645.**

The habit of drinking coffee, firstly for medicinal purposes and later on for pleasure, spread very quickly in Venice and coffee houses proliferated. The famous 'Florian' cafe was established in Piazza San Marco in 1720; the equally well known 'Pedrocchi' coffee house followed in Padua in 1831 and gradually coffee houses became established in all major Italian cities. The habit spread quickly through Europe where coffee houses were established both by Italians and by locals. For example, the oldest coffee house in Austria, where Mozart is said to have been taken quite often by his father, is to be found in Salzburg and is known to this day by the name of its founder 'Tomaselli's'.

The spread of coffee throughout Europe was very rapid. The first London coffee house is said to have been established in St Michael's Alley, Cornhill, under the sign of 'Pasqua's Head' in or about 1652, although the first coffee house in England was opened that same year in Oxford by a Jew from Italy.

Also towards the end of the seventeenth century, more precisely in 1689, a Sicilian nobleman by the name of Francesco Procopio Dei Coltelli (Lit. 'Procopius of the Knives'), from Palermo, opened the first coffee house in Paris which was appropriately called 'Cafe de Procope'. The establishment very soon became famous, especially because of his inventiveness. Apart from being a limonadier, he was also an apothecary, a distiller, and a grocer and, in his cafes, he sold not only liqueurs and sherbets but also perfumes and jams and chocolate.

Purely as an item of gossip, it was an Italian priest, Father Marco D'AVIANO, who is credited with having invented what is now known as a 'cappuccino', at some time towards the middle of the seventeenth century. It is claimed that he found coffee too bitter and made it more palatable by adding honey, milk and cream when the beans were being boiled. Our dieticians and doctors, who seem to change their minds as quickly as the wind changes direction, have now told us that we can only improve our chances of survival if we change to the Mediterranean diet. They have told us that carbohydrates are not fattening and are indeed necessary; that olive oil is better than butter, margarine and other fats; and that we should increase our intake of pulses, vegetables and fresh fruit. I must say, I knew this when I was very young; my mother taught me and it is what the Italians have been doing since at least the days of the Romans.

There is a long-standing argument amongst historians and dieticians as to whether it was the Chinese or the Italians who invented spaghetti. Put in that simple fashion, there can be no doubt that the 'spaghetto' can only have been invented by an Italian, although it would appear that noodles were known to the Chinese.

More modern research nowadays propounds to the view that it is a myth that Marco Polo came back with evidence of pasta having been produced in China. It is now said that pasta was first produced according to a recipe of the Bishop of Aquileia, in north-east Italy, in about the year 1000. The popularity of pasta is such that in 2003 Italy, its largest producer in the world, manufactured three million tonnes of it.

A number of other countries have jumped onto the bandwagon by trying to 'reproduce' pasta; United States, Canada, and so on.

350 If we take spaghetti, however, we have a fairly authoritative record. The Italian Gastronomical Academy at Bologna has established that they were first created on 28 May 1487 by Mastro ZAFIRANO, who was Chef to Giovanni II

of Bentivoglio, who then ruled the town. The event was the wedding of his son, Annibale, to Lucrezia d'Este, the daughter of Ercole Este, who was Lord of Ferrara.

What the Italians have done with spaghetti, the Chinese never succeeded in doing with the noodle. In other words, they raised its manufacture to an art long before it was produced on an industrial scale by the Neapolitans.

Spaghetti ought to be thick enough to break and thin enough so that the sauce can wrap it up; it should be wide enough to attract the right quantity of sauce but not too wide that it won't mix so well. However, there is no point in measuring it before it is cooked. The exact dimensions of the 'spaghetto' according to the Italian Gastronomical Academy, are to be taken after cooking and they are: width 6.5 mm and thickness 0.6 mm. The specification does not cover length: the longer a 'spaghetto' is, in theory at any rate, the better.

The variations on the pasta theme have now become so numerous that, from time to time, new words are coined to describe different shapes; it would not be in any sense a worthwhile exercise to consider them. For the curious, however, I merely record that the famous 'Tagliatelle' are said to have been so named because they resembled the cut hair of the famous woman poisoner Lucrezia Borgia.

The 'first' recorded below for the fabrication of pasta relates to manufacture on an industrial scale. Spaghetti and vermicelli (the thinner version) had been manufactured on a smaller scale many years earlier.

351 It is recorded that vermicelli were imported into the United States as early as 1751 (see *Virginia Gazette*, 19 September 1751) and

that in 1767 one Sam Brown applied for permission in England to establish a vermicelli factory (Privy Council Office, unbound papers, 1767). It is not clear whether he got it and, if he did, how successful he was.

352   It was in Naples, in 1800, that pasta was first mechanically produced.

Until that time pasta, and especially spaghetti, was made by hand and it is worth noting that, for something like three centuries before then, they were by no means considered a poor man's food. It is fairly well established that it was mainly the nobility and the rich who could actually partake of them.

353   The first factory to manufacture pasta was built at Sansepolcro in 1827 by Giulia BUITONI.

354   In 1896, Italo MARCIONI, an Italian immigrant to New Jersey, USA, created the first ice-cream cones.

However, an earlier creation of the edible ice cream cornet, stated to have occurred about 1850, is credited to another Italian, Carlo Gatti who is said to have made it by twisting pastry round his finger before baking it, when he was peddling ice cream in London from a painted cart.

355   What has now become popularly known as the 'moka' (sometimes 'mocca' or 'moccha') machine was invented by the firm of Bialetti in 1933.

356   The world's first espresso coffee machine was invented in 1946 by the company GAGGIA of Milan, production beginning in 1948. The machine revolutionized coffee drinking by establishing a

culture that was to spread throughout the world.

Gaggia machines were exported worldwide and contributed to the spread of American-style coffee houses which changed the pattern, established in the coffee-drinking boom years of the fifties, from the mid-nineties onwards.

The 're-packaging' of the drink with its numerous variants, American-style, as far removed from the genuine, traditional Italian coffee as Eskimos are from Neapolitans, is an undisputed fact.

The first coffee bar using a Gaggia machine opened in London's Soho in 1950.

The establishment of the Gaggia machine has been claimed by some as a symbol of Italy's transition from a rural to an industrial society: maybe.

It is beyond doubt that the Americans have appropriated the 'cappuccino' and other variations on the coffee theme to such a degree that many British persons actually believe that, like pizza and jeans, cappuccino and espresso coffee originated in the USA. . . . .

The people of Calabria claim that the first shop using the first of such machines was inaugurated at Via Florio 101 in Reggio Calabria. I have been unable to find documentary evidence of this.

The spread of coffee-based drinks, often with spurious Italian names, throughout the Anglo-American world is due in no small measure to Gaggia.

One wonders what would happen to present-day Western society without 'espresso' and 'cappuccino'. . . . . Italian versatility shows through even in this field since a number of Italian 'barmen' have now taken to spending time offering cappuccinos with fancy 'patterns' on the froth. . ., copying what has been done for years with Guinness.

It is worth noting that, in my opinion,

the Italians are probably the only people in the world who take their food seriously. By that, I mean not only that they have developed a culture of food, but also that they are exceptionally concerned and vigilant about its purity and integrity. I know the Germans are equally fussy about their beer, but that is it. Most other people, in my view, still function at a very basic level when it comes to food.

Foreigners, and the English-speaking peoples in particular, look either astonished or behave condescendingly when they hear of the concern manifested by the Italians as regards food. Speaking from personal, professional experience, I may say that I have found it very difficult to explain to the British public as well as the English judiciary that, for instance, Parma Ham is manufactured and cured to particularly exacting standards of quality and purity. The general reaction seems to be that these misguided foreigners have as usual gone over the top.

HOW TO MAKE A PIZZA

A similar reaction, although I detected signs of an improved approach on the part of the public, was manifested when (February 1998) the Italian authorities decided that it was time to stop the abuse by the rest of the world of the concept of the pizza and to codify into law the essential requirements (ingredients and cooking technique) for a true pizza. They have now re-stated that the fundamental ingredients of pizza are tomatoes, mozzarella cheese and olive oil *but* they have made it quite clear that the tomatoes must be plum tomatoes in 8 mm dice, the mozzarella must be made from buffalo milk, and the oil used must be extra virgin. If and insofar as salt is to be used, it can only be sea salt.

To make matters more difficult for all those corrupt pseudo-caterers and suppliers of pizza, the pastry must be tossed by hand and the pizza must be cooked in a wood oven at between 216 °C (420 °F) to 250 °C (480 °F). The crust must be thin and the pastry not overcooked.

Incidentally, there is nothing new about this. This is exactly the way the genuine pizza was always made until a number of establishments, especially in the United States and Great Britain, decided that they knew more about cooking than the Neapolitans who created the pizza.

Not a minute too soon, I say. I add that the extraordinary worldwide success of the pizza is another milestone in the journey that I have embarked upon when writing of our 'firsts'. As I have observed, it just shows how universally acceptable simple Italian concepts can be, and how everybody jumps onto the bandwagon once the Italians have given them the basic idea. I heard recently that it was claimed that pizza was not an Italian concept, but an American creation. There we go again. . .

The reader will have gathered by now how confident and proud I feel about the Italian contribution to gastronomical well-being.

For the record, one could say that the institutionalization of the pizza, at least of that which has become known as 'pizza margherita', dates back to June 1889. Of course, it had existed long before that date, since it was the food of the poor, but on one occasion Queen Marguerite of Savoy was visiting Naples (at the time Queen of Piedmont-Savoy, an independent Italian state). The world-renowned cook, Raffaele Esposito, was invited to the royal palace at Capodimonte and on that occasion, imitating the colours on the Italian flag (it was a time of high patriotic fervour celebrating independence), he prepared a pizza with mozzarella, tomatoes and basil.

Since 1989, when the first edition of this book appeared, we have witnessed throughout the world a consolidation of the reputation of Italian food in every sphere.

I always find it interesting to wonder what, in fact, the English (and for that matter, many other people. . . . .), at all levels of society, ate before they realized the numerous benefits of pizza and pasta. The matter does not end there, however, because a number of Italian dishes and foodstuffs have now become household names in the Anglo-American language. To choose at random, Cannelloni, Passata, Ciabatta, Focaccia, Fettuccine, Lasagne, Mortadella, Tiramisú and the ten essential 'p's (pandoro, pannacotta, panettone, Parma ham, parmigiano, pasta (alla carbonara, all'amatriciana, etc.), pecorino, peperoncini, pizza, polenta and prosciutto).

One need only consider the impact that the Italians have had on eating habits worldwide. Despite the various misspellings created by Americans and others, the 'Pizza' (a Neapolitan creation) has demonstrated how successful the Italians can be with the simplest possible ingredients; but more about it later.

The variants on the themes of Mozzarella cheese, the basil herb and salsas of all kinds need hardly be mentioned.

I am reassured by the fact that over the past two decades so many Italian products have been 'falsified' especially in the United States and Canada. From 'Parma ham' to 'Parmigiano Reggiano', from 'Mozzarella' to 'Mortadella', imitators throughout the world, but especially in the United States, Canada and Germany, have jumped onto the bandwagon of affixing the Italian tricolor band or using an Italian description for products which are as far removed from the original as chalk is from cheese. Apart from the fact that the majority of these mis-described products contain ingredients which are, in my view, dangerous to one's health, let alone the colorants and additives which abound, they are a bad introduction of a fairly ignorant general public to Italian food, whose quality and purity are incomparable.

Therefore, I unhesitatingly reach the conclusion that our expertise and inventiveness in this field is very great indeed. Given that the saying 'imitation is the sincerest form of flattery' (or words to that effect) must be correct, I am reassured in making this last statement by the fact that there was published on 8 August 2004 by the European Commission a list of all the countries, then members of the EEC, showing the percentages of fruits and vegetables where the amounts of pesticides were found to be above the maximum permitted by European regulations. Top of the list with 11% came Austria, France was third with 8.3%, the UK thirteenth with 2.8% and bottom (or top, in this case, thus endorsing what I've been maintaining so far) was Italy with 0.09%.

'Buon appetito!'

☐

The reader should not be tempted to think that in so doing the Italians have gone over the top. The reason, whether we are dealing with pizza, Parma Ham, or any other form of cooking, regulated by law or by custom, why the Italians are so fussy about food is quite simple. There are only three things in life that are important to an Italian, and they are food (and wine) women and beauty (and art). The fourth one used to be the family, but I am inclined to cross it off my list at the moment, given the introduction of divorce and exasperated feminism into Italy.

From the remarks made by me elsewhere in this book, it will be apparent that I believe that if you eat well, you perform well in bed, and once these two aspects of your life are well taken care of, you can, because of that fact, indulge your appreciation of beauty and your artistic tendencies. It is really a matter of getting one's priorities right, and it is interesting to note that a lot of people are beginning to see things the Italian way. At the moment, it is the dieticians with the Mediterranean diet; but our time is coming. . .

In the early 1860s, a young Italian chemist from Corsica (Corsica was not French at the time), Angelo Mariani (not to be confused with his namesake opera conductor, who had a difference of opinion with the composer Verdi) infused coca leaves in wine creating the teas, pastilles and even a wine that became known by his name. He called it a 'Tonico alla coca del Peru', namely a tonic made with coca from Peru and he supplied it both to Queen Victoria and to the then reigning Pope, Leo XIII.

He made excessive claims for his creation, which according to him 'nourishes, fortifies, refreshes, aids digestion, strengthens the system, prevents malaria, influenza and wasting diseases'. Even Thomas Edison is alleged to have said that the Mariani wine gave a boost to his energies. So sorry. . . to disappoint the Americans, with their Coca-Cola!

It is claimed – but I found it somewhat difficult to retrieve documentary evidence of the fact – that it was the Italian immigrants to England in the early years of the twentieth century who developed what was to become the very typical British dish, 'fish and chips'.

GEMSTONES

357   In the early seventeenth century, Vincenzo PERUZZI (born in Florence) was the first to cut diamonds to make brilliants, by inventing the 58-facet form.

'Diamonds are forever': thus goes the well-known song and it is of course perfectly true that the popularity of diamond rings has continued unabated.

We owe them to the Italians. What an author (Charles Panati 3) calls 'this expensive custom', is said to have begun in the sixteenth century. Panati quotes as his authority a Venetian wedding document dated 1503 which lists 'one marrying ring having diamond'. This was the gold wedding ring of Mary of Modena and is indeed the first record of a betrothal ring featuring a diamond setting.

The tradition thus begun has continued for over five centuries, and I suppose the Venetians did not realize at the time how successful the concept of a diamond engagement/wedding ring would become.

358   In 1669, Nicola STENO was the first to note the regularity and constancy of facial angles of crystals.

359   In 1694, AVERAMI and TARGIONI were the first to fuse a diamond at the focus of a burning glass.

GLASS

The glasses of Venice are particularly well known and no visit to Venice is complete, it is said, without a short excursion to the island of Murano.

360 Colourless glass was first achieved by the Venetians.

In the year AD 1000, or thereabouts, the Venetians first developed their glass-making techniques. They later moved out to the island of Murano, either to avoid causing fires on the mainland, or to keep their techniques more secret and safe, or both. Despite draconian legislation to protect these secrets, several Venetians left Venice and built factories to produce clean glass in other countries.

Most people know of the existence of Chianti wine and have seen the straw-covered flask which seems to be a regular feature of Italian restaurants, genuine and artificial.

361 There are practical reasons why the typical Chianti flask is no longer used, but it is a matter of record that glass wine flasks were first produced in 1265 in San Gimignano. The town is referred elsewhere in this book for its sky-scrapers but is also well-known for its 'vernaccia', a noble white wine of great distinction. . .

The Chianti-type straw flask has been the subject of historical studies and one of the biggest producers of Chianti, Ruffino, has (November 1993) gone on record with the rather astonishing assertion that the straw-cladding for the fiasco was invented by Leonardo da Vinci and that some can be identified in certain of his sketches.

That the straw covering prevents the round bottomed bottle from falling and gives general protection is self-evident. It is also said that when the discovery of the atomic battery was made on 2 December 1942, Dr Eugene Wigner, its pioneer, celebrated it by uncorking a flask of Chianti. The label was fittingly signed by an Italian to whom credit is widely given in this book and elsewhere for atomic studies, namely Enrico Fermi.

362 The Venetians were the first people who developed the technique of making mirrors of glass backed with mercury and tin. They embarked upon this new venture about the beginning of the fourteenth century, and the new idea caught on so quickly that in a very short time the polished metal mirrors which had been in use for thousands of years, disappeared from circulation.

Venice and Murano are certainly of fundamental importance in the history of glass-making, and the reader who is interested in the silvering of glass, in particular to make mirrors, is referred to p. 369 of *Europe: A History* by Norman Davis, Oxford University Press, 1996.

363 In 1530, the Venetians first developed their 'cristallo'-type glass, which twenty years later they allowed on patent to dealers in Belgium.

The success of Venice in this field prompted many to try and steal its secrets. A number of Venetian workers were enticed away to foreign countries, including England where the Duke of Buckingham employed them in his glass-works.

364 In 1612, Antonio NERI (1576-1614) published his book known as *L'Arte Vetraria*, 'the first systematic account of the treatment and pre-paration of raw materials to make glass. Fifty years later it was trans-lated into English and becomes very influential.' (Bruno)

SPECTACLES (EYE GLASSES)

365   **These first appeared in Pisa in 1291. Their invention is attributed to one Alessandro SPINA from Florence, a Dominican monk who first used convex lenses to cure myopia.**

This attribution has been challenged (see Frugoni), it being suggested that Spina was beaten to it by his compatriot Salvino Degli Armato in 1285.

Since the third edition of this book, my attention has been drawn to the fact that perhaps this attribution should go to Salvino Armato, an optical physicist from Florence. Charles Panati (*Panati's Extraordinary Origins of Everyday Things*), Harper & Row Publishers Inc, New York, 1987) records that around 1280 Armato had injured his eyes whilst performing light refraction experiments and turned to glass-making in an effort to improve his sight; in so doing, he devised thick, curved, correcting lenses.

This fact appears to be confirmed in a book published in 1289 by Sandro di Popozo (*Treatise on the Conduct of the Family*) in which it is recorded that eye glasses 'have recently been invented for the benefit of poor age people whose sight has become weak'.

I don't mind either way. . . . .

366   **In 1352, Tommaso da MODENA was the first painter to depict spectacles.**

In 1480, Ghirlandaio depicted Saint Jerome using an eyeglass. (Saint Jerome is the patron saint of the London Guild of Spectacle Makers.)

367   **In 1738, the Florentine Domenico Maria MANNI published the first book on the history of spectacles. It is interesting to record that Manni ascribed the invention of spectacles to the Florentine Armali, and he claimed that it occurred somewhere round about the year 1300. (Morton's 5991).**

6. POLITICS & WAR

BUREAUCRACY

It is hardly surprising that bureaucracy was founded in Italy where it has become a curse upon the country.

Italian bureaucracy is accused of being inefficient and corrupt. Inefficiency promotes corruption in order to get things done. It is, of course, both, but that is easily explicable.

It is inefficient because too many incompetent people are recruited who have to justify their existence in their posts. They are all poorly rewarded and therefore easily open to corruption. The mentality of officials is medieval.

However, it is clearly not the case that bureaucracy is corrupt only in Italy. It is patently corrupt in Italy; it is latently corrupt in other countries.

As I have said before, the corruptibility point is merely a function of one's general appetite and the amount of food that is available to one's family. It is quite easy to do a job without having to insist that bribes should be offered when one is in a position of power, so to say, or if one has enough to eat. It is easy to be honest when your wallet is full of bank notes. Not so easy to be generous, because wealth often engenders meanness. But certainly, the temptations are fewer when one is not too badly off or, to put it another way, the point at which one yields to temptation becomes more difficult to achieve.

Corruption is universal and it produces the same results wherever it operates.

There is corruption which is brought about by monetary inducements and there is social corruption; the former is fairly widespread in Italy, the latter is perfectly normal in England. It is surprising what an Oxford or Cambridge or equivalent education, the right accent, membership of the right school or club or freemasonry can achieve in England that money cannot; and there are some perfectly respectable bureaucrats here would consider themselves affronted if offered monetary inducements who succumb daily to the blandishments of an accent or to membership of the right club.

In England, there is the old boy network; in Italy it is the poor-boy network. Corruption occurs everywhere; it is merely dressed up differently. What, however, is thoroughly objectionable about corruption in Italy is that it has become a way of life. Everyone expects everyone else to be corrupt; and corruption is proffered quite openly, as though it were the most natural thing in the world. The above was written by me in 1986 and I do not wish to resile from it in any way. I am however both pleased and proud to say that twenty years later the position has changed substantially in Italy. I'm not for one minute suggesting that there is no corruption or no fraud because that would be inaccurate; but I should say that Italians nowadays are more affluent, more socially conscious and much more cosmopolitan. Things have improved.

368   1390 can be taken as the date of origin of bureaucracy in the

Western world. It was invented by Gian Galeazzo VISCONTI at his Milan court when he created a special class of paid clerks and secretaries for various departments in his court. They kept ledgers regarding income, expenditure and taxes and dealt with his correspondence.

DIPLOMACY

Italians are not always good strategists, but on the whole they are exceptionally good tacticians. In a negotiation where diplomats are brought in, the strategy is already laid down for them; they are left to deal with tactics. That is why I think Italians have always been successful diplomats.

In addition, there is the question of manner and suavity. There is also the lack of dogmatism and the ability to see a number of sides to each argument. Furthermore, a healthy dose of cynicism is essential. All these are qualities which, generally speaking, the Italians have in abundance.

Finally, for a diplomat, the Italian has an outstanding virtue because on the whole he will never really, in negotiation, slam a door shut in the face of his opponent. He will certainly push it hard, but he will always leave a little bit of it open. And that I think is fundamental for a diplomat worth his salt. Indeed, one can think of a number of present-day politicians and leaders whose careers might well have developed much more successfully had they adopted a less dogmatic and doctrinaire approach to their dealings.

The Italian bankers who were so successful in London in the fifteenth and sixteenth centuries must have been born diplomats in any event to survive. One thinks also of all the clerics sent out from Rome by the Church to different parts of the world.

369 In 1585, Alberico GENTILI (see also Law) had written his *De Legationibus* which, based on his lectures at Oxford, was the first textbook on diplomacy. He dedicated it to Sir Philip Sidney whom he considered the ideal Ambassador.

It is interesting to note that what prompted Gentili to write his book was the fact that a conspiracy against Queen Elizabeth I had been discovered to which the Spanish Ambassador was a party. Gentili, who was a well-known lawyer lecturing here at the time, was consulted by the British Government as to how the matter should be viewed from the standpoint of international law.

Gentili was well known in legal and diplomatic circles and he was a protégé of Walsingham. He was a friend of that John Florio, who is referred to elsewhere in this book, a leading exponent of Italian language and culture in Elizabethan England.

370 The first diplomat ever to be on record (and here I am ignoring the numerous Venetian ambassadors and spies) was Guido BENTIVOGLIO (born in Ferrara) who in 1607 went to Flanders as the first accredited papal nuncio.

POLITICAL POWER

371 According to Luigi Barzini (*The Italians*, Penguin, 1964, p. 141) the political cartoon is attributable to an Italian. Barzini discovered

that in the middle of the fourteenth century the Roman tribune, Cola di RIENZO, had pictures painted on walls to make political points.

372 The political writer *'par excellence'* was Niccolò MACHIAVELLI (born in Florence, 1469). He is the founder of political and analytical science in Europe. He popularized the concept of state in his book *The Prince* and took state sovereignty for granted.

No-one influenced the arts of politics and of government to a greater degree than did Machiavelli. His outspokenness was a fundamental teaching for leaders of all time.

He was responsible for the popularization of a theory, which he never really meant, that the end justifies the means. As a result, his name has ever since been used in a pejorative context which has been associated with Italy. Contrary to popular belief, he was in fact a patriot and behind his cynicism his heart beat for a united Italy.

Machiavelli's work was continued by Giuseppe Guicciardini (born in Florence) but, although they were both Florentines, they did not have very much in common.

373 Although it is doubtful to what extent he himself was concerned with Europe as a whole, as distinct from Italy, it is to the Italian patriot, Giuseppe MAZZINI, that we owe the prototype of the European Economic Community.

After his failure to invade the kingdom of Savoy from Genova in 1834, compounded by the reluctance to fight by his mercenary General Ramorino, Mazzini organized from his bases in Switzerland and in London, what he called the 'young Europe'.

Mazzini's movement aimed at over-turning the tyrannical governments which prevailed in the Europe of the time and at replacing them by 'beneficial federal republics' organized within the framework of a European democracy. Most historians agree that the European revolutionary movements of 1848 were the fruit of Mazzini's teaching.

David Lloyd George is on the record as saying of Mazzini:

> I doubt whether any man of his generation exercised so profound an influence on the destinies of Europe.

Not technically a first but, in my view, worth recording. Way back in 1814, the Frenchmen C.H. de Saint-Simon and A. Thierry, in their book *The Reorganization of the European Society* had put forward proposals for 'a federation of people in a sole body politic, each of them conserving their national independence'. There is nothing new about the idea of a common Europe, for it was advocated by a number of people, each with different political views. One may mention in passing G. Mazzini, P.J. Prudhon, Carlo Cattaneo, Otto Bauer, Luigi Einaudi. But I believe that the first 'modern' restatement of the said two Frenchmen's proposals, in the form of a political manifest for a united Europe, is due to two Italians, Altiero Spinelli and Ernesto Rossi. They were militant anti-Fascists who had been arrested by the Mussolini regime and 'exiled' to the penitentiary on the island of Ventotene. In 1941, they wrote their *Manifesto per un'Europa Unita e Libera*. This became known as the *Manifesto di Ventotene* and formed the basis on which there was constituted in Milan, on 27 August 1943, the European Federalist Movement.

374 Another first, but one can take little pride in it. In the 1920s, MUSSOLINI began talking about

his 'ferocious, totalitarian will'. This was a phrase that was coined to represent a new kind of tyranny in which the State was everything and the individual nothing, compared to which the tyrannies of the past faded into insignificance.

The new political creed proceeded in theory from support of the masses who, instead of being enlisted to support democracy, were indoctrinated with concepts of tyranny.

Because of Italy's historical background (and although Mussolini could not be taken seriously – his ability to be both a bully and a clown was a serious handicap in the historical context), Fascism became quite successful there and represented the inspiration and the model for totalitarianism throughout Europe. The list of people who followed it is long: Dollfuss in Austria, Pilsudski in Poland, Horthy in Hungary, Salazar in Portugal and Franco in Spain. But, in its most original form, totalitarianism settled in Nazi Germany and Bolshevik Russia.

375   Gaetano MOSCA (born in Palermo) elaborated the concept of a ruling minority present in all societies – whether military, priestly, oligarchic or aristocratic (whether by wealth or by merit).

Mosca proceeded from the premise that majority was, in reality, a fiction. His main work (*Teorica*) published in 1925, was seized upon by Fascists who failed to understand the points he was making.

TRADE UNIONS

376   Trade Unions were founded in Italy during the Renaissance with the establishment of the '*Arti*' and the '*Confederazioni*' of the principal Italian cities.

They became very powerful and, despite what one could term, by modern standards, restricted practices, represented the backbone of commercial activity in Florence.

They were also instrumental in encouraging works of art by actually paying for them. One of the most powerful of such 'confederazioni' was that of the wool traders and spinners: it paid for the beautiful doors by Ghiberti in the Florence 'Duomo' but, more particularly, for the construction of the octagonal dome for Santa Maria del Fiore.

I have been unable to find any authenticated records of strikes (lawful or unlawful) during that period.

But, even during an earlier period, there existed guilds of artisans and especially wool workers in Florence and there is evidence that they were already beginning to make their voices heard, for example by public demonstrations and by demanding the right to have their guilds recognized as early as the last decades of the fourteenth century.

377   The first 'official' protest by workers who wanted to form their own trade unions (at the time, 'guilds') occurred in 1378 when one Michele Di Lando led a mob of wood workers and other artisans in Florence who were insisting on their right to vote, thus precipitating a revolt which upset the local Medici ruler and resulted in substantial civic protest.

378   There was a first 'go-slow' in Florence in 1424 when the masons employed by Brunelleschi on the construction of the Duomo complained about his methods of building and the fact that he was a hard

task-master. (See 'Architecture' and 'Time and Motion Studies'.)

In 1428, for example, he had no qualms whatsoever about dismissing twenty-five master masons who objected to the new work practices that he planned to introduce.

TREATIES

379 In November 1190, the first recorded peace treaty ever concluded by England was with Tancred, King of Sicily. It was a Charter of Peace with a foreign power that took effect immediately and was intended to last forever.

Although it is by no means a first, it is interesting to note that on 15 May 1367, another treaty was entered into by England with Italy. Here, the term 'Italy', of course, is a misnomer, since Italy did not become a political entity until 1870. The treaty, in fact, was with Milan and related to the marriage of the Duke of Clarence with Princess Violanta of Milan.

WAR

It is my firm belief that taken as a whole, the Italians are less warlike and less feudal than most other people. For twenty-two years, Mussolini tried to inculcate into them a more militaristic spirit, but failed. Fascist Italy had the 'Cubs', the 'Balillas', the young 'avant-garde' members of the Fascist party. The uniforms might have been pretty and enjoyable, but the spirit was not there. The Italians are too resentful of authority and their historical development has made them highly suspicious of military power.

Machiavelli called all foreigners 'barbarians'. Our culture was such that all these barbarians who invaded us failed conspicuously to imbue the Italian spirit with their love of war and of chivalry. Feudal life and feudal hierarchies did not become settled in Italy at any time. As a result, the country was able to move out of the darkness of the Middle Ages faster than any other people in Europe.

The drawback, assuming it to be a drawback, was that when it did so, Italians were politicians, artists and scientists, but not soldiers. Our armies never meant very much.

If anything, Italians are sailors, but not soldiers. The four maritime Italian Republics (Pisa, Genoa, Amalfi and Venice) made an enormous contribution to sailing, discovery and politics. The next time you sun yourself in the Balearic Islands you may care to remember that Pisan sailors occupied them as far back as the year 1115. They had been preceded as conquerors by the Carthaginians (Mahon in Menorca takes its name from the Carthaginian General, Mago) and by the Romans.

As is commonly known, Venice left its mark throughout the Mediterranean, particularly in Cyprus and Crete and most notably in Heraklion, Rhethymnon, Chania and, to a lesser extent, Ierapetra in Crete.

Machiavelli, who knew the Italians well, in ending his *The Prince*, complained that they were intolerant of authority and could not fight well together. He said: 'Look at the duels and the combats between a few, how the Italians are superior in strength, in skill, in inventiveness, but when it is a matter of armies, they do not compare. All this because of the weakness of the leaders. Those who are capable are not obeyed. Everyone imagines he is competent.' (I am quoting from George Bull's translation of *The*

Prince in the Penguin Classics edition.) It is the very last sentence of what has been transcribed that is so revealing.

Even so, we have some bright ideas. It appears that the Italians made a notable contribution to weapons of war when the Duke of Montferrat landed at Tyre in 1188 with a small Italian fleet and a number of followers, almost an advance party in anticipation of what was to become the Third Crusade.

Readers may recall that the Third Crusade was convened by Gregory VIII after the fall of Jerusalem.

380   It is said that the Duke of Montferrat had a special contingent of troops coming from Acqui who were equipped with crossbows, thus anticipating the later English developments of the sixteenth century.

In fact, the Italian City States and their mercenary armies quickly adopted the weapon and it was well known that Genoese mercenaries, who had special knowledge of it, were much in demand.

The weapon came into its own also in the battles that the crusaders had with the Saracens.

The longbow then took over and it was said to be more efficient, as was proved at the Battle of Crécy in 1346.

Admittedly the crossbow was slower and less accurate than the longbow, but it managed to hold its own until the Arquebus was introduced in the late fifteenth century.

It has, however, outlived the longbow because it is still occasionally used nowadays in hunting and competitions.

381   In 1326, Rinaldo Di VILLA-MAGNA (born in Florence) developed the 'Bombarda', the first metal cannon that fired iron bullets.

A Florentine ordinance of that same year represents the earliest unequivocal evidence of the existence of such a weapon.

By definition, the 'bombarda' presupposed the existence of gunpowder at that time, for its explosion propelled the 'bomba', or projectile. If, which seems unproved still, the Chinese invented gunpowder as they claim, they did not use it in weapons before the Italians. However, it must be admitted that this still remains a contentious issue.

382   In 1450, Bartolomeo COL-LEONI (born at Salza BG) invented the gun-train.

383   In the fifteenth century, pistols were first manufactured in Pistoia, hence their name. There is also a later (1540) attribution of this invention to the gunsmith Camillo VETTELLI, also of Pistoia.

384   In 1475, Bartolomeo COL-LEONI pioneered artillery tactics by getting artillery to fire from the rear through gaps left by the infantry.

385   By 1495, a blow-gun known as 'Cerbottana' was in use in Italy.

386   In 1512, Niccolò TARTA-GLIA (born in Brescia), the mathematician, originated the science of ballistics.

We record under the heading of 'metallurgy' the manual by Vannoccio Biringuccio on metal fusion techniques applied to cannons and other offensive weapons. The valley of the River Po and that of the River Mella, better known as the Val Trompia, were famous in the sixteenth century for the smelting of iron ore. It has been claimed that at one time there were produced in the Val Trompia alone, some 25,000 barrels a year for use in early muzzle-loading firearms. The document, discovered not too long ago in the Venetian archives, indicates that as far back as 1526 one Bartolomeo Beretta was running a thriving business in the area and was a main supplier of weapons to the Venetian republic. Those interested in shooting will recognize the name of what is one of the oldest, if not the oldest, gun-making families in the world. It is not obviously a first in which one can take pride; but then, as often happens, it is the men who use them rather than the instruments themselves, whatever they may be, who must accept responsibility for weapons, motor cars and other instruments or mechanical devices which can cause harm.

Italian military engineers also worked out techniques for strengthening the bastioned walls of cities under siege against the ever-more popular cannon. It is a matter of record that by the middle of the sixteenth century they were on call to design fortifications in England, France, Spain, Hungary, as well as in East Africa, India and the Caribbean.

I have already stated that I hold the view that the Italians are amongst the least war-like people in the world, although the number of firsts in this section do not seem to support it.

387   In 1550, the Viceroy of Naples, the Duke d'AVALOS, worked out the concept of calibre.

388   The first illustrated book on military technical subjects is *De Re Militari*, a book on warfare by Roberto VALTURIO. It contains nearly one hundred wood-cut illustrations of contemporary engines of war for land and sea. (Bruno)

389   In 1588, Agostino RAMELLI (born in Maranza) wrote a book, *Le Diverse et Artificiose Macchine,*

describing all sorts of machines that could be used for war-like purposes.

Ramelli had a successful army career as engineer-in-chief to the Duc d'Anjou, later Henry III of France, for whom he designed equipment.

His inventions ranged from pumps, derricks and sawmills to continuous bucket conveyors and even an amphibious armoured vehicle. All his machines used water power and he elaborated on the conversion of rotary to reciprocal power, and all were meant for military use. Not all his ideas could be put into practice, as most of them were well in advance of his times and no tooling was then available for the kind of fine work that they necessitated. Nevertheless, his work *Le Diverse et Artificiose Macchine*, represents a landmark in technical publishing.

390   In 1588, RAMELLI described a new roller mill.

391   Also in 1588, RAMELLI, together with Veranzio, mechanized bolting mills.

392   A wire link-type driving chain was also first mentioned by RAMELLI.

Italian engineers were much in demand in this particular century. Apart from what has been recorded, they contributed substantially to the art of fortification to protect cities from the effects of artillery bombardment. Towards the middle of the sixteenth century, there became known the 'Trace Italienne', namely 'a sophisticated system of ditches, entrapments and low-angled bastions which denied the cannoneers easy targets and access while exposing them to withering counterfire' (see Norman Davis, op. cit. p. 519). The classic example was the fortification of Antwerp carried out by Italian engineers in 1568 and there is no doubt that the celebrated French military engineer 'De Vauban' learnt his art from what the Italians had done before him. It should not for one moment be thought, however, that the great contribution of the Italians to weapons of war and fortification engineering did not take into account what happened at sea. There is no doubt that:

> 393 . . . 'the changeover from medieval to modern naval power is marked by the emergence of the galleon. Contrary to popular belief, this was not a Spanish development but, like everything in the Renaissance of the arts and sciences, Italian'. This laudatory statement is taken from Sir Julian Corbett's *Drake and the Tudor Navy*, Vol. I, p. 24 and is quoted in A.L. Rowse's *The Expansion of Elizabethen England*, Macmillan, 1955.

It is possible that the conception of the galleon reached England through France, but the characteristic of the model, namely an average length of about three times its beam, was established by the Italians. It was on the basic Italian model that the English under Henry VIII carried out development which probably arose in close conjunction with the extension of commerce and maritime experience into the Atlantic.

Hawkins and Drake were closely associated with the adoption of the type of ship that was to fight the Spanish Armada successfully. The result was a sudden increase in the range of action of British naval power which allowed England to set itself up as the major world naval power.

It can be said, therefore, that when the English defeated the Spanish Armada, they were doing so with the help of Italian technology.

The striking of the top mast, the chain pump, the lengthening of cable that enabled ships to ride out stronger winds, the weighing of anchors by capstan, and the new varieties of sail were all Italian 'inventions'. The reader who is in doubt is referred to *Ralegh's Works* edited by Oldys and Birch, Vol. VIII, p. 253.

> 394 In 1605, LEONARDO invented the airgun, thus allowing his compatriot, Bartolomeo CRESCENZIO, to design a much more powerful weapon with a stronger spring.

> 395 In 1625, Giuliano BOSSI tried out fulminate of gold on explosives (an experiment that Samuel Pepys and Edward Howard both indulged in somewhat later) in order to provoke the kind of explosion that would prove suitable for percussion weapons.

> 396 In 1750, Duke Alfonso the Second D'ESTE invented the gun case.

> 397 In 1835, Giovanni CAVALLI (born in Novara) developed rear-loading guns and rifled barrels.

> 398 The first steam operated warship, 'Ercole' was built in 1843 at the behest of Ferdinand II, King of the two Sicilies.

> 399 In 1846, Ascanio SOBRERO (born in Turin) discovered nitroglycerine.

One of his direct descendants bearing the very same name, has taken me to task for showing Sobrero under this particular heading. He reminds me that Sobrero was a doctor and a scientist who really had no interest in warlike activities and that his discovery of nitroglycerine was almost accidental.

As soon as he saw its potential and its dangers, he lost interest in it completely and went on to other things. Nor did he ever seek any kind of recognition for what he had done, although the Nobel prize committee thought otherwise.

I believe that, of course, and I accept that the heading might be slightly unfortunate. Since, however, it has been followed throughout the previous editions of this book, I see no particular merit for changing it.

400   The automatic repeater gun was created in 1888 by Salvatore CARCANO (born Piossasco, Turin).

401/2   To him we also owe two more firsts:
1. The preparation of a detailed map of the planet Mars.
2. The identification of falling stars as fragments of comets traversing the solar system. (For authority, r. vol. 19, *Dizionario Biografico degli Italiani*.)

403   The first aerial bombing – on 1 November 1911, an Italian plane was recorded as dropping the first bombs used in war on Turkish positions.

404   The first military application in aeroplanes of MARCONI's wireless system occurred in September 1915.

On that occasion Marconi and his lifelong friend and colleague Luigi Solari (who had helped Marconi in the development of a more efficient Coherer) fitted the then still elementary Marconi apparatus to an Italian two-seater military biplane in which Solari flew as radio operator, communicating with Marconi who remained on the ground.

405   The Italian Gabriele D'ANNUNZIO, apart from being a well-known twentieth century writer and poet, was also a military man. During the First World War he actively pressed the Italian Government for permission to carry out what can only be termed as a publicity stunt and finally on the 9 August 1918 Italian planes flew over Vienna scattering half a million leaflets bearing a literary and probably incomprehensible message from him.

This was clearly unusual because those planes could just as easily have dropped bombs. It was done in an attempt to dispirit the enemy.

I record it as a first because in fact nothing like this had occurred prior to the said occurrence during a war. It shows once more how topical the Italians can be since they anticipated by more than twenty years what was going to happen during the Second World War.

406   The 'human torpedo', developed by the Royal Navy in the early 1940s, was an Italian invention. What have sometimes been referred to as the 'silent assassins' (namely, a cross between submarines and torpedoes manned usually by two men who would sneak under cover of darkness into harbours, attach the machine itself to stationary ships, for it to be later detonated after they had made good their escape) were first used by the Italians during the First World War, when in 1918, in the Yugoslav port of Pula, they sank certain ships of the Austro-Hungarian Empire.

These were refined and redeveloped in 1936 and used to great advantage against the British fleets in the ports of Alexandria and Gibraltar. The machine that was used in the Second World War became known as '*maiale*' (literally, 'pig') and was first used on the night of 18 December 1941 in the port of Alexandria when it was attached to the battleship HMS *Valiant*. The Italians involved in the escapade were captured by a Royal Navy patrol boat before the charge exploded and, ten minutes before the ship was due to be sunk, they revealed how they had attached the torpedo to the ship and the crew were safely evacuated.

The '*maiale*' was used repeatedly in Gibraltar, being operated from across the border in Spain, a wrecked oil tanker being used for cover.

The *Queen Elizabeth* and the *Valiant* were the only two allied battleships which were put out of action in the eastern Mediterranean. Both ships were refloated but the *Valiant* not until 1942 and the *Queen Elizabeth* not until June 1943.

Nevertheless, the British were impressed by the idea and after initial difficulties, in development and in usage, they succeeded in sinking the pride of Germany's fleet, the *Tirpitz* in a Norwegian fjord in October 1943. The British machines were called 'X-craft' and, when fully developed, made Churchill's life a lot happier than it was when he first learnt of the manner in which they were being developed and used by the Italians.

407   It is recorded that the first large-scale airlift of supplies in military history occurred during the Italian invasion of Ethiopia in the 1930s when General BADOGLIO ensured air drops of as much as twenty-five tons per day of equipment along the route to be taken by the Erithrean Corps (see p. 326 of *Lion by the Tail* by Thomas Encoffee, The Viking Press, New York).

408   During the same war, another first was achieved by the Italians, less memorable and much

less worthwhile. For the first time in history, Italian airplanes sprayed the poor Ethiopian population with chemicals. Nothing to be proud of, of course; as usual, Italians proved quite topical, anticipating by nearly half a century what the Americans did in Vietnam.

409   To Bruno ROSSI we owe the discovery in 1931 of cosmic rays. He made it easier for Enrico Fermi to develop his theory of beta-radio-activity, which subsequently resulted in the creation of the atomic bomb.

410   In 1934, Enrico FERMI (born Rome) developed the theory of beta radioactivity.

411   FERMI was the first physicist to split the atom and, for better or for worse, is considered one of the most important architects of our nuclear age.

His name is now permanently associated with the Fermi Constant (which analyses sub-atomic particle interactions), the Fermi-Dirac Statistics (to determine the statistical behaviour of atomic particles (an exercise defined by the Fermion) the Fermi Level (a measure of energy), the Fermi Surface (an abstract boundary for predicting electrical and thermal behaviour of metallic solids), the Fermi Energy (to determine the surface energy of metals) and the new chemical element of the actinide series, not occurring in nature, known as 'Fermium'.

412   In 1942, FERMI elaborated mathematical statistics for atomic phenomena.

413   FERMI also discovered neutron-induced radioactivity in 1942 and directed the first controlled nuclear reaction which was really

the heart of the modern reactor, thus becoming the father of the atomic bomb.

414 In 1942, FERMI gave his name to the neutrino and in 1950 was made a Fellow of The Royal Society.

I wonder whether Fermi appreciated the implications of his discovery of the '*neutrino*' (Italian for the 'little neutral one').

It would appear that scientists are becoming increasingly puzzled at the disappearance of 'neutrinos' in space and are finding it more and more difficult to explain what has become known as the 'vanishing mass' conundrum. Perhaps the geodesic dome placed into position at the Sudbury Neutrino Observatory (February 1997), 200 miles north of Toronto in Canada, will help.

On the campus at Chicago University there is a monument to Fermi with a plaque indicating the spot where he first split the atom.

It is interesting to find such a major contribution by an Italian to what ended up by being the most powerful weapon ever used in war.

Although it is true that Leonardo and Galileo helped their masters to develop machinery of attack and defence, it is a fact that Italians on the whole are not enamoured of war. This is not so much because Italians lack discipline or courage; it is much more because their cynicism prevents them from believing with sufficient conviction in any particular cause to the point where they are forced on the one hand to run the risk of losing life or limb and on the other of being distracted from their main pursuit, namely the

enjoyment of life and the pursuit of pleasure.

Going back to Fermi, however, we should record that in 1938 he won the Nobel Prize for Physics and there is little doubt that he established himself as a physicist of both theoretical and practical expertise.

He gave his name to the kind of question that is now known as a Fermi problem. The key to the solution to such problems being the principle that, even by making assumptions, one can still arrive at fairly close estimates because, in any string of calculations, errors have a tendency to cancel one another out and bad guesses tend to compensate for one another in the same way, so that results will converge towards the right number.

The reader who wants to know more about the practical implications of the Fermi technique is referred to an article in *The Scientist* (September/October 1988), New York, by Hans Christian von Baeyer.

415 Finally, we owe to FERMI the first suggestion of the mechanism which is said to explain the energy distribution of the cosmic rays. Fermi suggested that they are accelerated in interstellar space by bouncing from moving clouds of ionized gas containing irregular magnetic fields, thus possibly gaining energy in head-on collisions as though they were ping-pong balls bounced from one player to the other (see *Britannia*, Vol. 5, p. 205).

American recognition of Fermi's work has gone beyond the statue at Chicago University since he is now permanently associated with the Fermi Award of the Atomic Energy Commission.

7. SCIENCES

ASTRONOMY

When considering the following facts please bear in mind that the unique contribution to astronomy by Galileo is covered separately under the heading 'Physics'.

416   In 1364, Giovanni de DONDI created the first astronomical clock which, in addition to the time, showed the phases of the moon and the signs of the Zodiac.

417   De DONDI was Professor of Astronomy at Padua and in his treatise, *Tractus Astarri*, published in 1364, he provided the earliest detailed description of clockwork by presenting a seven-dialled astronomical clock which inspired a number of replicas.

418   We owe to Alessandro PIC-COLOMINI (1508-78) the first labelling of the stars with letters when in the chapter 'Libro Delle Stelle Fisse' in a book that he published by the title *Delle Sfere del Mondo* he shows the brightest stars in each constellation labelled with capital letters, thus making them easier to identify. (Bruno)

419   According to Carter's *Dictionary of Discoveries and Inventions*, p. 133, Gianbattista DELLAPORTA (a versatile scientist with many inventions listed elsewhere) is 'credited with formulating the idea of the telescope which was said to have

been made in Italy in 1590 before finding its way to Holland'.

420   In 1650, Giovanni RICCIOLI identified in the constellation of Ursa Major the star by the name of 'Mizar' (from the Arabic for 'wrapping') or 'Zeta Ursa Majoris', as the first multiple star to be discovered by telescope. It took, however, 227 years exactly for the first double star to be photographed. The discovery is important because both Mizar and its companion star have been classified as spectrosopic binaries, which means that each has a close companion which isn't visually capable of identification but can only be discovered through an examination of the colours of light emitted (see 'Ursa Major' in *Britannic Student Encyclopaedia*, 2004).

421   In 1636, Francesco FONTA-NA made the first drawing of the planet Mars.

422   In 1664, G.A. BORELLI (born Naples) was the first to suggest the idea of a parabolic path for heavenly bodies (see also 'Physics').

423   In 1666, Francesco CASSINI (born Perinaldo) was the first astronomer to identify the Polar Caps of the planet Mars.

424   In 1666, Giovanni SCHIA-PARELLI (born Savigliano) established the Mercurian year of rotation.

425   In 1666, Giovanni Domenico CASSINI (born Perinaldo) discov-

ered what is known as Cassini's Division as well as four of Saturn's moons.

426 He was the first to record zodiacal light.

427 He studied Jupiter and Mars and discovered the four satellites of Saturn known as Japetus, Rhea, Thetis and Dione. He became a Fellow of The Royal Society in 1672.

Cassini's discoveries were so important that King Louis XIV of France invited him to Paris in 1669 to join the recently formed Academie Royale des Sciences. There he assumed the directorship of the Observatory after it was completed in 1671 and continued the studies he had begun in Italy. Two years later he became a French citizen and died in Paris.

428 His son, Jacques CASSINI, born in Paris, also became an astronomer and compiled the first tables of the orbital motions of Saturn's satellites, succeeding his father as head of the Paris Observatory in 1712. He is on record as an ardent opponent of Newton's gravitational theory.

429 Giovanni Domenico CASSINI certainly set up a tradition of astronomy in France. His final success occurred in 1693, when he established the formulation of the laws that bear his name – three empirical rules that accurately describe the rotation of the moon.

430 Cassini's French successors were also notable astronomers. His other son, Cesar François, was renowned for the commencement of a major topographical map of France, succeeding his father as Director of the Paris Observatory in 1771, and his nephew, Jacques Dominique, completed his own father's map and also

became a Director of the Paris Observatory in 1784.

431 The 'French' Cassinis carried into effect Giovanni Domenico's discoveries. For example, in 1676 Giovanni Domenico had perfected a means of using Jupiter's moons to determine longitude, which he started applying to a world map and also to a survey of France. His son, Francesco, helped him and starting from the Paris meridian, they carried out triangulation exercises off high landmark points. By 1774, they had mapped 400 triangles over France.

Domenico's said grandson proceeded to publish an atlas of France (see *National Geographic* Magazine, Vol. 193, No. 2, February 1998).

432 Eustachio MANFREDI (1674-1739) was the first to observe the annual aberration of fixed stars and, indeed, to use the term 'aberration', namely, the apparent displacement of a star from its true position in the sky.

433 In 1669, the astronomer Geminiano MONTANARI (1633-1687) was the first to observe the changes in the brightness of the binary star Algol. (Bruno)

434 In 1728, Francesco BIANCHINI (born Verona) who also studied the moon and discovered three comets, was the first to measure the rotational period of Venus as twenty-four days.

435 In 1801, Giuseppe PIAZZI (born Valtellina) discovered the first minor planet known as Ceres (Neptune 2.8). In 1804 he became a Fellow of The Royal Society.

The work that Piazzi carried out

between 1790 and 1800 represented attempts in the main to measure the parallax of heavenly bodies: it was of fundamental importance.

As Mari Williams has observed ('Notes on some records of The Royal Society', volume 37, 1982/83, pp. 83-100): 'It was the beginning of more than thirty years of interest in parallax throughout Europe, culminating in the production in the late 1830s of acceptable values.'

Piazzi himself had been preceded in his studies by a compatriot, Eustachio Manfredi, who in the 1730s had made an extensive study of stellar positions whilst he was Professor of Astronomy at Bologna University.

436   Antonio SANTUCCI, at the beginning of the seventeenth century, was the first to explain to the public that comets were not mere atmospheric phenomena, contrary to what had been believed for centuries, but celestial bodies.

437   In 1838, Angelo SECCHI (born Reggio E.) was the first to apply the spectroscope to the study of stars.

438   The Italian astronomer MAIOCCHI was the first to photograph in 1842 the solar crown. Until that date, it had always been considered an optical phenomenon, connected to the moon.

439   In 1849, SECCHI made the first survey of the spectra of the stars and was the first to suggest the classification of the stars according to their spectral type.

440   He was a precursor of the Harvard classification of stars.

441   He gave his name to the Secchi Disc used to measure water transparency.

442   SECCHI also described the chromospheric layers viewed at the limb of the sun (the spicules) as a 'burning prairie'.

This is a poetic description for a scientific phenomenon (*Encyclopaedia Britannica*, Vol. 17, p. 804) especially considering that he was no poet, but merely a Jesuit priest. As such he was elected Head of the Pontifical Observatory at the Collegio Romano. (In 1856 he became a Fellow of The Royal Society.) He worked there for nearly thirty years, during which time he examined almost 4,000 stars.

443   SECCHI was the first to use photography to obtain a picture of the solar eclipse of 1851.

Together with Pietro Tacchini he founded Società degli Spettroscopisti Italiana, the first institution of its kind with the purpose of co-ordinating research on solar phenomena and celestial physics carried out by observatories around the world.

444   In 1861, Giovanni Virginio SCHIAPARELLI discovered the asteroid Hesperia.

445   In 1877, he discovered the 'canals' on Mars.

He had called his first discovery the 'Atlantic channel' and it was thus that he gave rise to nearly a century of speculation. Speculation centred on whether, because of the water that 'Canals' presupposed, there might be life on Mars. In 1890 Percival Lowell propounded his theory that there was in fact such life, a theory which became very popular and as a result of which, possibly, H.G. Wells created his *War of the Worlds*.

Schiaparelli called the markings he had seen '*canali*', a word which was erroneously translated into English as canals instead of channels, thus giving rise to speculation that intelligent life existed on that planet.

446 In 1866, he discovered the connection between comets and meteorites.

447 He was also the first to suggest that falling stars are of cometary origin.

He was Director of the Brera Observatory in Milan for thirty-eight years (1862-1900) and was elected to The Royal Society in 1896.

448 Giovanni Battista **DONATI** (born Pisa) was the first to observe the spectrum of a comet in 1864. It became known as Donati's comet.

BIOLOGY

449 Francesco **STELLUTI** (1577-1653) published in Rome the first book to contain illustrations of natural objects as seen through the microscope. More specifically, he provided an engraving of the exterior surface of the body of bees.

His work is also important for its inclusion of the Latin text of the satyrae of Aulus Persius Flaccus, which he translated into the Italian language. A versatile literary scientist.

450 In 1627, Gaspare **ASELLI** (born Cremona) observed for the first time the lymphatic system. He described the 'venae albae et lacteae'. (See 'Medicine')

To the Palermitan Giovanni Battista **ODIERNA**, who published in Palermo

in 1644 his book *L'occhio della Mosca* – which translates into 'The Eye of the Fly' – we owe two firsts.

451 Number one is the first microscopical section in biology to be discussed and illustrated.

452 Number two is the first description of the faceted eye of an anthropod. (Morton's 259)

453 In 1668, Francesco **REDI** (born Arezzo) made the first scientific study into spermatozoan generation.

454 In 1680, Giovanni Alfonso **BORELLI** demonstrated that muscular contractions are explicable in physiological and chemical terms. He was the first to determine how muscles are contracted on impulses travelling down the nerves from the brain.

He exerted considerable influence on William Harvey, who was impressed by Borelli's work *De Motu Animalium* (in two volumes compiled and published in Rome in 1680) in the particular section where, trying to explain how generation occurred, Borelli compared the movement of the semen to a magnet arranging particles in the field of force of the womb.

455 In 1684, REDI set out for the first time the germ theory of infection. (He was a writer and a very famous humorous poet in his spare time.)

Redi's scientific interests, well apart from his literary ones, were quite catholic. For example, he was a keen student of vipers. After extensive observations he found conclusively that their poison originated not from their teeth or their tail as had been commonly believed previously, but in a bladder-type container that covered their teeth.

He was very versatile in his scientific experiments going so far as to question the idea, prevailing at a time since about the middle of the sixteenth century, that tobacco was a plant that healed. It is a view he did not share and to challenge it he conducted scientific tests by injecting oil of tobacco into animals with the result that they all died.

This did not appear to stop people having faith in the plant upon which much research was carried out until in 1828 the alkaloid nicotine was discovered in tobacco leaves.

His studies on vipers and his conclusions are quoted on p. 160 of Volume 1 of the *Philosophical Transactions of The Royal Society* in the form of a report to that society by a French author who commented on experiments carried out by Redi which had not yet reached England and who states in turn: 'There is no place left for doubting after so authentick a testimony.'

456   In 1685, REDI also demonstrated that maggots came from the eggs of flies and set up one of the first experiments with proper controls.

457   In 1678, REDI recorded for the first time the fact that the electric shock of the torpedo fish may be transmitted to the fishermen through line and rod.

458   In 1728, Giovanni Maria LANCISI (born Rome) – who wrote on influenza, cattle plague, malaria and cardiac pathology – was the first modern hygienist.

459   LANCISI was the first to use the expression 'aneurysm of the

heart' which has sadly become so topical in this age of heart trouble. He also described in detail the part played by mosquitoes in spreading malaria.

460   LANCISI was the first to describe cardiac syphilis.

461   Agostino BASSI (born Lodi) was the founder of the parasitic theory of infection, which he developed in 1835 studying silkworms.

462   The first marine biological station in the world is to be found in Naples. It is the 'Stazione Zoologica' built in 1870 by German scientist Anton Dohrn with funds from several European countries.

The tradition of internationalization is quite strong as far as the station is concerned because various governments and scientific societies to this day pay annually towards the upkeep of a worktable there and have the right to nominate a scientist who works at the station.

463   In 1903, Adelchi NEGRI (born Perugia) discovered the Negri bodies in cytoplasm that are diagnostic of rabies.

464   In 1938, Guido PONTECORVO (born Pisa) discovered the process of genetic combination in fungus, opening the way to probing the nature of gene action and deserving the name of 'father' of genetic engineering.

BOTANY

Whilst it is true that the first modern botanical illustrations date back to 1530 with the publication of Opto Brunfel's

'Pictures of Living Plants', which was in fact the first book with illustrations made from direct observation, one should record at this point the work of Pier Andrea MATTIOLI (born Siena), otherwise known in England as Matthiolus.

This is done firstly because he gave his name to a number of plants but, above all, because he made a synthesis of all medical botanical knowledge in his 'Commentarii a Dioscoride'.

> **465** MATTIOLI was the first to systematize medico/botanical notions existing at the time and, in particular, to describe and draw over one hundred new species of plants. His work was soon translated in French, German and Bohemian.

> **466** Andrea CESALPINO (born Arezzo) wrote in 1583 *De Plantis*, which was the first botanical treatise to group plants according to their reproductive organs, thus paving the way for the more detailed work of Malpighi.

> **467** In 1592, the botanist Prospero ALPINI (born Marostica) was the first European to observe and report on the coffee plant. (See 'Gastronomy')

> **468** ALPINI was also the first to fertilize dates artificially.

> **469** In 1671, Marcello MALPIGHI (born Crevalcore) founded plant anatomy. He was the first to observe the stomata of plants.

> **470** MALPIGHI's treatise on silkworms is considered the first monograph on an invertebrate.

Malpighi also made various important discoveries in the sphere of medical science. (See 'Medicine')

> **471** In 1830, Giovanni Battista AMICI (born Modena) discovered the sexual process in flowering plants.

Amici had started work on the general aspects of fertilization in plants in 1823. In 1846, he identified the female agent in these processes, paving the way for the refinements brought both to his studies and to his techniques by cytologists more than fifty years later.

CHEMISTRY

> **472** Nitric acid was first produced from saltpetre and alum in Italy in 1150.

> **473** In 1603, the first investigation of luminescence (by studying barium sulphate) was made by an Italian cobbler called Vincenzo CASCARIOLO (born Bologna).

The Cascariolo research is a classic instance of the versatility of the Italian people. Here we have an ordinary cobbler who goes to the trouble of investigating luminescence. The Italians, in fact, will turn their hands to anything and will improvise on anything. We often make a mess of it but sometimes we have flashes of real inspiration. And herein lies the genius of the Italian people.

In the case of Cascariolo, he found near his home town white stones of barium sulphate and synthesized from them a material which, after exposure to the sun by day, glowed at night. He was an alchemist as well as a cobbler and it may be that he thought he had found at last the philosopher's stone that would enable him to turn things into gold. He had not: all he had found was the mineral barite.

Whilst he himself thought that he was

contributing to the production of the much sought after 'philosopher's stone', the compound which he had created (barium sulphate with powdered coal) became very popular for crucifixes, icons and rosary beads. It was described as a sun stone ('lapis solaris') and was probably used for the first time on children's toys.

He is said to have used his material on a number of artefacts and amulets as well as on some toys.

Although it would appear that we owe to the Dutch the conversion in the sixteenth century of the more primitive systems of wine distillation into commercial enterprises it was, in fact, in Italy round about the beginning of the twelfth century that wine was first distilled to make brandy. (Bruno)

474 The alambic is recorded as having been in use ever since the twelfth century, at least in Europe. Raimondo LULLO was the first to use the term 'aqua vitae' to describe the alcohol resulting from distillation. The term stuck and was picked up in most Latin languages (aqua vitae in Italy, acquavite, eau de vie in France and so on. . . . even whisky was first known as aqua vitae.)

475 Adamo FABBRONI published in 1787 in Florence his book entitled *Dell'Arte di Fare il vino*, in which he showed for the first time that air was not necessary for fermentation to take place, generally, and more specifically in wine.

476 In the late eighteenth century, an Italian named ALESSIO mixed white wine with a blend of bitter herbs (like artemisia – wormwood) and bitter oranges (later to become known as 'Turin bitters') inventing 'Vermouth' which began to be sold

to the public towards the end of the 1780s. The French then gave it the name Vermouth, a noun related to the English 'wormwood', also an ingredient of a popular and highly damaging French liqueur, 'absinthe'. The English word is, in turn, a corruption of the German 'Wermut' which means 'courage' simply because it was thought that the herb artemisia had certain aphrodisiac effects.

477 FABBRONI was also the first to regard the ferment as an albumenoid substance. Pasteur considered his work the beginning of modern ideas on fermentation.

As an aside, he studied the development of chicks in order to find clues to human embryology. (Morton's 2467).

478 In 1811, Amedeo AVOGADRO (born Turin) formulated his hypothesis that elemental gases are groups of atoms and elucidated the number of atoms in a given volume of gas.

479 AVOGADRO was the first to propound the theory that, given the same circumstances of temperature and pressure, equal volumes of all gases contain equal numbers of molecules.

His was 'a brilliant conception ignored for 50 years'. (See *Biographical Dictionary of Scientists*, ed. Pitman, London, 1969.) He laid down the fundamental method of chemical formulae.

His discovery is sometimes attributed to Ampère who, to his credit, admitted Avogadro's paternity of it.

480 In 1836, Raffaele PIRIA (born Scilla di Calabria) discovered salicylic acid by the oxidation of salicylic aldehyde present in a fairly

common herb known as meadow-sweet (Latin name 'spiraea ulmaria').

Fifteen years after that, Gerhardt discovered acetylsalicylic and he and Piria paved the way for the Germans Rolke and Lauterman to create aspirin.

It would be nice to think that the very name if this medicament comes from Piria, but I believe this to be a coincidence: all that has been done is that the Latin name 'spiraea' has been turned into aspirin.

Even so, the next time you take an aspirin, you might spare a thought for Piria who is not normally given credit for his discovery.

Piria came from Calabria, but he died in Turin in 1865. He was one of the very many Italians of all descriptions who were more able to develop their personality in the smoky environment of Northern Italy. It is possible that the sun of the '*mezzogiorno*', which undoubtedly promotes the appreciation of many fine things in life, as well as sexual prowess, is not conducive to scientific studies.

481   In 1850, Francesco SELMI (born Vignola Novarese) published the first systematic study of inorganic colloids.

482   In 1858, Stanislao CANNIZ-ZARO (born Palermo), as part of a process of rehabilitation of his predecessor, gave the first representation of Avogrado's hypothesis.

Cannizzaro became a Fellow of The Royal Society in 1889. The name may be familiar to some Londoners. 'Cannizzaro House', now an hotel and formerly the home of the Sicilian Duke of Cannizzaro who lived there in the eighteenth century, can be seen lit up at night across Wimbledon Common.

483   Helium gas was first discovered on earth in 1882 by Professor PALMIERI.

484   Giulio NATTA (born Imperia) invented polypropylene in 1954. It was first marketed throughout the world by Montecatini under the brand name 'Moplen'.

485   NATTA also discovered polymers in 1957. In 1963, he was the Nobel Prize Winner for Chemistry.

GEOLOGY

486   In 1760, Giovanni ARDUINO (born Caprino Veronese) was the first to classify rocks and to establish bases for stratigraphic chronology by defining the four major layers of earth as primary, secondary, tertiary and quaternary.

487   ARDUINO also pioneered the use of fossil and chemical methods to determine the age of rocks.

MATHEMATICS

488   In 1202, Leonardo da PISA, otherwise known as Leonardo FI-BONACCI (the son of Bonacci), wrote the first textbook ever on mathematics. It was called the *Liber Abaci*, a book he revised in 1228 and dedicated to Michael Scott. In it he set out the sequence of numbers henceforth known as the Fibonacci Sequence, which has proved to be inexhaustible, and formed the basis of all future number games.

489   FIBONACCI also introduced

Hindu-Arabic numbers into mathematics.

Although written in 1202, this book was not well known until after 1450, when it was printed by Luca Pacioli and brought to the knowledge of the general public. It is to his credit that he kept mathematics alive during the Dark Ages and there is no doubt that he did all the groundwork in preparation for higher mathematics and developments in physics, astronomy and engineering. It is usually said that he was the greatest mathematician of his time. It has been remarked (Joseph Gies of *Encyclopaedia Britannica*) that 'future scholars will in time give Leonard of Pisa his due as one of the world's great intellectual pioneers'.

He illustrated his sequence with the problem so well known to mathematicians and philosophers of how many pairs of rabbits placed in an enclosed area could be produced in a single year from one pair of rabbits if each pair gave birth to a new pair each month starting with the second month; he ended up with the conclusion that the ratio of any two consecutive numbers in the sequence approximates 1.618 or, inversely, .618, after the first four numbers.

We have already recorded how essential his sequence has proved in the world of ciphers (see 'Cryptography') but his modernity does not stop at ciphers. The sequence of Fibonacci numbers keeps recurring in nature and in music and has been applied in cyclical form to the Elliott wave principle used on the Stock Market, particularly in Futures Trading, and generally in the commodity market.

490   FIBONACCI should also be credited with the first use in 1202 of the 1/2 fractional line.

491   He also introduced calcula-tions by reference to fractional numbers, and established the study of trigonometry and algebra. Very little was added in the field of mathematics to his work for at least four centuries.

492   The percent sign (%) was established by Italian commercial usage round about 1425.

493   In 1494, Luca PACIOLI, a monk, who established the 'Lucas sequence', published his *Summa de Arithmetica Geometria Proportioni et Proportionalita*, the first printed book on geometry.

494   To PACIOLI is attributable the first use of the sign 'p' meaning 'plus'.

495   At about the same time, BRUNELLESCHI (born Florence) (see also 'Architecture & Buildings') the famous Florentine architect, applied mathematics to his principles for the use of perspective in building.

Britannica records that 'Brunelleschi's optical and mathematical discoveries in this field are reflected in Leon Battista Alberti's (q.v.) *Della Pittüra*', the 1436 (Italian) edition being dedicated to him.

496   In 1510, Scipione del FERRO was the first to find the solution to cubic equations.

497   In 1512, Niccolo TARTAGLIA (born Brescia) was the first to find the solution to quartic equations.

Tartaglia is said to have obtained his surname from the Italian verb '*tartagliare*' which means to stutter because, according to tradition, when he was young, he received an injury to his lips by French soldiers who at that time were invading his home town of Brescia. He was a versatile man.

498   In 1543, TARTAGLIA published the first translation of Euclid in Italian.

In *Nuova Scienza*, which he wrote in 1537, he dealt with the theory of gunnery, applying mathematics to it. His interest in artillery was so great that in 1546 he wrote and dedicated to Henry VIII a whole volume on artillery and fortification.

499   TARTAGLIA determined the rule for dividing a number into two parts such that the continued product of the numbers and their difference is a maximum. (See *Biographical Dictionary of Scientists*)

500   In 1540, Ludovico FERRARI (born Bologna) was the first to find an algebraic solution to the quartic equation and he competed publicly with the said Tartaglia to solve the cubic equation.

501   In 1545, the formulae for cubic and quartic equations were put forward for the first time by Niccoló TARTAGLIA, Ludovico FERRARI and Girolamo CARDANO.

502   In 1572, Rafael BOMBELLI (born in Bologna 1526, died 1573) published the first three of his five books entitled *Algebra*. He never completed the last two volumes because he died shortly after. This is the first thorough account of the algebra known at the time. Bombelli was the first person to write down the rules for addition, subtraction and multiplication of complex numbers, of which he can be said to have been the inventor, at least in the sense that nobody before him had elaborated a system

for complex numbers or had considered their value. In his book he describes 'imaginary roots' and thus laid the foundation for a better knowledge of imaginary quantities and numbers. (Bruno)

Two authors (J.J. O'Connor and E.F. Robertson) have stated that 'Bombelli's Algebra is one of the most remarkable achievements of sixteenth century mathematics and he must be credited with understanding the importance of complex numbers at a time when clearly nobody else did.'

In, perhaps, belated recognition of his contribution to mathematics a lunar crater has been named after him.

But we should not forget his contribution to geometry which is contained in the last two books – the manuscripts of which only came to light in 1923 in a library at Bologna and were published by Bortoletti in 1929.

503   In the early seventeenth century, Girolamo SACCHERI adopted the 'reductio ad absurdum' argument on Euclid's axioms.

504   In 1613, the mathematician Pietro Antonio CATALDI (1552-1626) published his *Trattato del Modo Brevissimo di Trovare la Radice Quadra delli Numeri* in which, not only does he discuss square roots as the title implies, but also his invention of the common form of continued fractions. (Bruno)

505   In 1678, Giovanni CEVA (1647-1743) wrote his book *De Lineis Rectis* (literally, about straight lines) in which he sets out what became known as Ceva's theorem.

506   In 1711, he published his *De Re Nummaria* the first clear mathematical text books on economics. (Bruno)

507   In 1635, Bonaventura CAVA-LIERI (born Milan) fashioned the geometry of indivisibles. The Cavalieri theorem takes its name from him and it involves the use of logarithms. He anticipated both integral calculus and the modern theory of calculus, and exerted profound influence on the later studies of Leibnitz and Newton.

508   In 1640, Evangelista TORRICELLI (born Faenza) was the first to find the length of the logarithmic spiral. He is also the inventor of the barometer (see 'Physics').

509   In 1646, Evangelista TORRICELLI described the asymptomatic point 'O'.

510   In 1668, Giovanni CEVA (born Mantova) established the geometric theorem known by his name. It concerns lines intersecting at the common points of a triangle.

511   In about 1670, Pietro MENGOLI was the first to analyse convergence and divergence.

Mengoli determined certain features of the harmonic series before Jacques Bernoulli and also produced a series of logarithms. 'His definition of definite integral is similar to that propounded by A.C. Cauchy 100 years later.' (See *Biographical Dictionary of Scientists*.)

512   In the year 1700, Girolamo SACCHERI (born Sanremo) was the first to develop hyperbolic geometry.

513   In 1712, Iacopo Francesco RICCATI gave his name to the equation otherwise known as a second-order equation.

514   In 1728, Guido GRANDI (born Cremona) analysed the rhodonea curves.

515   The eighteenth century also saw the first woman mathematician, Maria Gaetana AGNESI (born Milan), who was noted for her work on differential calculus.

A child prodigy, who mastered several modern languages at an early age, in addition to Latin, Greek and Hebrew, a philosopher and a scientist, she became known for the so-called Agnesi Curve, or 'versiera' curve which, through a bad translation ('versiera' also being capable of meaning 'witch') became known in English as the 'witch of Agnesi' (see *Britannica*, Vol. 1, p. 139).

516   Luigi la GRANGE (born Turin) was the first to apply mathematical criteria to mechanical sciences. In 1761, he was recognized as the greatest living mathematician. In 1788, he published his major work, *Mecanique Analytique*, which, ignoring completely metaphysical concepts, provided a review of mechanics of the past 200 years.

517   In 1799, Iacopo Paolo RUFFINI (born Valentano) showed for the first time that there is no algebraic solution to the general quintic equation.

518   In 1857, Enrico BETTI (born Pistoia) wrote the first book on topology.

519   BETTI also gave the first exposition of the theory of equations which was later developed by the Frenchman Galois.

520   In 1860, Luigi CREMONA (born Pavia) originated graphical statics, the study of forces in equilibrium, using graphical methods.

521 In 1868, Eugenio BELTRA-MINI (born Cremona) was the first to observe the correctness of Lobatchevsky's postulates in Euclid's geometry.

522/23 In 1880, Gregorio RICCI (born Lugo) developed absolute differential calculus, called after him Ricci Calculus. RICCI also created the first systematic theory of tensor analysis.

524 In 1885, Giuseppe PEANO (born Cuneo) established the Peano axioms as a series of geometrical calculus and mathematical logic.

His work gave Bertrand Russell the idea for *The Principles of Mathematics*, the first draft of which was finished at the end of 1900 just months after his meeting with Peano.

Russell was a great admirer of the Italian mathematician whom he described as the 'great master of the art of formal reasoning among the men of our day'.

525 In 1890, Ernesto CESARO (born Naples) developed the theory of divergent series.

526 In 1900, Vito VOLTERRA (born Ancona) created functional analysis. He was elected to The Royal Society in 1910.

527 In 1908, Ernesto ZERMELO gave the first system of axiomatic set theory.

528 In 1917, Tullio LEVI-CIVITA (born Padova) developed the notion of parallel transport and together with Cumbastro Gregorio RICCI was the first to formulate absolute differential calculus (otherwise known as tensor analysis). Levi-Civita was elected to The Royal Society in 1930.

529 In 1930, G. TONELLI (born Gallipoli), L. CESARI and E. DI-GIORGI were the first to study multiple integral surfaces.

530 Federico FAGGIN (born in Vicenza) should have the gratitude of all computer users. To him is due the world's first microprocessor, the Intel 4004, which he devised himself, allegedly solely with the use of a slide rule, in 1971 as a result of his attempts to bring the silicon chip to reality. He is officially recognized as the inventor of the MOS Silicon Gate Technology, the basis of all computer chips and all microprocessors. In 1988, he was honoured for his invention when he received the International Marconi Fellowship Award. Intel 4004, the world's first microprocessor, is in fact signed with his initials, F.F.

531 To him we also owe the CPU, namely the central processing unit of a computer which contains the circuit for performing and controlling the execution of instructions in a single minuscule chip.

MEDICINE

This is a field where the contribution of the Italians is probably not so well known as in other fields such as arts and music; it is usually substantially underrated and, as a matter of recorded fact, happens to be truly outstanding.

The lists recorded in this section cover most spheres of medical expertise and knowledge.

From the Middle Ages to at least the eighteenth century, the major centres of medical learning were to be found in Italy. The universities and colleges at Bologna, Padova, Venice and Pavia were frequented by all European doctors-to-be. Harvey went there, and learnt the principles which later enabled him to enunciate his theory on the circulation of blood. Vesalius was also there and acquired indispensable knowledge.

I can state unhesitatingly, therefore, that Italian medical knowledge, developments and expertise represent the foundations on which the medicine of the Western World is based.

The authorities for the statements made are, as usual, either contained in the Schedule to the book or under the relevant 'first'. The references to the *Encyclopaedia Britannica* have already been addressed. The references to 'Morton's' are to *Morton's Medical Bibliography*, 5th edition by Garrison and Morton, 1991, made available to the writer by courtesy of The Wellcome Institute in London and the number that follows identifies the relevant paragraph in the handbook (e.g. Morton's 4279).

532   The first public physicians employed by the community emerged in Italy in the Middle Ages. They were called '*Medici Condotti*'.

533   The first public contract recorded for one of them is dated 1211 and was signed at Reggio Emilia which is not too far from Bologna, where a similar one was executed in 1214.

(We have already recorded Bologna as the oldest university in the world having been founded round about the year 1000.)

By 1300, public physicians were to be found in all the large towns in Italy, but we have to wait until the 1500s before civil doctors were appointed to other European countries such as France, Flanders and Germany (see Roy Porter, *The Greatest Benefit to Mankind*, Harper Collins, London, 1997).

534   In 1221, the first medical school of the Western world was founded in Salerno. It was licensed by Frederick II of Sicily in 1224, the same year as the university was founded.

He decreed that the only people entitled to practise in his kingdom were those who had been publicly approved by the master teachers at the Salerno School of Medicine.

535   The first post-mortems of the Western world were carried out in Salerno by Mondino de' LUZZI and Da VIGEVANO.

The Salerno Medical School was already in existence before the above date, for there seems to be evidence that it was considered as 'ancient' three centuries earlier. It continued to be well known until about the sixteenth century.

A number of medical students flocked there from all parts of the world. The principal purpose was to obtain a diploma from the Salerno School which entitled them to practise their profession in every country of Europe.

Patients, too, came from all over, including soldiers who had taken part in the crusades: in fact, it was the practice to give the crusaders a 'vade mecum' before leaving – a sort of *aide-memoire* of what they should do when they were no longer in touch with their doctor. This 'vade mecum' is in Latin but there is an amusing English translation of it made by Sir John Haryngton which was published in London in 1607.

Haryngton himself is connected with Italy in a different way because in 1591 he translated *Orlando Furioso*. (A man of some versatility, since he had also invented the water closet in 1589.)

This is not the place to go through the various rules which, according to the

School of Salerno 700 years ago, were supposed to keep one healthy. By modern standards, some read a bit strangely. However, one of the principal ones is a rule of conduct of universal application, namely that the best medicine consists in a mind that is happy, rest and food in moderation ('*Si tibi deficiant medici, medici tibi fiant haec tria: mens laeta, requies, moderata diaeta*' which is cheerfully translated by Sir John Haryngton as 'Use three physicians; first Dr Quiet, next Dr Merryman, and Dr Diet'.)

There are also a few gems of a different kind which have now been rediscovered as part of modern medicine; for example, that if one had too much to drink the previous night, a drop of the same stuff first thing in the morning would redress the balance (I am told that a number of cures for allergies acknowledge this principle); or that plums are very good for you and your system, as our grandmothers knew only too well; or that the herb sage is excellent for most ills, as are nettles, hyssop, watercress, leeks and rosemary.

536 Finally, feminists might like to note that as far back in time as this, there practised an obstetrician at the Salerno School of Medicine, a woman by the name of TROTULA.

537 At some time between 1175 and 1230, RUGGERO OF SALERNO, otherwise known as Ruggero Frugardo, wrote his treatise on surgery, probably the first textbook on surgery ever compiled; its editor was Guido d'Arezzo. It was, of course, written in Latin but a copy of it translated into Anglo-Norman French is in the possession of Trinity College, Cambridge.

The book contains many expressive drawings and shows the techniques used by doctors at that time, either in preparing potions or in viewing the ailments of their patients. It dominated European surgery techniques until the Renaissance.

538 The post-mortems carried out at, or in conjunction with, the Salerno School of Medicine were not ever formally recorded. The first formally recorded post-mortem or judicial autopsy was performed in Bologna in 1302, having been ordered by the local court to decide a case of suspected poisoning. (Bruno)

539 In 1296, the Italian surgeon Guido LANFRANCHI, otherwise known as Lanfranc, wrote his book *Chirurgia Magna* in which he describes for the first time a cerebral concussion.

In the same book, he also studies the breast and differentiates between hypertrophy (benign) and cancer (malignant). It is said by Bruno that: 'His chapter on the symptoms of a skull fracture is considered a classic.' (Bruno)

540 By 1400, there were practising in Florence graduates from Padua, Bologna and Rome, and it is in Florence that as early as 1236 we find the first medical guild in the Western world, taking up responsibilities for apprenticeship exams, as well as supervision of drugs, foods and herbs. (Roy Porter, op. cit.)

The Italian pre-eminence at the time is confirmed by the fact that surgery was included in the academic curriculum of Italian schools – a notable event in Europe – and it is a matter of record that in Frederick II's regulations for the Kingdom of Italy dating back to about 1231, it is recorded that a licence to practise medicine could be gained only after five years' study, such study to include surgery. The period of five years is, perhaps coincidentally, still the time it takes to obtain a medical degree in Italy.

541   In 1275, Guglielmo da SALI-CETO (1210-80), who was a major surgeon and Professor of Surgery at Bologna University, wrote the first treatise on surgical anatomy, which was officially printed in Venice in 1474. This was the first book on surgery ever written, containing the first known treatise on surgical anatomy. It is worth noting that one of his pupils was the founder of French surgery, namely Lanfranc of Milan (Morton's 5552).

542   Italy was undoubtedly at the forefront of medicine in the Middle Ages. The first efficient hospitals are to be found in medieval Italy, mainly in Milan, Siena and Florence.

543   It is recorded that in Florence alone, a city which at the time had about 30,000 inhabitants, there were over thirty religious foundations catering for the sick, some admittedly with only a small number of beds, but others having more than 100. By 1288, Santa Maria Nuova in Florence, the first hospital among 'Christians' as it was termed, had expanded from twelve beds to a stage where it had a staff of ten doctors, a pharmacist, several assistants and even a female surgeon.

In his book *The Evolution of The Grand Tour* (Frank Cass, London, 1998) Professor Edward Chaney, in a comparative study of Catholic and Protestant charity, observes that the 'high standards of the Italian hospitals were clearly a novelty to sixteenth and seventeenth century English travellers'. More particularly, all those who wrote letters or books about hospi-

tals in Italy, and especially Thomas Hoby, were constantly struck about the standard of care in the major cities such as Milan, Venice, Genoa, Rome, Florence and Naples.

It is beyond the scope of my small work to consider this aspect of the matter further, save to observe that the 'Albergo de'Poveri' in Genoa, the 'Ospedale Maggiore' in Milan and the 'Annunziata' in Naples were particularly important. I have mentioned above S. Maria Nuova for Florence, but I should not omit 'S. Spirito' for Rome (there were many more, particularly in Rome, of course).

One of the most notable comments comes from Johann Keysler, a Fellow of The Royal Society, who in a work in four volumes, summarizing his travels throughout Europe, discussed the comparative merits of the hospitals that he found in the various countries visited.

He is on record as saying that 'no country in the world equals Italy in the care of the poor and the sick'. (*Travels*, London 1756)

544   In 1377, there are recorded the first known quarantines on land imposed at Reggio Emilia as a check against the spread of the plague. The system ensured that all visitors 'suspected of being infected by the plague are required to spend a designated amount of time at appointed places outside the city'. (Bruno)

545   Simone CARDO (otherwise known as Simone of Genoa) (1270-1303) compiled the first printed medical dictionary. Unfortunately, in the Bodlean Library in Oxford, only a fragment of twenty-one pages is available of the version printed at Ferrara in 1473. (Morton's 6788).

546   In Milan in 1410, there was

established the first board to co-ordinate public health measures. By 1450, it had on its staff a physician, a surgeon, a notary, a barber, two horsemen, three footmen and two grave-diggers. Milan was followed in 1486 by Venice, in 1527 by Florence and in 1549 by Lucca.

547 We owe the first isolation 'hospitals' (or areas) in the world to the Venetians. As a result of the increase in trade with the Orient in the fifteenth century, they decided to isolate on an island in the Adriatic fronting the city of Venice those whom they believed were affected by contagious diseases. The area was known as 'lazzaretto' ('lazzaretti' in the plural).

The word is derived from the Italian 'lazzaro', meaning beggar or leper. The period of isolation was initially for thirty days ('trentina') but later became standardized at forty ('quarantina', from which our noun quarantine is derived). (See *Britannica*, Volume 15, page 326.)

548 It was left to Antonio BENVIENI (1440-1502) to establish in 1507 the concept of pathological anatomy when he described for the first time 'how the dissection of cadavers can be used to study the internal causes of disease and to determine the cause of death'. (Bruno)

549 Paolo BAGELLARDO (born Padova) published in Padova in 1472 the first printed book dealing exclusively with paediatrics.

550 His *De Infantium Aegritudinibus et remediis* is also the first medical treatise to make its original appearance in printed form, rather than having prior circulation in manuscript. (Morton's 6315)

The Italian word 'ghetto', accepted in other languages, is a variant on the Venetian 'gheto' meaning 'foundry'. This was the name given to one of the many small islands in the Venetian laguna (where Jews were relegated in the sixteenth century) because there used to be a foundry there. (*Britannica*, IV, p. 522).

551 The name still remains as a description of an area in Venice itself, 'gheto novissimo'. Forced segregation of Jews first occurred in Muslim countries in the thirteenth century and spread to Europe in the fourteenth and fifteenth. It was in Venice, however, in 1516 that the name 'gheto' was first used to describe an area specially set aside for Jews.

The Venetian arrangement became a model for ghettos both in Italy and elsewhere, especially because, despite the fact that there were Christians watching over them, Jews were free to organize themselves autonomously with (as *Britannica* observes Vol IV, p. 523) 'their own religious judicial charitable and recreational institutions'.

552 Dorotea BUCCA who lived in the fifteenth century and died quite young, was remarkably successful because she became the first woman lecturer in medicine, at the University of Bologna.

553 Benvenuto GRASSI in his book published in 1474 established the earliest printed book on ophthalmology. (Morton's 5816)

554/5 The existence of universities made it easier for lecturers who travelled from town to town to develop. It is a matter of record that one of the first lecturers in surgery was to be found in Bologna in the fifteenth century. He was BEREN-

GARIO da CARPI (1460-1530), who is also recorded as having been the first surgeon to carry out a post-mortem on a pregnant woman (see Roy Porter, op. cit.).

This was quite a significant event, firstly because, as a general rule, religious taboos forbade human dissection but, more particularly, because the internal workings of women's bodies were even less well-known than men's.

556 Giulio Cesare ARANZI (otherwise known as Aranzio or Arantius) (born in Bologna) was the first to record, in or about the year 1500, a pelvic deformity. (Morton's 464)

557 Bartolomeo MONTAGNA-NA of Padua is recorded as being credited with having discovered Senna powder.

558 Antonio BENIVIENI (born Florence in 1443) 'the father of pathological anatomy', was the first physician to request permission of his patients' relatives to perform autopsies in cases where there was some doubt as to the cause of death.

559 His book *De Contagione* published in 1546 gave the first descriptions of the dissemination of tuberculosis, anticipating to some extent the work done on cavities in lungs by his compatriot G.B. Morgagni (q.v.).

560 In his book 'The Hidden Causes of Disease' he was the first to give extensive consideration to the practice of post-mortem examinations. (Morton's 2270).

561 In 1483, the Italian surgeon Giovanni ARCOLANI (otherwise known as Arculanus) published his book *Practica* in which, for the first

time, he recommends the filling of teeth with gold. A novelty at the time, of course, but not entirely unexpected from a pioneer of dentistry whose said work contains also a description of the dental instruments available at the time and who was well-known for his work on surgery of the mouth. (Bruno)

562 In 1502, Gabriele ZERBI (1445-1505) published a book which was 'the first systematic detailed examination of the human body since Mondino (q.v.)'. (Morton's 363)

563 He also wrote the first book concerning the anatomy of the infant, treating infantile anatomy as a separate area of medical knowledge. (Bruno)

564/5 Da CARPI, in his 'Commentaria' published in Bologna in 1521, provided the first mention of the Vermiform Appendix as well as the first good account of the thymus gland.

It is worth recording that other features in this work are extensive descriptions of both the male and female reproductive organs as well as the valves of the heart (Morton's 367).

566/7 Guido GUIDI, otherwise known as Vidius (born Pisa in 1508), a Professor of Philosophy of Medicine at Pisa University, discovered the 'vidian nerve' and the 'vidian artery'. (Morton's 380)

568 Girolamo CARDANO (born Pavia in 1536) published the first account of typhus, which he described as 'morbus pulicaris', namely the disease of the fleas. (Morton's 152)

569 In 1530, Girolamo FRACAS-TORO (born Verona) was the first Westerner to describe syphilis.

He was mistaken inasmuch as he did not believe that it came from America and called it the 'French disease'; but I suppose his mistake is understandable because the plague that had started in Naples in 1495 was spreading throughout Europe on an epidemic basis and he may have believed that it came from there and that the French were responsible.

He thought at one stage it also came from the air and suggested that it be cured with quicksilver.

He was quite a character because he wrote a whole book on it in rhyme (by the title *Syphilis sive de morbo gallico*).

It is interesting to record that until Fracastoro could compose his book, which is essentially a poem about a shepherd called 'Syphilus' who is struck down by this particular illness, syphilis had no official name. Italians, Germans, Poles and English all called it the French disease, whereas the French called it the Neapolitan disease. The Neapolitans, who hated their conquerors, the Spaniards, called it the Spanish disease and the Portuguese, for analogous reasons, called it the Castilian disease. Even the Turks could not resist the temptation of a tit-for-tat and called syphilis the Christian disease.

According to Norman Davis (*Europe – A History*, op. cit.) the Spanish doctor who first came across it called it the 'Serpent of Hispaniola'.

570/1 FRACASTORO was the first to study epidemiology and is credited with being its founder. He propounded the germ theory of disease and anticipated Pasteur by 300 years.

He also anticipated Copernicus by postulating the planets revolved spherically around a central point, in his work *A Single Centre of the Universe*, published in 1538.

In the Victorian era his studies were of great help to the famous scientist John Snow, when he had to determine that the cause of a cholera epidemic was to be found in the water supply being polluted by raw sewage.

Fracastoro was a very influential humanist, apart from being a famous physician, and, with Copernicus, had studied at Padova University. He anticipated Leibnitz and his 'monads', when he established his 'semina' as primary philosophical concepts similar to atoms – thus giving the idea to his compatriot Bruno.

Fracastoro must surely be one of the greatest names in Italian science. All that he said and did in 1530 is extraordinary and I am sure that one would be hard put to believe it were it not for the authority of the *Encyclopaedia Britannica*, Volume 12, p. 109.

We now come to the father of modern medicine, namely, Matteo Realdo Colombo (born Cremona).

572 In 1540, COLOMBO was the first to describe clearly the pulmonary circulation. He thus anticipated Harvey who acknowledged him as the discoverer of pulmonary circulation.

573/6 COLOMBO was also the first to describe the mediastinum, the pleura, the peritoneum, and the action of the heart, namely its two phases of systole and diastole.

He was exceptionally well known as a physician during his lifetime and was a close friend of Michelangelo, whom he treated from time to time, particularly in his old age, when the artist suffered from dysuria and gall-bladder problems.

Colombo also claimed in 1543 that he had discovered the clitoris. He was wrong about this because, as Fallopio properly proceeded to show some twenty years later, both Avicenna and Albucasis had referred to it in their works and, in any event, it was already known to the Greeks.

577 Leonardo BOTALLO (born Asti in 1519) was the first to describe hay fever, which he called summer catarrh. He is also credited with the 're-discovery' of Botallo's Duct, Botallo's Foramen and Botallo's Ligament. The term 're-discovery' is used because the Duct, the Foramen and the Ligament had already been identified earlier on by Galen, Falloppio and Vesalius respectively (Morton's 2581).

578 Gianni Battista CANANO was the first to publish in 1541 a book in which each muscle in the human body was separately described (Morton's 373).

579 In 1546, FRACASTORO wrote the first textbook ever on contagious diseases, where, for the first time, he correctly identifies infection as the passage of minute bodies from the infected person to another, although it was left to his compatriot Redi to formulate the germ theory of infection (see 'Biology').

580 In 1552, Bartolomeo EUSTA-CHIO (born Sanseverino) laid his claim to posterity through his unpublished book *Opuscola Anatomica*. He is now known generally because of the tube in the human ear which bears his name. But he did much more.

581 Specifically, in 1563, EUSTA-CHIO published a book *Libellus de Dentibus* describing the teeth in great detail. He pointed out the first and second dentitions, the outer tissue and the soft inner structure of teeth, as well as the sensitivity of the tooth's hard structure.

His book was written in 1552, and is otherwise known as the *Tabulae anatomicae*. Eustachio was born in 1510 and died in 1574, but his work remained unpublished and forgotten in the Vatican Library until it was discovered in the seventeenth century and presented to Pope Clement XI who passed it on to his own personal physician, G.M. Lancisi (q.v.). Lancisi published it in 1714, together with his own notes on it.

It is worth transcribing what Morton has to say about Eustachio's work: 'The copper-plates were more accurate than those of Vesalius. Singer was of the opinion that had they appeared in 1552 Eustachio would have ranked with Vesalius as one of the founders of modern anatomy.'

For the sake of the record, the other 'firsts' of Eustachio are the following:

582/3 The description of the *thoracic duct* and the *azygos vein*, thus anticipating Jean Pecquet by a century.

584/5 His discovery of the *adrenal glands* and the *ganglion chain*.

586/9 His detailed descriptions of the *uterus*, *cochlea*, the muscles of the *throat* and of the *larynx*.

590/1 The origin of the *optic nerves*, and the structure of the *kidney*. Many of the concepts that he established and the description that he provided were developed more fully by others, especially by Vesalius.

592 Apart from the Eustachian tube, he also identified the *tensor tympani* (Morton's 391, 801, 1093, 1139, 1228, 1312, 1538 and 3668).

Apart from the fact that he was the first to describe in scientific form anatomical variations, Eustachio did much work on muscles, showing their nerve supply, as well as on the brain and on the sympathetic system.

Are you ever bothered, when you go to the dentist, by the sound of the drill? Have you ever tried using earplugs to muffle it? If so, you will know that it does not work: the sound and the vibration get through to the ear, come what may. The reason is that the teeth conduct sound.

593/4 This discovery was made in the sixteenth century by the Sicilian Giovanni Filippo **INGRASSIA** (1510-80) who noted the sound recording capacity of the teeth for the first time. In addition, he discovered the *stapes* – the stirrup-like bone in the human ear.

595/601 In 1561, Gabriele **FALLOPIO** (born Modena), who was the most illustrious of the sixteenth century anatomists, studied particularly the ear and the genital organs. He discovered the *tubes* that now bear his name and was the first to name the *vagina*, the *placenta*, the *clitoris*, the *palate* and the *cochlea*. He also invented the *condom* as has been noted elsewhere.

602 Alvisio **LUIGINI** (born Udine) spent some time on venereal diseases and particularly syphilis and was effectively the first to write more than one book about it. In 1566, he wrote his *De Morbo Gallico* which was the first summary of world knowledge and techniques of treatment for syphilis and in 1599 his *De Lue Venerea* treatise on V.D.

603/5 In 1573, Constanzo **VAROLIO** (born Bologna) published in Padova his study on the *optical nerves*. He gave his name to the *Varolio 'bridge'*, the transverse part of the brain, and was the first to teach that when dissecting the *encephalus* one had to start from its base.

606 Gianni Battista **CARCANO-LEONE** was the first to publish in 1574 an exact description of the lacrimal ducts, giving the exact position of the lacrimal gland as well as identifying the route taken by tears (Morton's 1479).

607 Ulisse **ALDROVANDI** (born Bologna 1522), apart from being famous for his work on monsters, later picked up by Fortunio Liceli (q.v.), provided the first detailed description and illustration of bladder exstrophy (Morton's 290).

He was professor at the University of his home town and he instigated the establishment in 1567 of the Botanical Garden there. His is one of the earliest pharmacopoeias, by the title *Natural History*, in fourteen volumes, only four of which were published before his death, the remainder made available to the general public from his manuscripts.

608 Marcello **DONATI** provided in 1586 the first description of angio-neurotic oedema, now known as Quincke's Oedema (Morton's 4011).

609 He also provides the first description of a gastric ulcer.

610 In 1588, using drawings which originated in Egypt, **DELLAPORTA** (many other firsts recorded elsewhere) designed the first incubator.

Andrea CESALPINO (1525-1603) preceded Harvey in studying blood circulation and it is suggested that Harvey must have known his work.

611/2 **CESALPINO** was the first to tie in a vein and record the centripetal flow in veins in a book published in Venice in 1593 (Morton's 756).

613   Gianbattista SILVATICO (1550-1621) published in 1595 in Milan the first book on feigned diseases (Morton's 2667).

614   Geronimo Scipione MERCURIO, in a book published in 1596 (incidentally, the first Italian book on obstetrics, which sets out in great detail the history of caesarean sections) was the first to advocate the caesarean operation in cases of a contracted pelvis (Morton's 6144).

615   Girolamo FABRIZIO, in a book that he published in 1600 at Acquapendente, recorded for the first time the dissection of several embryos. He was a professor of pathology at Padova University where he taught Harvey.

616   It is to FABRIZIO that we owe the discovery of venous valves; in 1603 he published his work *De Venarum Ostiis*, a work which was certainly known to Harvey and which must have influenced him in his experimental efforts on blood circulation.

Fabrizio also taught a compatriot, Giulio Casseri, whose book published in 1600 is according to Morton's 'the most beautiful book ever published on the ear and throat in man and in lower animals' (Morton's 465).

617   Ercole SASSONIA published in 1604 a book entitled *De Pulsibus*, in which he gave the first description of a heart block (Morton's 2726).

618   Santorio SANTORIO (born Capodistria) was the first to employ instruments of precision in the practice of medicine.

619   In 1614, SANTORIO published his *De Statica Medicina*. This represented the first systematic study of basal metabolism. Well ahead of his time, his instruments were not introduced until a century later and the implications of his research were not realized until the nineteenth century.

620   In 1622, Gaspare ASELLI (born in either Pavia or Cremona) discovered lacteals, namely the lymphatic vessels that serve the small intestine, which he described as 'white and milky veins'.

Aselli also made an extensive study of the digestive system and in particular of the absorption of food in the mesentherium. He laid down the foundation for those studies which the Frenchman, Pecquet, was to develop more fully.

621   Giovanni COLLE (1558-1631) published in 1628 a book in which he provided the first definitive description of a blood transfusion (Morton's 2011).

622   Fortunio LICELI (1577-1657) expanded on the work carried out by Aldrovandi and is credited with the earliest medical classification of deformities *De monstrorum causis natura* (Morton's 534).

623   In 1632, Marco Aurelio SEVERINO (born Naples, 1580) published the first textbook of surgical pathology, dealing with abscesses, neoplasms and sarcomas. His work is particularly relevant to modern times because the section that he devoted to tumours of the breast was very extensive and one of the most important parts of his book.

624   Apart from this, SEVERINO's work was the first book to include within the text illustrations of lesions.

625 In 1621, the Roman physician Paolo ZACCHI, well known in the Vatican, was the first to contradict Aristotle's views on embryology by stating that they were nonsense; since life began at the moment of conception. This has remained a tenet of the Catholic faith.

626/7 Giovanni Alfonso BORELLI (born Naples, 1608) was the first to identify the *neurogenic theory* of the movements of the heart and the first to suggest that *circulation of the blood* in reality resembles a simple hydraulic system.

628/9 Furthermore, BORELLI was the first to insist that the *heartbeat* was the result of a single muscular contraction, as well as the first to provide measurements of *masticatory force* (Morton's 762 and 3669).

630 In 1628, Giovanni COLLE provided the first printed description of blood transfusion improving on the rather vague references which followed upon William Harvey's discovery that blood circulates through the body in a closed system.

631 Sebastiano BARDO (otherwise known as Baldi) (born Genova) was the first to show in about 1640 that 'fever bark' was introduced into Spain in 1632. He was a keen student of the virtues of Peruvian bark (Morton's 1826).

Another book by Marco Severino, published in 1645, shows how many animals he had dissected and how well he realized that improvements to the microscope would be of enormous benefit to mankind (Morton's 2273).

Marcello MALPIGHI (see also 'Botanical Gardens & Botany') made many major contributions to medical science.

632 In 1661, MALPIGHI discovered the capillary vessels which connect arteries and veins; he also described in detail the structure of the human lung, brain and spinal cord.

633/5 As a result of his discoveries, MALPIGHI's name is associated with the epidermis (the *Malpighi layer*), the spleen (the *Malpighi corpuscles*) and the kidneys (the *Malpighi tufts*).

He studied the lungs of frogs with the microscope. In so doing, he discovered that the inner surface of the lungs is actually covered with tiny capillaries which are very close to the skin; through these, arteries on one side are connected to veins on the other. He wrote: 'I could clearly see that the blood is divided and flows through tortuous vessels and that it is not poured into spaces but is always driven through tubules and distributed by the manifold bendings of the vessels.' He thus gave scientific confirmation to what Harvey had already intuitively determined, but had been unable to prove.

636/40 He studied in detail both *red blood corpuscles* (which he first found in the lungs of a frog using a microscope) and the *cells of muscles* as well as the structure of *secreting glands*. He discovered the *papillae of the tongue* and the *cortex of the brain.*

The depth of knowledge he developed as to the fertilization of eggs and the development of the chick can be gauged from the very beautiful drawings that are preserved in the archives of The Royal Society where seven of his papers were published in the *Philosophical Transactions.* The first true Italian scientist, Malpighi was admitted as a Fellow of The Royal Society on 4 March 1668. (The first

Italian to become a member of The Royal Society beat Malpighi to it by just three months; he was Count Carlo Ubaldini about whom, however, nothing seems to be known.)

641 MALPIGHI was the first to use the microscope for detailed analysis and study.

He gave his name to the Puerto Rican Cherry tree (the Health tree) – 'Malpighia Punicifolia' – whose acerola berries are one of the richest sources of vitamin C.

642 Lorenzo BELLINI (born Florence) was the first to describe the excretory tubes of the kidneys (still known as Bellini's tubes).

643 BELLINI was only nineteen years old when he made this discovery in 1662 – three years later he described the human organs of taste.

644 In 1670, for the first time SANTORIO attempted to cure TB sufferers with transfusions of blood of mutton. (See entry under 'Physics'.)

645 I am not sure whether feminists will rejoice or not, but it is a matter of record that the first woman to obtain a degree in medicine was Italian. On 25 June 1678, Elena Lucrezia CORNARO PISCOPIA graduated at Padova University. There is a statue of her recording this event in the medical school building there.

646/7 Giovanni Cosimo BONOMO (born Livorno), together with Giacinto CESTONI, was the first to observe the scabies mite and in 1687 in Florence obtained the first clinical and experimental proof of infection by a parasite, thus paving the way for later researchers into

parasitic problems. Thanks to him, the theory of an objective exogenous pathogenic agent as a causation factor of diseases became established (Morton's 2529).

648/9 Tommaso ALGHISI, (born Florence in 1669) a pupil of Bellini, was the first to use an indwelling metal catheter to drain urine away from the wound after lithotomy. He was also the first to suggest the inclined position of the patient with the head raised during interventions on the bladder (Morton's 4279).

650 In 1696, Georgius BAGLIVI published in Padova a medical text where he advocated for the first time a 'direct surgical assault on a diseased lung'.

651 In 1700, Antonio Maria VALSALVA (born Imola) discovered how air pressure on the pharynx can cause the Eustachian tube to open. This is the same reflex of which we are too well aware when we fly.

652 VALSALVA was also the first to describe the aortic 'Sinus of Valsalva' (Morton's 803).

653 Giovanni Guglielmo RIVA (born Asti) was the first to carry out blood transfusions.

654 Giacomo PILARINI (1659-1718), inoculated three children in Constantinople with the smallpox virus in 1701. According to Morton's (5409) he should be credited with the medical discovery of variolation, and is thus the first 'immunologist'.

A compatriot, Emanuele Timoni, followed in his footsteps and a few years later, in 1713, wrote a letter to The Royal Society in London, in which he described the Turkish practice, which he, too, had found in Constantinople, of inoculation by incision which Pilarini had established, as above recorded.

655 **Antonio VALSALVA (see above) in his book on the ear, published in Bologna in 1704, describes minutely the muscles and nerves of the human ear. He was the first to describe the ear by classifying it into external, middle and internal.**

656/8 A pupil of Malpighi, VAL-SALVA is probably better known for his method of inflating the middle ear, which is still practised today, and is known as 'Valsalva's Manoeuvre', and for his association with 'Valsalva's Dysphagia' (Morton's 1546). Furthermore, Valsalva was the first to mention the cerebro-spinal fluid, although it was left to the Neapolitan Cotugno (q.v.) to provide an exact description of it.

The son of an aristocratic family he became a doctor of medicine in 1687 and was Malpighi's favourite pupil. His studies ranged from endocrinology to madness, from surgery to forensic medicine and throughout his life he entertained an extensive correspondence with colleagues, both in Italy and abroad.

As stated, to him we owe the 'Valsalva's manoeuvre', sometimes undertaken to rectify a cardiac arrhythmia. He published in 1704, that is to say about 150 years after his great predecessor, Bartolomeo Eustachio, wrote his book on the human ear by the title De Aure Humana.

He also discovered what has now become known as Valsalva retinopathy, namely a kind of blurred vision, caused by small haemorrhages on the retina, brought about by vigorous exercise.

659 **In 1714, Bernardino RAMAZ-**

ZINI (born Carpi) was the first to publish a systematic account of trade diseases.

660 **Amongst the diseases thus identified by RAMAZZINI in his compilation by the title De Morbis Artificium Diatriba was the affliction which is now commonly known as RSI (Repetitive Strain Injury).**

Whether this ailment which today affects those who use amongst other machines, computer keyboards, actually exists as a distinct medical condition in law, appeared to be in some doubt, as a result of a decision at first instance in the UK (October 1993), when the second edition of this book was published. The matter now appears to have been put beyond doubt and repetitive strain injury is acknowledged as something which can affect those who abuse their bodies in intensive mechanical activities. It might be called a sort of modern 'tennis elbow'.

It shows how modern some 280 years ago Ramazzini was, for he identified problems which, whether for factual or psychological reasons, now appear to afflict a growing number of people.

Ramazzini's work was translated into a number of languages, but was especially popular in England and inspired Adam Smith to say that each trade had its peculiar infirmity. His Christian name was, in fact, Bernardino, even though he is often referred to as a result of the Anglicization of Christian names, a practice to which reference has been made elsewhere in this book, as Bernard. See for instance p. 209 of John Rule's The Vital Century England's Developing Economy 1714-1815, Longmans, London & New York, 1992.

661 **To him we also owe the first book on artesian wells. De Fontium**

Mutinensium contains not only diagrams explaining the nature of artesian wells (dug into springs from which water flows under natural pressure, i.e. without being pumped out) but also their origins.

662   Another first is his suggestion of an addition to Hippocratic teaching to the effect that, when visiting a worker, a doctor should also ask for that patient's actual occupation in order better to formulate a diagnosis.

663   Carlo Francesco COGROSSI (born Siena in 1682) published in 1714 his formulation of much of the modern theory of infection as a result of his experience as a doctor in an epidemic affecting oxen in the Po valley.

In his book he deals with microscopy, the isolation and destruction of personal effects if contaminated and he analyses the spread of bacteria through manure (Morton's 2529).

664   Bernardino GENGIA (born Urbino in 1665), published in Rome the first book devoted entirely to surgical anatomy (Morton's 384).

We now come to 'the father of modern pathology', (here I am using the words of the *Encyclopaedia Britannica*), namely Giovanni MORGAGNI (born Forli).

Morgagni revolutionized medicine by his thorough studies and teaching of the human body. He was the greatest pathologist of the eighteenth century and his worldwide fame resulted in his being elected to The Royal Society in 1722.

665/7   MORGAGNI discovered the so-called pockets of the larynx, he made extensive studies of the urethra, he was the first to identify the anterior cervical muscles and the nodules of the arterial valves of the heart.

His analysis of the human body and its organs, consequent from his numerous dissections, was much more thorough even than that of Leonardo. In one of his publications dated 1761, Morgagni described 700 postmortems.

It has been said that if the totality of his anatomical discoveries had, in fact, been named after him, about a third of the parts of the human body would bear his name.

His interest ranged from the organs of procreation to the fluid of the cornea of the eye but, above all, he was a great teacher and a very active person who was still busy at work when he died aged eighty-nine. His contribution to human wellbeing is very great indeed.

He was already exceptionally famous throughout the eighteenth century. Samuel Johnson himself (see Boswell's *Life of Johnson*, aetat. 59 Spring 1768) refers to him ('the great anatomist Morgagni') as the only man whose word he would accept to decide whether the scorpion is capable of committing suicide by darting its sting into its head, or not.

668/70   Giovanni Domenico SANTORINI (born Venice in 1681) published in 1724 his book of anatomical observations. He is known for at least four major discoveries that all bear his name, that is to say 'Santorini's Vein', 'Santorini's Cartilage', 'Santorini's Duct' and 'Santorini's Caruncula' (Morton's 392).

671   The first book on the surgical treatment of breast cancer was published in 1746 by the Florentine, Angelo NANNONI.

672 SERTOLI gave his name to the 'Sertoli cells'. These are a necessary part of the body and they have the function of transporting the sperm cells within the testes. They are necessary for good sperm formation and when they decrease, this function becomes deficient and is one of the manifestations of male hypogonadism. (See *Britannica* 9, p. 415.)

673 Vincenzo MENGHINI published in 1746 a book where he recorded his discovery of iron in the blood (Morton's 862).

674 CHIARUGI (1710-90) was the first to abandon the use of chains and fetters in mental hospitals which he ran with a benevolent eye, providing hygienic rooms for the inmates as well as segregation of the sexes. He was also the first to practise humanitarian treatment of the insane in the two Florence hospitals of Santa Maria Nuova and San Bonifazio (Morton's 4920).

675 Domenico COTUGNO (born Ruvo di Puglia in 1736) was the first to describe in 1764 the fluid surrounding the spinal cord, as well as to suggest for the first time in medical history that such fluid was in continuity with the ventricular and subarachnoid fluids. To be fair to a fellow Italian, he followed upon a mention of this fact made earlier by Valsalva (Morton's 1382).

In 1786, he published at Louvain, in Latin, his *De Sedibus Variolarum Suntagma.*

676/9 Lazzaro SPALLANZANI (born Modena), a priest and biologist, showed for the first time that *spermatozoa* were necessary for the reproduction of mammals. He established *animal artificial insemination* and in 1776 laid down the technique of *sterile cultures*. He was the first to show that the *tissues use up oxygen* and give off carbon dioxide.

He was a truly brilliant biologist. His experiment with frogs is admirably described by Joseph Bellina and Josleen Wilson (Penguin's *The Fertility Handbook*) as follows:

In 1775 he came up with a colourful experiment. Spallanzani dressed up a bevy of male frogs in little taffeta trousers. He then put the frogs together with female frogs. The male frogs clasped the females in amorous embrace and released their sperm. Instead of falling upon the female's deposit of eggs, the semen was caught in the froggy pants. When eggs failed to produce tadpoles, the inventive Italian knew he was onto something. He collected some of the frog semen from the trousers and mixed it with the female eggs. The eggs became fertilized.

Spallanzani himself did not make the obvious connection because he allowed his priestly background to override his scientific judgement. In fact, he concluded that there was an embryo of a tadpole already existing inside each egg and that the seminal fluid was no more than an activator in making the tadpole grow. We now know that this is not strictly so, thanks to later studies by Hafez, Petrucci, Steptoe and Edwards. But he went a very long way indeed. On 7 May 1780, he discovered that an infinitely small amount of semen sufficed for fecundation. Much earlier than that, in 1771, he applied his mind to the action that the heart had on circulation and two years later he undertook his studies on rotifera. In his manuscripts for May 1781 are to be found a proposal for 161 new tests on the artificial fecundation of frogs.

680   His were the first experiments and deductions on the subject of ovulation.

For example, SPALLANZANI wrote on 2 April 1780 'it becomes clear that the ova are not fecundated in the womb; that the sperm cells after emission remain apt for fecundation for a certain time, that the vesicular fluid fecundates as well as the seminal, that wine and vinegar are opposed to fecundation'.

681/2 He also carried out experiments on salamanders and he was the first to record the now well-established fact that if you cut a salamander's leg off, it will re-grow; and it will do that more than once.

683   Spallanzani was a very versatile scientist: in 1792 he published a work on vulcanology in which he describes the Italian volcanoes (Etna, Stromboli, Vesuvius and Vulcano) and he can certainly be termed a pioneer in the subject of vulcanology for which he suffered, physically, more than once; he was burnt whilst measuring the flow of lava and he was overcome by fumes on Mount Etna. (Bruno)

Over 200 years ago, and well in advance of modern scientific developments of the past few years, Spallanzani contributed profoundly to the question of whether spontaneous generation of life exists. He was elected a Fellow of The Royal Society in 1768.

684   SPALLANZANI was also the first to obtain gastric juice for analysis. He did this by tying a sponge on a piece of string and then allowing it to be swallowed (Morton's 981). Finally, we owe to him the first determination of blood pressure.

685   Francesco GENNARI (1750-1797) was the first to demonstrate the laminar structure of the cerebral cortex discovering in 1776 what became known as 'Gennari's Stria', otherwise 'the line of Gennari' (Morton's 1384).

686   Michele Vincenzo Giacinto MALACARNE, published in 1776 in Turin the first detailed account of the anatomy of the cerebellum, creating the use of such terms as 'tonsil', 'pyramid', 'lingula' and 'uvula' (Morton's 1382).

687   Paolo MASCAGNI (born Pisa in 1752) wrote his *Anatomia Universale*. This is a record as the largest of all medical books in format (Morton's 409).

688   Antonio SCARPA (1750-1832) was the first to introduce the concept of arteriosclerosis.

689/90 Giuseppe Angelo FONZI (1768-1840) produced the *first sets of individual porcelain teeth* mounted on a base and also discovered the means of partially imitating a semi-transparent tint for teeth.

691/2 Giuseppe BARONIO was the first to carry out scientific research in his history of plastic surgery which was published in Milan in 1804 under the title *Degli Innesti Animali*. He was also the first to attempt transplantation and experimental surgery in animals (Morton's 5736).

693   Agostino BASSI (born Mairago in 1773) was the first to demonstrate the parasitic nature of the muscardine disease of silkworms and is generally regarded as the founder of the doctrine of pathogenic micro-organisms. Ac-

cording to Morton's 2532, 'he is rather neglected by medical historians'.

694 It is recorded (see Charles Panati) that whilst the first scientific trials with fluoridated drinking water took place in America in 1915, the idea comes from Italy. 'In 1802, in several regions surrounding Naples, Italian dentists observed yellowish/brown spots on their patients' teeth.' They noticed that those who had such spotted teeth had no cavities and they attributed that to an interaction between 'natural variations in human tooth enamel and a high level of fluorides occurring in local soil and water'. So much so, that by the middle of the nineteenth century both in Italy and in France dentists were suggesting, though perhaps not many believed them, that from an early age one should suck lozenges made with fluoride and sweetened with honey. . . . .

695 In 1809, Luigi ROLANDO (born Turin in 1773) recorded his discovery of the fibrous processes of the brain and identified the 'sulcus' namely the rather marked fissure on the outside of the cerebral hemispheres dividing the frontal from the parietal lobe, which even today takes his name.

696/9 Prior to that ROLANDO had published in 1809 in Sassari a book in which he describes what have since become known as 'Rolando's substance' and 'Rolando's tubercle'. He gave the first description of ablation experiments for brain localization. He was also the first to allocate motor activity to the cerebral hemispheres (Morton's 1388).

700 To Bartolomeo PANIZZA (1785-1867), we owe the localization

of the visual function in the posterior part of the cerebellum.

701 In 1835, Filippo PACINI (born Pistoia) discovered the corpuscles of the digital nerves that are nowadays known as *Pacinian corpuscles.*

702 In 1852, PACINI began studying the pathology of cholera and shortly thereafter he identified the *vibrios of cholera* as bacteria.

His contemporaries, however, did not attach much significance to what he was doing. It was left to R. Koch in 1884 to identify finally the bacillus of cholera and to earn a Nobel Prize for doing so.

703 In 1850, Angelo RUFFINI (born Arquata del Tronto) described the *endings* that are known by his name in nerves, ligaments, joints and subcutaneous tissue.

704 In 1851, the Marquis Alfonso CORTI (born Gambarana PV) was the first to describe a fundamental part of the inner ear which is now known as the organ of Corti.

705 Cecilio FOLLI (born Modena) was the first to describe accurately and exhaustively the structure of the ear.

706/7 More specifically, FOLLI discovered the long process of the malleus, he accurately discussed the general configuration of the middle ear, identifying both *round and oval windows*, and he delineated the three *ossicles* (with the so-called fourth ossicle, the semi-circular canals and the cochlea) (Morton's 1542).

708/14 Francesco RIZZOLI (1809-1880) was a famous surgeon at Bologna who introduced a *com-*

pressor for aneurysms, a tracheotome, cystotome, lithotrite, enterotome, osteoclast and performed *acupressure* as early as 1854 (Morton's 5610).

716 In 1862, Pietro PELLIZZARI (1823-92), provided for the first time truth of the possibility of the transmission of syphilis by blood transfusion (Morton's 2388).

716/7 Giulio BIZZOZERO (born Varese in 1846) gave the blood platelets their name and was the first to identify the part played by platelets in blood coagulation (Morton's 881). He also discovered the haemopoietic properties of bone marrow.

These are the only two 'firsts' that Morton's records. No mention is made of the fact that Hayem claimed the discovery of platelets as his own, quite wrongly, as the *American Journal of Pathology*, Volume 92, 1978, page 776, and *The Lancet* of 7 April 1984, page 804, confirm.

718/20 BIZZOZERO was also a great histologist and there are other 'firsts' that have to bear his name, namely:
1. The construction, in the late 1860s, of an instrument which he called '*cromo-citometro*', which served the purpose of establishing the relationship between the content of haemoglobin and the transparency of blood diluted with saline, which he used in cooperation with his compatriot Golgi (q.v.)
2. His evolution, at about the same time, of a new system of *violet staining of bacteria*, and
3. His classification of the reproductive ability of cells as labile, stable and permanent which, as every medical student knows, is still current.

721 BIZZOZERO's major claim to fame, however, is related to what is termed a modern discovery, but which is a 're-discovery' – in connection with gastric ulcers. In 1983, two Australian doctors, Robin Warren and Barry Marshall, of the Royal Perth Hospital, reported in the *Lancet* of 4 June the existence of 'unidentified curved bacilli on the gastric epithelium in active chronic gastritis'. As a result, the modern cure of gastric ulcers no longer relies on chemical powders, drinks, and other forms of treatment or diet restrictions, but merely on the elimination of the helicobacter pylori. The first description of the helicobacter species in the stomach of a mammal was made on 18 March 1892 by Giulio Bizzozero at a lecture that he gave at a meeting of the Medical Academy of Turin. This is recorded at some length, together with the relevant bibliography, in Volume 1, No 1, 1996, of the magazine *Helicobacter*.

Bizzozero was a much under-rated scientist. His papers were published in Italian, rather than German, French or English, and even though the Helicobacter Paper did emerge in German in 1893, in the *Archiv fur Mikroskopische Anatomie*, published by Springer in Berlin, the English-speaking world had some difficulty even in acknowledging his work on platelets (although the *Lancet* carried a full page report on his work in the 21 January 1882 edition, no sources were given for the information on Bizzozero's studies).

On 3 December 2005, the two Australian doctors mentioned above received the Nobel Prize for Medicine. No mention was made on that occasion of Bizzozero's discovery.

722/3 Angelo MOSSO (1846-1910) invented the ergograph, an instrument to measure muscular fatigue. He showed that fatigue in the muscles was due to the creation of a toxin produced by muscular contraction. His name is associated with careful *investigations of breathing at high altitudes* and the effect of such breathing on heart movement.

724 **Luigi Maria BOSSI (born Malnate VA in 1859) was the first to use the method of induction of premature labour by means of the forced dilation of the cervix (Morton's 6201).**

725/8 In 1873, Camillo GOLGI (born Cortena) (PV) commenced his studies of the nervous system and *discovered the silver nitrate* method of staining nerve tissue. He also identified the *Golgi nerve cell*, the *Golgi tendon organ* as well as the *Golgi apparatus*. He was awarded the Nobel Prize in 1906, for Cytology.

729/30 GOLGI's work was truly revolutionary. From his discovery of the nitrate impregnation staining method (1873) to that of the *nervous tendon spindle (1888), on to the division of tendon cells by 'arborescence'* in 1898, his contribution to medical science was exceptional.

731/3 GOLGI was a scientist who made possible for the first time a clear conception of the whole of the nervous system. Apart from his studies of nerves, he was also the first to differentiate between the *tertian and quartan parasites* in malaria by the periods of their respective developments, showing how they differed. He also discussed at length the action of *quinine* on parasites and on fevers caused by them (Morton's 1277).

More topical, perhaps, in the twenty-first century are his studies of the central nervous system, which some have described as 'seminal'. They clearly contributed to the development of the more modern anti-depressants such as Selective Serotonin Reuptake Inhibitors (SSRIs). In 1994, to honour him, a 750 lira stamp was issued in Rome.

He owes much to the work he carried out in the laboratory of experimental pathology directed by Giulio Bizzozero, referred to above, one of whose nieces, Lina Aletti, he married.

734 **Luigi Maria CONCALO (born Padova in 1825) was the first to describe in 1881 the tubercular inflammation of the serous membranes and gave his name to 'Concalo's Disease'.**

735 In 1884, Edoardo BASSINI (born in Pavia 1844) carried out the first surgical operation on inguinal hernia, developing the technique which, ever since that day, is tied to his name, and establishing the principle of the surgical reconstruction of tissues.

736/7 BASSINI had studied in London during his formative years, but the Bassini method of operating on hernias is now renowned the world over. He also developed special surgical techniques for nasal polyps and certain aspects of hysterectomies. He was made a Senator in 1904. The authority is: pp. 144-145 *Grande Dizionario Enciclopedico* and *Dizionario Enciclopedico dell Italiano.*

738 Vincenzo CERVELLO (born Palermo in 1854) was the first to introduce in 1884 paraldehyde into therapeutics as a narcotic (Morton's 1877).

739   The principle of bacterial antagonism was stated in 1885 by Arnaldo CANTANI (see Roy Porter, op.cit.).

740   In 1889, Carlo FORLANINI (born Milan) devised the first pneumothorax to cure congenital tuberculosis.

He had interrupted his medical studies to fight in Garibaldi's army. An author (Thomas Dormandy, op. cit. p. 254) has described his papers as 'full of bold insights and audacious (if usually unfeasible) proposals'.
His work on the pneumothorax was continued by his compatriot Maurizio Ascoli.

741   The linking of human malaria to the anopheles mosquito is due to Giovanni GRASSI, who established it in 1891 working with his fellow Italian, Amico Bignami. This is admittedly a controversial discovery because Ronald Ross claimed it as his, denouncing the 'Italian pirates', and got a Nobel Prize for it in 1902.

The award of the Nobel Prize to Ross outraged the Italians and embittered Grassi — not an unusual situation for Italians, as we have seen with Meucci for the 'phone — who did not get any reward for his work.
An English writer (see Roy Porter, op. cit.) has endeavoured to put the record straight by stating 'certainly Ross reached the conclusion before Grassi that mosquitos transmitted malaria but Grassi first identified anopheles as the agent of transmission and elucidated the complete sequence of steps in the life-cycle of the parasite'. I suppose they ought both to have got the Nobel prize!

742   In 1872, Luigi ARMANI

showed conclusively how tubercules could develop in animals inoculated from the tuberculous lesion of a recently dead patient (see *The White Death – A History of Tuberculosis*, Thomas Dormandy, the Hambledon Press, London, 1999, p. 132).

743   Emilio RESPIGHI provided in 1893 the first description of hyperkeratosis excentrica, porokeratosis (Morton's 4115).

744   Prospero MANDOSIO published in 1896 the first book on the lives of papal physicians (Morton's 6703).

745   At the end of the nineteenth century, Enrico STASSANO, the brother of Ernesto Stassano (q.v.) was the first to re-discover and describe in detail the virus of syphilis, which he called 'spirochaeta pallida'.

746   He is on record as suggesting that one way of reducing epidemics of typhoid was to boil milk at very high temperatures. The milk that was thus boiled in his time, namely the first decade of the twentieth century, became known as 'stassanizzato' milk. It is not too clear how the process of boiling milk at high temperatures later acquired the description 'pasteurization', clearly derived from the French scientist Pasteur's name. Technically, however, Stassano got there first.

747   In 1896, the sphygmomanometer was invented by an Italian doctor, Scipione RIVA ROCCI.

748   In a book published in Florence in 1898, Giuliano VANGHETTI (1861-1940) is stated to be the first to suggest the use of muscu-

lature remaining above the amputated stump to form a motor unit for artificial limbs (Morton's 4474).

749 His compatriot, Antonio CERCI (1852-1920), was the first to carry out surgical interventions on the lines suggested by Vanghetti (Morton's 4475). His work was improved upon by Vincenzo Putti (Morton's 4477).

750 Gaetano RUMMO (1853-1917) was the first to draw attention in a paper published in Palermo in 1898 to the downward displacement of the heart, thus tying his name to 'Rummo's disease'.

751/2 Guido BANTI (1850-1925) apart from describing the pathological changes that occur in the spleen as a result of anaemia, was the first to give an account of cirrhosis of the liver as a sequel to an earlier stage of spleen anaemia, thus providing the description of 'Banti's Syndrome'.

753 Alessandro CODIVILLA recorded in 1905 the first known attempt at a lengthening of limbs (Morton's 4375).

754 In 1907, Francesco CENCI wrote a book in which he recorded the first use by him of convalescent serum in prophylaxis against measles (Morton's 5447).

755 Early this century, the scientist, Count Aldo CASTELLANI, identified the streptococcus in sleeping sickness (see Roy Porter, op. cit.).

Morton's (5276) records that Castellani 'failed to appreciate the significance of his discovery, despite having found the trypanosoma gambiense in the human cerebral spine fluid'. Fortunately for the reader, we ourselves shall not get involved in any discussion relating to this aspect of the matter, and our sole concern is to record the arguments.

756 Despite this particular failing mentioned by Morton's, there is no doubt that CASTELLANI was the first to determine that toxoplasmosis, which until then was believed to be solely a disease of animals, could in fact be carried by humans (Morton's 5535).

757 Guido FANCONI (1892-1979) gave his name to 'Fanconi's Syndrome', namely the congenital hypoplasia of the bone marrow as a familial disease (Morton's 3142).

758 Carlo CRUZIO was the first to differentiate between scleroderma and the three ailments it used to be confused with, namely leprosy, ichtyosis and keloid (Morton's 4014).

759 In 1937, the first applications of electroconvulsive therapy were elaborated by two Italian doctors, Ugo CERLETTI and Lucio BINI as a treatment for schizophrenia.

760 Ettore BOCCA (born 1914) provided the first test for disorders of the central auditory function.

761 Renato DULBECCO (born 1914) shared a Nobel Prize in 1975 with D.N. Baltimore and H.M. Terrin for his discoveries concerning the interaction between tumour viruses and the genetic material of the cell.

762 In 1944, the naturalized Italian pharmacist (originally of French/Swiss parents) Daniele BOVET discovered mepyramine, following it up with investigations that resulted in the production of a synthetic form of the South Amer-

ican Indian poison known as cur-are. For his work in the fields of physiology and medicine he was awarded the Nobel Prize in 1957 (see Nobel Prizes heading).

763 To him we also owe the opening of the way to the discovery of the important anti-histamine drugs of which we are quite often reminded when we suffer either from sinusitis or hay fever. His discovery had a revolutionary effect on anaesthetic practice.

764 As recently as 1950, Rocco de NICOLA provided the first implan-tation of silicone rubber to replace the urethra (Morton's 4203).

765 Claudio FERMI was the first to use the chemical treatment of tissue suspension of fixed rabies virus for the preparation of vaccine which bears his name (Fermi's Vaccine) (Morton's 5484).

766 In 1990, a psychiatrist at the University of Pisa, Donatella MAR-AZZITI, discovered that so-called obsessive compulsive disorders are linked to the brain messenger che-mical known as serotonin.

767 It was announced on 18 April 2005 that Professor Cesare GALLI of the University of Bologna had, for the second time, succeeded in cloning, in Cremona, a champion race stallion. A predecessor in the cloning system, a filly called 'Pro-metea', had successfully been pro-duced two years previously. The newly cloned animal weighed 42 kilos.

METALLURGY

768 In 1350, gold wire was first made in Italy.

769 In the sixteenth century, Van-noccio BIRINGUCCIO (born in Siena) wrote the first book on the subject. He was particularly inter-ested in the application of metal fusion techniques to cannons and other weapons and he wrote what is probably the first book on such applications, namely his *Pirotechnia*. He described in detail the mining and industrial techniques of his day. (Incidentally, the word cannon comes from the Italian 'cannone' which means a large bamboo.)

770 BIRINGUCCIO was also among the first to provide cannons with ornamentation (scrolls, figures, etc.) and in 1540 was the first to make mention of boring machines for cannon.

771 In 1805, BRUGNATELLI was the first to gild silver coins.

NOBEL PRIZES

Italian performance as far as winning Nobel Prizes is concerned is indifferent, if not poor. To date, we have a total of fourteen prize winners.

Compared to Britain which has eighty-one and to the United States of America which has 150, Italy's results are not so impressive. I would make two observa-tions.

1. The Swedish Institute and the Nobel Foundation started awarding their prizes in 1901. By then, most of the spade-work in the fields of universal

knowledge had already been done by the Italians. In all fairness one may ask the question 'How many prizes would Italy have got if the Nobel system had come into operation in the year 1001 instead of in 1901?'

2. No Nobel Prizes are awarded for mathematics. It is conceivable that under this heading Italy might have picked up a further three prizes. Even so, I suppose that what the following list shows is that the Italians of the past centuries were much better than those of the twentieth century. Evidently, quality is deteriorating.

1906	Giosué CARDUCCI – Poetry
1906	Camillo GOLGI – (Cytology) – Medicine
1906	Ernesto MONETA – Peace
1909	Guglielmo MARCONI – Physics (Radio)
1929	Grazia DELEDDA – Literature
1934	Luigi PIRANDELLO – Literature
1938	Enrico FERMI – Physics
1957	Daniele BOVET – Physiology (synthetic curare)
1959	Emilio Gino SEGRE – Physics
1959	Salvatore QUASIMODO – Poetry
1963	Giulio NATTA – Chemistry
1975	Eugenio MONTALE – Poetry
1984	Carlo RUBBIA – Physics
1985	Franco MODIGLIANI – Economics
1986	Rita LEVI-MONTALCINI – Physiology
1997	Dario FO – Literature

PHYSICS

This section includes such diverse ideas or discoveries as diving, incubators and electricity. There is no real causal connection between them, but it was a matter of convenience to encompass them all under a single heading.

I must confess that in compiling the Physics entries I experienced my greatest surprise. I remember that when I was still very young and studying in Rome the then Fascist government had caused to be published a book entitled *Da Leonardo a Marconi* which listed all the achievements of the Italian people in the artistic and scientific world. Regrettably, my recollection of it is limited to the two names of the title and I never realized until I embarked upon the present exercise how noticeable the Italian contribution has been in the scientific field. I began to appreciate it a little more when trying to ascertain what had been done in the fields of chemistry and medicine. But when I came to physics I was very pleasantly surprised.

There are, to my mind, four Italians whose names stand supreme in the world of knowledge and art. They are in order of seniority: Leonardo Da Vinci, Michelangelo, Galileo and Verdi. They represent what is best and most noble in Italy and, in particular, Leonardo and Galileo have made a contribution to science which can never be equalled. This is not to minimize the scientific impact of the four subsequent Italian Nobel Prize-winners, namely Marconi, Fermi, Rubbia and Levi-Montalcini. But when you consider Leonardo or Galileo, you are almost referring to something superhuman. Because of this I have listed their contributions separately.

However, before we get to them consider the following facts:

772 **The first recorded application of a cam in the Western world occurred in a fulling mill on the River Serchio in Tuscany roundabout the year 1000.**

773/5 **In the early part of the fourteenth century, Giacomo DONDI of the Dondi Family to which reference is made elsewhere in this** book (otherwise known as de Dondi), a physician and astronomer, wrote his *Tractatus de Causa Salsedinis* (literally, a treatise on the cause of salinity). The text establishes three firsts: (1) the first discussion on the salinity of the oceans; (2) the first suggestion that salts could be extracted from mineral waters for medicinal purposes; (3) more importantly, that the sun, the moon and the planets have an effect on the tides here on earth.

776   In the early part of the fifteenth century, Marco ZIMARA was the first to devise a machine that recycled wind energy by using a windmill with sails. The idea was sound but he was unable to derive sufficient power from it, probably because of gear reduction difficulties.

777   In 1420, Giovanni da FONTANA sketched jet-propelled fish, birds and rabbits. He proposed the use of jet propulsion for measuring water depths and air heights.

778   In 1490, Francesco di GIORGIO described a ball and chain centrifugal governor.

779   Five years later, di GIORGIO designed jet-propulsion petards on wheels and floats.

780   He was also the first to sketch a boat with paddle-wheels, anticipating the paddle-steamer.

LEONARDO DA VINCI (1452-1519)

Leonardo was born in Vinci in 1452, quite coincidentally in the same year as the person who was to become one of his patrons, Ludovico il Moro (Ludwig the Moor – in this sense 'Moro' is used as the 'dark one'.) the Master of Milan, whose

service Leonardo joined in 1482 (staying seventeen years). For Ludovico il Moro he built canals and war machines but one must not forget his artistic bent. Leonardo survived Ludovico il Moro by eleven years.

At the age of fifteen he had joined the School of Lorenzo il Magnifico as a sculptor and in 1498 he had illustrated Luca Pacioli's Essential Book on Mathematics *De Divina Proportione.*

LEONARDO was the first man to:

781   Provide the first study of mechanisms as a separate concept to that of a machine. Before him, machines were designed and built. He was the first to study mechanisms *per se.*

Furthermore, his notebooks contain the first systematic study of friction. Indeed, his graphic representations of his enquiries are also valuable for their aesthetic qualities and technological ingenuity.

782   Work, experiment and design on diving. For example, he actually designed a diving tube and suit.

783   Analyse the flight of birds.

784   Analyse the rectineal propagation of light.

785   Design a dredging machine.

786   Design a screw-operated automatic printing press.

787   Design a machine for cutting screws.

788   Design a paddle-boat long before those that started plying the Mississippi.

789   Design a webbed glove to facilitate movement through water

thus anticipating the idea of using the same system for feet propulsion.

790 Sketch spur, bevel and worm gears.

791 Design roller ball and bearings.

792 Study fluid-flow engineering.

793 Design a propeller (in reality, an endless screw which if turned rapidly would rise into the air: the principle adopted by helicopters).

794 Design the first porous hygrometer.

795 Design a rotating double crane.

He anticipated Clerk Maxwell's findings on electromagneticism by describing air as being made up of rays of light crossing one another without interfering with path lines so as to form a predictable pattern.

796 Carry out underwater exploration.

797 Design a gas and a water turbine.

798 Lay the foundations of photometry.

799 Design a tank with a small cannon.

800 Design a three-tier moveable machine gun.

801 Design a multiple crossbow.

802 Draw a repeater-type gun.

803 Design a bicycle.

This is a blunt statement, for there continues to remain some doubt on whether the design which is found in

the *Codex Atlanticus* at folio 48 r.b. is his or is merely a later design by Pompeo Leoni.

804 Develop a rope-making machine.

805 Design a retractable undercarriage.

806 Anticipate explosive bullets for firearms.

807 Design a machine for the transmission of motion to an axle, anticipating the rear axle of a motor car.

808 Describe a submarine.

809 Sketch the first tensile-testing machine.

810 Devise a handsaw for cutting marble.

811 Sketch a disc-grinder.

812 Sketch internal and external grinders and polishers.

813 Design a parachute.

814 Sketch and describe the use of airbags (*baghe di vento*) as a safety aid when flying.

815 Design a mechanism for converting alternating motion to continuous motion.

816 Design and build the first 'modern' distillation plant.

817 Build the first automotive four wheel vehicle anticipating (without the internal combustion engine, of course. . . . .) the modern motor car (see *Codex Atlanticus* folio 296 v.a., and folios 812 r 17 and 114 r).

818 Describe capillary action for

the first time, in or about the year 1500.

819   He was the first to design a swing bridge.

820   Devise an efficient system for creating the spark that would allow flintlock guns to fire.

821   Describe how to make a wax cast of the brain (of an ox). This act is considered as the initiation of a technique that became widely known, and practised and, indeed, accepted, namely the injection of solid matter for the purpose of examining the form of body cavities.

822   His studies on the effect of vortices in fluids, the first known, both by reference to air, water and blood circulation have all been confirmed by modern science.

823   He was the first to build a model of the heart and of the aorta. His sketches for them correspond exactly to what we know today and what is confirmed on a regular basis whenever any surgery is carried out to the heart. The extent of his impressive genius is highlighted by these designs, especially if we bear in mind that he did not have access to scientific aids such as X-rays and magnetic imaging.

And just to recap Leonardo firsts listed under other headings, he was the first to:

- Design a flying machine.
- Elaborate a 'camera oscura'.
- Invent lock gates.
- Describe a fusee for clocks.
- Invent the airgun.

824   The design of the gearing shown in the *Madrid I Code* at Folio 10 resulted in the Chiaravalle Clock, the first to show hours, minutes as well as the position of the sun and the phases of the moon.

825   As Charles Panati has recorded, we owe him what can best be described as: 'history's first high-intensity lamp. A glass cylinder containing olive oil and a hemp wick was immersed in a large glass globe filled with water, which significantly magnified the flame.'

Leonardo's genius was of a unique nature, his imagination equally so, his curiosity boundless. He could take the same trouble over the human body as he did over the drawing of a leaf or a rock. His interests were extraordinarily wide-ranging; from making wax impressions of the interior of the human brain to drawing fairly accurately a womb with an embryo inside. The drawing of the mitral valve which Leonardo contributed to the 'paper museum' (see the heading 'Accademia dei Lincei') is so accurate and perfectly detailed that it has enabled modern cardiac surgeons to make an incision which is of great help to them in heart surgery, so much so that it is now technically known as 'The Da Vinci Cut'.

His concern with causation and the way things work is exceptionally modern: his confidence in his ability to understand anything ran counter to the then teaching of the Church. Whether considering why leaves are arranged in a particular manner on a stalk or what the effect was of the movement of the wings of a dragonfly, in anticipating to some extent both Copernicus and Galileo, he pioneered studies on the nature of sound and light, hydraulics, optics, meteorology, the use of air as a source of power and innumerable war machines.

It has been suggested (see *The Times*, 15 March 2004) that Leonardo went as far as inventing a form of plastic similar to Bakelite, even in colours. . . . . Obviously the technology was not available at the time to make his invention useful on a large scale. The leader writer on that date was prompted to recall Elbert Hubbard's observation that: 'One machine can do the work of fifty ordinary men, but no machine can do the work of one extraordinary man.'

It is interesting to observe that modern scientists have, over the past few decades, gone back to his designs and sketches in an endeavour to ascertain to what extent they were workable, engineering drawings, rather than expressions of his fertile imagination.

In 2003, a wind machine was built in England copying his designs. It was found that it could rise to sixty feet, travel one hundred yards and stay in the air for about a minute, operated like a hang-glider by an experienced woman flyer.

Admittedly some of his designs, when put into practice towards the end of the twentieth century, have not always worked; but it has been said, and I believe correctly, that this was probably due not to the fact that the design in itself was faulty but rather that the construction of the relevant gadget was not as Leonardo had envisaged it. This, in fact, happened with the crossbow: a very big one was built but when the required tension was achieved, it broke.

Water and air seem to have fascinated him. His approach to fluid dynamics has still not ceased to puzzle modern scientists. Over five centuries ago, his contribution to the development of gliders, parachutes, the helicopter and retractable landing gears and wheels is such that one can only consider him truly unique. It is impossible to compare him with anybody.

He has been called the essential 'Renaissance man' simply because of the breadth of his interests which ranged from analysing the possibility (which he denied) of squaring the circle, to his studies of optics, to making maps of Europe, studying clocks and establishing a primacy at the time in the field of military engineering.

(The maps prepared by Leonardo for Ludwig the Moor in his Milan period are the precursors of modern topography.)

The changes he made to the design of Archimedes' screw and his design of a barometer anticipated later developments.

More particularly, although in the text I attribute the invention of the modern barometer to Torricelli, there is no doubt that Leonardo's barometer, consisting of wax on one side and cotton wool on the other, is a major contribution to horology.

I have recorded the more commonly held views of Leonardo's achievements but they are not shared by some, and more particularly not by Terence Kealey, Vice Chancellor of the University of Buckingham. He disputes a number of Leonardo's 'discoveries'. For instance, he claims that only twenty-five years after Leonardo's death, Vesalius's dissections and anatomical sketches proved that they contained a number of errors. As to the invention of the submarine, namely Leonardo's 'method for staying under water', Terence Kealey maintains that it was another Italian, Cesare Cesariano, who invented the submarine by submerging it in Lake Como in 1508, Leonardo having obviously only plagiarized that design.

Kealey gives Leonardo no credit for the aerial screw either and ascribes the invention of a flying machine to Roger Bacon of Oxford.

As to the parachute, he claims it wasn't Leonardo's creation but that of one

Arman Firman who had jumped off a minaret in Cordoba, Spain, so that 'every one of Leonardo's designs can be traced to an earlier progenitor'.

I mention the above for the sake of the record.

GALILEO GALILEI (1564-1642)

Galileo was born in Pisa in 1564 and died in Arcetri in 1642. In fact, Galileo was born more or less on the day when Michelangelo died and died in the year that Newton was born.

13 March 1610 saw the publication of his book *Sidereus Nuncius* in which he set out most of the discoveries he had made in the sky and, effectively, laid the foundations for the antagonism towards him by the Catholic Church and his trial for heresy twenty-three years later.

Galileo was the founder of modern mechanics and experimental physics. Most students remember him for re-stating in scientific terms the argument as to whether the sun rotated round the earth or vice versa, but he did much more. He was a great astronomer and a real scientist and his list of firsts is truly outstanding:

His primary merit, some might term it his essential intuition, was to decide that mathematical concepts could and should be applied to physical phenomena establishing a framework within which both mathematicians and philosophers, especially Descartes and Locke, could operate.

826   Galileo was the first man to construct and use a workable telescope.

827   He was the first man to consider the implications of the movements of the pendulum. In 1583, he discovered that the oscillation period of a pendulum is virtually independent of the amplitude of the swing.

828   He was the first to state informally the principles embodied in Newton's first two laws of motion. (Effectively, he discovered that acceleration, which was previously believed to be circular, occurred in a straight line.)

829   In 1604, he proved the law of uniformly accelerated motion (thus disproving Aristotle who had stated that heavier bodies fell faster than lighter ones).

830   He was the first to prove that air has weight.

831   He was the first to discover and observe the four satellites of Jupiter.

832   In 1610, he was the first to observe that the planet Mars was not, as had previously been believed, round.

833   He anticipated the law of inertia.

834   He constructed lenses for his telescope and invented the microscope.

835   He set out the law of freefall.

836   In 1610, he observed Saturn and started his study of the phases of Venus which spread over many years.

837   He was the first to establish the law of parabolic fall, although studies on the theme were made before him by the mathematician Bonaventura Cavalieri.

838   He was the first to establish the concept of energy.

839   He was the first to analyse the principle of odds when playing dice.

840   He was the first to use the term 'probability' in a mathematical sense.

841   In 1610, he explained sunspots, which he had discovered, as solar phenomena: by measuring their motion he proved that the sun was rotating.

842   He was the first to set out the concept of relative motion.

843   In 1592, he invented the thermoscope, forerunner of the thermometer.

844   The expanses he saw on the Moon he thought were water and he called them 'maria', i.e. seas. They said he was mad!

845   He was able to show that, apart from air resistance, a projectile's actual velocity would remain constant. His discoveries enabled Newton to restate the principles of gravitation.

846   He can be deservedly described as the 'first scientist' for his application of theory to practice.

847   He was the first to elaborate a device known as a compass, namely a graduated metal instrument that could be used to calculate the elevation of guns. Ultimately, although in a different context, he could be said to have anticipated the creation of the pocket calculator.

848   His book, *Two New Sciences* was the first *modern scientific* textbook. In it he explained how the universe was governed by understandable laws and driven by forces that could be mathematically determined. He was the first to set out the concept of relative motion.

849   He was the first to set out the

probability theory in a paper by the title 'Sopra le Scoperte dei Dadi' (on playing dice) which, against his will, he was forced to write by his employer the Grand Duke of Tuscany (see P.S. Kruger, *Industrial Engineering – Rooting for Roots, Hankering for Heroes*, p. 140).

He revised and improved Leonardo's hygrometer, which was later to be improved again by Francesco FOLLI.

There is no doubt that Galileo was one of the greatest Italians who ever lived and that the debt that the scientific world owes him is enormous. Again, what did his compatriots do to him? The Church banned him to Arcetri and in 1633 he had to recant. Italian boys are taught that even after he recanted he kept saying *Eppur si muove* (and yet it moves) referring to the earth, and maybe he did say it. But for practical purposes he was treated in such a manner that his recantation marks the end of scientific development in Italy for about 200 years.

In fact, the Catholic Church dealt with him by the same constraints that had been applied thirty years earlier to Giordano Bruno, who was eventually burned at the stake.

He had the ability to combine theory with practice and he studied projectiles for his employer, the Grand Duke of Tuscany.

Galileo had considerable influence during his own lifetime. In 1611, for example, there appeared the first published poem of John Donne under the title 'An Anatomy of the World'. It was a disturbing poem which was directly inspired by Galileo's demonstration that the world was no longer the centre of the universe. This caused John Donne to remark that the world was 'All in pieces, all coherence gone.'

Two further contributions are also

sometimes attributed to Galileo, but I believe them to be doubtful. One is that he discovered that the Milky Way consisted of a multitude of separate stars and the other is that he invented the pendulum. As regards the former, it is possible that this was believed before him and as regards the latter there is the argument that its inventor may have been the Dutchman Huyghens. In the circumstances, I have not recorded either as a first.

By applying mathematics to physics he contributed to scientific development generally. I would suggest that Descartes's philosophy could not have developed without Galileo's inspiration; his studies also influenced the English philosopher John Locke.

(It took the church just over three and a half centuries to recant in the same way as they had asked Galileo to do. In 1992, Pope John Paul II officially conceded that Galileo was right when he stated that the earth revolves round the sun, rather than otherwise.)

So much for the great Italian firsts in Physics. Now to some lesser ones:

850   The true theory of the rainbow was explained by Antonio de DOMINIS in the sixteenth century.

851   In the second half of the seventeenth century, Antonio VALLISNIERI provided the 'first definitive statement on the origin of springs' when he described how spring water gushes from mountains as a result of rain and snow falls.

852   Also in the sixteenth century, Geronimo FABRIZZI was the first to apply mechanical principles to the anatomy of muscular movements (v. Girolamo Fabrizio).

853   The precursor of the modern drilling machine in elementary and cumbersome form is said to have been created in the sixteenth century by an Italian from Bologna called Taddeo CAVALLINI.

854   A bucket-type dredger was patented in 1561 by VENTURINO of Venice.

855   In 1595, Fausto Venanzio di SEBENICO designed a cart which was fitted with a very primitive form of shock absorber.

856/7 Prior to that, in 1551, Girolamo CARDANO, who was also a mathematician, had invented the universal joint or cardan shaft as well as the gimbal suspension.

It was Hooke who later developed a more modern form of the universal joint devised by Cardano and, as a result, such a joint is usually referred to in English texts as Hooke's joint.

858   In the sixteenth century, Francesco MAUROLICO, a great optical mathematician, preceded Kepler in many of his ray reflection theories.

859   In 1612, Santorio SANTORIO (born Capodistria) elaborated Galileo's thermoscope to invent the first medical thermometer.

860   SANTORIO was the founder of the modern study of metabolism. He spent most of his life weighing himself and the products of his body, attributing great importance to the individual's pulse rate.

861   At a time when watches had no seconds hand (and probably no minutes hand either) he devised (1602) a method of measuring the pulse not by its rate but by its

strength and rhythm. He devised a machine called a pulsimeter.

Santorio was quite technically minded, since he elaborated machines to weigh the human body and its discharges, he did work on hygrometers and even designed a device for bathing a patient in bed.

862   The first gas turbine (using steam as its medium) was built by Giovanni BRANCA in 1629.

863   In 1630, Bruno CASTELLI and Evangelista TORRICELLI founded modern hydraulics.

864   CASTELLI was the first to measure running water with a water meter.

865   Building upon William Gilbert's experimental work on magnetism, in 1629 Nicoló CABEO, an Italian physicist, was the first to describe electrical repulsion.

866   In 1641, FERDINAND THE SECOND, Grand Duke of Tuscany, developed the first sealed-in liquid glass thermometer by replacing water with wine vinegar. He also developed one of the first chicken incubators.

867   The barometer was invented in 1641 or thereabouts by Evangelista TORRICELLI.

Viviani, a Fellow of The Royal Society (1696), himself an engineer and mathematician of repute, assisted Torricelli in this work.

868   TORRICELLI was the first man to create a sustained vacuum.

Torricelli got to know Galileo in the last few months of his life. It was Galileo who put to him the task of determining why water in a well could not be pushed up more than a certain height. Torricelli determined that it was because of the weight of the atmosphere pressing on the water and he tested his idea by using a tube of mercury.

He was a great mathematician (his is the famous theorem bearing his name that deals with the speed of water); he was an expert on fluid motion and also studied projectiles.

In 1640, he succeeded in grinding telescope lenses which came near to optical perfection.

The perceptive reader will, no doubt, realize how significant the contributions of Galileo and Torricelli (thermometer and barometer) have been in enabling the study of weather patterns to commence. There would be no meteorological science but for these two fundamental discoveries.

869   In 1648, the mathematician, engineer and architect, Alessandro CAPRA (born Cremona) created a machine which, fitted to horse-drawn carriages, calculated the distance travelled in kilometres.

870   In 1660, G.A. BORELLI (born Naples) and V. VIVIANI first measured the velocity of sound by the cannon flash and sound method.

871   In 1660, Francesco Maria GRIMALDI (born Bologna) discovered the diffraction of light.

Grimaldi made it clear that 'light was propagated by reflection, refraction and diffraction'.

872   GRIMALDI was also a good physician and was the first to observe the weak sounds produced by muscle contractions.

But he remains particularly well known for his fundamental experiments in the field of optics.

873 Towards the end of the seventeenth century, Luigi Ferdinando MARSIGLI (1658-1730) otherwise known as Marsili, published his *Histoire Physique de la Mer*, the first complete book dealing with the sea.

874 Apart from that, we owe to him another first, namely the description of a naturalist's dredge. (Bruno)

875 In 1664, Giuseppe CAMPANI (born Castel San Felice) established himself as a technician in lens production. He improved on Torricelli's method and refined the grinding of lenses to such a degree that he managed to build telescopes that were better than those built by Huygens. It was Campani who supplied G.D. Cassini with the telescope that enabled Cassini to study the rotation of Jupiter and Mars and to discover the four satellites of Saturn.

876 In 1678, Stefano LORENZINI, a doctor from Tuscany, published his book titled *Osservazioni Intorno Alle Torpedini*. He gave his name to the 'ampullae', namely electrically sensitive organs which are found on sharks, rays, skates and other members of the elasmobranch family (selachii and amphibians). These are special sensory organs found on the side of such fish.

877 In 1680, Domenico GUGLIELMINI (born Bologna) studied rivers and was the first to understand the equilibrium between water and the resistance of the river-bed to flow. He was the founder of the Italian School of Hydraulics.

Not bad for a researcher who, together with his brother Lorenzo, a mathematician, spent twenty years imprisoned in the fortress at Volterra for his political views. (*Treccani* Vol. XXI, p. 500 and *Britannica*, 11, p. 804).

878 Giovanni Battista VENTURI (born 1746 Bibiano) invented the Venturi Tube, an important instrument in the field of water and aeromechanics as well as acoustics.

879 In 1762, Paolo FRISI (born Milan) wrote the first engineering textbook, 'A Treaty on Rivers and Torrents'.

Alessandro Volta is credited with the discovery of static electricity and the battery elsewhere ('Motor Vehicles', 'Telegraph') but he was a scientist of some resourcefulness.

880/1 In May 1784, VOLTA invented the audiometer and in November of that same year he had discovered the production of hydrogen in organic fermentations.

882 In 1792, Volta constructed his great conductor.

883 During the years 1776-78, Volta was the first to isolate methane gas.

884 Tradition has it that it was Luigi GALVANI experimenting with frogs on the balcony of his house who made the discovery of 'animal' electricity; and there are drawings that show him, a grey-haired gentleman, examining a number of frogs strung up on a metal wire from one end of his balcony to the other.

I am not certain how reliable this story is, but it is a very picturesque one and as such worthy of being retained if not for its factual accuracy, at least because it makes children so much more interested when they first learn about the discovery of electricity by Volta or Galvani as the case may be.

885   In 1771, Luigi GALVANI was able to identify the fact that nerve impulses were a travelling wave with chemical and electrical changes that affected the membrane of the nerve cell. The impulses involved the passage of sodium and potassium ions across the nerve cell membrane.

886   In 1802, Giandomenico RO-MAGNOSI (born Salsomaggiore) observed the magnetic effect of electric currents.

He was not only a scientist but also a lawyer and he reported his discovery that an electric current flowing in a wire affected a nearby magnet in the Gazetta del Trentino on 3 August 1802. He was ignored and it was left to Hans Christian Ørsted in 1820 to be credited with the discovery.

887   In or about 1810, Giovanni BECCARIA (born Mondovi) discovered the electrical stimulation of muscles.

888   In 1820, Macedonio MELLONI (born Parma) discovered that heat rays are also light rays.

889   In 1832, with Leopoldo NOBILI, MELLONI invented the thermo-multiplier. He became a Fellow of The Royal Society in 1839.

890   In 1824, Ignatio LEMENI invented the mechanical wine press operated by rollers or cylinders. Hand-operated presses were known to the Egyptians, who used a wooden type with two screws.

891   Between 1827 and 1828, Francesco Giacomo LARDERELLO

(born Vienna), an Italian nobleman of French extraction, was the first to use on an industrial basis thermal power for the manufacture of boric acid.

He developed the waterpools of Larderello in Maremma (Tuscany) to produce this result and even had ammonium hydrate of boracic acid named after him ('Larderellite').

Further refinements to his technique occurred after his death, thanks to his family and to other Italian scientists. Nowadays, the Japanese, keen as always to develop new sources of electricity, are investigating thermal energy with their customary thoroughness. When, as seems likely, the technique will have been mastered and they and probably the rest of the world will have become less reliant on oil as the major source of supply of electricity, maybe some acknowledgement greater than this writer can provide will be given to the work of Count Larderello.

892/3   Around 1830, Giovanni Battista AMICI (see also 'Botany') built the Amici Prism for prismatic spectroscopes, constructed the first microscope with achromatic lenses and suggested the system of water immersion for improved vision through the achromatic compound microscope (Morton's 266).

894   We are all accustomed to hearing references, in weather forecasts, to anticyclones, whether of the Azores or from elsewhere. The identification of them is thanks to the nineteenth century Italian meteorologist, Luigi de MARCHI.

Chang Heng, a Chinese scholar, is credited with having invented a seismoscope that registered the occurrence of an earthquake, as early as the year 132 and in the seventeenth century a device which involved water spillage caused by the movement of the earth, was evolved in Italy.

895   But it was only in 1855 that Luigi PALMIERI designed the modern form of seismometer, consisting of several 'U' shaped tubes filled with mercury and oriented towards the different points of the compass (see *Britannica*, heading 'Seismograph').

896   The first luminous submersible chronograph capable of resisting to depths of 1,000 metres (3,281 ft) was built in Florence in 1860 by Officine Panerai

897   In 1866, Felice MARCO patented his principle of electric generation by water power.

898   At the Vienna Universal Fayre of 1873, Angiolo MENICI of Livorno exhibited his 'bagno a pioggia' namely the first shower consisting of a machine where, by putting pressure on two foot pedals, the bather could control the amount of water passing through the showerhead; the machine itself was made of detachable pieces which could be carried around.

899   In 1875, Augusto RIGHI (born Bologna), who was Marconi's teacher, discovered that Hertzian waves are also light waves.

Righi was Professor of Experimental Physics at the University of Bologna and was elected to The Royal Society in 1907.

900   To Alessandro CRUTO we owe the invention of the electric bulb with a carbon filament, first exhibited as the result of an experiment carried out by him on 5 May 1880 at Turin University.

His success was endorsed at the Munich Exhibition of 1882. The streets were lit up with his bulbs in 1884, the event ante-dating by eight months the illumination by Edison of Place de la Concorde in Paris. (For authority, v. *Dizionario Biografico degli Italiani* vol. 31.)

901   In 1889, Galileo FERRARIS (born Livorno) discovered alternating current.

902   In 1894, Arturo MALIGRANI invented the phosphorous 'gettering' process to assist in creating a vacuum in electric lamp bulbs.

903   In 1898, Ernesto STASSANO invented the electric arc steel furnace.

904   In 1914, EMANUELLI invented the first oil-filled electric cable of the high-tension type.

905   In 1951, Luigi GEDDA published in Rome, *Studio Dei Gemelli*, the first *comprehensive* scientific study of twins.

906   Emilio Gino SEGRE (born Tivoli) was the co-winner in 1959 of the Nobel Prize for Physics. Together with three other physicists at the University of California at Berkeley, USA (Chamberlain, Wiegand and Ypsilantis) Segre produced technetium, that is to say, the first man-made element not found in nature. In 1940 he discovered astatine and a little later plutonium 239.

8. SPORT & LEISURE

ANIMALS

You may be one of those people who believes that Italians are not too fond of animals; for example, they shoot birds indiscriminately and eat grilled sparrows greedily.

You are quite right, they are not. Do not be misled by the fact that at Crufts in early 1986 the top prize went to a charming Italian lady breeder; it was a one-off. Nor should you be misled by the fact that it is now very popular in Italy to have dogs around the place: they are used mostly as guard dogs and in choosing them people are concerned more about their wealth and possessions and rather less about any affection they may have for animals.

This is understandable. Italy has been until recently, and still is in many areas, an economically poor country. In poor countries, people do not have enough to feed themselves: hence they cannot spare food for their animals. If the animals perform a useful function, then they are cared for; if not, they are disposed of.

Indeed, the animals themselves become food for their keepers. To an Italian an animal, like nature, is merely ancillary to man. Man is the centre of all activity and animals and plants only serve his purpose.

From this follow the many uses to which animals have throughout our history been put as a result of erroneous or superstitious beliefs; snakes and mice killed for their special properties, or, as was done at one stage, dogs cooked in a saucepan in order to cure rickets. Most animals have throughout Italian history been considered as having some special properties.

These beliefs are common to most primitive people. In Asia, for example, some people think that the horns of rhinos have aphrodisiac properties.

There is no sentimentality in the way an Italian looks at animals; particularly in the south, the animals themselves appear to be different. They are thinner, neglected, they look haggard and old; ultimately, they are neither cared for nor fed.

You need a romantic outlook on life to be truly fond of animals and economic pressures are not conducive to a disinterested approach to our four-legged friends in particular. In case you are in doubt, may I remind you that on 18 February 1986 all British newspapers reported the complaint of The Royal Society for the Prevention of Cruelty to Animals that the number of cases of cruelty to animals in Britain had gone up by one-third in the previous year. In 2004, according to the RSPCA, 109,985 complaints were investigated (as against 64,678 in 1985 and 47,362 in 1984).

In 2004, there were 1,665 convictions and in 1985 there were 2,112 convictions for cruelty to animals, a post-war record (in 1984, there had been 1,889). Is it a coincidence that our standards of living dropped in the same period?

I am not trying to blind you with statistics nor am I advertising myself as someone who does not love animals. I have two German shepherd dogs, three cats and a number of other domestic animals, so I record the above with sadness.

The Italian approach to animals is somewhat ambiguous and I think it stems not only from the poverty of the country but also from its cynicism. Animals do not serve a terribly useful purpose unless they work. And I can already hear the protests of animal lovers of Italy that the picture I paint is wrong.

It may be, but it is the picture that I paint. I am comforted in it by the fact that I cannot find many writings in Italian literature that relate to animals and even though the Patron Saint of Italy, St Francis of Assissi, talked to the birds, he was a saint and, according to his preaching, hardly an Italian.

Almost in contradiction to what I have been saying, it is worth recording what is, perhaps, an unexpected item of information: the Italian Society for the Protection of Animals (Ente Nazionale Protezione Animali) was founded in 1871 in Turin by the initiative of Garibaldi, his personal physician Dr Timoteo Rimoldi and Mrs Anna Winter.

You may be wondering what facts of significance relate to this topic. I can find only three, and they are not much to boast about.

907   In 1738, Antonio FRANCONI (born Udine) standardized the diameter of the circus ring at thirteen metres, which is exactly what it is today

908/9 FRANCONI was also the first lion-tamer and the first person to exhibit trained canaries in a circus.

Franconi came from a noble Venetian family and fled to France when he was accused of murder for having killed an opponent in a duel.

He was a famous trick-rider of horses and was assisted by his two sons, one of whom, Victor, established the first open-air Hippodrome in Paris.

The Franconi circus tradition greatly influenced American circuses, especially Barnum.

BOATING

910   In 1300, the first boat race was organized in Venice.

As may be seen from the section 'Ships & Navigation' Italians were from the very inception of their history, competent and innovative sailors.

Just as the Vikings gained the advantage of surprise by the speed of their oarsmen, so the Venetians were able, by their oar power, to transform themselves into a major political and maritime entity despite being no more than a city state built on water.

However, as the previous reference to the first boat race shows, the Venetians were also able to transform the oar from a weapon of politics into one of fun and entertainment.

It is recorded that as early as 1315, the Doge Soranzo decreed that on the 29 June, the feast of SS Peter and Paul, there should be racing for youths; thereafter, this became an annual event.

911   At the regatta held on 17 May 1569, in honour of the Archduke Charles of Austria, women competed as well.

It is to be presumed that they had started to compete earlier than that; in fact, towards the end of the fifteenth century there is a reference to an earlier event in which women participated, probably for the first time. (See *The Story of World Rowing*, published by Stanley Paul.)

BOWLING

912 The Italian game of '*Bocce*' was a precursor of bowling. Played initially in the Italian Alps about 2,000 years ago, it consisted of the underhand tossing of stones. It was then exported to Germany in the form of bowling at pins where it was developed around the third or fourth century AD.

FENCING

913 Rapier fencing was invented by an Italian.

As Lawrence Stone recorded (*The Crisis of the Aristocracy 1558-1641*, Clarendon Press, Oxford, 1965, p. 244) whereas the duel with rapier and dagger had taken hold in Italy and France by the middle of the sixteenth century, it was not till the 1580s that it became generally accepted in England.

914 In 1576, the first fashionable fencing school was set up in Blackfriars by the Italian, Rocco BONETTI, who advertised his social success by hanging the coat of arms of his patrons round its walls. By the 1590s, the English had at last taken to the rapier.

One of the most famous Italian swordsmen was Vincenzo Saviolo.

The two acknowledged masters of the technique of fencing with light sabres were Giuseppe Radaelli and Italo Santelli.

Domenico Angelo was a famous fencing master who spent quite a while in London in the eighteenth century. He is recorded as having lived at No. 3 St James's Place, SW1, from 1758 to 1762 and as having had quite a high-class clientele.

The Italian contribution to the sport of Fencing is very aptly summarized on p. 224 of Volume 7 of *Britannica* in the following words:

'The Italians are said to have been the first to discover the effectiveness of the dextrous use of the point rather than the edge of the sword . . . they may therefore be credited with being the originators of true swordsmanship that emphasizes skill and speed rather than force.'

The Italian School of Fencing found some competition in the seventeenth century from the Spaniards who specialized in rapier fencing based on complex movements, a method which was never adopted as widely as that of the Italian School.

GAMING & GAMBLING

915 Gambling chips were first created in Italy around the beginning of the thirteenth century. They were minted as coin-like counters to be used on abacus tables and soon became a very popular way of keeping count. Being cast or thrown onto a table, they became known as 'Jetons' from the French verb to throw ('jeter') and were a mark of class distinction because the poorer persons' counters were made of copper whilst those of the well-to-do were cast in silver and showed the relevant coat of arms of the family.

Interestingly, perhaps, the word was adopted into the Italian language and converted into 'gettone', a noun still very much in common use initially for telephones and nowadays for various machines. (Bruno)

> **916** The picture-type playing cards – as distinct from the number cards which are probably a Chinese invention – originated in Italy. The first reference to them occurs in 1299.

These picture-cards were called '*Tarocchi*', a word that was later converted into the German 'Tarok' and the French 'Tarot'.

Games, especially card games, are quite popular in Italy. It is no coincidence that the Italians were world bridge champions for nearly twenty years.

Card games are still played often in Italy. It was not unusual to find youngsters playing them in the streets or older men outside a bar or an 'osteria', in the same way as Greeks and Turks play backgammon.

They are in a sense part of the Italian scene, although I am not sure to what extent the Italian is temperamentally a real gambler.

> **917** At some time in the thirteenth century the Dominican Friar Giacomo di CESOLE (otherwise known as Jacopo de Cessolis) wrote a book where he described the customs of the nobility (*Liber de Moribus Hominum vel Officiis Nobilium*). In another work (*Ludus Scaccorum*, a manuscript of which, dated 1468, is in the Vatican Library) he described for the first time the game of chess.

> **918** In 1526, Girolamo CARDANO (born Pavia) worked out the odds on casting dice and was probably the first to propound the probability theory. He also contrib-

uted to the discovery of both cubic and quartic equations. (See '*Mathematics*'.)

Cardano, the illegitimate son of a lawyer, published in 1545 his *Ars Magna*, which is a cornerstone in the history of algebra. As *Britannica* records, he was the most outstanding mathematician of his time. In terms of his computation of probabilities, he anticipates Pascal by one hundred years.

It has been suggested that Cardano was an inveterate gambler, a bit of a rogue (possibly because he was illegitimate), a bit of a heretic (since he was arrested for daring to cast a horoscope of Jesus Christ) and all in all, not a nice fellow – maybe. However, he was appointed Professor of Medicine at Pavia in 1543 and at Bologna in 1562 and perhaps the image that is projected of him is due to the dislike and envy that some of his contemporaries and indeed his successors, felt for him; perhaps he was too far ahead of them. . . . .

> **919** **CARDANO** was also an astrologer and a physician; and in this latter capacity, he was the first to provide a description of typhus fever. In the Anglo-American world he is known as Jerome Cardan.

(I wonder whether it has ever occurred to you, either when playing the football pools or bingo or even buying Premium Bonds, that they all stem from an Italian idea.)

> **920** In 1890, Giuseppe AIROLDI, who wrote under the pseudonym of Inno Minato, invented a crossword puzzle.

> **921** In 1530, there was held in Florence what is believed to be the first public lottery to have paid out prizes in the form of money, '*Il lotto*

di Firenze.

Of course, the gambling instinct is as old as mankind and examples of the use of the concept of chance to determine events can be found both in the Bible and in Roman history.

But the Lotto of Florence was an organized event which represented the starting point and I suppose we can also trace back to it today's gambling casinos.

There is no doubt that 'Lotto', the Italian National Lottery, formed the basis of subsequent games like lotto, keno, bingo, etc. Indeed, on a national scale, Italy would come first even in modern times had it not been beaten to the post by Australia which had lotteries as early as the nineteenth century.

The first National Italian Lottery was created in 1863; others followed. The Irish Sweepstake goes back to the 1930s, France followed in 1933, the Malta Lottery is well known and in some countries (England, Hungary and Malta, for example) even the name 'lotto' was imported.

It is due to the innate cynicism of the Italians that Italy has always been fairly successful in exploiting for economic benefit the weaknesses and foibles of human beings.

I am not sure to what extent one ought to be too proud of the next first, but there it is.

922   In 1638, the first official gambling house or, as they call it nowadays, 'casino' was opened in Venice. It was named 'il Ridotto' and soon became exceptionally popular and drew a great number of foreigners who swelled the number of visitors who came to the city not only because of its uniqueness, but also for its well-known carnivals.

GARDENS & HORTICULTURE

Everybody knows how successful the Italians have been with the formal garden and the general impact of Italian gardening on Europe is referred to later. For present purposes, suffice it to say that Italy influenced France extensively: it provided the model and inspiration for Louis XIV and gave him an appreciation for gardens like those of Versailles and the Tuileries. Both Marie and Catherine de Medici had taken Italian gardeners to France with them.

When John Evelyn first went to Italy, he was most impressed by the gardens of the Doria family in Genoa, which were very well known for their terraces. Indeed, at first sight he thought that the gardens extended from the sea to the mountains and he so described them.

In 1622, the Danvers brothers started to pioneer the Italian garden in England.

Apart from this general background, there are a number of firsts.

923   In 1305, Pietro de CRESCENZI (born Bologna) who for the previous thirty years had been a judge, and who had retired officially in 1299, wrote his *Liber Ruralium Commodorum*. De Crescenzi originally wrote the work in Latin. It was translated into Italian in the latter part of the fourteenth century and it was published in 1471. Soon after, it was translated into French and German.

This was the first gardening book, for in it he deals at great length with the size and shape of trees and plants and, above all, garden furniture and statuary.

Book IV of the text has the title: 'De vitibus et vineis et cultu earum, ac natura et utilitate fructus ipsarum', which freely translated reads 'About vines, wines and their cultivation, nature and uses to which they can be put.'

924   In it, he described for the first time the liquorice plant ('regolizia') (although it was already known in Germany by the eleventh century) simply because it was becoming extensively cultivated in Italy in his time.

925   He was the first to mention the cultivation of the white and purple irises, flowers which, though originating in the eastern Mediterranean, became very popular in the area around Florence (it is hardly a coincidence that the ancient arms of the city of Florence show what has always been described as a white lily but which could just as easily be an iris). There is a variety of Iris called 'Florentine' (Iris germanica 'Florentine') which has white flowers tinged with pale lavender blue; orris root, used to fix colours, for making pot-pourri as well as in perfumery, is nothing else but dried ground root of the iris plant. Tuscany is the principal region in Italy given over to the cultivation of iris but although there are several varieties of orris root available commercially, the finest is still that derived from Florentine Iris, known locally as 'giaggiolo' or 'giaggiuolo'.

926   In the fifteenth century, the Italians were the first to lay out parterres.

The approach, based on formal layout, is reflected also in the extensive use made by Italians at a very early date of arbours or fruit tunnels, i.e. the covering of areas or walks by plants or trees trained over lattice work. Here there was a pioneer.

927   In 1467, a Dominican monk Francesco COLONNA wrote the *Hypnerotomachia Poliphili*, roughly translated in English as 'The Dream of Poliphilus', which represents the first gardening encyclopaedia.

Apart from describing elaborate work in the construction of tree tunnels in the book, he deals at great length with landscape gardening, the layout of orchards, woodland, of vegetable gardens, pergolas, garden furniture and fountains, plant utilization, the use of old stones and the topiary of myrtle and cypress trees.

Any reader of Boccaccio's *Decameron* knows the extent to which gardens are described by him and how in particular he refers to arbours planted with climbers. Obviously Boccaccio antedates Colonna, but to Colonna we owe the systematization of gardening techniques. Colonna's book was beautifully printed by Aldo Manuzio and it is possible that it even antedates the *De Re Aedificatoria* by Leon Battista Alberti (see 'Architecture') which dealt at length with the siting of villas in gardens.

928   The first 'public garden', that is to say a garden established by a private individual and opened to the public on payment of a small fee, was established by Bernardo RUCELLAI of Florence in 1480 in the garden of his villa at Quaracchi. He struck on the idea of 'inviting' the public into his garden so that, with the admission fees, he could help with the maintenance charges. (*Grande Dizionario*, UTET, 1959 ed.)

929   The study of plants appears to have commenced in ancient China and was well known to the Indians and to the Greeks but it is a historical fact that the first university chair for the specific purpose of studying plants was set up in 1533 in Padova.

930   We owe to Bernardo BUON-TALENTI (born Florence 1536), referred to earlier on in connection with ice cream, the introduction of 'grottoes' in gardening. It is impossible to document that he was the first garden designer but he was clearly quite versatile because he is described in *Britannica* (Vol. II, p. 373) as a stage and costume designer, a builder of palaces and fortresses, a theatre architect and a stage technician, who entered the service of the Medici family and was patronized by them for the rest of his life.

The first grotto he created was in the gardens of Boboli, near Florence, and he glorified the event by giving a position of honour to Michelangelo's famous 'prigioni'. (v. *Encyclopaedia Biografica*, Treccani, 1960 repr. 1997)

931   The Italians were the first to use ornamental marble benches as a feature of princely gardens, a practice that started during the Renaissance.

932   The first herb garden was laid out in Pisa in 1543. Florence and the University of Padua followed suit in 1545 and Bologna in 1567. (See John Hale, *The Civilization of Europe and the Renaissance* op.cit.)

933   In 1545, Daniele BARBARO (born Venice) was the first to establish a conservatory. He put it to the use of the Botanical Gardens at Pavia; an open fire provided heat during the winter.

In 1593, he wrote his principal book *Corrections to Pliny*, underlining the significance of Greek and Latin experience of the Mediterranean and arguing that the culture of East and North Africa did not necessarily have much meaning for the rest of Europe.

Conservatories were already common features of the Italian gardens of the Renaissance. A versatile person, Barbaro. He also anticipated the invention of the camera (see 'Photography').

934   Giovanni Battista CERLETTI (born Chiavenna), in 1877, was the first to establish at Conegliano, near Venice, a School of Viticulture and Oenology.

935   Many English gardeners have to be grateful for the supply of Italian seeds (rocket, sorrel, cardoons, artichokes and sundry varieties of differently coloured lettuces). But there's nothing new about this because purchases of this nature, not always successfully it must be admitted, were made way back in the early eighteenth century (*The Country House Kitchen Garden 1650-1900*, Sutton Publishing, 1998).

GYMNASTICS

936   Girolamo MERCURIALI (born Forli) published in 1753 the first illustrated book on gymnastics (Morton's 1986).

HOROSCOPES

937/8 Cardano, already mentioned in connection with Gaming, is also deserving of a place in history as the first publisher of the horoscopes of (one hundred) outstanding men of his century; a very versatile scientist, he claimed to be the first to be able to draw horoscopes by looking at faces.

HORSE-RIDING

The Italians have always been closely associated with horse-riding. Leaving on one side all the representations of the horse in drawings and in sculpture (from Mantegna and Romano to Verrocchio, Gattamelata and Colleoni) they have made a very great historical contribution to the glorification of the horse.

939   For example, from about the fifteenth century, the ruling family in Mantova, the Gonzagas, formed a stud, whose stallions sired the horses for 'Haute Ecole', creating a precedent for the kind of riding school of which the most celebrated modern exponent is the Spanish Riding School in Vienna. As we observe elsewhere in this book, the school uses horses (Lipizzaner) whose name is, itself, derived from Italian.

Mantova, in particular, was exceptionally well known thanks to the Gonzagas; the 'Loggia delle Muse' and the 'Sala dei Cavalli' of the 'Palazzo Te' in Mantova are perfect records of the glorification of horse breeding. From Mantova, such glorification spread to other Italian courts, so much so that Baldassar Castiglione (referred to elsewhere in this book as well) makes it clear in 'The Courtier' that by 1516 fashioned horse-riding had replaced tournaments as one of the recreations of the Italian nobility.

The stallions from Mantova became famous and were crossed with horses from Spain, Tunisia, Jaffa, Constantinople, as well as from Tuscany and Sardinia.

940   In 1550, Federico GRISONE (Neapolitan) published *Gli ordini di cavalcare*, in which he attempted to combine Greek principles with the requirements of mounted combat.

941   At about the same time Giovanni Battista PIGNATELLI (also born in Naples) cooperating with the said Grisone laid down the practice and principles of horse-riding which were to be developed three centuries later by the Spanish Riding School in Vienna.

942   And whilst on the subject of horses, it should not be forgotten that the nobleman Carlo RUINI (born Bologna 1530) was the first to write a book on the anatomy and the illnesses of the horse (*Dell'anatomia et delle Infermitá del Cavallo*). It was published in 1598 and is to be considered the first veterinary text book.

The book was a great success, it was reprinted many times and translated into a number of languages, also because it was illustrated by sixty-four beautiful tables which are attributable to one of the Carracci brothers, famous painters.

It is interesting to record in this connection that the first book in the English language on equine anatomy, (that is to say 'the anatomy of an horse') published by M Flesher in London in 1683 and written by Andrew Snape Junior, is described by Morton's (298) as 'largely a translation of Ruini'.

943   In 1895, Frederico CAPRILLI (born Livorno) revolutionized the mechanics of locomotion and created the forward seat position which is now in universal use. It was his pupil, Piero Santini, who popularized Caprilli's new idea.

KITES & GLIDERS

944   Although the kite as such originated in China over 3,000 years

ago, the diamond-shaped kite was first described by DELLAPORTA in 1620.

MAGIC

945/6 In 1780, Giuseppe PINETTI (born Orbetello) established himself as the first stage magician. He was the first to introduce a number of tricks, including the second sight trick; he also founded the classical School of Magic.

The Italians have long been well known in England as expert magicians.

On 8 April 1779, Dr Johnson refers to their abilities, quoting from King James's 'Daemonology' to the effect that the Italian magicians were 'elegant beings'.

MOUNTAINEERING

There is little in the old authors about the subject. Apart from minor references in Herodotus and Thucidides, it is the Latin writer Sallust who records the first attempt (in the year 106 BC) to climb a mountain.

In his history of the Longobards, Paolo Diacono records the first *failed* attempt to climb the Rocciamelone mountain which is 3,537 metres high and stands in the Alps near Susa in Piedmont.

947 The first historical document on mountain climbing is to be found in Petrarch's Letter to Father Dionigi (*De Rebus Familiaribus* IV). Petrarch himself in 1336 climbed the Ventoux mountain which is 1,912 metres high.

948 But the first recorded, suc-

cessful attempt to climb a mountain over 2,000 metres occurred in 1358. In that year, Bonifacio Rotario D'ASTI climbed the Rocciamelone mountain, thus becoming the first recorded mountaineer to climb over 2,000 metres.

949/50 A much more recent (1980) first should also be recorded here. The first person in the world to have climbed all the world's-8,000-metre peaks is an Italian (from the north), Rheinhold MESSNER (see also 'Skiing'). He was also the first to climb Everest alone and without the assistance of oxygen tanks.

951 In 1954, Achille COMPAGNONI and Lino LACEDELLI, as part of an Italian team of nineteen men headed by Ardito DESIO, reached, for the first time, the summit of K2 in the Himalayas, the second highest mountain in the world in the Karakorum range.

I shall not get even remotely involved in the controversy as to whether K2 may be higher than Everest. . . . . A matter which, in any event, appears now to have been settled beyond any doubt by the Italian expedition to Everest of November 2004 which, with the most up-to-date measuring equipment, has established that the true height of Everest is just over two metres greater than was initially thought. It now stands at 8,842.70 metres.

Compagnoni and Lacedelli crowned the unsuccessful attempts by a number of other teams, which had started way back in 1902.

SKIING

952 Rheinhold MESSNER also achieved another first, together with

the German Arved Fuchs. **On 13 November 1989 the two of them set out from the Ronne Ice Shelve in Antarctica to ski alone all the way to the South Pole and from there to cross over to Scott Base where they arrived in February 1990, after a journey of ninety-two days covering 1,550 miles (2,800 km), having been the first to traverse Antarctica without the aid of either dogs or machines.**

There is no need to quote any authority for this. It is common knowledge. It was an event that was publicized in the Press and very many pages were dedicated to it in number 5 of volume 178 of *National Geographic* Magazine.

953 At the Winter Olympics of 1992 in Albertville, France, Alberto TOMBA scored two firsts: On 18 February, he was the first athlete successfully to defend an Olympic Alpine Title when he won the Giant Slalom at Val D'Isere, with an advantage of .32 of a second over Girardelli of Luxembourg.

954 On 22 February, when TOMBA won a Silver Medal in the Slalom (being beaten by Jegge of Norway by a mere .28 of a second) he became the only man to earn four Olympic Medals in Alpine Skiing, namely, three Gold and one Silver.

The Authority for the above can be found in many daily newspapers throughout the world for 19 and 23 February 1992. And whilst on the subject of skiing, an Italian woman has decided to compete with Tomba's records. On 20 February 1998 Deborah Compagnoni won the Women's Giant Slalom at the Nagano Olympics. In doing so she earned a gold medal for the third successive winter games, having won her first gold in the Super Giant Slalom in Albertville in 1994, and her second in the Giant Slalom in Lillehammer two years later, thus setting up a world record. The schedule for the Winter Games was changed, hence the gap of only two years.

SOCCER

955 This is possibly a more contentious sphere since the origins of soccer are said to be found in China (third and fourth centuries BC) as well as in Scotland, where there exists an Edinburgh print that shows something looking like a game of soccer. Whilst, of course, it is true that soccer became standardized by the English with the formation of a football association in October 1863, it is a fact that way back in Florence in the sixteenth century a game was played with thirteen players per side which looked very much like soccer. Indeed, the rules of that particular game were codified in a manual of 1580 under the title *Discorso Calcio* which fact entitles me, I believe, to add this particular claim to the many others contained in the present work.

9. TRANSPORT & TRAVEL

CANALS

956 The first major canal system established anywhere in the world was built in Milan in 1179 and is still known now by the name it had then, namely 'Naviglio Grande' (The Great Navigation Canal).

In 1179, other nations were thinking of the Crusades whilst the Milanese were concerned with their amenities.

Much later (in 1496), Leonardo da Vinci was involved in the construction of the famous canal which links the rivers Adda and Ticino. (Even at this time, most people of northern Europe were no better than uncouth barbarians.)

957 The previous year, 1495, LEONARDO had invented lock gates and he used them in 1497 in the form of mitred lock gates on the Milan Canal. (Carter, *Dictionary of Inventions and Discoveries*, p. 98.)

FLYING

958 In 1507 at Perugia, Giovan Battista DANTI was probably the first man to attempt to fly. In 1560 Giovanni Damiano (John Damian) made a further attempt to fly, this time at Stirling in Scotland. Before that, Leonardo had designed a flying machine, a sort of helicopter actuated by a worm screw, as well as a parachute. (See 'Physics')

In 1600, Paolo Guidotti also attempted to fly. He constructed two large wings of whalebone which he covered in feathers and, having thus converted himself, as he thought, into a bird, he jumped from a great height hoping to fly. He did not really, and although the large wings slowed down his fall, he ended up on the roof of a nearby house and broke a leg.

The desire of man to imitate the birds, at least in the sense of moving about in the sky, antedates Guidotti. Long before him, legend tells us that Icarus (and his father Daedalus) who flew from Crete to Naples is said to have made it to the sky but to have been struck down by the gods when carried away by his excitement and conceit. He flew so close to the sun that the wax that kept his feathers together melted: he ended up in the Aegean sea.

Everybody knows both Icarus and Leonardo but not many know of another valiant contributor to 'air travel'. He is Tiberius Cavallo, who was born in Naples and was admitted to The Royal Society on 9 December 1779.

Cavallo was quite well-known in England as a scientist and spent most of his life in London in Little St Martin's Lane.

In 1780, he gave his first Bakerian Lecture at The Royal Society and did so annually for the next twelve years; in this respect he is probably one of the very few, if not the only Member to have given so many such lectures.

The lectures ranged from the observation of meteors to detailed electrical and magnetic studies, as well as to comments on the then most recent development in the field of electricity, namely Volta's plates.

He is to be remembered principally, however, for the lecture delivered on the 20 June 1782 under the title 'Common and inflammable airs penetrate the pores of paper', an eighteen-page dissertation on the lightness of gases. It is recorded at The Royal Society under the reference 'L & P VII, Lecture 263'.

It may be interesting to quote an extract from it: 'The experiment was to construct a vessel or sort of bag which when inflated with inflammable air might be lighter than an equal bulk of common air and consequentially might ascend like smoke into the atmosphere.'

959 He practised with 'some fine china paper' and with different kinds of bladder. The exercise, which he himself called 'a diverting experiment', is significant because it showed for the first time what could be done once a suitable type of vessel was found that would contain nitrogenous gases. This was achieved exactly one year later by the Montgolfier brothers.

The encyclopaedia *Treccani* records Cavallo as an innovator in the field of lighter-than-air gases and studies, as well as thermo-metrical observations; *Britannica* does not mention him at all. This is surprising because The Royal Society library contains eleven printed works by Cavallo as well as papers that he published in its *Philosophical Transactions*; in addition, it holds twenty-five manuscript letters and other papers relating to Cavallo.

Another figure who was quite a success in the field of ballooning and who followed closely in the wake of the Montgolfier brothers was Vincent Lunardi.

960 On 15 November 1784, LU-NARDI took off in a balloon from the Artillery Ground at Finsbury Square in London in the presence of 100,000 people. This was treated as an exceptional feat at the time; it was certainly something that London had never seen before even though two years earlier the Montgolfier Brothers had staged the first balloon flight of all time in France. Lunardi's was the first aerial voyage in Britain in a hydrogen balloon.

He touched down briefly at Welham Green, near Hatfield, having flown for a little while, but a hostile reception from local people forced him to take off again, which he did immediately, travelling north-eastwards.

That the event was one of major significance can be elicited from the fact that there is a granite stone within railings in a meadow at Standon Green End at the commencement of Parsonage Lane, North Mymms (now better known as Welham Green) in Hertfordshire, which commemorates the landing of Lunardi in a metal hinged flap providing an inscription about the flight. One hundred yards down the road, we now find Vincenzo Close, a quasi-suburban street in the Hertfordshire countryside.

Lunardi's flight earned him an audience with George III and the Prince of Wales presented him with a watch.

It is interesting that *Britannica* does not mention Lunardi either, although he was evidently well known to the English public at the time; indeed, to English literature because Sir Walter Scott actually used Lunardi's name to describe something like a balloon in his novel *St Ives*.

Exactly a month after Lunardi, on 15 October 1784, the Frenchman Francois Blanchard made his ascent from Chelsea. Horace Walpole records having watched him from the window of his Round Tower at Strawberry Hill.

961 The first night flight in a balloon was made in 1803 from Bologna to the Istrian coast by Count ZAMBECCARI, Dr GRASS-ATI and Pasquale ANDREOLI. (Carter, *Dictionary of Inventions and Discoveries*, p. 16.)

Although, as we have observed, Leonardo was the first one to sketch a parachute in his notebooks, and his compatriot Fausto Veranzio to publish a description of a workable parachute as early as the year 1595, the said BLANCHARD is the first man who is credited with actually having used a parachute. In 1785, one year after the ascent that we have just recorded, he dropped a dog in a basket, to which a parachute was attached, from the very same type of balloon high up in the air. Blanchard himself claimed that he had descended from a balloon in a parachute in 1793, breaking his leg upon landing.

962/3 Mario de BERNARDI (born Venosa), an engineer and above all pilot, patented in 1924 a cable to ensure the landing of an aircraft on aircraft carriers and ships.

In 1926, he won the Schneider Cup at Norfolk, Virginia and in the following six years he set several other speed records.

In 1934/35, he evolved the first automatic pilot for aircraft (*Dizionario Biografico degli Italini*, Volume 33, 1987 edition).

964 Believe it or not, America's first woman pilot employed by a major airline was an Italian, Bonnie TIBURZI.

965 The first jet aeroplane that flew was designed by CAPRONI-CAMPINI in 1941. It flew 300 miles. (Carter, *Dictionary of Inventions and Discoveries*, p. 7.) It had previously, in August 1940, made a very short – ten minutes – run.

966 The first hydrofoil biplane was designed by Aldo GUIDONI in 1911.

967 Enrico FORLANINI was a pioneer in aircraft technology. In 1879, he had already designed a helicopter driven by a steam engine, which actually flew. (Carter, *Dictionary of Inventions and Discoveries*, p. 5.)

968 In a similar manner in which the Italians treated Marconi who had to go abroad to develop his invention, an energetic engineer from the Abruzzi region, Corradino D'ASCANIO, was the first to build the precursor of the modern helicopter. Leonardo may have designed it, Forlanini had followed, but D'Ascanio actually built it. In 1927, his machine lifted and flew for eight minutes forty-five seconds at a height of thirteen metres over a distance 1.78 km. The officials of the Air Ministry at the time didn't appreciate what he was doing and provided no encouragement and the project died a more or less natural death. His name is better known for the creation of the motor scooter Vespa (q.v.).

969 In 1912, Mario CARDERARA built and flew the first seaplane (or hydroplane) at La Spezia. This was quite an event especially because at the time the particular craft was the largest aircraft in the world.

970 In the field of power plane sports, Italy's design achievements in the 1930s were outstanding. In 1933, an Italian aircraft (the Macchi) set a 440-mile per hour (708 km per hour) seaplane speed record that still stands (see *Britannica*, Vol. 7, p. 401).

971 Not entirely under the right

heading, perhaps, but the reader might like to be told that the automated airport notice board announcing arrivals and departures now found all over the world was patented in 1948 by Messrs. SO-LARI of Udine in North-East Italy.

To this day, in some countries, especially the USA, the revolving 'dials' on such notice boards are referred to as Solari.

HORSE-DRAWN CARRIAGES

972   **Ever since the thirteenth century, horse-drawn carriages have been popular in Milan. In fact, the first travelling wagon known as a 'cocchio' was manufactured in Italy in 1288.**

Initially, the 'cocchio' had no suspension but by the sixteenth century this had been remedied and it is recorded that when Isabella D'Este was a guest there, she was astonished by the fact that Milan could boast no less than sixty carriages drawn by four horses and hundreds drawn by two. This should be compared with what went on in Paris at the same time, for at the Court of Francis I, there were only three carriages: one for him, one for Diana of Poitiers and one for a courtier of his who was somewhat overweight.

973   **The Italians were the first to protect the travellers in such conveyances by applying windows to carriages; this was done in the early part of the seventeenth century.**

MOTOR VEHICLES

After good food, nothing else except clothes and the motor car reflects the taste and the temperament of the Italian nation more effectively. It is not surprising, therefore, that Italy can lay claim to quite a few 'firsts' regarding the development of the 'automobile'.

I do not mean first in racing or in success or in line, although there can be no question that there is a prestige attached to some Italian cars (Ferrari, Maserati, Lamborghini, Alfa Romeo) which is unique.

Italians love motor cars, for they equate them with women. There is an old Italian expression: '*Donne e motori, gioie e dolori*', which freely translated means that women are like cars; they give both joy and pain.

In Italy, more than in any other part of the world that I know, the car is the manifestation of the driver. It transmits his taste, his aggressiveness, his manners; it is almost a mirror of his personality. And very few people drive with the same abandonment and panache as the Italians.

It is of course true that Italians drive like madmen, or so it appears to the foreigner with little knowledge of local conditions. It is certainly true that they drive in a selfish manner; and one needs only to be caught in the Rome rush-hour or in traffic in the centre of Naples to realize what a dreadful place both those cities can be in particular circumstances.

And yet, one must often wonder why the number of serious accidents both in Rome and Naples is consistently smaller than it ought to be judging by the way people actually drive. There seems to be an inherent ability in the Italian to control a motor car which I do not think I have seen shared by any other Europeans. So, what are the facts? The Italians have contributed inventions in connection with the motor car that are fundamental.

974 Although stretching the imagination somewhat to see this as a first in connection with motor vehicles, it is nevertheless true that Guido da VIGEVANO, apart from being a doctor, also wrote a treatise in the fourteenth century containing drawings of men working what is believed to be the first known crankshaft inside a vehicle.

975/6 In 1775, Alessandro VOLTA created the electro-phorus, a device to generate static electricity. He followed this up in 1800 when he invented the first electric 'pile' which was the forerunner of the battery.

977/8 In about 1800, Giovanni Battista VENTURI (born Bibiano RE) invented the Venturi meter to compute flow volume. The Venturi effect has many applications, such as in the carburettor.

Little did Venturi realize that his 'principle' would find somewhat unexpected applications. There is now in existence a US patented shower head which, by narrowing the width of the holes, increases the flow rate of the water generating negative pressure. The result is that air is sucked in through the nozzles and it is claimed that, consequently, the mixture of air and oxygen in the jet of water is not only more powerful, but contributes to a sense of freshness and revival, apart from saving both energy and water. Fantastic what these Italians get up to. . . . .

The carburation system based on the Venturi principle is used in motor cars, airplanes, and wherever motor engines

are installed. (He gave his name to the phenomenon known as the Venturi effect, which occurs where fluid flows through a horizontal pipe of varying cross-sectional areas and which results in the static pressure changes of the fluid being least where the cross-section is smallest.)

979 In 1853, Eugenio BARSANTI (born Pietrasanta) and the Marquis Carlo Felice MATTEUCCI (born Ravenna) deposited at the Florence Academy of the Georgofili a report on what is considered the prototype of the internal combustion engine.

In the report, Barsanti and Matteucci refer to a 'chamber' where there is to take place 'the ignition of the mixtures of gases, the expansion force of which activates at each stroke of the camshaft which is at its bottom'. I know that priority for this claim is attributed to Otto Van Langen at the Paris Exhibition which took place three years later. But I think that the seminal idea was Italian.

Visitors to Santa Croce in Florence will see the monument dedicated to the said two inventors and situated along the left-hand side of the nave.

980 In 1858, Giovanni PACINOTTI (born Pisa) invented the dynamo which was patented ten years later by the Frenchman Gramme. It was the first practical electrical machine. (Pacinotti also developed one of the first parachutes.)

A physicist of varied interests, not merely confined to electricity and electromagnetism, he published in 1860 the details of what he called his 'macchinetta' (little machine) which could be used either as a direct current motor or as a generator. A copy of the original machine is still kept in the University of Pisa.

Britannica ascribes the invention of the

dynamo to Gramme but Pacinotti got there at least five years before Gramme. Siemens called (in a letter which he himself wrote to Pacinotti in 1875) Gramme's claim to the invention of the dynamo a 'usurpation'. What is true is that Gramme was the first to market dynamos in 1871 but one cannot deny Pacinotti the merit of an invention which can be said to have opened the era of industrial electrical engineering since it marks the beginning of the development of electrical power on an industrial scale.

981   In 1884, Giuseppe PIRELLI (born Como) made the first electric cable.

982   In 1889, the same PIRELLI made the first motor car tyre.

So, the next time you look at any motor car – and not only when you look at an exciting Ferrari or an expensive Lamborghini – you might bear in mind that that machine would not be there but for these various and important Italian firsts.

When you next use the motorway please remember that:

983   The first motor car race took place in 1895. It was a road race from Turin to Asti, and back; it was won by a Daimler.

984   The first motorway was the Italian 'Autostrada'. It ran between Milan and Varese, was inaugurated in 1924 and would later connect Turin with Venice.

It is a common misconception that it was thanks to Hitler that the first motorways were built. It was even repeated in the first episode of an outstanding BBC series that ought to have known better, 'The World at War'.

This is clearly wrong. Hitler may have concentrated on the autobahn but he got his example from Mussolini's Italy.

985   Whilst it can be argued that the moped originated in Germany, the motor-scooter was developed by the Italians soon after the Second World War. In 1946, a revolutionary two-wheel vehicle was presented at the golf club in Rome by Enrico PIAGGIO and his designer, Corradino D'ASCANIO (an aeroplane and helicopter engineer). It was called 'Vespa', which means 'wasp', presumably from the noise it made and its ability to go practically anywhere.

1946 was the year in which Europe began to emerge from the tragedy of the Second World War. Whilst it saw the discovery of cortisone and streptomycin and the publication of Dr Spock's guide book on babycare, as well as the first edition of the Cannes Film Festival and the establishment, terminologically and practically, of the 'Iron Curtain', as far as Italy was concerned, 1946 was a particularly significant year. The country desperately needed movement from city to city to re-establish itself, and its motor industry had not yet recovered from the war. The Vespa manufactured by Piaggio, and soon after the Lambretta manufactured by Innocenti, set the tone of private transport in Italy for many decades, at the same time as the 'Scala' in Milan was re-inaugurated by Arturo Toscanini after the war bombings, the Italian Republic was proclaimed, and the first 'Miss Italia' beauty contest was established. One looks back nowadays on Silvana Pampanini and wonders how present-day tastes have changed, but at a more artistic level, Rossellini's 'Rome Open City' did manage to win the best foreign film prize at Cannes.

The Vespa was a uniquely Italian

representation of entrepreneurial spirit, revival and creativity which led *The Times* to write in the early 1950s that the Vespa was 'the Italian vehicle "par excellence", whose like we have not seen for centuries, since the age of the Roman chariot'. To equate the Vespa with a Roman chariot may be thought by some to be carrying glorification of things Italian, somewhat unusual in *The Times* newspaper, to extremes. On the other hand, there is little doubt that it became a unique symbol of the '*Joie de Vivre*' which was to become associated with the so-called '*Dolce Vita*' years.

The Vespa fans, known as '*vespisti*', soon formed a band of people young and old, men and women, of a universality which defies classification and which enabled the Vespa to become a great success, especially in Third World Countries.

Not a first by any means, but it might be worth noting under this heading, that the first long-distance motor vehicle road race, the Peking-Paris, was won in 1907 by Prince Scipione Borghese. This was quite an event for its time, since it covered a distance in excess of 9,000 miles and took two months to complete. He acquired instant fame, particularly because, in his Itala motor car, he got to Paris three weeks before any other competitor.

986 The fondness of Italians for motor cars allowed them to establish the Formula One World Championship in 1950; Italian drivers triumphed seven times in the years 1950-60.

Interestingly, the 1950s were quite important for the Italian motor industry not only because of the production of scooters like the Vespa cited above and the Lambretta (which had in fact pre-ceded the Vespa, since the first one was manufactured in 1947), but more particularly because the decade saw the first mass production of a 'V' six cylinder engine, the Lancia Aurelia produced between 1950 and 1955. In May 1954, Alfa Romeo produced the Giulietta Sprint designed by Nuccio Bertone which was a forerunner of all the GT motor cars and which even today, over fifty years later, is a brilliant example of Italian sport style and line.

One year later the Fiat Seicento was born (four million cars built and sold) and in 1957 the smallest car in the world, the Fiat 500 type (1.33 m, width 1.32 m, length 2.97 m and a mere 479 cc engine).

987 In 1957, Enrico MATTEI (born Matelica) was the first to negotiate separate oil treaties with Third World countries.

He founded the Italian National Hydrocarbon Agency, ENI, and the petrol company AGIP, represented by the six-legged dog breathing fire on a yellow background which must be well known to anyone who has travelled through Italy. Whether his death in 1962 in a plane crash was an accident or not remains a question mark.

988 AGIP was the first petrol company in Europe to provide a comprehensive range of services at its petrol-filling stations and more particularly to endeavour to maintain a high standard of cleanliness in their toilet facilities. The standard thus set has been imitated ever since, as have the bar, restaurant and motel facilities that MATTEI originated.

989 One fact, however, is worth mentioning in reference to the use of two wheels, namely that Giacomo AGOSTINI set a record which is, to this day, unbeaten: in motorcycle road racing, he won fifteen World Championships between 1965 and 1976 (in two different classes). More recently, Valentino Rossi has excelled in the same field but so far Agostini is still unbeaten.

RAILWAYS & STEAM ENGINES

As *Britannica* records (see Vol. IV, p. 436) three-fifths of the world's entire railway track relies on the so-called standard gauge of 4 ft. 8.5 in., which originated with George Stephenson's pioneer Liverpool & Manchester line in 1829. From Britain it was exported to Europe and the United States as part of a package which included British locomotives built for it.

Whilst it is true that a number of countries do not have the same gauge (the Soviet Union, Spain, Japan, and others operate on two or even three different systems, for example, Australia, India, Pakistan), it is interesting to note that the 1.4 metres standard measurement is exactly the same as that left by the existing roadway tracks in the excavation at Pompeii.

It is almost impossible to determine whether Stephenson actually copied the dimension although there are a number of train historians and engineers who believe that he did. If this is true, the Romans were merely anticipating another Italian first.

990   The records show that it was Thomas Savery who patented the first commercially successful steam engine in 1698. This is absolutely true, but he got the idea from an Italian. It was Giambattista DELLAPORTA, a Neapolitan, (see

'Photography'), who, in either 1601 or 1606, first described a steam engine, thus anticipating Savery by nearly a century.

991   Naples can claim another record, however, in the field of railway communications. In Europe, outside England, the first commercially-operated publicly-owned railway was that inaugurated in 1832 in Italy, running between Naples and Portici. It covered a distance of only eight kilometres but it was considered a most exciting development.

992   Another small first for Naples. On 6 May 1880, the first funicular railway in the world was inaugurated to climb Mount Vesuvius. At the same time, the Neapolitan song 'Funiculì Funiculà' came into being, soon to become known worldwide, being cited also by Richard Strauss.

SHIPS & NAVIGATION

993   By the mid-twelfth century, Genoese ships had two decks and the best sails were made in Genoa. Hence the term 'Genoa sail' to describe a particular type of quality sail. Related terms are the 'Genoa lead block' and the 'Genoa' car.

Genoese and Venetian sailors set examples which the English mercantile and war fleets followed. It is said that the first ships that sailed up the Thames as far as London were Italian. (For examples of Italian sailing expertise used in England see 'Travel & Exploration', CABOTO.)

994   The 'Lanterna' at Genoa was probably the first lighthouse of the modern world (apart from the light-

house at Alexandria in Egypt, which was built in 285 BC and was visible for over forty miles).

995 In the Middle Ages, perhaps as early as the thirteenth century, but certainly by the year 1300, charts created by Italian sailors were the precursors of maps and harbour guides. These were effectively sailing handbooks called '*Portolanos*', or Portolan Charts, from the Italian word for harbour guides and mark a sharp tack in Western map-making. They were probably the most useful map-making innovation in the Middle Ages and identified a need by Italian sailors to find their way back to port. They antedated the rediscovery of Ptolemy by map-makers of the fifteenth century.

The Italian contribution to charting the various ports and inlets of the Mediterranean started in the eleventh century and the first consolidation of that work found its outlet in the so-called 'Portolan' charts.

996 The first real maritime map was made in Italy towards the end of the thirteenth century and it was known as the '*Carta Pisana*'.

It was so-called not because it was made by Pisan sailors but merely because it belonged to a family from Pisa. According to researchers, it was almost certainly drawn up by a Genoese. It is undated.

997 The first dated map (1311) belongs to Pietro VESCONTE who was also a Genoese.

These maps were used by all Italian sailors (Pisan, Genoese, Venetians and Neapolitans) and the accumulated experience was obviously extensive. It is recorded that Venetians traded with

London from Italian ships as early as 1240.

998 The compass was, according to tradition, invented by Flavio GIOIA (born Amalfi) in 1302. (Columbus is said to have used it when he sailed to America in 1492.) In turn, it is said that Gioia got his idea for the compass from the Arabs.

As a rule, Italians have always made better sailors than soldiers.

As history shows, the four Republics of Genoa, Venice, Pisa and Amalfi at one stage ruled the Mediterranean in the same way as five or six centuries later Britannia ruled the waves. Before the discovery of America and the sea route to the East, the known world centred around the Mediterranean.

This is hardly surprising: Italy's coastline is very long indeed; it is about 2,600 miles if one only considers the mainland and over 5,000 if the islands are included. And all of it is within the cradle of civilization, the Mediterranean.

Throughout its history, Italy, until the nineteenth century, relied almost exclusively on its ports as outlets for trade or points of communication. The conformation of the country to the north, protected to some extent by the Alps, reinforced this reliance. The Italian side of the Alps is much more difficult than any of the other sides, with the result that the exit from Italy through the Alps has always been more arduous. This explains the comparative ease with which Italy was invaded at regular intervals.

On the other hand, apart from the raids by the Normans, the Saracens and the Arabs, and also excepting the Allied landings at Pachino and Anzio during the Second World War, the Italian coastline has never represented a major point of invasion. On the contrary, it has represented a point of escape and a trading post. This may help to explain why the naval tradition in Italy is strong, the military is weak.

999   The Venetians were the first to elaborate shipbuilding management and production systems, anticipating modern developments by 500 years. This happened at their 'Arsenal'. Founded originally around the year 1100, it had remained reasonably small until 1300 when the growing pressure from the Turks, following upon the fall of Constantinople in 1453, provoked the Venetians into building a further shipyard – what was known as the 'Arsenal Nuovo'. The construction, which began in 1460, was not completed until 1525 but it had the effect of doubling the size of the shipyard.

Such an increase necessitated a better definition of the shipbuilding progress. As a result, the Venetians evolved systems whereby the taskforce was disciplined, gang bosses were involved in the planning process, budgets were established, inventories of ships and materials and components were carefully monitored together with work in progress and cost control. Venetian ships were reconditioned and refitted on an assembly line system with weapons, munitions and gear being installed by specialized groups of skilled workers at different work stations as the ship moved along a channel.

The Arsenal included docks, covered slipways, powder mills, as well as a rope factory and employed some 3,000 workers.

In effect, the Venetians may be said to be the forerunners of strategic planning. (*Shipbuilders of the Venetian Arsenal*, Baltimore, Johns Hopkins University Press, 1991 and Frederic Lake, *Venetian Ships and Shipbuilders of the Renaissance*, Glenwood

Press, Westport, Connecticut, 1975.)

1000   In 1584, Fabiano MORDENTE (born Saluzzo) wrote his first work, *Il Compasso et Riga*, where he describes his invention of the eight-point compass.

1001   In 1591, Bartolomeo CRESCENZIO (born Rome) – a naval officer for the Pope – wrote *Il Proteo Militare* in which he illustrated a kind of nautical instrument which improved on Gioia's and which was in effect the precursor of the precision compass invented by Galileo.

There seems to be some doubt about the precise timing of the invention of the compass, since it is recorded that sailors from the city of Amalfi were using a wooden box with a needle placed on a small sheet of paper, which they then proceeded to move about with a magnet. Quite clearly the compass was already in existence when Dante (1265-1321) wrote his 'Divine Comedy' because he refers to the needle of the compass pointing towards the North in his work (see *Paradiso*-12, 28-30).

1002   In 1602, the same CRESCENZIO drew a 'Portolan' chart in which he showed with extreme clarity and for the first time all the inlets of the Mediterranean suitable both for sailing ships and for oar vessels.

1003   The first shipping company was founded in 1823 by Neapolitan businessmen during the reign of Ferdinand II, King of the two Sicilies.

The ship's capstan was already known to Columbus who referred to it as '*cabestante*'.

1004   The *Dizionario Biografico*

Degli Italiani credits CASELLI (see firsts under other headings) with the invention of the electromagnetic automatic pilot for ships, around the middle of the nineteenth century.

1005 The first successful hydrofoil was built in 1906 by Enrico FORLANINI.

TRAVEL & EXPLORATION

1006 In 1271, Marco POLO (born Venice) started on his journey to the East. He was the first great traveller and explorer and wrote the first travel book (*Il Milione*), in French. Niccolo' and Matteo Polo had started out ten years before him.

Marco Polo belonged to a Venetian family of merchants and diplomats and as a result of his travels, after his father and uncle had left with him on their second expedition to the Court of Kublai Khan, the ruler of Mongolia and China, he was away from home for a total of twenty-five years. With his father and uncle he spent nearly seventeen years in the service of Kublai Khan.

His book made an enormous impression at the time and it alerted Europe to the existence and importance of the East. Its writer, however, remained throughout his life very much a merchant and a traveller: he records more than he comments or moralizes.

Apart from the knowledge of the East which Marco Polo brought back from his travels, he also made available in 1292 in the West, a combination of 75% potassium nitrate, 15% charcoal and 10% sulphur, which the Chinese had been using as 'gunpowder' and allowed his compatriots to develop what was to prove one of their most successful industries, that of fireworks.

Of course, despite their reputation for extravagance and artistry in firework displays, the Italians have to acknowledge that the Chinese got there first. But one novelty which has proved extremely successful is, in fact, due to the Italians, and it is the substitution of potassium nitrate with potassium chlorate. The replacement of the former by the latter, I am told by those who understand chemistry better than I, resulted in a more substantial amount of heat being produced and, as a result, in much better definition and purity of colours being obtained. This occurred in Naples in 1830 and from that date onwards the Neapolitans proved their mastery of the particular medium.

Some Neapolitans emigrated, especially to the USA, where in 1892 the Zambelli family established itself in Newcastle, Pennsylvania, and endorsed, by its spread and notoriety, the Neapolitan mastery of the art of pyrotechnics.

Marco Polo was one of the first to introduce cashmere wool to the West. He brought back to Venice the famous cashmere ring shawls, which he had obtained during his travels to the East. These were so called because it was claimed that they were so fine that they could be drawn through a lady's finger ring.

He also gave his name to a breed of sheep and was the first to note the abundance of oil in the Caspian region. (See *National Geographic*, May 1999, Volume 195, No. 5).

It has been suggested by Prof. David Selbourne that Marco Polo was not the first to reach China, having been beaten to it in 1721 by a merchant from the Marches, Giacobbe D'Ancona, thus an ticipating Marco Polo by four years. (v. *The City of Light*, Little Brown & Co., London, 1997)

However, recent research points to the fact that despite all that we have said about Marco Polo, he may not even have been the first great traveller, always assuming that the facts he recorded in *Il Milione* are true. It now appears that in 1245 Giovanni di Pian del Carpine was sent by Pope Innocent III to pacify and get to know the Tartars.

He left Lyon in France to travel to Mongolia. It took him a year to get there. He stayed and acquired knowledge, and it took him a a year to get back.

1007/8 **In 1291, the brothers Ugolino and Vadino VIVALDI circumnavigated Africa, and are said to have anticipated Columbus by reaching America; other members of the same family founded the first trading posts of the Western world in India during the fourteenth century.**

1009/10 **Francesco Balducci PEGOLOTTI (born Florence) was the first writer of books that, in addition to describing places and trade routes, also provided glossaries of foreign terms, the names of marketplaces and description of imports and exports of the various regions involved as well as generally giving information on marketing. His principal book was called *Pratica della Mercatura*.**

1011 **In 1338, a Franciscan Friar called Giovanni dei MARIGNOLLI (born in Florence) became, after Marco Polo, the second great world traveller. He was the first to stay at the Court of the Mogul Emperors and become a notable traveller to the Far East.**

1012 **Italians discovered America and gave it its name.**

We were all taught at school that America was discovered by Christopher Columbus and that it was named after Amerigo Vespucci who followed him in 1497 and who made known to the world the fact that it was not the Indies, but a new continent.

We are now told that it is possible that what we were taught at school was not correct and that, just as it has been speculated that Shakespeare was an Italian, or a Russian, America had been discovered previously by the Venetians or the Vikings, or some 10,000 years ago, by migrant Asians or Chinamen. In any event, this argument is irrelevant as Columbus's voyage was the one which initiated the subsequent European move towards America.

We are told that even in the event that it was Columbus who discovered America, he was not an Italian but he was a Jew; or a Spaniard; or a Spanish Jew.

For the sake of what follows, however, I shall assume that he was an Italian born in Genoa and known as Cristoforo Colombo who, after sailing from Spain in three little ships made available to him by the Spaniards, discovered America. When he set out from Palos, he did not mean to discover America because he was looking for a through sea route westwards to the Indies. It could be said that, like all Italians, he did not really know what he was doing even though he had the benefit of the use of a compass, invented by another Italian (Flavio Gioia), who had got the idea from the Arabs.

Another point worth mentioning is that in Italy, Columbus's voyage is seen both in a positive and negative sense: positively because of his exploits and the significance of the discovery; negatively because economically it was the turning point in world history. The economic centre moved away from Italy and the

Mediterranean and shifted to the western Nordic countries facing the Atlantic Ocean – all this in a relatively short period of time.

It does seem to be a national failing of the Italians that they make great discoveries without always realizing exactly the implications of what they are doing and, even though they may understand the significance quite well, once they have made the discovery they cease to be interested.

I have, of course, the greatest respect for Christopher Columbus, as we refer to him in English, whoever he was. The next time I am in Pavia I shall certainly go to the university library there and stare at his ashes; that is where the Italians claim that they are preserved. I know that there is an alternative claim that they are to be found in the cathedral in Santo Domingo: who knows? The Spaniards maintain that his remains are to be found in Seville cathedral where he was initially buried in 1506. They admit that in 1546 his bones were removed to Santo Domingo from where they travelled firstly to Havana cathedral and thence to Santiago De Compostela, ending ultimately in Seville cathedral in 1902.

(The Italians themselves seem to be in some doubt about the point since it is also claimed that part of his ashes are in an urn contained in the 'Palazzo Tursi' in Genova – the same Palazzo has in its custody Paganini's violin.)

Theories as to where Columbus was born emerge at regular intervals. The last two dating to 2005, are to the effect that (1) he was born in San Marino. . . . . and (2) a revival of the theory that he was born in Barcelona, the surname 'Colom' being obviously Catalan. I use the words advisedly because the Catalans themselves have always maintained that he was one of their own, as witness amongst

other things the impressive statue dedicated to him on the seafront in Barcelona.

It must be admitted that those closest to the idea that Columbus was not Italian are, of course, the Spaniards. For the year 2006, they have set up a commission to celebrate the five-hundredth anniversary of the death of the man they call Cristobal Colon. The latest theory, however, is that he didn't originate in Cataluña as some have claimed but was born in Galicia and was a historian and naval captain. In support of this, it is claimed that a number of names given to the lands conquered in Venezuela, Jamaica, Haiti, Cuba and so on, correspond to those still extant on the coasts of Pontevedra. Quite recently, there has been a similar claim by the Chinese, which appears spurious. Will anyone take pride in claiming not to have discovered America?. . . . .

1013 **The groundwork for the British claim to Canada was laid in 1497 by an Italian, Giovanni CABOTO. He is otherwise known as John Cabot, a name which may lead a number of people to believe that he was British. He was not. He was born in Genoa, but moved to Venice when still young. His son Sebastiano was born in Bristol, England, and both of them led the earliest English expeditions across the Atlantic.**

1014 **It was Giovanni CABOTO who discovered Newfoundland and indeed who anticipated Columbus by reaching this part of the new continent first. He was sailing in a British ship but he was at heart an Italian, so much so that he dug into the soil a standard with both the British flag and the rampant lion of St Mark. (Sir Humphrey Gilbert later claimed Newfoundland for England, in 1583.)**

It seems to be the destiny of Italians that they are not appreciated in their own country. Columbus sailed in a Spanish ship, Caboto in a British one and a number of other Italian sailors rendered service under the British flag. Filippo Albini had been in the service of King John and Leonardo Pessagno in that of Edward II and the two brothers Oberto and Niccolo' Usodimare had been in the service of Edward III.

Marconi had come to England to conclude his experiments with radio waves (see 'Communications') as did Pontecorvo with his genetic engineering.

For the Canadians, Marconi and Caboto are associated in a different sense. In 1901, Marconi received the first Transatlantic wireless radio signals from Poldhu in Cornwall on Signal Hill, at St John's, Newfoundland. The spot is next to Cabot Tower, a monument to Caboto.

1015 In 1524, Giovanni da VER-RAZZANO (also born in Florence) explored the coasts of North America and was the first European to sight New York (where a bridge is now named after him).

Verrazzano set sail on his remarkable voyage – he coasted the whole of North America from Florida to Newfoundland – from the Italian colony at Rouen in France. If Francis I had not been busy at the time making war in Italy, this might well have been a French venture instead of an Italian one.

1016 In 1579, a Jesuit Priest by the name of Alessandro VALIGNANO travelled extensively in Japan. He was the first to do this. His travels extended to the Far East generally and there he introduced Christianity. He was a forerunner of and assistant to Matteo Ricci.

Valignano was a very objective appraiser of Japan and Japanese culture. He remarked on how polite they all were and how well behaved in particular the Japanese children appeared to be. In fact, he reached the conclusion that everything that he saw in Japan was the reverse of what he saw in Europe, so that there was no similarity between Japanese and European people. The differences ranged from food, to language, and clothing, but above all, it was the social instincts and differences of the Japanese that he found most striking.

1017 In 1582, another Jesuit Priest, Matteo RICCI (born in Macerata), an early visitor to China, was the first to gain entrance to China's interior which at the time was closed to foreigners. He was a pioneer in his attempts to foster understanding between East and West.

His map of the world printed in Beijing (Peking) in 1602 was sold at auction at Christies in November 1989 and fetched the sum of £209,000, thus establishing a record as the highest price ever paid at auction for a map.

1018 Giacomo Costantino BEL-TRAMI (born in Bergamo in 1779) was one of the many Italians who landed in the USA. In August 1823, he was the first to reach by canoe the source of the Mississippi, an event which he recorded in his book *A Pilgrimage* published in London four years later (Hunt and Clarke).

1019 BELTRAMI also published the first complete map of the head of the river and explored the Lake Ithasca region nine years before Henry Schoolcraft, who is normally credited with the discovery.

I have already recorded the thefts of

antiquities by Belzoni (see 'Archaeology'), but there is another first by Italians which is associated with the River Nile.

1020 In 1856, Romolo GESSI (born at Constantinople) was the first to study the Nile. He is known more especially for having served under General Gordon and for being the first man to circumnavigate and map Lake Albert in Uganda.

When Gordon received the successful Gessi back in Khartoum, having read his report, he used somewhat patronizing words and is believed to have been rather clumsy in congratulating Gessi, who felt slighted and returned to Italy. General Gordon is alleged to have said: 'What a pity that you're not an Englishman.' Which was, to say the least, tactless.

Gessi went back to East Africa in 1878 with an all-Italian expedition, in the course of which he is said to have freed some 30,000 slaves from the control of Suleiman Bey, an Arab potentate who was interested in the slave trade.

An Italian writer living in the USA, Don Fiore, has described Gessi as 'Africa's Garibaldi' when he claims Gessi struggled to bring a new spirit to Africa's people while serving the racist British Empire.

Mention should be made here of the pioneering work in the fields of topography and map-making of the descendants of Giovanni Domenico Cassini. Their success may be found under the heading 'Astronomy', because of the means by which they carried out their work.

1021 Pellegrino MATTEUCCI (born Ravenna) was the first European to traverse the whole of the African continent north of the Equator from Egypt to the Gulf of Guinea. His journey began in February 1880 and was completed in July 1881. (R VI, p. 696.)

1022 Luigi ROBECCHI-BRICCHETTI (born Pavia) was the first European to cross the whole of the Somali Peninsula (the Horn of East Africa) in 1890/91. (R VIII, p. 610.)

1023 The first to plant a national flag in the proximity of the North Pole was Luigi di SAVOIA, Duke of the Abruzzi.

A soldier and explorer, a great admirer of the Norwegian Nansen, he chartered in 1899 a Norwegian whaling vessel, the *Jason* and immediately changed its name to *Stella Polare*. With it, and a crew of eleven Italians and nine Norwegians, he sailed from Archangel in Russia having taken on board 120 sledge dogs. The expedition travelled to the Pole and at a latitude 86° 34' Luigi Savoia planted the Italian flag. He was a mere twenty-six years of age.

To him we owe another first, namely the reaching of 7,500 metres on the Karakorum, anticipating his compatriots Compagnoni and Lacedelli (q.v.).

1024 Umberto NOBILE (born Lauro, near Salerno) was a pioneer in Arctic aviation. In 1926, he started from Rome on a 13,400 kilometre long voyage in his dirigible (airship) 'Norge'. An advanced piece of engineering, the airship was 104 metres long with a cabin ten metres long by 1.80 metres wide.

His was a joint venture with Roald Amundsen, whom some consider the greatest land explorer ever. They were accompanied by eight Norwegians, four Italians, two Swedes and the American, Elsworthy, who financed the expedition.

Leaving the Svalbard archipelago on 26 May they flew over the North Pole, dropping a Norwegian, an American and an Italian flag. Possibly to Amundsen's distaste, Nobile took his dog with him (R VII p. 368).

PART II

REFLECTIONS ON
ITALY AND
THE ITALIANS

1
WHO ARE THE ITALIANS?

The Italian peninsula is long and narrow, running from northwest to south-east for a length of about 800 miles. Its land boundary is about 1200 miles; the remainder is coastline. Its coastline extends to about 2600 miles (5300 if one includes the islands).

It hangs in the Mediterranean Sea almost like a reversed appendix from the intestine: its usual description is a boot. Its northern part is clearly attached to central Europe, but its southernmost tip of Sicily is almost contiguous to Africa (it was once joined to the African continent). To the west, it is a long way removed from Spain, whereas to the east it is much closer to the Balkans. Its northern regions of Lombardia and Piemonte are fertilized by the River Po – one of the longest rivers in Europe, which intersects an almost rectangular plain well cultivated and irrigated, with good centres of activity and excellent communications with the rest of the world. Indeed, it is interesting to note that, despite the Alps, communications between northern Italy and Europe have always been good, even before the building of the more recent Alpine tunnels. Nevertheless, the Italian side of the Alps is much steeper than the outside accesses and one of the consequences is that it is easier to travel into Italy from the north than out of Italy from the south: a well-established geographical fact which has had great historical repercussions.

The rest of the peninsula is so long, so lacking in centres of activity and so clearly cut into two by the Apennines, that the inevitable result was the isolation of certain parts of Italy. In the old days, as now, the rivers there were of no significance because they were mainly torrents and, until the advent of the motorway network, which is now fairly extensive, certain parts of the south remained inaccessible and totally isolated. Italy is largely a mountainous country (plains cover only 23 per cent of its total land mass), with about 1500 lakes, a wide range of soils and varying climatic conditions. Even some parts of the south can be bitterly cold, as the Eighth Army found to its cost in 1943/44.

This is Italy's geography in a nutshell. Now for a similar thumbnail sketch of its history.

☐

The Indo-European inhabitants of the Italian peninsula were firstly affected by the Greek colonization of Sicily towards the eighth century BC. Around the sixth century BC, this colonization spread northwards up the southeast tip of Italy and into Naples and the surrounding area. About the same time, the Phoenicians hopped over from Malta and the Carthaginians occupied the western coast of Sicily whilst the Venetians took over Sardinia.

Some time around 600 BC, northern Italy was occupied by the Ligurians and the Venetians, whereas south of the Po was the domain of the Umbrians, further south the Etruscans, and, close to the Tiber, the Sabines and the Latins. West of them were the Samnites and in Apulia the Iapigians. The two principal civilizations of Italy at this time were the Etruscan and the Greek.

All these different populations were ultimately consolidated into what became the Roman Empire which lasted for about nine centuries. But when that empire collapsed, the pressure of the barbarians along its boundaries ultimately became impossible to resist.

The Goths, led by Alaric, were the first to sack Rome in the year AD 410; they were followed by the Huns led by Attila, and then Jenseric's Vandals who in 455 took possession of Rome again. They came from Africa and it was easy for them to occupy both Sicily and Sardinia as well as rule the Mediterranean. As pirates, they met with no resistance.

But hardly a century had elapsed before the first German invasion occurred. These were the Lombards, so called because of their long beards, who had previously settled along the Danube. They created quite an impression. Their king, Alboin, entered Italy by the northeast in the Spring of 568, and moved south-west.

About two centuries later, the Lombards managed to come to terms with the Catholic Church but in turn were defeated by the Franks c.750. In the subsequent conquest of Italy by the Franks, Charlemagne exercised considerable influence over the country, now that it was once again part of a major empire. It ceased to be, therefore, the centre of gravity of the Western world as it had been basically since the time of the Romans. The Frankish occupation obviously made it very difficult for Italy to have any kind of autonomy. The result was an Italy split into the north held by the Franks, the centre held by the Popes, and the south still controlled by Byzantium.

The only benefit was that c.850 some of the Italian sea ports began to acquire a certain amount of independence. Naples and Amalfi, in particular, started to develop their fleets. Not a minute too soon because the Arabs from Tunisia began attacking Italy, taking possession of Sicily and pushing as far north as Rome.

This situation continued for 200 years, that is to say until the next lot of invaders, the Normans, turned up. By the year 1030, the Normans were settled in Naples and started attracting their brethren from the mist of Normandy to the sun of the south.

The next group to 'invade' Italy were the Crusaders. This was not an invasion of occupation and it resulted in a great exchange of business, information and culture between East and West. Italy hardly took any part in the Crusades in the sense that it sent few of its men to fight. It did, however, deal with the logistics of transport and provisioning of the Crusaders and in this way it strengthened its importance as a business centre as well as allowing its maritime powers (Venice, Genoa, Pisa, as well as Naples and Amalfi) to prosper.

The greatest contribution to the Crusades came from the French knights. They established certain concepts of chivalry which had no impact whatsoever on the Italians, save possibly in Sicily as a backcloth for the Mafia that was to develop later.

In 1194, Henry of Swabia was crowned Emperor in Palermo, concluding his campaign for control of Italy. The Germans were back. In 1266, Charles of Anjou was crowned King of Sicily. The French were back in southern Italy, but their occupation was not such a success. They had great problems with the locals and in 1282 the so-called War of the Vespers (which gave Rossini the idea for his 'Sicilian Vespers' opera) broke out.

When Charles of Anjou died, as a result of various dynastic complications Sicily and the south of Italy passed to the Spaniards. In 1494, Charles VIII of Spain took over. From this point onwards Italy ceases to have any significance in European history. The discovery of America and the route to the Indies had the effect of shifting economic power to the countries facing the Atlantic.

We have to wait until the war of Spanish succession for the next change. Effectively, as a result of the Treaties of Utrecht and Rastadt, the Austrians replaced the Spaniards. This may have been very useful from the administrative point of view because the Austrians were more efficient. But we were replacing one master who was inefficient with another one who was not quite so bad; we were still slaves and thus we remained, except for the short interlude that occurred from Napoleon's entry into Italy through the Great St Bernard Pass in May 1800 to his final defeat in 1815 when the Congress of Vienna consolidated the position of Italy, divided into a number of little states, as an appendage of Austria.

Indeed, it is true to say that the Congress of Vienna, which aimed at restoring the old order, seems to have been particularly keen to restore it for Italy; at any rate, in the sense that the hold of the Austro-Hungarian empire over northern Italy was considerably strengthened. Effectively, the most promising region of Italy had its development blocked. This prompted the French writer Lamartine to say Italy was 'the land of the dead' and Prince Metternich to call it a 'geographic expression'. That Italy was not dead was proved shortly after by the first revolutionary activity of 1820. Whether Metternich was right or wrong to call Italy a geographic expression must remain to this day a matter about which there can be a difference of opinion; but would not most readers agree it is a rather beautiful geographic expression?

There were further revolutionary movements in 1831 and, as is common knowledge, the first Italian war of independence started in 1848, continued as the second war in 1859 and resulted in a glorious end to that decade, for in 1860 Garibaldi conquered southern Italy for the Italian Royal House of Savoy.

The third war of independence took place in 1870 and it resulted in the fall of Rome (held until then by the Popes) on the 20 September of that year. To all intents and purposes, therefore, the first Italian State was constituted in 1861 and completed between that year and 1870. Other than by the Germans and the Allies during the Second World War, there were no further military invasions of Italy.

I must apologize to those readers who are 'historians' for the somewhat cavalier manner in which I have condensed nearly two thousand years of Italian history into a few paragraphs. The point is, I wish to remind the reader of the very simple fact, namely, that the make-up of the Italian people has been influenced by all those who ruled over the peninsula. The intermingling of blood ('native', barbaric, Muslim, Norman, French, German, Austrian, Spanish) by invasion is greater than has occurred in any other country of the world that I know. Let us now look at who the Italians are.

□

It would of course be too trite to say that the Italians are the inhabitants of Italy, a country, as we have seen, which in the opinion of Lamartine was dead and in the opinion of Prince Metternich was not a political entity. But according to one of our own, Vincenzo Gioberti, the Italians do not even exist. Writing in the nineteenth century, he went so far as to say that the Italian people were not a fact but an ambition, a hypothesis rather than a reality. They were so divided in terms of government, laws, institutions, speech, customs, tendencies and habits, that they could not be dignified by the term 'people'.

He was not being unkind. He was trying to awaken the national conscience. But, in so doing, he was reminding us of the very unusual political nature of the Italians. He was recalling how varied their nature is and how marked the regional differences. He was, in essence, being an Italian himself; but of the better kind.

This is hardly surprising, because there is no such thing as a typical Italian; there are a number of Italians diversified according to the part of Italy from which they come and the social class to which they belong. And in any event, it is usually easier for a foreigner to paint his own picture of a people. But, such pictures are invariably stereotypes; also because foreigners are so difficult to please.

In 1902 Edward Hutton (*Italy and The Italians*, Blackmore) wrote: 'The Italians! It was easier to find them twenty years ago than it is today. Today there are Romans, Florentines, Neapolitans, Venetians. . .' Who was right, I wonder: Gioberti or Hutton?

These stereotypes are fairly well established. For instance, according to R. Brown, in *Social Psychology* (New York, 1965) when students at Princeton University are invited to describe Italians, they say that they are 'artistic, impulsive, and passionate'. Other foreigners ascribe to the Italians certain characteristics which they feel are typical, namely that they are kind-hearted, intuitive, lazy and undisciplined, hard-working, sceptical, womanizers, and so on.

Italians are always described as paragons of Machiavellism and duplicity. Indeed, according to Ann Radcliffe who wrote *The Italians or the Confessional of the Black Penitents* in 1786, the typical Italian is 'a creature with arms and legs of enormous size, who always dresses in black with a large hat that covers his half-open eyes prone to betrayal'.

Some fifty years later, around 1820-24, Paganini was to be seen always dressed in black and often wearing dark spectacles. Radcliffe, therefore, could hardly have invented her stereotype. Furthermore, Italians, she states, are Machiavellian courtesans and Papists worthy of the Spanish Inquisition. That an educated English lady could claim to define an Italian in these terms some 200 years ago is clearly absurd. Stendhal thought that she simply did not know what she was talking about. She certainly displayed the (by then) well-established xenophobic tendencies of the British.

In the early nineteenth century, a Swiss writer by the name of Bonstetten in his work *L'Homme du midi et l'Homme du nord* commented that the Italian was basically a happy-go-lucky, cheerful and improvident peasant, the light-hearted fly that lives from day to day, and contrasted him with the man from the north who, having to spend most of his time indoors because of his country's inclement weather, had more time to plan his future and was in effect the wise virgin of the Gospel.

The descriptions are never-ending but it seems to me that what we may call the character or nature of the Italians changes according to the time and place of the analysis and, above all, it changes according to the point of view of the observer.

I believe that it is almost impossible to define the character of a people. The only way one can do it is negatively, by referring to their history. That is useful as a canon of construction of the people as a whole, but no guide whatsoever to the character of the individual. There is no relation, in my view, between the two.

Take, for example, the fact that Britain created a great empire. Is it to be believed that it succeeded in doing so because of its innate ethnic or racial superiority? It seems to me that the reverse is more likely to be true, namely that because it had established an empire, it was able to develop a kind of ethnic and racial superiority mentality which was perhaps latent and which would never have come to the fore but for the historical accident of the empire.

The same considerations apply to all peoples. We are what we pretend to be or, alternatively, what others believe us to be, or, in the last resort, what history has made us. In our case, those who have purported to analyse, describe or classify Italians have been foreigners who may have travelled through the country, historians purporting to identify a particular type of artistic or political behaviour or philosophers trying to make a synthesis of certain presumed common traits; they might also have been detractors, who found them inferior.

John Ruskin, for example, who after the initial shock of his first visit to Italy became a devotee of Italian art, was certainly less than flattering of the Italians. Upset by the apparent neglect of their antiquities and artistic treasures which he considered part of the patrimony of humanity as a whole, he wrote: 'Take them all in all, I detest these Italians beyond measure. . . : they are Yorick's skull with the worms in it, nothing of humanity left but the smell' (John Ruskin, *Works*, Volume XXXVI, p. 48). But he went even further. He looked upon the Italians generally as corrupt and decadent; he considered the ordinary Italian to be idle and totally unconcerned about his heritage. Elsewhere, he wrote that the ordinary Italian was 'lazy, lousy, scurrilous, cheating, lying, thieving, hypocritical, brutal, blasphemous, obscene, cowardly, earthly, sensual, devilish' (Letters to his Parents, 23 October 1845).

Italian postillions, douaniers and country people 'appear knaves of the first and most rapacious water' (*Ruskin in Italy*, ed. Shapiro, Clarendon Press, 1972, p. 50); Italian people 'seem bad enough for anything' (ibid, p. 51). 'Beggars, mosquitos, customs officers, priests even, were a great nuisance, evil, smelling, and vile' (ibid, pp. 86 & 160). Compared to the Swiss, Italians grumbled and swore: they were 'very barbarous', uncaring about art and about anything that was good (ibid, p. 114).

But that is not quite sufficient for Ruskin. He also finds the opportunity to say in very much the same vein: 'If I were the devil, I wouldn't buy these Italians to roast at a farthing a pound – they smell so abominably already' (ibid, p. 154); elsewhere: 'I am quite sick of Italy – the people are too much for me – it is like travelling among a nation of malignant idiots, with just brains enough to make them responsible for their vices – they have taken the whole feeling of the country away from me' (ibid, p. 194).

You may feel at this stage that Ruskin was going too far. Not so; here is another sample: 'Now, if I could put these Italians in a waterbutt with the top on, or roast them in sulphur a little, or wash them in steepdown gulfs of liquid fire, or in any other way convey to them a delicate expression of opinion, it would do my heart good, but as it is I am so sick that I believe I shall have to give up art altogether' (Letters to his Parents, 7 September 1845).

One hears echoes, in these unkind qualifications, of his complaisant Protestantism which came under pressure from Catholic art as soon as he set foot in Italy, one sees a reaction to his strict Chapel upbringing and one realizes how great the impact must have been on a northerner (arguably almost a Scot) – who had led a secluded life until about the age of twenty – of places bursting with beauty like the Alps, with history and art like Venice and with power and sensuality like Naples.

I wonder why, if he disliked the Italians so much, he felt he had to return to Italy from time to time throughout his life. It surely was not just for the cheap food. . . On one of his many stops on the road, he dined on 'macaroni soup, an excellent beef steak, a dish of fresh-cut asparagus, cheese, a bottle of lemonade, and wine of course, ad libitum' all for 2½ 'Paoli', about 13 pence. Not bad, I suppose, even though all he could see around him was 'ugliness, meanness, vice, folly, idleness, infidelity, filth, misery, desecration, dissipated youth, wicked manhood and withered, sickly, hopeless age' (*Ruskin in Italy*, op. cit. p. 51). To be fair to him, he did give the Italians credit for their music. Comparing them to the French, (*Ruskin in Italy*, op. cit. p. 242) he states that 'the music in the Italian churches beats them hollow. I used to think music was an art, but I am sure now it is nothing but an instinct, since those brutes of Italians have it in what God has given them as a substitute for souls.' Perhaps he should have remained in England; but no, he went abroad repeatedly. He enjoyed both France and Switzerland but, despite everything, Italy above all. His first trip to Italy dates from 1833-34 but he returned there in 1840-41, 1843-45, 1846-48, 1849-50 and 1851-52. In 1845 he went for the first time on his own, with a servant.

Up to this date, although he had been once to Rome and Naples, he had spent most of his time up north, especially in Venice. Ruskin was greatly attracted to the Alps. Perhaps in the majesty and whiteness of the scenery he saw a reflection of himself, 'everything pure and bright'.

He wrote in his diary for 23 November 1840: 'How often, in the monotony of the English scenery, I shall remember that panorama of snow and marble, with a wild, sick yearning – the desire of the moth for the star, of the night for the morrow.'

But there is probably a less romantic explanation. Ruskin suffered from consumption; the pure air of the Alps would have certainly proved more congenial to him than that of other parts of Italy.

The impact of the south, however, was of a different kind. It did not seem to be too immediate but it has been said that his first visit to Naples 'started trains of thought which did not take clear course till forty years afterwards'. (*The Wider Sea – A life of John Ruskin*, John Dickson Hunt, G. M. Dent & Son, London, 1982.)

Ruskin seemed to combine his enthusiasm for northern Italian art and architecture with his contempt for southern Italy, especially Naples, which he termed as 'the most loathsome nest of human caterpillars I was ever forced to stay in', adding that, in his view, Naples was certainly 'the most disgusting place in Europe'.

In 1854-56, he went back to northern Italy again, much taken by Turin. In 1860, he returned to Milan to copy the frescoes of Bernardino Luini. In 1869, he was back in Verona and Venice and he returned to Venice in 1870, the year in which he also revisited Florence, Pisa and Siena.

In 1871 and 1874, he made two more visits to Pisa. Also in 1874, he was in Rome and Naples and he travelled as far south as Sicily which he was seeing for the first time. In 1876-77, he was again in Venice and in 1882 he visited Pisa, Florence and Lucca once more. In 1888, he made his last trip abroad and visited Venice. But this was to be the last time. He died on 20 January 1900.

Unless I have got it wrong, he visited Italy fifteen times, on occasions for stays greater than two years. I wonder how he reconciled his view of the Italians with his love for Italy and Italian art. I am not being unkind to him, for he rendered Italy a great service by publicizing its deficiencies in caring for its artistic heritage; and he was a lover of the country, and as such worthy of the utmost respect. He also rendered enormous service to the English by imparting to them a true knowledge of Italian art in all its forms.

For present purposes, however, I am mainly interested not in his artistic leanings but in his judgement of the Italians and I find that it is suspect, since it was too obviously influenced by the deficiencies in his own personality and make-up: it lacks objectivity, it is too rhetorical. After all – and one does not need to be an iconoclast to make the observation – what was he if not an imitator and commentator, a teacher, and an interpreter? But he created nothing, either in the artistic or in the physical sense. He was a restless soul, he could never stay put in one place, except Italy, for longer than about six months; but his was the restlessness of impotence, not of creativity.

Are these the right qualifications for passing a thoroughly negative and highly critical judgement on a whole people? Did he perhaps consider that Luini, Carpaccio, Tintoretto, Veronese and Tiziano, to choose at random, were not Italian or, maybe, ought not to have been born such?

How Ruskin must have suffered, I have no doubt, when he thought it was these pale, effeminate, lazy, cheating, animal-eyed, listless , sulky, filthy, unhappy, sensual creatures who had been able to find that balance between beauty and everyday life which meant so much to him, who were able to live amidst the ruins of antiquity apparently entirely uninfluenced by and uninterested in them; and yet, who were the creators of the very art and beauty for which he longed, but which he could not either in his mind or in his body ever attain. (All the adjectives I have used above are taken from Ruskin's Letters to his Parents as applied to the Italians, especially of central and southern Italy. He was not so aggressive about northerners.)

As I have already observed, these hasty criticisms stem on the one hand from arrogance and on the other from an impacted psyche: the northerner's intellectual pseudo-superiority finds itself under pressure in the Mediterranean. It is hardly surprising that Ruskin should have concentrated on the brutality, obscenity, earthiness and sensuality of the Italians when he himself was impotent; his six-year-old marriage was annulled because of his incapacity to consummate it by reason of incurable impotence. The decree of nullity of his marriage weighed on him all his life and I am not aware that, even though he claimed it was wrong, he was ever able to prove otherwise.

Let us not forget that it was Ruskin who, apart from being so critical of the Italians or, I would argue, exactly because of his approach to them and to life, became guilty of the 'crime' of destroying hundreds of Turner's sketches after the painter's death, because he considered them pornographic.

It is entirely possible, of course, that some of the adjectives Ruskin used to describe the Italians in his time, could be true even today of some Italians. Incidentally, I wonder whether Ruskin would himself have obtained any notoriety whatsoever if he had not had the opportunity of studying and living in proximity to the works of those very Italians he failed utterly to understand.

(Ruskin's views must be interpreted in context: the British Empire was at its peak, and England was the most 'civilized' country at the time; on the other hand, Italy was at its lowest point, ravaged by wars, internal strife and conquest. The turning point was unification. What is remarkable is that in the space of about one hundred years, from 1870, Italy has emerged from being a downtrodden agrarian country to a modern industrialized country – economically one of the top seven in the world (G7).)

□

If I have spent an undue amount of time considering Ruskin's petulant observations it is because I believe that they represented the view that, on the whole, the Victorians formed about Italians. Put differently, Ruskin offset the great service he rendered Italian art by his assessment of what the Italian people were like. The caricatures he published permeated educated English society for the whole of the nineteenth and for part of the twentieth centuries. Indeed, it can be said that Ruskin's views retained their authority in England until the early 1950s. It was only then that with the advent of mass tourism the English were able to see for themselves what Italy and the Italians were really like and began to appreciate that despite her defeat in the Second World War, Italy was anything but dead. The vitality of Italy is a feature that strikes most visitors today: it is as though Italy were coming into its own, after centuries of slavery and comparative decay. But that is anticipating somewhat the conclusions that I shall be reaching. Let us first return to the nineteenth century for a few further observations.

About seventy years separate Ruskin's pronouncements from the escape to Italy of D.H. Lawrence, accompanied by Frieda Richthofen. If one reads Lawrence, the Italians have altered so dramatically that it is impossible to believe that they have changed in that period. Lawrence viewed Italy from an entirely different angle to Ruskin's: more working class, less inclined to rationalization, more reliant upon his instinct for common humanity and much influenced by his own sexuality.

There are a number of permutations to be considered here in order to explain the substantial difference between the judgements formulated by Ruskin and D.H. Lawrence. In the first place, it is possible that the Italians themselves had changed in the intervening seventy years. This, as I have said, is almost impossible to believe because the change is too dramatic and could not have been achieved over such a comparatively short span.

One must therefore consider whether either Ruskin or D.H. Lawrence saw the wrong picture. A decision on this is dictated by whether one prefers the view of the impotent or the dynamic, the assessment of a critic steeped in artistic beliefs to that of a man ready to be affected more or less objectively by the images he saw.

Lawrence was in Italy in the company of a woman and not on his own with a manservant, like Ruskin. He got on well in Italy. He still thought that the locals had a dark soul and he was perhaps too insistent upon what he called the 'phallic divinity' which he claimed marks the Italians' way of thinking. But he liked the common people and he understood the spirit of the country.

He was a keen student of things Etruscan and correctly identified the influence that those articulate, sensuous, pleasure-seeking, 'modern' people had exerted on the Italian spirit. He ascribed greater impact to Etruscan influences on Italy than to Roman; and he was instinctively in the right about this.

In a sense, however, he may have laid undue stress (*Twilight in Italy*, William Heinemann, London, 1956) on the all-pervasiveness of sexuality. From that outlook upon Italian life (op. cit., pp. 35, 45 & 137), he drew the conclusion that it was an absolute dedication to matters sensual rather than spiritual that was sapping the energies of the Italians, whereas the same was not happening in northern countries. This a typical northern judgement of southern races generally and is one which I cannot share, since it stems from a psychological northern obsession with matters sexual that fails to find a satisfactory physical outlet.

It seems to me that the sexual appetite, in so far as it represents primarily a physical need and only secondarily a psychological one, is satiated by its satisfaction in the same manner as hunger pangs are assuaged by the intake of food. It is only those who battle with sexuality who perforce have it constantly before their eyes.

Furthermore, I doubt that it is correct to overrate sensuality or at any rate to assume that powerful sensuality reduces strength of mind and purpose. I find this a common misconception: whether it arises from a failure to understand to what extent one can separate physical from mental activity or whether it is the main plank in the argument that, in certain intellectual respects, the northern races are superior, I have yet to determine.

For these reasons, I am not too sure how correct an analysis even D.H. Lawrence makes of the Italians. The distinction between sensuality and rationality, between the mind and the body, art and ugliness, beauty and technology, is as marked in Italy as the distinction between the sacred and the profane: they all coexist. It is a mistake to suppose that because conduct is capable of being classed as profane according to certain standards, one is therefore incapable of appreciating and attaining the sacred: St Augustine is the best example.

There is here a dichotomy that northerners who come to Italy because of their artistic leanings find somewhat difficult to explain. They are so enthralled by its art and beauty that they are reluctant to accept, as concomitants, poverty and ugliness, darkness and neglect. Such reluctance arises because they come to Italy with pre-conceived stereotypical ideas, almost divorced from feelings of common humanity: their enthusiasm for art is too great.

There is a certain type of foreigner, of which Ruskin is a classic example, whose avowed love or appreciation of Italy is no more than a reaction to a desperate need to commune with the country that has always been capable of communicating the message of its history and civilization to those who sought it in order to transmit it to their own country.

This search for the spirit of civilizations past is the outcome of a basic deficiency. Hence the anger and annoyance at the apparent neglect by the locals for their art.

The trouble is that when you grow up amidst art and antiquities, they become part of yourself and no longer have any extraordinary meaning. To the extent that they are absorbed by the intellect and the eye, they blend so intimately with everyday life and the landscape that they cease to have any especial significance. In a somewhat similar context, it is the converts to any religion who feel more strongly about it than those who were baptized or initiated into it at a very early age.

By this token, any judgement of the Italians made by those whose sole purpose in visiting Italy is to remedy their own cultural deficiencies rather than to comprehend its true spirit is, in my view, not worth very much at all. And it is extreme conceit on the part of such persons even to attempt to express an opinion.

Fortunately, not all Englishmen are like Ruskin or indeed Roger Ascham. Edward Hutton seemed somewhat more enthusiastic when he said: 'Without Italy I am beggared. Though God saw fit to make me an Englishman, it was in Italy I caught my first glimpse of heaven.'

And, in its Italian supplement for 21 March 1934, the *Times Literary Supplement* said: 'The world's debt to Italy is infinite: for these last two thousand years and more the influence of Italy, ancient, medieval and modern, has shaped the history of civilization and set the course of its achievements.' This comment is almost paraphrasing G.M. Trevelyan when he said that the cultural gain that England made at the expense of Italy represents 'a debt that England can never repay'.

Goethe was equally flattering. In his *Italian Journey* – 22 September 1786 – he remarks that the Italians 'consider themselves the finest people in the world, an opinion which, thanks to certain excellent qualities which they undeniably possess, they can hold with impunity'. How nice of him. He was less flattering on his second trip to Italy, perhaps because he saw things a little more clearly.

These totally opposed and contradictory judgements of the Italians highlight the difficulty in reconciling some of the features that they display, which are so multifarious as to defy classification and analysis.

The Italians themselves have not bothered to make a synthesis, historical or psychological, of these contradictions and it seems to be a fact that all the people who have put pen to paper to describe the Italians have in the main been foreigners. There is no doubt that only very rarely have they been Italian.

In the Introduction I have already referred to the lack of writing by Italians about Italians. In 1768, one of the Italians who spent a considerable time in England, Giuseppe Baretti, wrote his *Account of the Manners and Customs in Italy*. But his was an apologia of the Italians in comparison with the English. He was really trying to say that we were at fault because we were not more like the English. The other Italians writers who covered the same subject matter (Beccaria, Verri, Filangieri, Sismondi) were more concerned with the failings of our political institutions. For his part, Alfieri was in turn berating us because we were not more like the Romans; so, to that extent, his feelings were almost English, and perhaps that is why Byron admired him so much. In 1828, Leopardi was quite scathing about the Italians. He found them both divided and divisive, unworthy of being a nation.

It strikes me that all these Italian writers were highly critical of their fellow countrymen, and understandably so. But none of them, as far as I know, except for Sismondi, ever embarked on any analysis of the good that we have done. Take for example, the Italian republics of the Middle Ages, starting with the tenth century and ending with the defeat of Venice. Naples, Amalfi, Pisa, Genoa and Venice were the pillars of the then civilized world. In business terms, they were what today Japan and the United States night be. No-one gives Italy credit for them, especially not for little Amalfi.

I suppose it is true to say that many people know that Venice was once the Queen of the Adriatic, a major centre of business and a great political power.

Venetian sea-power and efficient government are too well known to require restatement by me. In terms of civic amenities, Venice was well ahead of its times: the first dogal ordinance to prescribe compulsory street lighting at night goes back to 1128. In pursuit of an ever more efficient navy, the Venetians thought up the idea of mounting cannons on ships and, anticipating Henry Ford by many centuries, devised also a form of assembly line in order that they might build galleys in a hurry.

Everybody knows Pisa because of its leaning tower. Equally, most people will have heard of Genoa for one reason or another; and if they are opera lovers, Simon Boccanegra reminds them of the conflicts within the Fieschi family. Genoese sailors and merchants have left their mark throughout the Mediterranean, from Mallorca and the Costa Brava, to Constantinople, Algeria and Tunisia. And of course, everybody knows Naples.

But I am confident it never occurs to the average tourist sunning himself on the beach of Amalfi that when in his own country his ancestors were eking out a meagre existence either as serfs or in any event as poor, uncouth peasants digging potatoes, the Republic of Amalfi was, as far back as the ninth, tenth and eleventh centuries, a major centre of civilization and culture.

I have already mentioned its rules of the sea under the heading 'Law' and the discovery or at least extensive use of the compass by one of its inhabitants. But in any event, as early as the twelfth century, business was thriving in Amalfi, Praiano, Positano and Ravello. The whole of the coastline from Naples to Salerno was punctuated by small towns and villages inhabited by rich merchants and sailors who lived in houses surrounded by gardens and fountains (see Boccaccio's *Decameron*, Day 2, Novel 4). Indeed, so great was the enterprise of the people of Amalfi that in the tenth century it had already established itself as one of the major commercial centres in the world, competing with Venice, even though it had no port, its ships being roped on to the beach by the people.

Nor should it be forgotten that to Amalfi we owe the Order of the Knights of Malta, formerly the Knights of Rhodes. In the year 1020, merchants from Amalfi obtained the right to establish a hospital and a church near the Holy Sepulchre. That was the origin of the Order which stretched its influence over the Mediterranean basin for many centuries.

Amalfi itself was a thriving town. Guglielmo Appulo wrote that during the eleventh century no town in the world was richer than Amalfi in gold, silver and cloth; it was a busy centre of trade and was frequented by Arabs, Sicilians, Africans and Indians.

Leaving history aside, it is meaningless to try and ask oneself who the Italians are and attempt to consider a people in isolation. It was Sir James Hudson who, in about 1864, is quoted as saying that the English were thoroughly well informed about Italy but in the most hopeless ignorance as to the Italians (cited in *The Golden Ring* by Giuliana Artom Treves, Longmans Green & Co., London, 1956). Such ignorance still prevails today.

Historically, Italians are an amalgam of different races and different needs. But, surprising though this may sound, they are a cohesive amalgam. Though the political bond may be tenuous, cultural ties are solid. There are historical reasons for this.

Of course, we all know who the Italians are. Obviously, the failed successors of the Romans, the allies of the Germans in the Second World War and the founders of the Mafia. That may give us some information about the history of Italy, but I believe it tells us nothing at all about the Italian male or female. In my view, any attempt to determine national character is doomed to failure unless it is related to the national character and culture of other peoples. It is only in this way, which is a somewhat negative way of looking at it, that we may be able to say that the Italian art of cooking is better than the English but the English have a greater civic sense than the Italians. Having said this, I am not quite sure exactly what is proved, save that the Italians are different from the English.

2

THE ITALIAN IMPACT ON ENGLAND

Much has already been written concerning the effect that Italian culture has had upon Britain (but England in particular) in so many different fields, including poetry, painting, architecture, landscape gardening or whatever. I decided that my approach, therefore, should be a practical, non-academic one with a view to demonstrating on the one hand how the English react to us and on the other that in the cross-fertilization of ideas that is inevitable in life, the usual two-way flow of influence between Italy and England has accrued to the benefit of the latter. This is not to say that the benefit has been only one way; but the impact of the Italians upon England has been greater and more beneficial than the reverse. And it has been quite substantial. I propose to provide an overall picture of that impact.

After all, it was an Italian who 'discovered' England, an Italian who brought it Christianity, and an Italian who taught it manners (Julius Caesar, St Augustine and Baldassar Castiglione, respectively).

When Julius Caesar invaded Britain in 55 BC, he established two firsts, one for Rome and the other for Britain. He annexed a new province, thus extending the boundary of an already impressive empire and he brought Britain out of pre-history and put it, as it were, 'on the map'.

His second invasion one year later and the expedition made by Claudius in AD 43 consolidated not only Roman power in Britain, but also a situation which was to last for a further 323 years from Claudius's journey, with significant consequences for the world, although they were not to become apparent until the sixteenth century and were certainly not appreciated at the time.

As they had done to other provinces, the Romans brought civilization to Britain. They brought their system of government, of law, of building, their art, their Greek medicine, all that contributed to establishing within the territories that they ruled a gentler society than they found, and a more settled one.

They built posts, forts, roads, camps, towns, baths, villas and palaces; they established agriculture, medicine, architecture and discipline.

They endeavoured to create that 'Pax Romana' which, centuries later, the

British Empire was to convert for its possessions into 'Pax Britannica'; they gave their citizenship in the same way as British nationality was later extended to all races in the Queen's dominions.

Above all, they came with a firm belief in their own ability to mould history, in their nobility of spirit and of caste and in their outstanding military techniques and dicipline.

It is interesting to note that when Britain found itself in a position to establish an empire of its own, it claimed and indeed displayed all the virtues which the Romans had brought with them many centuries before. As I shall observe later on, in the political sense there is no doubt whatsoever that Britain was the successor of Rome.

The Italians (or Romans, if you prefer) who filtered over to Britain in the three-and-a-half centuries that it remained a province of the Roman Empire were not only those in overall command. As well as consuls, or pro-consuls, there were army officers, soldiers, auxiliaries, farmers, technicians, doctors, road builders: they permeated all classes of British society.

The extant records make it impossible to decide now what the effect was in quantitative terms but, qualitatively speaking, it cannot have been negligible.

I wonder how many English people carry Roman blood. Nor should this be at all surprising, given the inevitable intermarriages; and it is hardly a coincidence that a psychological Roman heritage exists, given the fact that Britain was able to prove that it did by establishing a fairly close equivalent of the Roman Empire.

For present purposes, I discount, through my ignorance, the suggestion made by the English historian Goldsworth that King Arthur was in reality a Roman called Arturius who was at the head of the last legion that the Romans left in England when they decided to abandon it. He made himself King of the Saxons and applied his Roman war techniques to organize the local tribesmen.

It is said by Goldsworth that this was not too difficult because both he and his soldiers had in the meantime intermarried with locals. They formed their base at Camulodunum, which later became known in England as Camelot; they are said to have created the Round Table and its Knights.

One is reluctant to call the British Empire an atavistic regression to the time of the Britons' emancipation from primitive life; but the pride of Macaulay in his ancestors may have had justifications that went beyond the purely historical and that were of a more physical/psychological nature. Who knows?

In 1269, Henry III entrusted to an Italian ('Petrus Romanus') the task of building the new shrine of Edward the Confessor in Westminster Abbey and 200 years later Henry VII did likewise for his own tomb and for the sculptures that decorate the New Lady Chapel there.

As is common knowledge, most of the English country houses are indebted to Palladio, and Christopher Wren could certainly not have been in a position to design St Paul's had it not been for his knowledge of Italian architecture, and the influence that it had on him.

One of the other architectural imports from Italy was the style of the banqueting hall in Whitehall, outside which Charles I was publicly beheaded in 1649.

The Reading Room in the British Museum is the work of an Italian. Many more instances will follow of circumstances where the Italian effect on things English has been quite noticeable.

Let me be a little more specific.

Take poetry for example. One can talk of 'Italian currents in English poetry' (Lytton Sells, *The Italian influence in English Poetry*) but I am not aware of any reverse influences. Great though the English poets have been, their influence on Italian poetry is slight, if non-existent. It is true that Eugenio Montale, during one of his stays in England, was inspired to write a poem about Eastbourne on a wet day with the band playing 'God Save the King'. But it is his view of that seaside resort that was embodied in the poem and his style was totally unaffected; he could just as easily have written about Hong Kong and his poetry would have been exactly the same. One wonders, on the other hand, how different the poetry and style of Byron and Shelley would have been if they had never set foot in Italy. There, they were alerted to a new feeling for style and for life which intoxicated them.

Chaucer was in Italy in 1368, 1372 and 1378. (A man of some versatility, Chaucer, for in 1372 he went to Genoa to negotiate a naval treaty; he was a lawyer of the Inner Temple.) He 'took much from the Italians' (Dr Johnson – 9 April 1778.)

There is ample evidence (Sells, op. cit., pp. 19 to 67) that Chaucer got ideas there from the three great Italians of that period, namely Dante, who died in 1321, Petrarca and Boccaccio, both of whom were still alive when Chaucer was in Italy – ideas as to subject-matter, style and rhyming techniques. The reader who wants to know the details upon which the foregoing statements are made is referred to Lytton Sells as quoted above, but it is common knowledge that his *Canterbury Tales* are derived from the stories in Boccaccio's *Decameron* and his *Troilus* from Boccaccio's *Filostrato*. And many other English works were inspired by Boccaccio: there are numerous instances where knowledge of his writings is apparent in both Byron's *Childe Harold's Pilgrimage* and *Don Juan*.

Shelley enthusiastically translated some of Dante's work and is well known for displaying the same spiritual approach to woman as that of the noble Florentine.

English writers of the period equally appreciated Italian romantic poetry such as is to be found in Boiardo, Ariosto, Tassoni and Pulci. In particular, Ariosto had a very marked and direct influence on Sir Walter Scott, his 'Ivanhoe' being a successor, in feats and in style, of Ariosto's Paladin Knights.

Thomas Wyatt and Henry Howard learnt from the Italian love poetry of Dell'Aquila, Aretino, Alemanni, Trissino, as well as, of course, from Petrarca (op. cit., pp. 68 to 81).

John Cheke, William Thomas, and Thomas Hoby profited from their contacts with Italy: and Sir Philip Sydney could not have had the influence he exercised throughout his life unless he had been steeped in classical and Italian culture.

When it comes to Spenser, however, the ties become much closer. As Lytton Sells has pointed out (op. cit., pp. 152, 156 to 159, 160, 166, 167, 171 and 175) he borrowed extensively from Machiavelli, Castiglione, Petrarca, Boiardo, Trissino, Tasso, Ariosto and Sannazaro. His *Faerie Queen* echoes Ariosto's *Orlando Furioso*.

The influence of Italy on Shakespeare the poet is perhaps less noticeable than that on Shakespeare the comedy/tragedy writer; according to Lytton Sells it still exists.

When it comes to Shakespeare's language, any student will know the extent to which he relies on the kind of structure which originated in Latin and which Norman-French and Italian preserved.

But many words he uses are borrowed directly from Italian, for example:

Argosy from Ragusa; Bergomask, from the peasants of the Bergamasco, the area around Bergamo in Lombardy; Bezonian, from the Italian adjective 'bisognoso' (needy); Bona-roba; Canzonet, from canzonetta (a short song); Capocchia; Fardel (a bundle), from Fardello; Gaberdine, from gavardina, Hay, from hai; Monarcho; Traject, from Traghetto.

Quite apart from the linguistic aspect, the influence of Italian culture on Shakespeare the writer is very great. He was himself thoroughly versed in the classics, of course, and it was thanks to the Italian humanists that the studies of the classics had been revived. Shakespeare was no small humanist himself and he is in a sense the next link in the chain that started with Petrarca and continued with Boccaccio and Castiglione. Furthermore, it has been suggested (Frances Yates, *Giordano Bruno and the Hermetic Tradition*) that Shakespeare was extensively influenced by Bruno.

Far be it from me to interfere with the almost reverential approach that the English have always displayed when dealing with Shakespeare, but there is no denying that he was influenced by the work of John Florio in many ways. Furthermore, many of his plots had their inspiration in *Le Novelle* of Matteo Maria Bandello and the *Ecatommiti* of Giambattista Giraldi, whom we have already mentioned. The reader may wish to be reminded at this stage that *Romeo and Juliet* have literary, as distinct from geographic, Italian roots of some importance. It was Luigi Da Porto who got the idea of the story of *Romeo and Juliet* from Masuccio Salernitano (in the *Novellino*, novel 33).

Da Porto introduced into it the dantesque names 'Cappelletti' (later turned into 'Capuleti') and 'Montecchi' through a misreading of a verse in Dante's *Divine*

Comedy (*Purgatory* VI, 106). The same idea was picked up again by M.M. Bandello in 1554 and by Broocke in 1562 and ultimately made universally known by William Shakespeare.

Principally, however, it can be said that Shakespeare was essentially concerned with human character, problems and emotions, as Italian writers had been before him. He was very much an individualist and a realist, both obvious Italian traits.

His eighteen or more plays set in Italy or with Italian themes show him at his most charming and graceful. Ultimately, this is the debt that Shakespeare owes Italy, namely that its culture focused his imagination and awareness and gave it charm.

I have left the other major English poet prior to the eighteenth century, namely Milton, until last. If I believe Norman Douglas (*Old Calabria*, 1962 ed., pp. 173 to 185) then Milton's *Paradise Lost* is a copy of a sacred tragedy by the title of *Adamo Caduto* written in 1647 by Serafino della Salandra. The reader who wants to know the details is referred to *Old Calabria*. It seems that without Salandra's *Adamo, Paradise Lost* as we know it would not be in existence inasmuch as Milton copied not only the layout and the idea, but actually the precise words. It is conceivable, of course, that Norman Douglas is wrong, or perhaps is not in earnest: I have not indulged in the kind of research that would enable me to say with any conviction what the truth is, assuming it to be capable of verification. Nor do I quote the above in any critical sense of Milton; quite the reverse. It is highly flattering for an Italian that Milton should have done what Norman Douglas alleges he did. Fashions change, of course, and nobody except students, who are forced to do so, now bothers to read Milton any more than they read Salandra; but it is all part of the general picture that I am painting that Milton should be so greatly indebted to Italy.

Whether Milton did or did not copy Salandra, it is a fact, as Joseph Addison has remarked, that Milton could never have described the garden of Eden without having seen the gardens of Italy.

By the end of the sixteenth century it had become fashionable for English noblemen to harbour Continental refugees, including scores of Italians, who were especially welcome. Queen Elizabeth I liked them and she is known to have been very fond of the Italian language, which she often spoke in public.

Amongst these Italian refugees was Petruccio Ubaldini, a Florentine, who first came here in 1545 but did not finally settle in England until 1562. He is remembered for his account, in Italian, of the victory over the Armada, published within a few months of the event. He was liked by Elizabeth, who gave him a pension. He always wrote in Italian, a fact that was readily accepted at the time. Apart from his writings, he was a skilled illuminator and some of his manuscripts have survived.

Federico Zuccaro painted in 1574, the year of his arrival in England, the by now famous portrait of Queen Elizabeth I.

He also painted other important persons such as Sir Nicholas Bacon, the father of Francis, the Earl of Howard, and the Head of the English Secret Service, Sir Francis Walsingham.

The seventeenth and eighteenth centuries were not marked by any great literary influence of Italy upon England; Italian literature at this period was hardly known in England and remained so until the middle of the eighteenth century when Dr Johnson's friend, Giuseppe Baretti, began championing the Italian literary cause in England (more about him later).

I don't think I have any need to mention Byron, the two Brownings (the lovers of Italy 'par excellence'), Coleridge, Keats, Hunt, Hazlitt, W.S. Landor, Macaulay, Meredith, Rogers, Shelley, Southwell, Swinburne, Tennyson and Wordsworth, all of whom had their own favourite Italian concepts, haunts and style. Keats is buried in Rome, in the Protestant Cemetery that also has the ashes of Shelley.

Most of them, if not all, wrote about Italy. Byron exalted it in *Childe Harold's Pilgrimage* (see for example Canto no. 4) and his passionate 'Italia! Oh Italia! thou hast the fatal gift of beauty which became a funeral dower of present woes and past' – which recalls, strangely enough, our own Filicaia who, writing in the seventeenth century, had addressed his country by saying 'O fossi tu men bella o almen piú forte' (Would that you were either less beautiful or at least stronger) as well as his *Ode to Venice*. His *Don Juan* owes much to Italy. Italian history occupied Byron's mind in *Marin Faliero* and *I due Foscari*, and to a lesser extent in *Beppo*.

Robert Browning wrote *Old Pictures in Florence* and *Sordello*, Elizabeth, his wife, *Casa Guidi*, and many others, Meredith wrote *Mazzini's Doctrines* and *Italy Shall Be Free*, W.S. Landor *On The Slaughter of the Brothers Bandiera*, *Ode to Sicily* and *Milton in Italy* and Samuel Roger composed the ode *Italy*. Shelley is well known for his *Ode to Naples*, *The Cenci*, and *Lines Written Among the Euganean Hills* and Swinburne for writing *Halt before Rome*, *Songs before Sunrise* and *To Aurelio Saffi*, Landor for his Trilogy of plays on Joanna of Naples and Bulwer Lytton for *Rienzi*.

Nor should we ignore their contacts, physical or spiritual, with Italian women. Such contacts in themselves, whenever they occurred, must have had perhaps a greater impact on them than even the landscapes. After all, it is a fact that a man only knows another country, if at all, through contacts with women of that country; for in knowing the woman he knows her man; her wants are his deficiencies, her desires his failings, her passions his weaknesses. By knowing her we understand him; and vice versa. Contacts with persons of the same sex are not, in my view, quite so instructive; but perhaps I am looking at the matter purely from a heterosexual point of view.

When it comes to general knowledge of Italy, it is a matter of record that during the seventeenth and eighteenth centuries, but particularly during the

Victorian era, the Grand Tour was part of the English gentleman's education.

One of the first Englishmen who crossed the Alps into Italy as part of the process of discovery to which somewhat later the label of Grand Tour was pinned, was John Dennis: he looked upon Italy as 'a garden protected by the Alps'. Quite a few Englishmen crossed the channel into Italy as early as the seventeenth century. Sir Thomas Isham and the Earl of Exeter were probably the most prominent as collectors of antiquities and works of art, but there were many others: and most of them liked what they saw. Bishop Burnet, for example, after having seen the 'Isole Borromeo' on Lake Maggiore in 1685, wrote that they were 'the loveliest spot of ground in the world' (G. Burnet, *Some Letters*).

By the end of the seventeenth century, the Grand Tour had become an established part of education for the English gentleman, whether he took it to study the country or its life, paintings, architecture, ruins or prints. The well-known names who followed this particular itinerary are legion: Gray, Walpole, Manby, Lassels, Bromley, Addison, Lord Shaftesbury, Richardson, Bishop Berkeley, Kent, Burlington, the Earls of Leicester and Warwick, Smollett, John Ealing, John Brown and John Wilkes, the Ladies Hartford and Miller, and Boswell. Indeed, the only Englishman of any significance at this time who does not appear to have set foot in Italy is Dr Johnson, which is probably just as well, or he would certainly have found something to complain about. He had, however, been to France, and as a result (Wednesday, 13 May 1778 in Boswell's *Life*) he wrote that 'the French are a gross, ill-bred, untaught people; a lady there will spit on the floor and rub it with her foot. What I gained by being in France was, learning to be better satisfied with my own country.' Which, I suppose, sums up the real purpose of foreign travel: to appreciate one's own home all the more!

The tradition of travelling on the Continent and especially into Italy continued in the eighteenth century and into the nineteenth and was interrupted only by the Napoleonic wars. Soon after Waterloo, however, the English swarmed into Italy; it is as though, having been deprived of it by the wars with France, they needed the culture and the sun almost like a drug.

The avowed object of the Grand Tour was to broaden the mind by contact with the civilization of the Continent ('Home-staying youths have ever homely wits'). It is difficult to determine whether in its inception the Tour was an acknowledgement that the educational system in England was deficient (I think it was a a Frenchman, Alexis de Tocqueville, who had remarked that the English public school system strengthened the mind without broadening it) or whether it was an exercise in showing off, in its inception at any rate, a form of keeping up with the Joneses, by the wealthier English gentry. In a sense, the modern equivalent would be to fly off to exotic or distant holiday haunts instead of staying in Europe.

There were, however, some who stayed away from time to time (Byron was one of them) on the ground that Italy was too full of Englishmen, just as some of us avoid going to the Costa del Sol nowadays. Nothing ever changes.

The motives for travel to the Continent and especially to Italy were quite varied

We all know Dr Johnson's dictum: 'The man who has not been to Italy is always conscious of an inferiority, for his not having seen what it is expected a man should see. The grand object of travelling is to see the shores of the Mediterranean.' (Thursday, 11 April 1776.)

Culture was certainly the primary reason, at any rate the declared primary reason. But the slant was different over the three centuries. In the seventeenth and eighteenth centuries there is no doubt that the Englishman (and woman) who went to Italy acknowledged that the Renaissance was the fount of all Classicism; in the nineteenth century, however, the Victorians may have looked upon it differently. It is conceivable that many went because they felt that they had to commune with Roman civilization on the basis that the English were the successors of the Romans. Those animated by Protestant religious fervour may have gone to see for themselves the negative sides of the Catholic church, or if historically-minded maybe even to see the collection of Henry VIII's letters to Anne Boleyn housed in the Vatican Library.

Many went to improve their health. More than once it was said that the rheumatisms and the consumption brought about by the English weather could be cured in the Mediterranean, where one could avoid the English winter 'ending in July to recommence in August' (Byron, *Don Juan*, Canto XIII, stanza XLII). Even here, however, the position is not entirely clear because in the southern Mediterranean the traveller was subject to the risk of cholera, malaria and typhoid: bilious attacks and diarrhoea were common. Many died in Italy and a few were even buried there.

Some went on the Tour for business purposes, like Sir Henry Wootton; some for botanical purpose or to improve their classical reputation or knowledge or to study politics or to improve their techniques if they were artists or possibly even to add to their already established fame. Scientists were there: Davy, Babbage and Faraday, as well as politicians: Brougham, Liverpool, Peel and Russell.

Others went to improve their manners. Writing to George Augustus Selwyn, for example, the fifth Earl of Carlisle considered that foreign travel – he had just crossed the Alps – could serve to improve the manners of some of his friends. Some might even have gone to spy.

Many went because of the fatal allure of the siren, Italy. They went to the land of gaiety and sensuality where they believed that their behaviour would be less criticized than at home. This certainly applied to those English eccentrics who, coming from a wealthy background, could afford freely to indulge their whims in

Italy; but it applies equally to those English homosexuals who were escaping from the somewhat stringent laws then prevailing in England.

It is, however, questionable to what extent the search for a totally different environment and culture was the result of a penchant for knowledge rather than the satisfaction of a craving for new experiences, an attempt to shrug off one's own background and way of living which were felt as unduly restrictive, or boring, or even hypocritical.

As a result, when books were written about Italian travel, facts were somewhat twisted and Italy (and its inhabitants) were shown as the visitor intended to find them rather than as they really were: a balanced view seldom emerged.

Accordingly, one finds writers being either too critical of the locals, or too eulogistic of what, under a different sky and breathing the air of the Mediterranean, appeared to be virtues when compared to some of the traits of the people that had been left at home.

Nevertheless, it is a fact that as a result of the popularity of the Tour, Italian literature revived, as did the language. To have an Italian master in the house of nobility was a mark of distinction and good taste. Indeed, as Professor Vincent has so stylishly observed, with Palladian influence extending to the stonework, Canaletto's paintings on the walls, Canova's statues in the halls and the Italian opera in the Haymarket, it can fairly be said that no other country exerted greater cultural influence on the England of the nineteenth century than Italy.

The eighteenth century was a particularly important period for the Italian influence upon England, which ranged from paintings to gardens. The fashion for Italy is also manifested during this period in the use of Italian words which became more and more prominent, especially in the artistic field. The Dilettanti Club was formed in 1734 by a number of English literary 'virtuosi' and 'cognoscenti', Sir Francis Dashwood being their prime mover (the paintings of the first members of the Dilettanti Club still hang in the drawing-room and elsewhere in the building of Brooks's Club in St James's): all members of the Dilettanti Club had been to Italy.

In fact, having travelled to Italy was the qualification for membership. However, Horace Walpole said that whilst having been to Italy was the nominal qualification for membership of 'Brooks's', the real one was that of being drunk. Is this true? According to Bernard Darwin (*British Clubs* in the series 'Britain in Pictures', Collins, 1943), it is certainly not true. He explains away Walpole's cutting remarks on the basis that members of the Dilettanti Club were 'a hilarious group, inclined to friendly foolery'. The reader will form his own view anyhow.

Of course, the Englishman who could afford to go on the Grand Tour was educated and had plenty of money: he would hire either a 'vettura' in which he could travel in comfort, or a tutor or a guide (cicerone) or a combination of the three. It was certainly not the lower class Englishman who could bear the kind of expenditure involved, which was not negligible.

Depending on the Englishman's background, tendencies, and finances the Grand Tour either stopped in Germany and Switzerland or continued into the Mediterranean through Italy. Italy was a staging post, so to say, for Greece, Turkey, Cyprus, the Middle East and Egypt. The further away one travelled, the richer one had to be. Richer not only as far as money was concerned but also in time, because journeys of this nature, at least initially (until the Saint Gothard Pass was opened towards the middle of the nineteenth century and until either railways or steamers came into their own towards the middle and end of the nineteenth century) took a long time indeed. For example, John Evelyn left England for his Continental Tour in 1643 and was away nearly four years, mainly in France and Italy.

It was therefore only the nobility who travelled to the Mediterranean, the nobility of title and the nobility of education, with servants.

The scenery changed in more ways than one as soon as the Alps were crossed. The novelty in the weather and in the landscape seemed to bring about a change in the pattern of behaviour of the travellers. They suddenly became more extrovert, they felt that since the people with whom they were mixing were so completely different in every respect (tradition, culture, appearance, eating habits, social customs and so on) they need no longer maintain the strict standards of thought and behaviour imposed by the society that they were leaving, albeit temporarily. In other words, they suddenly felt free. All Northerners do, as soon as they cross the Alps: it's as though they are escaping from the cage in which their society keeps them and they are at last free to behave in accordance with their instincts.

This freedom provokes firstly a change in outlook; but it has further consequences. The change in outlook is a concomitant of a variation in behaviour which is manifested initially by an increase in noise level. The pitch of voice rises and this is accompanied by a general disregard for others. Such manifestations are common to northern people generally. Whether they be Swedes, Germans, Belgians or British, as soon as they cross the Alps or the Pyrenees, they display features which, whilst interesting to observe, are extremely irritating. One might think that it is the novelty of being in a different country; but not so. The very same people act in keeping with the patterns of behaviour that they have established in their own countries whilst travelling through Scandinavia, Germany, France, Austria or Switzerland. But as soon as they cross the Alps or the Pyrenees they appear to be almost compelled to raise their voices, make more noise generally, be utterly unmindful of the well-being and the peace and quiet of the inhabitants of those countries where they are but guests. It is as though on the one hand they feel that they have to adapt to local habits –

but few people make noise in Italy, Spain or Greece during the 'siesta' hours except the foreign visitors – and, on the other, that their stronger foreign currency provides them with certain rights of 'seigneurity' which are absent in their own countries. It is an interesting phenomenon which knows barriers neither of nationality nor of age: if they are from the north, this is the way they behave in the south.

I had initially thought that such a change in behaviour was due to alcohol. By this I mean that the general availability of cheap drink so interferes with established patterns of action and discipline that the urge to make noise and to be assertive becomes irresistible. I have now reached the conclusion that my initial assessment was wrong: alcohol does not figure in the psychology of the exercise, although it is a very potent factor in the practical problems that occur. The same people who are paragons of propriety in the suburbs of Dusseldorf or London, feel compelled to let themselves go when they find themselves in Italy, Spain or Greece. True, they have drunk too much because it was so cheap to drink so much: but the problem is primarily a psychological one and only secondarily a practical one provoked by alcohol.

It is the Mediterranean air, mood, mentality, tradition, impact, strength, and all pervasive aura. The Alps and the Pyrenees – Italy and Spain and, to a lesser degree, Greece – represent the geographical and cultural division between north and south and it is at that point that psychological barriers break down.

But what about France, you may be wondering? In my view the same does not happen there. France is not so markedly a Mediterranean country as either Spain or Italy, save in Provence which, in any case, was part of Italy until 1860 and is now becoming once more increasingly Italianate.

The northerner who goes to France feels he's in a different country, but does not make so much noise, does not consider deep down that he can let himself go quite so completely as he does, undoubtedly, as soon as he crosses the high peaks of Europe. Whether it is because there is an element of contempt for Spaniards, Italians and Greeks which does not apply quite so strongly to the French, or whether it is because the northerner considers that he will be allowed greater freedom and sympathy in these three countries, is a little difficult to determine.

The net result, however, is the same: today, the northerner in the Mediterranean is, on the whole, a noisy, ill-behaved person, who has little regard for the locals and whose appreciation of what is available there is a function of the rate of exchange. It is sad. However, let us not dwell too much on the present but return to the Englishmen on their Grand Tour.

It was a long journey, at times difficult, at times worrying; in those days, the travellers were not really concerned with the dangers of the journey; indeed, those very dangers added to the excitement.

The sermonizing of those who maintained that by mixing with the natives the visitors would be weakened did not seem to have much effect. True, there was a view in some quarters that by mixing with these instinctive, sensual and sometimes even slightly effeminate southerners, the aristocracy of England would be corrupted. But there seems to be no real evidence to support the theory that corruption affected those who did not wish to be corrupted.

Those who travelled to the south wanted to experience sensations that were denied to them in northern climes; they wanted to be light-hearted, when at home they had to be stern; they wanted to have fun, when at home they were miserable; they wanted to give free rein to their eccentricity, which at home had to be restrained; they tried to belong to the places they visited, so that Dickens may have preferred Genoa and Ruskin Verona; they wanted to have the heightened experience of the senses that only Mediterranean sunlight and life provide. As they crossed the Alps, they left behind them all social and psychological constraint; the bright light, I suppose, was the first major impression, and then the sounds, and the people.

Their attitude to the people, however, varied. Some thought that the Italians were charming and polite; others felt that they were dark and mischievous and that there were bandits and crooks everywhere. Byron liked them, Landor disliked them.

Some thought that the Italians were childish and simple; others that they were vicious and corrupt. Some loved all they found; others complained of barbaric habits and customs. Even Byron, a great lover of Italy, objects to the custom of fasting in Lent. In his *Beppo* (stanzas VII and VIII) he complains about having to live for forty days on 'ill-drest fishes' and recommends to those who intend to visit Italy that they should stock-up on 'Ketchup, Soy, Chili-vinegar and Harvey.'

But whatever view was taken, the northerner felt a great sense of liberation as soon as he got to Italy: he almost ceased to think and began to feel. If he was a nobleman who had been accustomed to strict hierarchies, he found that in Italy, and indeed throughout the Mediterranean, the structures of society were not so well defined; if he felt the so-called innate superiority of the Teutonic race, he began to realize that some of it would have to be left behind because, at least in the artistic field, that superiority meant very little in Italy and Greece; if he felt that the Church of Rome was corrupt, he was like Abraham the Jew in Boccaccio's second novel on day one: struck by the fact that the corrupt Church survived and attracted converts, despite the extensive superstition that was found particularly in the Italian hinterland; if he remembered the Inquisition, he was still bound to acknowledge the almost symbiotic life of Italian art with the Roman Church; if he felt that the Italians were degenerate, he still must have wondered whether their degeneracy did not have something to commend it. If one day the traveller felt like complaining about the natives' rudeness, dirt and uncivil behaviour, the next he would be surprised by their unexpected urbanity and restraint; after all, if, having stayed a while, he thought he knew what the Italians felt, he must have wondered how their ability to make themselves agreeable could be reconciled with their apparent inscrutability of thought.

All in all, he must have felt as though he was on a see-saw, enjoying the sun one moment and malaria the next.

Apart from the different weather, manners, customs, eating habits, superstitions and so on, one of the features of the country that the northerner must have found quite unsettling was the comparative lack of social differences. This is not to say that social distinctions did not exist in the Italy of the time. Indeed, the number of titled heads all over the country, and especially in the south, was very substantial.

But the great divide between the classes that may have existed in England, Germany or Sweden was not so marked in Italy: Italy was not then, any more than it is now, a class-conscious country. People knew, of course, that there were distinctions between the classes, that there was a nobility of blood as there now is a nobility of money; but the bond of common humanity could not easily be dislodged and whatever else Bonapartism may not have achieved, it did achieve, particularly in Italy, a certain levelling upwards, at least in the basic aspirations of the common people.

In addition, I find that where the sun shines strongly, people seem to be reminded more of their common humanity. Deep processes of thought are not so easy to maintain; even the amount of clothes to be worn is reduced; and living in the proximity of antiquity, art and history serves as a reminder of one's comparative insignificance. This insignificance is universal and is not limited to those who may not have a title or be penniless.

This kind of natural religion has a levelling effect and it must have been unsettling, to say the least, for those coming from the north to find that a number of the strictures imposed upon them by their own upbringing and class structure had no meaning whatsoever in the southern Mediterranean. As a result, the visitor to Italy learnt not only about antiquities but also about life; he broadened his horizons extensively, despite his complaints.

One feature, however, about which there never was any complaint or any argument was the Italian garden.

The Italian landscaped garden seems to have been particularly prominent at this period and the English landed gentry and patrons of the arts vied with one another in providing new ideas in gardening based on what they saw in Italy, some going even so far as to incorporate Roman arches or ruins. Others introduced terraces, grottoes, fountains, waterworks, statuary, descending stairways, separate courtyards, mazes, mounds, orangeries, loggias, stone terraces, arcades, parterres, follies, sunken pools and little islands in lakes.

The Duke of Devonshire laid out at Chatsworth the waters of the Derbyshire

Peak District in imitation of Tivoli.

Fountains Abbey was added to the local garden to give it character as part of a campaign to glamourize local ruins in the same way as the ruins of ancient Rome were used in Italy. In fact, such was the determination to follow the Italian pattern, that where there were no remains to incorporate into the new landscape, they would actually be created. This occurred, for example, at Scotney Castle which was partly pulled down to make it more like a ruin when the owner went to live nearby in order to give effect to his scheme. The operation was clearly artificial, but the search for what was natural was certainly genuine and heartfelt

James I was himself very keen on the Italian type of garden and he increased the interest that was already growing.

As John Dickson Hunt has already stated so eloquently (*Gardens and Groves*, Dent, London, 1986) all this was the result of Italian imagination: 'Italian gardens provided the imagery, the structures and the ideas for all northern gardens whether French, Dutch or English. . . there was indeed nowhere else whence such inspiration could derive.'

All this followed from the fact that the visitor to Italy saw many new types of garden on his tour, which he admired for the variety and the fullness of the design. Above all, he began to appreciate that they represented a world all of their own, self-contained as they were; and they were almost a theatre. Indeed, the owners of the gardens were the actors on that stage and many plays and operas were in fact set in the Italian gardens of the time. Niches, grottoes, pools, and other features were also added as if scenes from the theatre.

Just as the painters who went to Italy brought back their own vision of the country, so the visiting nobility who were impressed by Italian nature returned home with a particular idolization of the natural world in the garden. They even went so far as to imagine that the 'genius' of the place inhabited their restructured English garden.

Even when travelling through France, the visitor will have been struck by the Italian influence on gardens. In fact, it was the gardens of Palazzo Pitti in Florence that gave the idea to Louis XIV of France for those of Versailles. Understandable, since his grandmother was a Medici anyhow.

Alexander Pope held the traditional form of garden up to ridicule: nature came into its own in the English garden.

Gradually, however, the fashion faded. People began to feel that the Italian garden was too informal and that, as master of the universe, man should control nature in his gardens as well. Capability Brown then became famous, as the English type of garden took over with the claim that nature had been 'educated' in the garden.

This approach to gardening was exported from England to France with a similar impact on nature there, since the French were prevailed upon to change their mistrust of nature which had been the hallmark of their approach to gardening in the seventeenth century.

□

Right through the eighteenth and nineteenth centuries, Italy continued to be 'invaded' and plundered. At this time, of course, the invaders were more civilized and the plunder occurred not through force of arms but by the use of money, market forces and stealth. One example, which I consider a classic, will suffice. Please note that the authority for what follows is to be found in Hutton's *History of Derby* published in 1791 (pp. 195-208).

At about that time, only the Italians had developed the technology for silk-throwing and consequently enjoyed an absolute command of the lucrative international trade.

During this period, the wearing of silks was considered high fashion and Bntish merchants were obliged to meet the Italian merchants' exorbitant prices for silk.

It transpires that a local Derby man, one Crotchet, thought he would make a fortune by throwing silk himself and started a mill; but he soon found that he needed the Italian machines and went bankrupt.

Next onto the scene stepped John Lombe, 'A man of spirit, a good draughtsman and an excellent mechanic.' He travelled to Italy 'with a view of penetrating the secret'. There he corrupted two servants of the manufacturer of the machines, copied the details and learnt how they were assembled.

Lombe was discovered but managed to flee back to England with two of his Italian accomplices. In 1717, he settled in Derby where labour and water were plentiful. There he did a deal with the city corporation for the buildings and water supply and he continued profitably for some three or four years selling silk at a lower price than the Italians.

The influence of the Italians in the sixteenth century in the textile industries was very substantial and has been reviewed at length in 'Textile History and Economic History – Essays in Honour of Miss Julia de Lacy Mann', Manchester University Press, by Joan Thirsk in *The Fantastical Folly of Fashion*.

Literally, the Italians were already knitting a finer wool fabric from worsted yarn when in 1564 a pair of stockings knitted from this yarn was spotted by a smart young apprentice in London. They belonged to an Italian merchant from Mantua who lent them to the Englishman. He had them copied and thus, we learn from Stow: 'Were the first worsted stockings made in England.'

Cunnington and Cunnington report that 'within a few years began the plenteous making both jersey and woollen stockings, so in a short space they waxed common'. It should be remembered, however, that jersey stockings, which were still finer than ordinary worsted, were originally a speciality of the islands of Jersey and Guernsey.

Predictably, Lombe's operation began to undermine the Italian trade to the extent that the Italian merchants decided on revenge. They sent over to England a woman who found employment at Lombe's mill and then got together with one of the two Italians who had originally come over with Lombe. In 1718, John Lombe might have had the commercial foresight to apply for a patent which he did, but he certainly did not appear to have the wit to realize that the Italians would surely have their revenge, which they may well have done – he was poisoned two years later and died in agony.

The Italian woman was questioned but was not charged. John Lombe was only twenty-nine when he died but he was apparently already such an important local figure that he was given one of the most magnificent funerals ever held in Derby. Lombe, as it happened, died a bachelor, so his estate went to his brother William who, being of 'a melancholy turn' shot himself shortly after.

However, the mill prospered and 300 people were employed there.

The theft of the Italian 'patent' for the silk-mill machine was quite well known in England at the time. Suffice it to refer the reader to James Boswell's *Life of Johnson* (Friday, 19 September 1777) where the good Doctor is said to have visited after dinner, with Mrs Butter, 'the silk-mill which John Lombe had had a patent for, *having brought away the contrivance from Italy*'.

When John Lombe's patent expired in 1732 his cousin, Sir Thomas Lombe, successfully petitioned Parliament for its renewal. The Government decided the technology was a good investment for Britain and made available £14,000 (an enormous sum in those days) to develop it. Further mills were opened in Stockport and Nathaniel Gartrevalli, the second of the two Italians who had initially assisted Lombe, worked there. Gartrevalli, however, died in poverty, Hutton remarking that such was 'the frequent reward of the man who ventures his life on a base cause or betrays his country'. But the business prospered; indeed, it has continued to do so until recently. Silks for the mills came from Persia, Canton and Piedmont in Italy (pp. 278, 279).

Italy is quite accustomed to having things stolen from it. All its invaders obviously plundered it. This is part of the history of all empire builders and colonizers, and the traditional right of conquest in war. It is exactly what the Romans did with Greece. The difference, however, is that Italy was plundered when it was at peace, except for the German actions in 1943.

Ultimately, all conquerors have for those they have defeated a feeling more of superiority and contempt than of understanding and sympathy. The basis on which they can take what they want, is that they feel greater than the vanquished. The vanquished in turn are an object of contempt. They may look upon their antiquities with neglect and not care for them and leave them abandoned amidst ruins, lichens, moss and capers.

The conquerors' attitude is that they will take them and care for them by putting them in museums and galleries, on the basis that they know best. They do not look upon it as theft, but rather as a good deed. This is exactly the attitude of Britain towards the Elgin Marbles. The argument is that they are being preserved for humanity and posterity.

It must be admitted that there is some truth in this approach which, however, only stems from cultural conceit and not from true artistic sensitivity or appreciation. It is arguable that leaving works of art amidst ruins is more in keeping with history than to remove them to museums, just as leaving animals in their natural habitat is more consistent with nature than keeping them in zoos.

In the final analysis, this attitude is the outcome of a desperate psychological need. It is the result of extreme scarcity in the particular commodity which it is said should be preserved for posterity. It starts out as a whim of those people with money who, on the one hand, might have cared, and on the other were able to gratify their whims and their fancies as such. This renders the exercise laudable and to some extent more forgiveable.

With the passage of time, however, it becomes more difficult to justify this attitude, as the retention of the Elgin Marbles shows.

If all had to be returned to Italy which was taken from it, most major museums and private collections of the world would be denuded and some would actually cease to exist.

It also has to be said that the present constant copying of things Italian by the 'outside world' is truly a disgrace. It is within my own knowledge that a number of people throughout the world actually take great trouble to go, say, to the Milan Fair in April to see exactly what new ideas emerge from Italy. Of course, this is the nature of commercial life today and, in a sense, is highly flattering.

The copying of the machinery for silk throwing resulted in the establishment in England of the textile industry in the Midlands. History repeated itself in the case of Meucci for the telephone and Pacinotti for the dynamo and it is my own direct professional knowledge that there have been 'thefts' of design or know-how in respect of industrial machinery (cutters, staplers, etc.), furniture, perpetual calendars, and a lot more. Dishonesty, like fraud, is infinite and I have to accept the fact that Italy is by no means the only country to have had its ideas pinched.

On the other hand, it is not always easy to copy successfully. For example, the Victorians tried to copy Majolica and they produced nothing like the original. Nor could they: the artistic spirit was not there.

Even when the supreme styling of Italian cars has been copied either directly or, as is more common, indirectly in the sense that the lines are not reproduced as such but the overall concept is adopted, the results are hybrid and they do not have the clean cut of the original.

It is inevitable, because line is influenced by an overall view of style and of life which cannot be transplanted. One may certainly copy the practical features of any machine or motor car; but you need style to copy Italian styling and, if you had the style in the first place, you would have no need to copy.

In turn, the Italians too were quite expert at fraud. Many a fake painting or sculpture must have been sold to foreign visitors. On the other hand, I wonder how many masterpieces left Italy either without any payment or in consideration of a pittance. One need only think of Joseph Smith or Sir William Hamilton. 'The Italian Collections were stripped' says Scott-Fox (op. cit., p. 52). Nothing unusual in that.

In 1851, A. W. Franks reported to the trustees of the British Museum that 'the whole of Italy has been so ransacked by foreign dealers that it is useless to expect any number of specimens to be discovered in that country' (Wilson, op. cit.). He was referring to Majolica, but the same thoughts could be expressed about other artefacts. The unfortunate reality is that the Italians have always been careless about their artistic heritage. The reason is simple: people attach no value to what they have in abundance; we had then, to use modern terminology, a masterpiece lake or mountain and all those who could, helped themselves to it. More recently, the Italian Government has tried to tighten up the export of art from Italy, but, as in the case of currency exportation, it has acted too late and all it has done is to shut the stable door after the horses have bolted; and how many horses; and what horses!

(Nor should we be any more grateful to the Germans who, with the excuse that Italy had in 1943 become an enemy country, tried to smuggle out as many antiques and works of art as they could. Some have been recovered, but not all. That was unkind, because the Germans did not really deserve to have them; in a sense, much better that they should go to the English or to the Americans who at least, throughout our history have, on the whole, befriended us.)

One can go further and say that the modern appreciation of antiques and works of art is prompted more by venal than aesthetic consideration. It is the rarity of the item that provokes the desire to possess it in the first place; the rarity adds to the value and the combination of the scarcity/profit factor overrides all other considerations.

Those who have little of a particular (artistic) commodity are in my view the least well equipped to appreciate the true nature of the intrinsic value, as distinct from the market value, of the work of art or the chattel or whatever. It is a misconception to assume that because one is a collector of rare items, one understands their true value and their real nature. I find that the contrary is true, namely that it is the people who are surrounded by things of a particular kind or of a particular style, who, although superficially contemptuous of them because they have them in abundance and therefore attach no significance to them, are in reality the very people who have a deeper psychological inner understanding of what it is they are surrounded by.

In other words, I do not believe that because a northerner had the means of travelling through Italy and collecting rare items of art or beauty he, for that reason alone, had a better appreciation of what he was collecting than those from whom it was taken away. It is obvious that the uneducated locals who allowed the abstraction of what was of such apparent value to others had little understanding of its market value. But it does not follow that they had no appreciation of the intrinsic nature of what they were giving away. That nature was part of their make-up, psychological certainly and probably also physical; and could never be taken away.

Be that as it may, the greatest impact of Italy on England occurred through architecture. The debt England owes Palladio is very great indeed.

☐

Palladio was easy to imitate. His four books on architecture were easy to read, digest and follow since they proceeded from the premise that so much could be achieved by modular construction.

Inigo Jones spent two months in Naples in 1614 imbibing the style of the local architecture. Additionally, he always carried with him Palladio's *Quattro Libri* wherever he went. That particular version which contains Jones's own annotations is now kept in Worcester College Library, Oxford.

The English were quick to seize on this concept which produced immediate, impressive results without any need to strain a deficient imagination and the results can be seen in their thousands all over England. However, if anyone needs a reminder of the keenness of the English to follow the modular type of construction, the four telephone kiosks at the rear of the Law Courts in Carey Street, London, show that even to this day the modular, lego-type approach has continued.

Furthermore, Palladio's buildings, though derived from Rome, had certain static, almost severe effects that were eminently suited to a cold climate. London is to this day full of Palladian ideas: his solidity appealed to the British much more than the decadent, ornate Baroque style. But mainly, I suppose, his exteriors made allowances for the weaker northern light and enabled the features of a building to stand out even under a cloudy sky. In England, Palladio is still king, and English architects had to go to Rome and Vicenza to learn about his style, as well as architecture generally. Sir John Soane would not have designed the 'new Law Courts' or the Bank of England if he had not studied Palladio's work; Nash's Langham Place comes from the same source; and George Basevi's buildings on the Grosvenor Estate in Belgravia owe an even more obvious debt to Italy.

Nor should I omit to mention the bands of Italian travelling craftsmen such as stone masons, painters, intaglio experts, wood carvers and cabinet makers. They used to come over for specific jobs, stay the time it took – sometimes years – to complete their task, and then move on. As England had had its itinerant judges, so Italy had its itinerant craftsmen. Indeed, it still has them, as anyone who is conversant with the construction of major building works or petrochemical plants in developing countries well knows. (See 'Pottery' for the influence that Italian master craftsmen had on the English delftware industry.)

Italian influence on English painting is not so great for the simple reason that England has not produced any truly great painters. Or is it the other way round? Could it be that there are no great painters in England because Italian influence was slight? Possibly, I am not sure; perhaps there is something in the make-up of the English people that prevents them from attaining true greatness in the artistic field.

As I have shown, Hogarth adapted the caricature for his own ends. But even though Sir Joshua Reynolds knew Italy and its art, it is difficult to see where the Italian influence in him really occurs. (Incidentally, Joshua Reynolds lived in Rome for seven years; he loved it, but he didn't like the Romans!) True, Gainsborough was inspired by Italian landcapes and Turner studied Titian very carefully indeed. To a layman like me, however, Turner's Italian passion for light is offset by his disregard for line. In that, he certainly is not Italian and I think that he was influenced by the Mediterranean sun more than by Mediterranean art: but I am no expert on this point. Still, it is rather odd to see in one of his paintings Mount Snowdon against the background of the Roman 'campagna'.

Other than in their name, I personally see nothing Italian about the pre-Raphaelites either; but, here again, I am ignorant. The influence of the Roman and Neapolitan countryside upon the English water-colourists of the eighteenth and nineteenth centuries, of course, is indisputable.

Turning to prose, the English-speaking lovers of Italy who were all influenced by her are numerous. In alphabetical order they are: Butler, Compton McKenzie, Norman Douglas, Dickens, Disraeli, T.S. Eliot, George Eliot, E.M. Forster, Gissing, Augustus Hare, Hazlitt, E. Hutton, James Joyce, Macaulay, Ouida, Ezra Pound, F. Rolfe, John Ruskin, Scott, J.A. Symonds, the Sitwells, Swinburne, Thackeray and the Trollopes.

Each of them found something different in Italy. What is it, I wonder, that draws the Englishmen to Italy almost irresistibly like mosquitos to the light?

I am not thinking of the English tourist who flocks to the Italian beaches to enjoy the sun, some pasta and vino. I have in mind, when I say the Englishman, northern races generally. Basically, what I remark about the English also applies to, say, the Germans or the Scandinavians.

It is too easy to say that it is the sun or the music or the art or the ruins or the museums or the Vatican. All these are of course important but, apart from the Vatican, they can all be found in differing degrees in other countries. The attraction of Italy for the English lies in something totally different, namely in the fact that there the Englishman can afford to be himself, because on the whole that is exactly what the natives are doing, namely being themselves. It is also true that, generally speaking, the Italians are probably the most hospitable people in Europe; they are certainly friendly and extrovert and they believe in making guests, whoever they may be, feel at home. Indeed, sometimes that hospitality can be overpowering for those spirits who are incapable of opening up to warmth. But overall, nobody can accuse Italians of xenophobia.

We make people feel comfortable and we pander to their desires; we take them as they are, no matter who they are and we have found it very easy to do so because, until recently, our experience of foreigners has always been an exceptionally good one. Take the English, for example; the Englishman who came to Italy on his Grand Tour whether in the seventeenth, eighteenth or nineteenth century, or to study, was the better class of Englishman with plenty of money. There is no more enjoyable country to be in, when you have money, than Italy. I am not sure, however, what view Italians have of some of today's visitors.

Nevertheless, when he gets to Italy the northerner suddenly feels free. It may be that the sun forces him to be himself and the effect of the diet. It may be a combination of factors. But he is a different person and after a long stay he sometimes ends up by thinking the way Italians do; which may not necessarily be to his advantage: but that is another story. . .

It is this effect which ultimately produces the contrast in the hearts and the minds of the English and affects their judgement of the Italians. The English, as it were, cannot help loving us, because we, the Italians, are inherently lovable; and yet the English resent the love they are experiencing because they find that they are appreciating something which deep down is alien to their nature.

Their reaction to that is a form of dislike which sometimes turns to hatred and which always results in attributing to the Italians faults which are associated in historical terms with Italy but which are not always present nowadays and, very often, in ascribing to the Italians their own English vices, but acclimatized to Italy.

Hence the marked contrast between the views held by Ascham (see 'Manners') and John Ruskin (discussed earlier) on the one hand, and the enthusiasm of Robert Browning on the other when he said, 'Open my heart and you will see, graved inside of it, "Italy".'

Nowhere is this ambivalent attitude of the English more noticeable than when it is experienced by women. (I am taking the Englishman as distinct from the Englishwoman because I have never found that the Italians present problems for English women. They may not understand us; but they have no real, fundamental dislike for us. As a matter of fact, they quite often like us for what I may call 'technical' reasons.)

In the case of the Englishman, however, things are different, basically for two reasons:

The first reason is that the Englishman learns as part of his everyday language an Italian word which represents all that he, as an Englishman, is incapable of being; that is to say, he knows what Casanova was and did and represented. I believe that the Casanova myth is one of the greatest exercises in public relations that the Italians ever indulged in. I cannot believe that a Venetian could be as good as Casanova makes himself out to be in his memoirs; nor do I accept that his indefatigability was a fact. Decency, however, prevents me from going into detail over this and in any event, it is not an important point.

The fact remains that whatever my beliefs are about Casanova, the Englishman is brought up to believe that, generally speaking, the Italian male scores pretty highly on the 'Casanova' scale. Nothing could be further from the truth.

But herein lies the problem. This belief is one of the sources of tension in the relationship between the two nationalities. It arises from the fact that the Englishman has what I would call a complex in sexual and amorous behaviour where he feels that the Italian is more at ease. He is bothered by our easy way with women, by the apparent facility with which we flatter all and sundry, by our spontaneity and our apparent brilliance. He would like to imitate us and be more demonstrative but on the one hand he does not think he should and on the other he feels that he would do it without conviction; and therefore, not quite so well. Hence this constant tug-of-war in feelings and emotions to which I have already referred.

You will have noticed that when I consider 'womanizing' I refer exclusively to Casanova and not to Don Juan. There are two reasons for this. Firstly, I am concerned only with Italians and not with Spaniards. Secondly, I find that there is a difference between the two types of lovers. Casanova is Mediterranean, Don Juan is affectively northern; Casanova is truly erotic, Don Juan is only intellectually sensual; the former has always seemed to me more human, the latter is a devil and as such he is portrayed by Mozart; Don Juan seems to enjoy the thought of possessing a woman whereas Casanova appreciates the actual possession; and is considerate and friendly to those he has relations with.

There are libertines both in Mediterranean and in northern countries, but their motivation is different: for the northerner, the ravishing of a woman is a manifestation more of pride than of love. In my opinion, Casanova had on the whole more tender feelings than Don Juan, and, because of this fact, had probably a greater understanding of women.

Such fundamental difference between the two renowned seducers is reflected in the duality of approach which I am considering, and underlines it. According to his servant, Don Juan had had at least 1,003 women in Spain alone; it is a pity that one cannot ask them what they felt after the event.

The second reason is historical. If one reads the poems of Macaulay one cannot help feeling that his admiration for ancient Rome is so indiscriminate that it amounts almost to veneration. He, like Kipling, correctly believed that all the virtues which he attributes to the Romans (strength, discipline, respect for authority, patriotism, etc.) were the very same that made the Victorians great. It was obvious to him and many others that the English were, in political terms, the successors of the Romans.

The English had in fact created an empire which could compare with that of Rome; they had extended their citizenship, as Rome had done, to all those who lived under the British flag and they had created respect for that citizenship.

All this is perfectly true. To that extent, the English are the true political successors of ancient Rome. Or rather, were; and just as Rome fell through the corruption of its body politic, so the British Empire crumbled away when Britain had fulfilled its historical function.

If then a proud Englishman looked to Italy, he found that those who should have been the natural successors of the Romans were in a sorry state indeed because, after the fall of the Roman Empire, they had failed conspicuously to reassert themselves. The people seemed incapable of national unity, the country itself was more like a cemetery. Looking at Italy through the rose-tinted spectacles of Romanticism, one saw a lot of art, of course; but mainly ruins. Ruins everywhere; ruins punctuated by trees. But in the arid south or the Roman 'campagna' or throughout Tuscany, so much favoured by the English, what was the principal tree? The Cypress, the tree of the dead. The tree of the dead in the land of the dead. Byron started the idea, Ruskin repeated it; they meant it kindly, of course. Lamartine, however, meant it most unkindly; whether through a misunderstanding of the real position or because of the gentle antipathy that has always existed between the Italians and the French, I cannot say.

But there seemed no doubt at the time that the country was in a sorry state and that the Italians were not up to much. They were quite incapable of formulating any coherent policy for their own nation and this state of affairs could be said to have continued right up to the twentieth century.

The Italians, therefore, cannot be the successors to the Romans, for they display none of the civic qualities that made Rome great. So the English think, forgetting that England has been a united country since 1066 and a democracy since 1688 whereas Italy has been a united country, basically, since 1918 and a democracy only since 1948. And it is easy enough to ignore the fact that throughout the whole of our post-Roman history we have been slaves; that we had to suffer over two centuries of Spanish domination; that we have never known until recently what it means to be masters in our own home. In fact, all in all, considering our history, we could have been a lot worse and much more incapable.

Nevertheless, in political terms, this assessment is perfectly correct. In historical terms it is inevitable. In economic terms it is irrelevant. But in cultural and psychological terms it is totally untrue. And it is the Roman culture in which Italy was and still is steeped and the Roman heritage, factual and psychological, that has provided some of the redeeming features of the Italian nation. The Italians are of course the cultural successors of the Romans. These contradictory features of history have always appeared mystifying to the English and have been a constant source of irritation to them. They have always failed to understand how one can be motivated by culture and not by political ambition or efficiency: Italian reactions and traits have always been a mystery.

The English have criticized us, correctly, for our lack of civic sense, but they have ignored the fact that our feeling for beauty is virtually unique. They have smiled, understandably, at our lack of stable Government, but have not considered that our cultural heritage is rock solid. They have caricatured, with justification, the number and proliferation of political parties in Italy but have taken no note of the significant fact that 80-90 per cent of those entitled to vote in general and local elections in Italy actually take the trouble of going to the polls.

It is a fact that apparently we have no self-discipline; but if necessary, we can fight for our families as well as the next man, if not better.

There may have been little historical merit, and even less ability, in conquering Abyssinia; but great strides have been made in overcoming poverty and illiteracy.

It may be taking us a long time to eradicate centuries-old evils like the 'Mafia', but the fact that police chiefs and judges are killed from time to time in the fight against organized crime, and yet are replaced, shows ultimately the strength of a system where the investigating magistrates ('pretori') emerge as the storm-troopers of justice.

And so it goes on.

Generalizations are born of misunderstandings.

On this subject of generalizations, I beg your indulgence in making one further digression.

Earlier on, I mentioned that I would come back to one of the many commonplaces amongst the English that concern the Italian male, namely bottom-pinching.

As I have already said, I do not believe this sterotype to be true. Some generalizations obviously have an element of truth in them, but I think this one is no more correct than many general beliefs that the Italians hold about the British.

For example, did you know that until, say, the early 1950s, when the Italians started to take a keener interest in Britain as a holiday country – and indeed, they have continued to do so in ever increasing numbers, sometimes hordes, to this day – Italians believed that the English had five meals a day? This rumour was set about by the Mussolini regime, in the days when that regime had to justify its invasion of Ethiopia, to explain to the poor Italian peasant that he should support a cause that provoked the British, since the British were doing so well when he, the poor peasant in southern Italy, was not; so well that they were having five meals a day when that peasant struggled to have one. Italy had to have its own back over perfidious Albion. It might have been true of the eighteenth-century English aristocracy but is a nonsense today. In fact, by Italian standards, the modern Englishman is thoroughly underfed and it is a matter of doubt whether he has two proper meals a day.

Did you also know, for example, that until recently the Italians had always believed that English cities and London in particular were perpetually shrouded in fog, the kind of fog described by Edgar Wallace in his thrillers; that numerous Jack-the-Ripper-type criminals roamed the streets of London; and that Englishmen on the whole went about molesting very young girls?

All dreadful stereotypes.

It is exactly the same with the Italian bottom-pinching stereotype. I have a theory that this is a rumour which is spread by both northern men and women. It is a kind of conduct which northerners think is in keeping with the picture they have of southerners, as it corresponds to what they would expect southerners to do; and it is a regrettable fact of life that people are more inclined to believe that others would behave in the manner in which they expect them to behave, than otherwise, regardless of factual evidence.

May I also say that I have never met any northern woman – and I have met many, in some form or other – who, when the subject was mentioned, could answer affirmatively to my question as to whether she had ever experienced bottom pinching. It was always someone else who had. I think what happens is that some crass Italian men do take advantage of what they believe to be the willingness of the northern woman, to caress her bottom. Caress, not pinch; I am very keen to put the record straight. The former may elicit a slap, a giggle or an upset look; the latter elicits contempt. Let us not confuse the two.

□

Coming on to the fields of general culture and manners, we start really with Henry VIII who was a great patron of the arts and encouraged Italian culture. Indeed, we are told that he spoke Italian well and that he appreciated the then famous Castiglione and Virgilio, as well as ensuring that his daughter Elizabeth should learn Italian.

Earlier, I discussed the impact of Italy upon Shakespeare. Throughout the Renaissance, Italians were employed at the English Court as secretaries, riding and fencing masters, and as musicians; they were particularly well established as physicians.

The influence of Italy declined dramatically in the seventeenth century; amongst other reasons, the association with Popery was too much for the Puritans. It is hardly surprising that Addison did not like the Italians at all.

Things changed in the eighteenth century. Baretti arrived in 1751 and by the end of the 1790s Italy was fashionable again.

Furthermore, English taste in the eighteenth century was quite Italianized by Paolo Antonio Rolli, a Roman who, as master to the English Royal household for nearly thirty years, had quite an influence both on it and on England. In the same century, many Italian perfumiers were to be found working and living in the Haymarket and in Pall Mall; and the odd 'castrato' was always to be found in London at about the same time.

The list of Italians who spent time in England being appreciated here and contributing to English culture is very long indeed. Some of the more prominent were John Florio, Francesco Algarotti, Alessandro Verri, Vittorio Alfieri, Ugo Foscolo, and then the painters and the sculptors (right up to the present day Paolozzi and Annigoni), the architects, the musicians, the singers. To mention them all would be well outside the scope of this short summary. But certainly anyone who has visited Westminster Abbey knows the impact of Torrigiani, the sculptor; and the statue of Richard the Lionheart opposite the House of Lords is by another Italian, Carlo Marocchetti.

GENERAL COMMENT

As is known, Elizabeth I was a great lover of all things Italian and of course of the Italian language, which she spoke fluently. She continued the custom inaugurated under Henry VIII of using Italian doctors. For example, one Pietro Adelmare who had already been physician to Mary Tudor and who was said to have been paid most generously a hundred pounds per visit. . . . .

More particularly, Cesare Sacco was personal physician to the Queen, who also wrote on his behalf a letter to the Venetian Doge asking him to look after the business interests which Sacco had in Venice and which were left unattended whilst he was caring for her.

But architects and writers coming from Italian also prospered in the London of the sixteenth century. Federico Zuccaro, who first landed in England in 1574, is known for his famous portrait of Queen Elizabeth as well as those of other prominent members of that society.

At the same time, the practice of speaking Italian amongst the upper classes was revived and became widespread. Lord John Russell, Charles Fox and Lord Holland all wrote and corresponded in Italian. According to G. M. Trevelyan, Gladstone's knowledge of Italian was 'An essential part of his soul'.

Another Italian who had an impact on England was Giordano Bruno from Nola near Naples. But his influence was of a totally different kind. He came to England in 1583 and spent two years here. He went to Oxford and took part in disputations there but did not get on at all well despite being befriended by Gwynne and John Florio as well as Greville, in whose house he spent some time. They disliked him in Oxford, whether because of his religious views or his neoplatonism or his animistic view of the world, does not seem too clear. Certainly, his outspokenness as to the barbarity of the London populace and his criticism of the amenities of London which he describes as being full of mud and puddles, with no lighting, or the table manners of both the more humble folk and the nobility, as well as his having compared the mentality of certain English doctors with that of a ploughman, were not made to endear him to his hosts.

It is, however, difficult to blame Bruno when one considers certain practices prevailing in England at the time which were (for an educated Italian) quite objectionable. For example, after dinner when the ladies had left, it was customary for the men to get out the chamber pots stored in the sideboards, and relieve themselves in them. But Bruno's criticisms went beyond this display of grossness in personal habits. More particularly, his ridiculing of Petrarca ran counter to the admiration that learned English people of the period had for our greatest lyric poet. Still, he was an admirer of Elizabeth I, whom he called the 'diva Elisabetta'; and this admiration cost him dearly, for such praise for a 'heretic prince' was thrown at him by the Venetian inquisitors when he went on trial at a later date.

Bruno was able brilliantly to expose the new astronomical views of Copernicus and his criticisms of Aristotle and of orthodox theology anticipated the modern mind. Kant and Schelling followed in his footsteps.

According to one writer, 'In the course of his demonstrations and deductions Bruno anticipated Descartes's position of the identity of mind and being; he supplied Spinoza with the substance of his reasoned pantheism; and Leibniz with his theory of monadism and pre-established harmony. He laid down Hegel's doctrine of contraries and perceived that thought was a dialectic process. The modern theory of evolution was enunciated by him in pretty plain terms, thus anticipating Darwin. He had grasped the physical law of the conservation of energy. He solved the problem of evil by defining it to be a relative condition of imperfect development.' This is a much shortened version from John Addington Symonds. Bruno appears in Italian textbooks as one of our three major philosophers of the sixteenth century. The English, except for John Florio (but was he an Englishman?), did not take to him, and in his *History of Western Philosophy* Bertrand Russell does not even mention him. Oversight or policy? The latter, I suppose; he was being quite English and the English did not, and still do not, like Giordano Bruno. And yet, as has been said, Bruno's reflections on infinity were not in vain: they represent one of the most important beginnings of modern consciousness (C.G. Jung, *The Structure and Dynamics of the Psyche* in Volume 8 of his *Complete Works*).

Perhaps Bertrand Russell did overlook him. . .; on the other hand, Coleridge was very keen on Bruno whom he compared, I believe, to Milton.

A special mention should be made at this stage of Giuseppe Baretti, who spent a great deal of his life in England. A friend of Dr Johnson, he was a sensible, temperate man and as such he appears in the portrait of him by Sir Joshua Reynolds which still hangs in Holland House, painted in 1774.

He was a great Anglophile and wrote much about the Italians for the English public. He was also a keen observer of the English scene.

He wrote, for example, that London in his time contained over 10,000 prostitutes (I wonder how he managed to calculate that figure) and was 'the centre of all virtue and all vice'. He repeatedly compared his compatriots to the English and, generally, the Italians came out of it worse. According to Baretti, the Italians were superior to the English in only four things: painting, sculpture, architecture and music. In every other respect, the English were better and all Italians ought to strive to emulate them. Hurrah for Baretti!

But let us carry on.

The nineteenth century was the time when most Italian patriots and political exiles came to England.

The list is long and some of the names are well-known.

The poet Ugo Foscolo arrived in 1816. He is the best known of the Italian exiles and had been preceded by his fame.

His was a long stay in England. He died, in poverty, at Turnham Green, 10 September 1827 and was buried in the churchyard of Chiswick Parish Church according to his wishes. His remains were transferred in 1867 to the Church of Santa Croce in Florence.

Foscolo was extremely popular with the ladies and, surprisingly, also with their husbands. He was a regular frequenter of the centres of Whig influence – Holland House and Lansdowne House. Indeed, Lord and Lady Holland had just returned from Italy when Foscolo first set foot on English soil.

He loved England. He did not really miss the sun of Italy and, in common with other exiles, he took the view that the sun that shone in England was the freedom of the country and not that big 'omelette that lights up the oversize frying pan of the sky', as an earlier Italian poet had put it.

Indeed, on occasions, he seemed not to care very much about Italy nor, as he proved, about his Italian nationality. In his writings, he complained bitterly about all Italians, arguing, with some justification, that their factious nature would for ever prevent their liberation. He did not even approve of the revolutionary movements and in a letter of March 1820 he used terminology that, 150 years or more later, strikes us as odd. He said: 'Italy is a corpse with no hope of resurrection.'

In 1820, he was not sufficiently ill that one could forgive him for a faulty judgement. It seems to me that he was most probably swayed by what he saw in England. If he compared the magnificence and the power of England with the divisions that tore Italy aside at that time, he must have found it very comforting to be in a country where he was revered and welcomed wherever he went – which is more than would have happened to him in his own country – and where everyone was free to express his view. In addition, he mingled with the nobility who, recovering from the Napoleonic Wars, were enjoying a reasonably pleasant and financially secure time. Whereas, Italy was in turmoil. . .

This view of the country that gave him hospitality, fame and freedom, through rose-tinted glasses, is shared by the other patriots and exiles who followed in his footsteps. Guglielmo Pepe, fresh from the revolutionary attempts in Naples, arrived in 1821; Santorre di Santarosa in 1822; Gabriele Rossetti in 1824; Giuseppe Pecchio, escaping an Austrian charge of high treason, in 1833. Shortly thereafter, Giovanni Berchet and Ferdinando dal Pozzo also settled in England, as did Beolchi and Mossotti.

Mazzini was here, after he was expelled from Switzerland to which he had retreated when things became a little too hot for him in Austrian Italy; and at later dates, Cavour, the father of the Italian state, and Garibaldi, possibly better known in England for his biscuits than for his contribution to Italian unity. Canova came, as did Gino Capponi and Count Confalonieri.

I suspect that the impact on England of these Italian intellectuals was not very great – except perhaps, for Garibaldi, who made an impression on the masses; the others moved in the rarefied circles of literature, poetry, good taste, nobility and politics. It is true that they kept alive the flame of Italian independence; but I should be surprised to find that the man in the street had any knowledge about most of them.

There is, however, one Italian who came to England in 1823. He is also almost totally unknown to the general public but his contribution to English cultural life is very substantial; his name is Antonio Panizzi.

Panizzi was an exile from the Grand Duchy of Modena which also took a dim view of early nineteenth century patriotic fervour. At first, he earned a living by teaching Italian but soon got to know the lawyer Henry Brougham, who was to become Lord Chancellor seven years later. Through him, he was appointed to the first Chair of Italian Language and Literature in the newly opened University of London in 1826 and then, as a naturalized British subject in 1832, he joined the staff of the British Museum where he distinguished himself for his zeal and administrative abilities. He introduced the card-index system for cataloguing and was instrumental in strengthening the copyright law which requires that a copy of every book published in England is deposited with the Museum (today, the British Library).

Although a private Act of Parliament made him a British citizen, he remained closely associated with Italy and its slow progress towards emancipation. He is said to have contributed to Gladstone's enthusiasm for Italy.

It is to him that we owe the Reading Room at the British Museum, which he designed himself, and which was opened in 1857, above the doorway to which sits his bust. When he died in 1879, having been made a Baronet by Queen Victoria, the British Museum had completely catalogued more than a million books.

I wonder how many people who use the Reading Room at the British Museum today are aware that they owe it to an Italian. *Britannica* records his efforts on p. 864 of Volume R.X., but the reader who is interested in discovering more about this period of Italian exiles should read Margaret Wicks' study, *The Italian Exiles in London 1816-1848*, Manchester University Press, 1937.

The other examples of the impact that Italy has had on England are on the whole of a much more modern and less cultural nature. They can be summarized very briefly in the 'Dolce Vita', the Mediterranean diet, the open air enjoyment of food and wine, and the impressive post-war record of Italy in matters of style: cars, clothes, furniture, shoes, fashion, design, domestic appliances, etc.

There is a whole aura about things Italian which is seized upon by advertisers and marketers even to the extent of inventing Italian-sounding names for motor cars and other consumer goods. It is a revival which reminds one of what happened in England in the early part of the nineteenth century, especially after the defeat of Napoleon, when the constant decline since the seventeenth century in the fashion and study of things Italian, was halted. The Victorians in particular were wont to use Italian words and phrases in their conversation and letters, as a mark of distinction and taste, in the same manner in which English authors took to quoting from Dante, Boccaccio or Metastasio.

After about 1850, however, Italy and things Italian gave way to an interest in France and Germany until about the 1950s.

Over the past few years, I have even detected a form of snobbery in the revived use of Italian words of greeting, for example, or in other contexts. I do not consider it a cultural development by any means; it is more what I might call an environmental reaction which follows from the ever increasing tendency of the English to take holidays abroad, especially in the Mediterranean, and a form of wishful thinking.

I cannot leave this section without returning to one aspect of Italian influence on Britain which is so often overlooked, namely – the film industry. Indeed, it has been so much forgotten that when a review of the British film industry spanning more than four decades was recently shown on television, the person with whom I shall be dealing shortly was hardly mentioned; he certainly did not receive the prominence he deserves – summarized in the words of Laurence Olivier who said of him: 'I know of no-one else in British films so kind, generous, imaginative and courageous.' The person he was referring to was Filippo Del Giudice.

Olivier had good cause to be thankful to Del Giudice because it was through him and the filming of *Henry V* that Sir Laurence won his first Oscar. The following passage, borrowed from *The Oliviers* (Felix Barker, Hamish Hamilton, London, 1953) shows how conscious Olivier was of Del Giudice's contribution:

'For Olivier, who was given his first "Oscar", the award of the Academy of Motion Picture Arts and Sciences, it was an artistic triumph, and for Del Giudice, who had fought so many battles on behalf of his ideal, its success was particularly sweet. Conscious of all the Italian producer had done to make the film possible, Olivier went to visit him at Sheepcote, his home on Wooburn Common, one day in 1947 just after he had received the Oscar from Hollywood. When he arrived, Del Giudice noticed he was carrying a parcel, but had no idea what it contained or why Olivier took it into the study on the first floor; not until he joined Olivier a little later did he find out the answer. Standing on his desk was the golden statuette. "I wish you'd have it, Del," Olivier said to him. "Henry V would never have been made without you, dear fellow." It was a gesture which, coming at a time when Oscars were not so profuse as they are now in the Olivier household, Del Giudice has never forgotten.'

Del Giudice kept Olivier's Oscar until he died. After his death, Sir Laurence asked the Executors for its return, and they agreed.

This particular character, for a character he undoubtedly was, who became known in his time in the cinema world as 'Mr Del', was a refugee from Fascist Italy, who first came to London in 1932 as a penniless lawyer, aged forty. When war broke out he was interned as an enemy alien, but released after about three months, probably through the intervention of Mrs Churchill and her daughter Sarah. He then drifted almost by accident into films and rose to be managing director of Two Cities Films Limited.

In 1941, with England at a low ebb and with the English film industry practically non-existent and swamped by the prestige and the money of Hollywood, Mr Del decided to set about reviving the ailing local cinematograph business. He had great imagination and great flair, but no experience of films whatsoever. His first film, *Unpublished Story*, was released in 1941. It was not particularly distinguished. But soon after, with the assistance of the Ministry of Information and the intervention of Noel Coward, he produced *In Which We Serve*, described by Alan Wood in *A Study of J. Arthur Rank and British Films*, (Hodder & Stoughton, London, 1952) as 'one of the crucial films of the British cinema and the starting point of many careers'. Quite so. The then unknown actors John Mills, Richard Attenborough, Bernard Miles, Celia Johnson, and the director, David Lean, made their first appearance. *In Which We Serve* was followed very quickly and successfully by *French Without Tears*, *The Gentle Sex*, *This Happy Breed*, *The Way Ahead*, *Blithe Spirit*, *The Way To The Stars*, *Odd Man Out*, *Henry V* and *Hamlet*, all the work of Del Giudice who, over a period of only four or five years, was able to bring together scriptwriters like Noel Coward, Eric Ambler, Peter Ustinov and Terence Rattigan, as well as actors like David Niven and Trevor Howard and director Carol Reed. Del Giudice was the first to bring Shakespeare to the screen: the forerunner of the screening of the literary masterpieces, and of opera.

Del Giudice's greatest contribution, in my view, however, lay in his ability to determine at an early stage that what British films needed was more money spent on them. He was good at overcoming obstacles and brilliant in succeeding where others had failed or had failed to try; but his greatest ability was in raising finance. By the time *Henry V* had been completed, nearly half a million pounds had been spent on making a single film. England had never seen anything like that before and, in context, half a million pounds in those days was a very substantial sum of money indeed.

The British film industry owes him a debt that can not easily be forgotten. And yet, the entry that refers to him in one of the major books of reference, Leslie Halliwell's *The Film goers Companion*, dismisses him in two lines as 'Italian Producer who settled in England and became the Managing Director of Two Cities Films Limited.' But then, England has always been the country of the understatement.

Opinions on Mr Del vary. Some consider Del Giudice as one of the founding fathers of the British film industry; others dismiss him as an adventurer.

I find the notion of Del Giudice as an adventurer an amusing one. Indeed, it is my experience that the word 'adventurer' is applied almost indiscrimately by English-speaking people to those whose abilities and success they cannot understand.

I suppose both Drake and Raleigh were adventurers of sorts. No doubt Clive of India was as well. It is an interesting label to apply and it is the result, in my opinion, of on the one hand a complete inability to understand the motivation of the person to whom the label is appended and, on the other, of a sense of inadequacy and failure.

The fact that he succeeded where others had failed, and possibly his exuberant nature and flamboyant style, caused quite a few raised eyebrows.

Mr Del had his share of problems with the J. Arthur Rank Organization and to all intents and purposes withdrew from the film industry in 1947, retiring to the Italian Riviera. He ended his life in a monastery. Even so, a larger-than-life character, overtaken by people like Arthur Rank, Alexander Korda and John Davis, but certainly not outshone by them.

I conclude: 'It is in the cinema that Italy has probably made its most significant contribution to art on an international scale'. (See *Britannica*, Volume 9, p. 1112).

3

THE CAUSES OF ITALIAN FAILURES AND SUCCESSES

FAILURES

If you couple the discoveries made by the Italians with their contributions to knowledge, science and art generally, it is a record that is very difficult to match. Indeed, there is no field of human knowledge or endeavour where the Italians have not left their mark – except in the fields of symphonic music and theatre: so far, the Italians have not been able to produce either a Beethoven or a Shakespeare.

This is to me a cause of considerable regret. If one could claim Shakespeare and Beethoven as Italians, then I have no hesitation in saying that the cultural and scientific primacy of Italy would be incontestable. As it is, that primacy is still there, but the absence of a major contributor in these two fields does allow those who do not like Italians to dispute it. But then, I am not sure who can be substituted for the Italians. Can the French match the Italian record? Can the Germans or the British?

Fortunately for the reader, I shall not indulge in any analysis of the French or German contribution nor indeed of that of any other culture because the purpose of this section of the book is to attempt to consider the reasons why the Italians are as they are, and not to determine whether they are the best.

Take for example the question why the Italians have been unable to produce either a Beethoven or a Shakespeare. It is an interesting one and it does lead us on to causation quite directly.

First, music. Everyone knows that the Italians are musical. Indeed, it has been said repeatedly that they are the most musical people in the world. I believe that statement to be perfectly true, but the reasons for it are not simple. It cannot just be to do with the Mediterranean climate or the sun, because the Welsh, too, are said to be a musical people, yet the rainfall in Wales is quite high.

It is also a commonly-held view that the Italian language is the most musical language in the world. That statement is equally true but there are good scientific reasons for it. For example, the seven Italian vowel sounds are basic and they occur quite freely and abundantly. Indeed, there is an Italian word — 'aiuole' (it means flowerbeds) – which consists of all five principal vowel sounds and only one consonant. (There are, in fact, five vowels, but two have two sounds.)

Furthermore, the Italian language has no harsh notes. All the consonants are pronounced simply and there is an abundance of soft doubled consonants such as l, m, and n, which produce some perfectly natural, flowing and easy sounds like 'palla', 'mamma', 'nonna, etc.

And finally, in order to speak Italian properly, you have to open your mouth in the shape of an O. It is a natural movement, but less exaggerated than the one you make when you go to the dentist or the doctor. You do not have to twist your mouth, or smack your tongue against the palate or the teeth, or move your lips in an awkward direction, either as if you were grimacing or as if you had swallowed a hot potato, as indeed you have to do if, for example, you are speaking French, German or Russian.

And I am not the only one to make this observation. In his *Beppo*, stanza XLIV, Byron has this to say about Italian:

> I love the language, that soft bastard Latin, which melts like kisses from a female mouth, and sounds as if it should be writ on satin, with syllables which breathe of the sweet South, and gentle liquids gliding all so pat in, that not a single accent seems uncouth, like our harsh northern whistling, grunting guttural which we are obliged to hiss, and spit, and sputter all.

So it is clear that there are technical reasons why Italian is a musical language.

When it comes to music, however, all we can say is that the Italian approach to it is what I call a purely melodic one. Music for an Italian does not exist unless there is a melody, preferably but not necessarily an easy melody, that he can sing, hum or whistle. Indeed, there are some people, of whom I am one, who maintain that you cannot call anything music if in fact you cannot whistle it, sing it or hum it.

It was Arturo Toscanini who used to keep telling his orchestra that, when they were playing, they had to sing. All the time, they should be doing nothing else but singing; not with their voices but with their instruments. Indeed, he is recorded as saying that 'Music, unless you sing, is nothing.' (See Bernard Shaw, *The Orchestra Speaks*; the same concept is re-stated in Howard Taubman's *Toscanini*.)

Italians, therefore, only appreciate music if it is pleasant to listen to or is simple in outline. When we listen to a melody we do not wish to listen to anything else, for we are being transported into a world of fantasy where we can forget the more sordid features of everyday life. We are moved by the music, which strikes the hidden chords of our psyche.

Ours is an emotional reaction and not an intellectual one, as the melody is associated with sound and the sound is associated with the person who utters it. That is why the Italians have been so successful with their operas because sounds have been coupled to persons and to characters, to their passions, to their laughter and, essentially, to their humanity. There are no demi-gods or gods in Italian opera; there are only human beings, heroes or villains, but always human beings. Sound divorced from the human voice and the human theme has no particular meaning or significance for an Italian.

That is for me the principal reason why we have been quite incapable of providing a Beethoven.

There are of course other reasons, namely the lack of patriotic enthusiasm, of religious concern or of spiritual excitement. These are not on the whole national traits; and we are deficient in them.

What there has always been, however, is great feeling, great sensuousness and, all the time, melody, even in passionate situations.

But passions have never been allowed to become too great and even where they have not been kept under control (like Othello's jealousy or Manrico's heroism) they have never reached peaks of Teutonic perseverance. This is ultimately due to the fact that Italians are quite incapable of taking most things too seriously, as I have already remarked more than once, except their culture and their families.

Nor should we forget, John Addington Symonds has pointed out that we are a smiling people. We can boast of a smile all our own – '*Il sorriso Italiano*'; it is part of our charm and does not detract from what we do.

We can be quite engrossed in something important, or serious, in which we are wholeheartedly involved; and then, a moment later, we can stand aside from it and smile at our seriousness. It comes naturally to us to do it; a northerner, for example, cannot, unless perhaps, he is in Italy, or has had too much to drink.

It is an asset, of course, since life is not worth taking too seriously. After all, one of our greatest men, Verdi, could end his last opera, *Falstaff*, composed when he was eighty years old, with the fugue '*Tutto nel mondo e' burla*' – 'Everything in the world is a joke'.

It must be admitted, however, that fewer people nowadays smile in Italy than used to be the case. Italians are becoming a less happy people. In a strange sense, they are slightly more introverted and much less friendly. It may be just a phase. It is really too soon to tell.

Furthermore, it is a cause for regret that we are not always able to smile inwardly. On the whole, I do not think we find it so easy to laugh at ourselves since it is so much easier to laugh at others.

We have a tendency to take ourselves much too seriously and there is a certain innate susceptibility in us that causes us to fail totally to appreciate the jokes that others make at our expense.

Nevertheless, our smile is an asset, despite the fact that in Italy life has always been something of a tragedy and no-one ever felt the need to glorify its tragic features in writing. On the contrary, starting with Boccaccio, Italian writers have enjoyed underlining its funnier sides.

When it comes to our failure to produce great drama, the national characteristics are equally to blame. The obvious first Italian contribution to writing is the 'Novella'. A number of great contributors exist here, as you will no doubt recall: Boccaccio, Straparola, Giraldi Cinzio, Machiavelli.

They all wrote interesting and entertaining stories, or comedies, but they attained no great heights. Nor could they. There was no real centre of learning from which these writers could operate. There was no capital city, no large city like Athens, Paris or Elizabethan London to hear them, apart from Florence. The greater part of the Italian public lived in the country, and could hardly read or write, so that only the scholars and the members of the various courts in the individual towns had any knowledge of their language. The general public was ignorant. There were no leaders, no sense of power, no feeling for history other than in the sense that the Romans were our predecessors, and no political enthusiasm of any kind. We were, and still are, far too sceptical; we were, and still are, not too religious nor too profound.

It is not that the material was not there. Ample material was available to Boccaccio and others; so much so that if there had been anyone of sufficiently great intellectual calibre, he could have turned to excellent advantage the very features that militated against Italy developing drama as England did. The disunity of the people, their suffering, the Naples plague, their extreme ignorance and poverty, the very sinister religious revivals which resulted in the growth of Italy being stunted by the Catholic Church in the second half of the sixteenth century. (If you have read Italian history you will recall that Carnesecchi, Paleario and Bruno were burnt alive in Rome in 1567, 1570 and 1600, respectively; Vanini was burnt at the stake in Toulouse; Gentile was executed by Calvinists in Berne; Campanella was kept in prison for nearly thirty years in Naples in the Castel Dell'Ovo; Galileo was forced to recant; and Sarpi was knifed, although he survived that.)

All these facts, tragic in themselves, could have elicited a tragic response; but they did not because, as already noted, the Italians have never taken life too seriously. After all, as Symonds reminds us, the nation had witnessed the slaughters of the Viscontis, the cruelty of the Sforzas and the poisonings of the Borgias: these were all Italian tragedies which in their own way gave the English great enjoyment. Marlowe, Webster and Shakespeare thrived on Italian themes, whether happy or villainous. Indeed, as we have seen, no less than nineteen of Shakespeare's works are set in Italy or are inspired by it. But the Italians were not moved.

There is a further reason, which has nothing to do with history but with personality. The Italian is constantly being both himself and playing a part. He plays a part in his love life and in his job and he has learnt at an early age to be an actor. He is, as Barzini has observed, a small showman; and that is why for twenty-two years he appreciated Mussolini, who was a big showman. Because, no matter what else you may hear, the Italians did approve of Mussolini. There were some independent spirits who decided they could not put up with a dictatorship and went abroad: Toscanini is the first example that springs to mind but there were many others, less well known. Many came to England; others emigrated to the USA and to South America.

But the majority of the people were pleased with what they had. If you speak to those in their seventies who were around at the time, they will disclaim any love or even acceptance of Fascism. But their disclaimers sound somewhat hollow.

The Italians at the time appreciated what Mussolini was doing; he was restoring the glory of Rome, he was, they thought, making Italy great. They felt that he was giving them back dignity in international affairs and they accepted him in the same way in which the Austrians and the Germans accepted Hitler. They accepted him because he was strong, and Italians will always admire and respect power in preference to goodness or justice; and because he was one of them, in the sense that he displayed, to a very marked degree, all the virtues and, even more, the faults of the Italian people. If this judgement seems harsh, consider for a moment the following facts. Mussolini proclaimed himself a dictator, suppressed freedom and constitutional rights, condoned the killing of Matteotti and wantonly attacked Abyssinia: he withdrew political rights from the Jews and declared war on England. The Italians applauded these deeds which were all contrary to their own tolerant nature. Why? Because he made them feel good.

In other fields, Mussolini was conceited, as most Italians are; he loved the sound of his own voice, as all Italians do; he proclaimed himself a believer in God but that did not prevent him from sinning, a normal feature of Catholic Italy; his bark was worse than his bite, and that is not too unusual in Italy either; he was a good father and probably also a family man but he had no compunction about keeping mistresses: indeed, he died effectively in the arms of one. No, do not believe those who say that Mussolini was not wanted by the Italians. If it be an historical fact that people get the government they deserve, then the Italians at the time thoroughly deserved Mussolini.

Returning to the point, however, I should say that the Italian's feelings are not, on the whole, repressed; therefore, he feels no need for any extra, greater theatricality on stage. That is the reason why, generally speaking, Italians do not make great tragic actors, although they have provided one of the greatest comic actors of all times, Eduardo De Filippo.

Great acting and great tragic works belong to the English, or to other northern people, who repress their personality in everyday life and who, therefore, enjoy acting out on stage, or in choral societies, all the feelings that they have so repressed, whether they are sincerely felt or not. In exactly the same way the English love to dress up or play a part, whether in the Territorial Army, the school play or in amateur theatrical groups. Anything in order not to be themselves. (I should add that this is a common feature of northern peoples in any event and is not only confined to the English.)

The ultimate reason is that in Italy life has always been something of a tragedy and no-one ever felt the need to glorify its tragic features in writing. On the contrary, starting with Boccaccio, Italian writers have enjoyed underlining its funnier sides.

This almost carefree approach of the writers reflects the attitude of the people as a whole. They have no wish to be serious for too long: they want to feel, not to think. It is almost as though one were afraid that thinking might cause the brow to furrow, that it might produce premature ageing. There probably is something in this approach: if you think too much or too hard, you grow old more quickly. One should remain a child at heart, I suppose.

The same attitude emerges if one considers the discoveries made by the Italians. Once made, interest is lost in them and the scientist, artist or whatever he might have been classified as, went on to something else. This lack of perseverance and continuity, this perpetual search for something novel or different, this desperate attempt to escape from the boredom of routine and repetitiousness is another facet of the tendency of the Italians not to be serious for too long. Foreigners call it levity or flippancy; I prefer the adjective 'fickle'. Perhaps neither description is accurate; the answer may be that if at heart you are a cynic and yet love life, the only way to survival and to psychological salvation is not to take things too seriously.

Historically, Italian tragedy went into realistic painting, as anyone will appreciate who has looked at the Sistine Chapel ceiling. It is only in his Rondanini Pietá that Michelangelo gets close to abstraction in a desperate attempt to express the inexpressible. I suppose it is ultimately true that, if one is surrounded by tragedy, one does not wish to read about it.

It is a pity, of course; just imagine how exciting an Italian Shakespeare or an Italian Beethoven might have been. Or perhaps not; perhaps the fascination that the south holds for all northerners is not something that can be turned upside down.

And so, regrettably, here are our two cultural failings. The reasons for them are to be found in ourselves, in our history and in our make-up.

SUCCESSES

O ne can really divide the history of Italy into several parts: pre-history, the Greek phase, the Roman phase, the Middle Ages; after that, taking as a starting date the year AD 1000, there is a further sub-division up to about the year 1500. Thereafter, we have the period of the Renaissance and then a further period from, say, the beginning of the eighteenth century to the end of the nineteenth (I am ignoring more modern history).

They are historically convenient periods since they highlight some of the principal phases of Italy's development as a country; but the three last periods are particularly relevant to the development of Italy as a nation.

The first of these last three periods includes such events as the travels of Marco Polo and the initial contributions by Italians to science and knowledge. Before we deal with this period we must try and visualize what had happened from the fall of the Roman Empire up to its beginning. Italy, as has already been established, was invaded by all and sundry. Let me repeat the list of invaders, for it is long: Arabs, Goths, Vandals, Lombards, Franks, Huns, Normans, Spaniards, Swiss mercenaries, French, Germans. The world was aghast when Rome was sacked by Alaric in the year 410; but that was only the beginning.

The first thing that the Italians had to learn, therefore, was survival. Each town or area developed its own techniques.

They had to learn when to make way for the invaders and retreat to the hills or to the mountains with their families and their cattle, and when to stay and fight or negotiate with them.

One finds signs of fortifications all over Italy. There are castles and defensive walls in all the major cities. The Sforzesco Castle in Milan is a classic example, but there are many others; from the tip of Italy (Castel del Monte in Puglia) to Naples (Mastio Angioino) through to Rome (Castel Santangelo), Florence and Bologna.

With the passage of time, the fortifications became in themselves a means of expressing the personality of the inhabitants and style was applied to them; but they started out as purely functional means of defence.

Even in Venice one finds a form of fortification, as the inhabitants retreated onto the islands from the mainland, thus escaping the invader.

All these defensive needs developed what I would call a siege mentality. People who retreated within the walls of the city in the face of the invader, often resisting sieges lasting for weeks or months, and sometimes years, had to learn two essential virtues which have been an Italian fundamental characteristic ever since; resourcefulness and improvisation. (Incidentally, have you noticed how this same mentality is reflected in the Italian style of soccer playing? The players retreat almost to a quadrangle, which is very difficult to penetrate and where they show all their defensive skills and resourcefulness. Thence they make sorties, at speed, to score. Having scored, they retreat to defence again. It is a classic example of the mentality that I am describing.)

Gradually, each city found an activity that was useful for its survival in exactly the same way as Venice found that it had to retreat to the islands, or the Jews to control money which in turn can buy those who wish to harm them.

It is of course true that, at about the same time, cities started fighting one another. This in-fighting obviously brought about one of the classic faults of the Italian, namely the constant bickering between one another. This has in turn developed into something of an antipathy towards his fellow human beings which is not always too successfully disguised by his easy manner and his gregariousness.

On the other hand, one has to be a little careful not to exaggerate the extent of this internecine fighting. It was frequent rather than occasional but the frequency was not proportionate to the intensity. Fights went on for years between one city and the next; take Florence and Pisa, who fought each other for decades; or Venice and Genoa, who did so for centuries. But there were more prisoners than casualties, for the particular reason that they were used for ransom.

In a sense, the in-fighting between the various factions in the individual cities (Florence is a particularly good example) was much more bitter, as fights between neighbours usually are. But peace was made as often as war and even in these local internecine battles the numbers killed were not so great: each faction being able to run for shelter to its own 'palazzo'. Indeed, we must remember this was the period when Italian cities were at their most prosperous – demographically, artistically and economically.

At the same time, this very in-fighting was also one of the sources of improvement for those individual characteristics of resourcefulness and inventiveness which have served the Italians in good stead. After all, hostility stimulates imagination and there is nothing like the need to survive to excite mental ability. In any part of the world the need to survive sharpens the intellect. In England, that old saying 'necessity is the mother of invention' sums it up nicely.

The constant invasions also explain the great love the Italians have for their homes. Every time an invader dislodged them or destroyed their villages, these were rebuilt with stubborness and determination, almost as though the home represented survival against future perils.

By concentrating on his own ability to survive and to rebuild what was destroyed, the Italian also developed, at a very early date, two characteristics which, in modern times, would represent probably his principal social and political drawbacks, namely his contempt for the state and his utter disregard for authority. The reasons are not far to seek: since the state, or whatever was the equivalent at the time of constituted authority, had been unable to prevent his territory being invaded and his home destroyed or his family molested, it could not obviously be worth very much. The individual, on the other hand, derived great strength from the fact that, despite the destruction that occurred around him, he found himself quite capable of surviving. Hence, the natural sequence of the individual considering himself better than the state; and in Sicily, the Mafia.

On the positive side, this concentrated, dogged resolve to rebuild and regenerate, led to the development of a technical and aesthetic sense that blossomed into the full flower of domestic, religious and public architecture, both during and after the Renaissance.

Since one could find some sort of protection from greater numbers, the houses were rebuilt each time in greater densities – hence the rapid early development of Italian cities.

These desperate, instinctive needs and ability to survive account for many contradictory and at times humiliating features of Italian history. They explain how one can revere a dictator for twenty-two years and then, having shot him and his mistress in tawdry circumstances, allow his body to hang in Piazzale Loreto for the benefit of the mob. (Here one almost hears faint echoes of what happened to Cromwell and to Cola di Rienzo.) They explain the almost inconceivably ruthless reaction of Italians in circumstances where their own survival instinct is paramount.

The average Italian, single or married, is constantly on the lookout for changes, whether in his job or surroundings, which might result in betterment to himself or his family. He lives like a pointer, his nose up in the air, sniffing the wind. Whether it be the more or less gentle wind of change or a real gale, it is always an ill-wind against which he must seek protection. It brings no good news and therefore he must remain on the alert.

This hypersensitivity to change and to surrounding circumstances raises survival ability to a fine art, but it also has drawbacks for him. It causes him to throw overboard without too much compunction those whom he believes will only prove to be ballast, or whose usefulness is becoming less noticeable – and, in so doing, often results in his backing, metaphorically, the wrong horse – as well as to behave in a manner which, if it were not essentially fickle, could be said to be cruel and short-sighted. He adopts a policy of 'shoot first and ask questions later': such a policy, in peace as in war, may be understandable when it is a matter of survival but it is not too efficient at guaranteeing that one does not shoot down the best people, or at any rate those who might ultimately be better for one's future than others who it is believed may be taking over from them. Hence the Italian's apparent disregard for people: 'When the Pope dies we elect a new one.'

In personal terms, this attitude to life (and death) often makes for short-lived friendships since the relationships themselves appear to be based on the notion of usefulness rather than conviction or commitment: in political terms, it makes for short-term solutions, as we have already seen, and in moral terms it is machiavellism refined: the end always justifying the means.

This same attitude explains how a separate peace could be made with the Allies leaving the Germans to fight on. It is true, of course, that the alliance with Germany was ill-matched; one cannot conceive of more diametrically opposed characters and temperaments than those of the Germans and the Italians. But the welcome given to the conquering Allied Armies, though undoubtedly genuine, was totally disproportionate in circumstances where, until a few months previously, the same Allies were the declared enemies of Italy.

I was in Rome at the time and speak from personal recollection. I suppose the hosannas to the British and American tanks were a reaction to many months of terror by the Germans. I suppose, too, that people who have been without food will kiss the hand that at long last feeds them and be quite unable to appreciate that with corn and sweet potatoes came not only 'K-rations' (meat and vegetable stew in a tin is excellent stuff when you have been starving, I promise you) but also cigarettes. One of the consequences was that the starving bodies were filled up at the same time as an addiction was encouraged which would kill many by lung cancer. All this was done, it is true, in the name of democracy and well-being. But the reality is that the power in marketing and advertising terms of the Americans never allowed any other voice to be heard such as would have been the case in truly democratic circumstances.

Italians sold their souls and prostituted their bodies for cigarettes. The same situation has recurred in the poorer countries of the world like Greece, Turkey, the Philippines, Thailand and South Korea, where youngsters were set to copy American filmstars. Cigarettes became their stance and Coca Cola their habit.

☐

If one goes back to Roman history, one is reminded of the fact that Hannibal, that great warrior who had the ingenuity and resourcefulness to bring his elephants across the Alps, was ultimately conquered when he got to Capua near Naples, not by any army, but by sloth. There, he found that the more genial weather and the local sensuousness caused him to slow down and relax and unwind. Unfortunately for him, he stayed long enough to allow the Romans to re-group, with the result that he was ultimately defeated on the other side of the Peninsula at Cannae. One wonders whether the course of history in Italy might not have been different if the Carthaginians had managed to conquer Rome. I suppose it can be said that one of the minor contributions of the south of Italy to Italian history was indeed to conquer Hannibal by means of its pleasure-loving techniques.

Nor was Hannibal the only one to be so affected by Naples and its district.

Lord Acton and Lord Nelson, each in their own way, felt the extraordinary fascination of the area, although in the case of Lord Nelson it was insufficient to enable him to behave as a gentleman either in the personal sense or in the political one. In the personal sense because, as is well known, he caused great scandal by his open affair with Emma Lyon; and in the political sense because, in restoring the Bourbon dynasty to Naples, he arranged the court-martial and hanging of Admiral Caracciolo, a brilliant Neapolitan who, apart from being a patriot, had also served under him.

It may be worth reminding ourselves of what happened. The Neapolitans, inspired by the French, had revolted against their Bourbon king. Caracciolo, who was an admiral in the Bourbon navy and as such had also served under Nelson when the two navies had joined forces earlier, decided that he would go over to the revolutionary side. In a sense, he was wrong in doing so because he had sworn allegiance to the Bourbon king; even assuming that his sympathies lay with the revolution, he should not have taken up arms against his previous ruler. But then, regrettably, Italian history displays many instances of this kind where a complete 'volte-face' takes place. Having said this for the sake of historical accuracy, Caracciolo certainly did not deserve his end; after all, if the revolution had succeeded, he would have been a hero.

Nelson's attitude to the revolutionaries, according to his historians and biographers, was ambiguous. He wavered, which was unusual for him: first he decided to destroy them, then he granted an armistice which forbade reprisals; he then went back on his word, and hastily hanged Caracciolo in addition to hundreds of other Neapolitans.

English historians are clearly in a difficulty here. On the one hand, there is the fact that Nelson is a national hero, was a great sailor, the victor of Aboukir, the Nile and Trafalgar; a legend in his own lifetime. On the other, he had given his word that the terms of the armistice which forbade reprisals would be honoured. Many Neapolitans fleeing Naples, took Nelson's word as his bond. A major contradiction here which no-one, as far as I know, has succeeded in explaining away.

It is the consensus of historical opinion that Nelson was influenced by his mistress. She was, after all, quite close to Queen Caroline, who had been deposed and was being restored to power thanks to the British navy. Perhaps she even felt that what she was doing on behalf of the queen would have been appreciated by her and by the British government. Perhaps there was in Emma a streak of cruelty. It must be remembered that she had had what one can only call, if we wish to use a euphemism, a somewhat chequered past. She had been one of the girls of Mrs Charlotte Kelly, the well-known procuress, whose establishments in Arlington Row and Duke Street, St James's, in late eighteenth century London were much frequented by the wealthy and the nobility. Much easier, I suppose, to blame a woman, particularly one with Emma's past, than besmirch the character of a national hero.

It has also been suggested that Nelson may have been jealous of Caracciolo's seamanship. This seems less likely, although nobody can tell: it is more likely that the reverse is true.

In a recent biography of the admiral (Tom Pocock, *Horatio Nelson*, The Bodley Head, London, 1987), there is a suggestion that Nelson may not have fully appreciated what he was doing since he was still recovering from the head injuries he had suffered at the battle of the Nile. This is also quite possible since there appears no real evidence of cruelty by Nelson until the Naples incident.

I accept that strange things happen in war and, as I have remarked, from a technical point of view Caracciolo could be said by some to have betrayed his king. However, whilst after having been tried by five Bourbon officers brought together by Nelson, and convicted, Caracciolo was being hanged in full public view at 1700 hours on the 29 June 1799, on one of the ships of the British fleet (*Minerva*), the Admiral was having dinner on board his new flagship, the *Foudroyant*, with the Hamiltons and other friends.

Furthermore, his body was thrown in the sea; being found a few days later, it was buried in the church of S. Maria della Catena at Santa Lucia, a suburb of Naples. In his home town, one of the principal streets is dedicated to him and Caracciolo has also passed into history for having had attributed to him the statement that 'in England there are sixty different religions, and only one sauce'. . . . .

I refrain from deciding whether Nelson's conduct on this occasion was an example of phlegm or of callousness: nobody will ever know. I can only assume that when the British government encouraged the first patriotic movements in nineteenth century Italy, at the time occupied by the Austrians, they may to some extent have been endeavouring to atone for Nelson's behaviour at Naples.

Not too far away, the people of Nola – better known as the birthplace of Giordano Bruno and of the brigand Pascalone – had for centuries indulged in orgies that were well known to the locality, especially at harvest time, and compared to which we are told the phallus-carrying processions of the Greeks pale into insignificance (interesting accounts of Nola and its varied celebrations can be found in Thomas Ashby's *Some Italian Festivals*, London, 1929). Sensuousness surrounds one in Naples.

Goethe could not deal with it either. On 16 March 1787 he wrote (*Italian Journey*): 'Naples is a paradise: everyone lives in a state of intoxicated forgetfulness, myself included. I seem to be a completely different person whom I hardly recognize. Yesterday I thought to myself: either you were mad before, or you are mad now.' Goethe was not alone. Thomas Nugent thought

Naples was the most pleasant Italian town, struck as he was by the gaiety and exuberance of the locals.

☐

B ut to return to the point, it is often said that Italy civilized its conquerors. This is certainly true if one means by the statement that Italy taught them manners and appreciation of the finer things in life. But the national genius that was born as a result of the constant tug-of-war between the cities and their constant fights with invaders also brought in its turn something to Italy, namely the virtues and vices of the invaders themselves. After all, most of the invading people must have had characteristics that encouraged and ensured their success. The Normans who went to Sicily had a very long way to travel, as had the hordes of Huns and Goths: they were all strong, cruel people: their individual genius matched the local ones. Italian genes embody all theirs, Italian psychological heritage is partly theirs.

The trouble with Italy's national genius, however, is that the clash between civic duties on the one hand, and private and family business on the other, is too great; individualism causes the pendulum between the two to swing too far in a particular way, always in favour of the 'particulare'. That is the reason why individuality does not lead to national unity: indeed, the situation is quite the reverse.

Each coin, as usual, has its two sides. The strength of the English people has lain in the willingness of the Englishman to sacrifice his individuality to the well-being of the community as a whole. For example, there is no way in which a disc-jockey could be successful in Italy, as the immediate reaction of an Italian would be to consider that no-one had any right to impose his choice of records on others.

On the other hand, the English have always accepted that ability can often result in eccentricity or failure to conform and have indeed encouraged such forms of eccentricity. It is not too far from the truth to say that in the days when English eccentrics were an acceptable part of the English establishment, England had an empire; it no longer has an empire now that we frown upon anything which results in deviation even in the slightest degree from the norm. The power of compliance and uniformity has become so all-embracing nowadays that it is hardly surprising that individuals have lost their sense of direction.

Italians often say, quite mistakenly, that they like the Englishman as a person but dislike England and its history. This is a highly superficial assessment. It seems to me that the Englishman as an individual is not necessarily any more or less worthwhile than any other individual of a different nationality. It is Great Britain as a whole, as a nation, that is a great historical fact, the greatest nation that has ever existed after Rome. It is a nation that conquered the world and brought its language and its civilization to distant lands. A nation worthy of respect as none of its individual components could ever be. A nation with pride and conviction, until post-Second World War times, when it lost its sense of history.

It is not for nothing that the saying 'My country right or wrong' has become established in Britain. It is interesting that there is no such equivalent of any description in the Italian language. If one had to be coined, it would read 'Right or wrong, my culture': our culture and our way of life are our patriotism. An Italian would never say 'My country right or wrong,' but he might say to his neighbour 'I am right and you are wrong.' And herein lies the difference between the two nations. The revival of learning which occurred in the sixteenth century put Italy at the forefront in the Western world because it had already developed a language and a culture that, although never consolidated into any form of political unity, represented continuity with the Roman tradition. And although there was no national unity at the time, there was political freedom combined with considerable academic freedom. There was also a great amount of commercial prosperity at a time when other nations were still semi-barbarous: so, if one can put it differently, the second phase of Italian development, the Renaissance, was almost predictable.

The revival of learning was also encouraged by some of the movements of the people and the establishment of the great Italian families that gradually replaced the communes. Nevertheless, it is odd to consider that the first democratic movements known to the Western world, after those of ancient Greece, occurred in the Milan Commune. In 1037, for the first time, the people there decided to be represented in a local sort of parliament by what you might call members of parliament known as consuls. From there were selected the members of the Gran Consiglio (if you like, a sort of Inner Cabinet) and from those members a 'Credenza', a sort of Privy Council. All were more or less supervised by the Bishop; but even so, it was a democratic process of sorts.

There were other examples. In 1212, in the village of Abbadia San Salvatore in Tuscany, the inhabitants complained about the rule of their feudal lord who lived in the local castle. They were granted certain rights to be represented, such as the right to elect consuls or the right of succession through direct lineal descendants rather than forfeiture to the local Vassal or the local Abbot, and the right to make a money payment in place of feudal labour. This, as Edward Hutton (*In unknown Tuscany*, Methuen, London, 1909) reminds us, was three years before Magna Carta.

One does not wish to belabour these early stirrings, these seedlings of democracy because, in effect, they did not amount to very much. The system did not work. And that was to be expected: the Italian virtues all have their corresponding faults and these faults are, on the whole, incompatible with democracy.

Gradually, therefore, the more capable families in each city took over and established their own form of government. Dictatorships, in the political sense; but very paternalistic dictatorships as far as the arts and learning were concerned.

As the great families took over from the old communes, they also made war upon one another and that in turn resulted in constant changes in government. Such constant changes taught men to fend for themselves, thus sharpening their ingenuity and their intelligence. At a time when moral considerations were not relevant, the versatility thus acquired was all-embracing. It led to the ruthlessness of the leaders and the ruthlessly political thought of Machiavelli, but it contributed above all to the formation of an original character and many-sided intellects in greater profusion than in any other nation in Europe.

Furthermore, there was not then, any more than there is now, any great hierarchy of classes in Italy: those who came to the fore were people of merit and they were all individuals. This is very well evidenced by each town having its own expertise. Genoa, Venice, Pisa, Amalfi were all great maritime powers; Florence went into banking; Milan developed state techniques; Naples was well known for the appreciation of the finer things in life and for its comforts (it was, after all, the city that inspired Boccaccio, even though Boccaccio was born in Paris of a French mother): the great intellectual freedom of the Renaissance stirred the imagination.

If there is one thing that the Italians have in greater abundance than any other people I know of, it is imagination. It has, of course, in the past led them to great crimes. One is only too well aware of the sophisticated poisoning techniques of the Borgias. More recently, say over the last two hundred years, it has also led them to sophisticated forms of criminal association and vindictiveness (the Mafia and the Camorra are classic examples.) But, when applied to practical life, it has allowed them to be at the forefront of most human activities. Love, hatred, lust and business are all feelings and activities where Italians display a great deal of imagination.

It is interesting to note that this exercise of imagination has not led Italians to any exciting writing. The Italian is not romantic enough to be introverted nor morbid enough to turn to melancholy. Boccaccio is possibly the best example of this, practical and open as he is; his novels are bawdy, but sound in commonsense; he is witty but never gross. (Thank God they did not allow him to burn his manuscripts, as he intended to do in his old age.)

Nor has it made Italians go and search for new political solutions; we are not revolutionaries. It took us twenty-two years and a defeat in the Second World War to get rid of Fascism. Partly because of our cynicism, we are inclined to accept the existing order on the basis of the French saying that 'plus ça change, plus c'est la meme chose'.

It is true that in Boccaccio's day adultery and unnatural passions were somewhat commonplace; but this was the price that had to be paid when the spirit was given an unbridled rein and it is a fact that people of great culture and considerable aesthetic temperament develop a sort of high intellectual approach to their vices, when they indulge in them.

On the other hand, this intellectual quality of the Italians has its redeeming features. For example, Italians enjoy drinking; but drunkenness is not a problem amongst us. The reasons are firstly that we adopt too epicurean an approach to food and drink and, secondly, that in psychological terms we have no need either to forget what we are doing or to project a different image of ourselves. Indeed, the Italian approach is always practical and we like to be in possession of our faculties in order to enjoy the pleasures of our senses to the full.

Again, the northerners went to the crusades in the Middle Ages because they were religiously enthusiastic about them; the Italians, particularly the Venetians, made money out of the crusades as contractors and as merchants. In the Middle Ages, the northern races were poor and barbaric and they lived for the most part in villages; Italy on the other hand had a wealth of experience behind it and developed its own civilization in towns and cities which were centres of learning and a high quality of life. In a strange sense, its political disunion encouraged and stimulated intellectual growth because each town competed with its neighbour. Each despotic family wanted to show the leaders of other cities that it was better, that it entertained more interesting artists, that it spent more money, that it was more powerful because it had better armies or better mercenaries. The leaders at this time were all people with very marked personalities.

The world has reason to be grateful that Italy did not at that time develop as a nation for, because of this failure, it was able to give the world its culture. It was a very humanistic culture that replaced patriotism at every level. It was also an outward-looking culture. It had to be, because of its multifarious origins. In the south, the Arabs and Islam; throughout the north, Venice and Genoa through their maritime contacts brought news of different civilisations. In particular, Venice maintained close relations with Turkey, as Shakespeare confirms in Othello. In the centre, the business interests of Florence and Pisa.

At this particular moment in its history, Italy also reached its trading peak. It was at the centre of all European trade because it stood in the centre of the Mediterranean. At this time, Italian fleets (whether from Genoa, Venice, Pisa or Amalfi) controlled that sea; it was in the true sense of the word 'mare nostrum', for Italian sailors had taken over from the Arabs and the Muslims and also exercised a kind of policing function to weed out the pirates. Textiles, spices, corn and salt were practically a Venetian monopoly. Genoa and Pisa did very well on the commercial side, too, the former holding Corsica and the latter Sardinia. Despite the fact that they made war upon each other they still developed their trading interests. Indeed, Venice ended up by controlling all the Ionian Islands, some of the ports in the Peloponnese, the greater part of the Aegean Islands, Crete and even a part of Constantinople, which enabled it to trade with Bulgarians and Hungarians. By the beginning of the thirteenth century, it had extended its trading activities to the Asian Muslims as well as Africa.

It had taken the Italian maritime cities time to reach their hegemony. They had to fight the Saracens and the Africans. (Pisa led a victorious expedition to Africa in 1088; the Genoese dealt with the Cypriots, obtaining trading posts there.) Ultimately, Genoa beat Pisa and then fought it out with Venice.

All this resulted in the Italians developing a great knowledge of the peoples with whom they came into contact. The Italians also had great familiarity with the mixed races of Spain, including the Jews there; they traded with all northern nations.

A different type of people, I suppose, from those today. Or perhaps not. Perhaps it is a misconception to consider the Italians temperamental; perhaps we are more cold and calculating than we are normally given credit for.

I have already referred to one description of our characteristics as a people, as being artistic, impulsive and passionate. I am not sure that this is the picture that emerges from what I have been saying. The archetypal Italian in my view defies analysis, and, for this very same reason, so does the Italian nation. Nevertheless, the picture that emerges is of a concrete, practical people, with no romantic quirks and no great mysticism, proud of its Roman heritage, its great civility and its great knowledge. A people that, as has been said, was born old and as such was incapable of illusion and thrived on cynicism. In a strange sense, a solid people that ought to have been much more successful than it has as a nation when it ultimately became one. A people with two feet firmly planted on the ground and much peasant good sense. (Incidentally, it is interesting that one of the Italian proverbs, 'contadino, scarpe grosse cervello fino' equates a fine mind with the peasant.)

The language itself owes much to peasant jargon. This is by no means unusual: even in the twentieth century most languages retain expressions derived from an era when there were no rockets to the moon, and no television. In English, as in Italian, we go looking for needles in haystacks long after the stacks themselves have disappeared and have been replaced by silage pits; stables are no longer so common as they used to be, but we still shut the stable door after the horse has bolted; we still fall from the frying pan into the fire; and so on.

In Italian, these recollections of times past are even more marked than in English. For example, Italians still use idiomatic expressions that describe handwriting similar to hens' legs ('zampe di gallina') or the sleeping hours of hens ('andare a letto con le galline'), all the verbs defining either aggression or masculinity which are derived from the cockerel ('fare il gallo', 'ringalluzzire', ('to get cocky') 'alzare la cresta'), the trapping of pigeons with broad beans ('cogliere due piccioni con una fava') or the terminology taken from the movements and habits of cats or dogs ('sgattaiolare', ('to sneak off') 'scimmiottare', ('to ape') 'scodinzolare', ('to wag one's tail') 'fare la gatta morta', ('pretending to be dead') 'menare il can per l'aia'). Even the poplar has been prayed in aid by the Italian language ('appioppare'.)

All these are matters for those who study etymology and semantics but there are very marked examples that identify a culture which is tied to the land. As I have already observed, not for nothing even in the twentieth century, Italian parents say to their male children 'moglie e buoi dei paesi tuoi', i.e. choose your wife in the same place where you buy your oxen.

During the Renaissance, toleration and compromise prevailed. This resulted in the extinction of any kind of moral conscience. Ultimately, it represented a culmination of twenty-five centuries of history in Italy.

In the Renaissance, Italy reached its peak. And what a performance. It was, however, accompanied by immorality and corruption, but, strangely enough, the Italians seemed to thrive on it and the circumstances surrounding them ultimately stimulated their artistic impulse. In everything that they do there appears to be something different and individual. As one of our best poets, Torquato Tasso, put it, there is 'Un non so che,' something one cannot quite describe.

Our Roman tradition governs us much more than we are prepared to admit. The fact that Italy has a civilization which antedates that of any other people in Europe makes it slightly anomalous. Indeed, as Curzio Malaparte has pointed out, in Europe we represent 'A live element of opposition to the triumphant spirit of the nations of the north; we are duty bound to defend an ancient civilization which derives its strength from the values of the spirit against a new heretic and false outlook which relies upon physical, material and mechanical values. . . ; to assimilate this modernity would lead us to irreparable decadence.' What pride, what conviction; and yet, he was only half Italian: his father was German, his mother from Lombardy. Malaparte was baptized Kurt Erich Suckert.

This reluctance to assimilate modernity, this ability to remain almost entirely unaffected by technological change – and indeed, by that most frequent of events in Italian history, namely political change – has resulted in a certain constancy of pattern of behaviour in the Italians who, on the whole, appear to have changed throughout the ages less than most other peoples.

Overall, Italians tend to emerge as quite conservative, in thought as well as in behaviour and, to some extent, also in attire. This conservatism is a feature which foreign observers usually fail to identify; and when they do, consider very puzzling indeed. Less surprising, perhaps, is the effect that Italy's geographical situation may have had on the physical and psychological make-up of the Italians. I have in mind in particular the nature of Italy's soil and diet, and the effect of the sun.

And so we come to the third phase of Italian development, which really started in the second half of the sixteenth century when Italy's growth gradually became stunted. Whether the fault for this temporary atrophy is to be attributed to the Church, or to nearly three centuries of Spanish domination, or to the fact that the effort had been so great that Italy had exhausted itself, or to the increasing modernization and progress of other European countries, or to something completely different, is a question about which historians, particularly social historians, have written volumes. Whichever way one looks at it, however, one has to wait until at least the nineteenth century before one can detect any signs of a revival in Italy. The revival came to the fore with the Risorgimento, reached a patriotic peak in the First World War and to all intents and purposes appeared to end with the arrival of Fascism and the Second World War.

SOIL, SUN AND DIET

Whether sun and soil go hand-in-hand, or not, their effect is joint and considerable. It is easier to make a general statement of this nature than to explain it away. It certainly cannot be explained away in terms of a grading of the soil according to the Ministry of Agriculture classification, or of an analysis of its acidity. It is not the pH of the soil of Italy that I have in mind, but its intrinsic physical/philosophical nature.

Think of the countless people who have trodden it, whose bodies are buried there, whose blood has fertilized it. Visualize a powerful Mediterranean sun baking the soil and actually sealing-in all the energy and vibrations of millions of people over thousands of years.

And it is a different sun that shines in Italy. The air is different from any other part of the world, as is the light. If we ignore modern pollution, it is the same light that can be found in certain parts of Greece and on the Spanish Plateau. In Greece, however, the temperament of the people is totally different. The Spanish Plateau, on the other hand, is a long way from the sea; it is a harsh part of the world, unsoftened by sea breezes; and harsh are its inhabitants.

On the contrary, every part of Italy, except for the Alps, is close to the sea, because of the very shape of the Italian peninsula jutting out into the Mediterranean. You may counter that by saying that England is surrounded by the sea and the sea breezes are on the whole not too far away. Regrettably for those of us who live in England, the same sun does not shine there. As a Neapolitan (the Marquis Caracciolo) once said: 'There's more warmth in the moon of Naples than in the sun of London.'

I do not for a moment believe that the statement that sun, soil and sea have influenced our development can be supported in scientific terms. I am not aware of any instrument that can measure the amount of energy or of blood baked into any soil, or its energy-giving qualities. If we are looking for scientific, demonstrable facts supported by any kind of authority, then the foregoing statements can be considered as the ravings of a lunatic.

And yet, there *is* something about the soil of different countries (not just the soil of Italy) about the way things grow in it, how plants develop, the flavour that the soil, combined with the sun and the air, imparts to fruits (and wine), vegetables, herbs and human beings. Yes, even human beings have a flavour. This is demonstrably so, in physical as well as in psychological terms. Its demonstration in scientific terms is a little more difficult.

Let me give you a small example. In recent years the English have learnt to grow basil. It is a herb which is now a well-established part of English cuisine and it forms part of a number of recipes which, as I have already indicated, have been 'borrowed' from Italy. You can buy the plant even in greengrocers' shops and garden centres everywhere.

But I assure you that the basil that is grown in England has a completely different taste from that which is grown in Italy, even when exactly the same seeds are used. Any good gardener or cook will be able to verify this simple statement. I can tell you with certainty that the leaves have a different colour, a different texture, a more pungent aroma, a different taste and, all in all, are dissimilar. The same can be said of other vegetables like courgettes, peppers and aubergines.

Whence does this difference arise? Some gardeners I have spoken to maintain that it is not derived from the soil but rather from the sun. I disagree; this is not to say that the sun is unimportant but even in the hottest summer England has experienced in recent years (in 1976) the basil that I grew in my garden tasted very different from that which I sampled in Italy, even though the seeds were exactly the same.

Some of you may think that I have been imagining things: I am not so sure.

There is a feeling about certain places that can only be explained in terms of some physical or magnetic energy being present which we cannot identify in scientific terms, but which we can certainly feel. I am somewhat comforted in my view by the recent development of the science of geo-biology, whose aim is to identify points of cosmic energy.

Furthermore, science has not yet explained why the same vine transplanted to California or Australia produces wines with different taste. The wine-making techniques are the same as in France, Germany and Italy; the root-stock is the same; the age of the vine is often the same. But the continental shades of flavour cannot be matched. What else can it be if not the different quality of the soil?

Has it never occurred to you to meet someone and shake hands with them – to be, in other words, somewhat closer to them than you normally would – and suddenly feel for no apparent reason a flow of either dislike or coldness from them? Or even, to be in a place where there is no-one else and still feel the presence of someone there? If so, does this 'energy' come from the air, the person or the soil or a combination of the three? I myself do not know nor pretend to know and no-one that I have spoken to does either. But that is not to say that the feeling one experiences has no justification or no cause.

I am not sufficiently blinded by science to acknowledge that if something cannot be proved in scientific terms, it does not exist.

There is more in my theory about the soil that I can neither prove scientifically nor have the ability to convey. I believe it to be true, but leave you to formulate your own judgement. I am nevertheless comforted by the fact that other people have considered what I would call the mystery of the earth. Others, more informed than I, have found no paradox in the above concept. I am reminded that in America the skull and pelvis measurements of all the European races began to indianize themselves in the second generation of immigrants. That is the mystery of the American earth. The soil of every country holds some such mystery.

We have an unconscious reflection of this in the psyche: 'Just as there is a relationship of mind to body, so there is a relationship of body to earth.' (C.G. Jung, 'The Role of the Unconscious' in Volume 10 of his *Complete Works*, p. 13.)

This would explain why no-one really conquers a foreign soil, as Italy has demonstrated throughout its history: it has always assimilated its conquerors.

If Jung is to be believed (ibidem, p. 49) the ancestor spirits of the conquered reincarnate themselves in the newcomers. The Americans who invaded us in 1943 and 1944 are living proof of this: they went back to their home country carrying with them Italian leanings and habits which, particularly for the humbler folk amongst them, were to prove a reminder of better days.

In or about 1945, there was a popular jingle in Rome – I recall it exceptionally well to this day – which, to the tune of 'Yankee Doodle' captured both the same concept and the Romans' cynical appreciation of 'KP' rations and baked beans. In verse, it pictured Johnny's changed behaviour the moment he got back in the United States after his stay in Rome. He has acquired Roman habits (eating broad beans with 'pecorino' cheese, drinking wine and 'stuffing himself' with spaghetti), he looks back nostalgically to his dinners at the Grand Hotel, to his drunken bouts and to the dinner dances at Pighetti's. And as he lights a cigarette stub he has picked up from the gutter, he reflects sadly on the many packets of Chesterfields which he could buy freely and cheaply at the Tor di Nona black market!

The doggerel verses ended somewhat sadly by reminding us that, as he reverts to doing his job as a shoe-shine lad in New York, he remembers the Roman youngsters who were always hoping he would let them shine his boots for a pittance.

□

The fact that because of its geographical position Italy has throughout the centuries had the benefit of a temperate climate has in its own way contributed to some of the Italian characteristics.

One does not have to go as far as some of the ancient peoples who thought that the sun was God. It is easy to understand why they should have reached such a conclusion, in the absence of any revelation as to what the true religion might be.

But one can take it for granted that the sun has a beneficial effect not only on plant life and ecology generally, but particularly upon human beings. We are all affected by it, each in our own way.

The face of London, for example, changes completely on a sunny day. I suppose it is the same everywhere. People become more extrovert, more loquacious, more inclined to smile, they spend more time in the open. People actually become friendlier when they have the opportunity of living in the open. They see things in a better light, their shape is more marked, their line is more significant, the aesthetic value of things becomes more prominent and capable of better appreciation.

A blue sky has an extraordinary effect on most human beings. Some of Shelley's best poetry was written under the sky of Rome – *Prometheus Unbound* – 'the bright blue sky. . . in that divinest climate', as he puts it himself. I for one find the Roman climate enervating, and there is no doubt it has a similar impact on many foreigners.

A blue sky also slows down physical activity. The northerners' passion for work or at least for activity has to be moderated in a very hot climate. In moderating it, they provide for themselves more time to reflect and to philosophize; they begin to learn a few things about the meaning of life which had escaped them in the hustle and bustle of a rainy or cold or hectic environment. This is inevitable, for the northerner has to alter his reactions and go back to square one: he has to re-learn what life is.

In his own country, most of his time is dedicated to work. There is after all not much else to do in the cold and the rain. He becomes ever more industrious and his only solace lies in recourse to alcohol.

The southerner, on the other hand, even if poor can live like a king, for he needs fewer clothes, less housing, less work. This prompts the belief that southerners are lazy: not true. They merely work to live, and rather than live to work they live to enjoy themselves. It is a question of choice, but then choice is dictated by the weather. Sunshine and joy of life go hand in hand.

In a different sense from alcohol, the sun heightens one's aesthetic sense and reduces one's inhibitions. That is why the Italians are always intoxicated: it is not alcohol, it is the sun.

One of the direct consequences of this is the extraordinary sense of light and line that appears in and guides everything Italian. In a different sense, the sun gives realism. On a bright sunny day, the colours are exactly as they should be: white is white, black is black. If there is a grey, it has a life and tonality of its own and it does not occur simply because white or black cease to be perceived as such. This makes for realism, and Italians on the whole are realists. This allows things to be called by their proper names; and on the whole, Italians are capable of doing this.

This enables Italians to sin quite blissfully without confusing beliefs and thoughts with high-fangled doctrinaire or romantic notions. After all, it was Horace who put it quite bluntly: 'Video meliora proboque, deteriora sequor' (I see good things, and I approve of them; but I do worse things).

So, on a personal level, the sun enables one to provide a more constant pattern of personality. It is interesting that as far as the English are concerned, the Latins, and the Italians in particular, are said to be volatile and unpredictable. This is true as regards their mood but I am not too certain that it is correct as regards their character. More constant and reliable weather patterns result, in my view, in a more constant and reliable pattern of personality.

In a strange sense, I find the English much more unpredictable than the Italians; and I have reached the conclusion that this follows from the instability of the English weather.

The effect of the sun is quite clear on Italian buildings. They have line, style, are pleasing to the eye and are open. This is very marked in the original style of Palladio.

The sun obviously has a marked effect on food. First of all, one has more time to appreciate it and therefore one approaches it with more of a cultural outlook. The food itself is tastier because of the combination of sun and soil, as I have already pointed out. This in turn has an educational effect upon people, at any rate as far as their taste-buds are concerned.

In conclusion, therefore, it can fairly be said that the sun has affected the Italian temperament and character in a number of ways. It has enabled us to judge things more clearly, it has made us realists, and it has given us a taste for good things. The combination of these factors has also resulted in our being happier and kinder then most other peoples. The sun gives us that sublime appreciation of beauty that puts us in a tender mood and protects our hearts from the sorrows and the bitterness of life.

Fortunately, the next item, the Italian diet, is capable of scientific proof. The case is proved abundantly by all the recent publications on food allergy. It is a fact that a number of illnesses, or so-called illnesses, do not always originate in the mind even though for many years they were inexplicable. Food allergy is now established as a branch of medicine.

If, therefore, food can influence you negatively by causing you to become hyperactive or come out in spots or be sick or whatever, it must by definition be able to influence you positively. I do not need to labour this point too much: food is all important.

Obviously food is essential for survival. But surely how you survive is also relevant.

Under 'Gastronomy' I have already made my position clear. It is that you are what you eat. It is your diet that determines your reactions and influences your temperament; that provides mental and physical energy, and sexual drive. Put differently, can you imagine what drive of any description you would have if your diet consisted of nothing else but bread dipped in milk, as we say in Italy? I am sure you would survive; but how? Equally, a diet of stodgy foods and fats may give you some physical energy but I wonder how much intellectual strength is really provides.

We are now assailed from all angles by dieticians who tell us that our diet ought to be balanced. I believe that the Italian diet has been balanced for centuries; obviously the poorer people have not fared quite so well: but vegetables, fruit and olive oil have been available in abundance to all Italians.

This diet has created a certain type of physical make-up. I am not saying that this make-up is better then other people's because the diet of any people is obviously related to the climate in which they live. I am sure that an Italian diet, even assuming it to be available, would not be of too much use to an Eskimo; and vice versa. But it must be a fact that the dietary intake of your body affects your overall performance and your personality, as well as your outlook on life.

If I am right, the Italians are due for a change: a MacDonalds has recently been opened in Piazza di Spagna in Rome.

Also, it occurs to me that perhaps what we eat does ultimately affect how we think as well. After all, there is little doubt that there are major dietary differences between the north and the south of Italy. Is it diet that determines our destiny? Look, for instance, at the differences in output between different regions in Italy.

In this context you will recall that, in the facts section, I have recorded whenever possible the place of birth of the people whose names are listed. I have done so partly for my own benefit because, when I started out on this exercise, I was not too knowledgeable about the extent of the individual contributions of the various regions of Italy.

For the purposes of understanding this contribution, after I had collated the evidence, I proceeded to divide the country into three parts, namely, the north, that is to say the totality of the northern regions down to approximately Bologna; the centre, that is to say, all that part of Italy from Bologna southwards to Rome; and the south, that is the remainder of the country including the two major islands.

If we are thinking only in terms of numbers, the contribution made by the centre of Italy is double that of the south and that made by the north is double that of the centre. I am not considering quality; for example, Galileo comes from the centre of Italy, as does Leonardo; Marco Polo and Christopher Columbus come from the north; the south saw the Salerno School of Medicine, two Nobel Prize winners (Deledda and Pirandello) and Piria who discovered salicylic acid. It is difficult to draw firm conclusions from these findings save to this extent: the contribution of the south has been more of an historical, philosophical and literary nature, that of the centre more of a cultural, intellectual and aesthetic kind, and that of the north more of a positive, practical and scientific type.

The southerners, of whom I am one, may complain about my way of putting things. They may wish to remind us that when the north of Italy was still in a semi-barbarous state, then the central part of Italy knew the civilization of Etruria, and the south and Sicily that of the cities of Magna Graecia. Indeed, some towns in southern Italy and Sicily were centres of civilization when Rome was still a village; Pythagoras was born more than a hundred years before Plato, Archimedes came from Syracuse, and the Temples at Paestum, south of Salerno, antedate both the Parthenon and the Great Wall of China. Southerners may also wish to point out that in the seventeenth century Naples had over 300,000 inhabitants and despite a major eruption of Vesuvius in 1631, the Masaniello revolt of 1647 and the virulent plague of 1656 it was, after Paris, the most important city in Europe.

Southerners *would* say this, and there is no denying the facts as so stated. But those facts merely prove that the south had a very ancient civilization and not that the southerners' contribution, over the last 1000 years, to the discoveries that I have recorded previously is that substantial. Progress and civilization are not the same thing and there may be a reason for this comparative failing on the part of the southerners. It is possible that southern climes are conducive to theorizing and philosophizing more than to action and positive thought. Hence the common accusation levied against southerners, namely, that they are lazy. I do not believe this to be true. They are not. They are, however, indolent, because the sun makes them so. But when the southerner emigrates to the north of Italy, he proves that he can work quite hard.

It is interesting that within the framework of the general ambivalence that the English show towards the Italians, there is very marked ambivalence towards southerners.

Lord Nelson's family and heirs are still Dukes of Bronte, in Sicily, and Lord Acton enjoyed his stay in Naples. On the other hand, others have been scathing about Neapolitans; for example, hear what Hutton has to say: 'Less civilized than ourselves, perhaps, the Neapolitan is at least never vulgar in our fashion. He may be a villain, but he is a courteous one; he may be a thief, but he steals politely; he may murder you for less than a lira, but he does it with perfect grace. Even his curses seem magnificent. Altogether, he is not to be despised.'

Altogether, not an unfair assessment of some perception; but I cannot forgive him the 'perhaps'. Whether one likes Naples and its inhabitants or not, its civilization is the oldest in western Europe. But on second thoughts, I shall be magnanimous; I shall forgive him even the 'perhaps', because he was a lover of Italy. And what he says about the Neapolitans can to some extent, be generalized to include many other Italians.

Still, the myth of laziness persists. Even such a knowledgeable and sympathetic writer as Constance Stocker Giglioli (*Naples in 1799*, John Murray, London, 1903) makes the same point: 'the Neapolitans, lazy by nature, were born in manifold servitude, bred in darkest ignorance, inured to suffering and privation, devoid of ambition. . . .'

Perhaps the circumstances described above explain away the laziness. . . but I retain my own view: not lazy, but indolent.

Nevertheless, that we are prone to theorizing and philosophizing in the south is well established. It can hardly be a coincidence that all Italian philosophers (Bruno, Telesio, Campanella and Croce) come from the south. Indeed, more famous Italian writers came from Sicily than probably from any other part of Italy (Pirandello, Verga, Capuana, Sciascia, Tomasi di Lampedusa, and many others.) Their 'verismo', simple tales of real life and descriptions of fate and injustice, are renowned the world over.

It is conceivable that those who are favoured by the kind of weather that will allow them to spend almost the totality of the year in the open air will be less inclined to sit at a desk or in a laboratory trying to unravel the secrets of life in the physical sense.

And yet, I wonder why this should be so, because if one has a scientific mind then it does not matter where he is to be found: science and the cold climate do not necessarily go hand in hand.

I am at a loss to explain this obvious imbalance between north and south for, to be objective, it must be recorded that northerners have achieved four times as much as southerners in the field of scientific discoveries.

The imbalance surely exists. It may be the diet, or it may be history: probably both.

Without going into too much detail, it is nevertheless understandable. The ancient civilizations of the south and of Sicily occurred at a time when there had been little opportunity of making great scientific progress. The first real kind of scientific progress was made by the Salerno School of Medicine.

But that School had no means of advertising its courses the way universities and colleges do nowadays. It must have taken decades for people to get to know of its existence and many weeks, if not months, of travel for those interested to reach it.

By the time we get to the Renaissance, and beyond, the south had remained fairly isolated. The isolation of Sicily is apparent from the fact that it is an island; the isolation of the rest of southern Italy is underlined by the Apennines that ultimately divide the country into two and also, to some extent, serve to separate the centre and the south of the country from the north.

Whereas the northern plains of Italy were open to all influences, especially trade and the general movement of goods and people, the south continued to live in a world of its own. If you add to that three centuries of Spanish domination or rather repression in the south of Italy, which only ceased in 1707 with the entry into Naples of the Austrian Army, coupled with the strictures imposed upon scientific research by the Catholic Church, the feudal organization of society and agriculture, the Neapolitan Camorra equivalent of the Mafia and the general apathy, in the political sense, of the southerners, who are all highly sceptical of authority and of the State, it becomes easy to realize that it was almost impossible for the south of Italy to make any true scientific contribution to its development.

Furthermore, the southerners were the last Italians to become emancipated politically. They clung to the monarchy as they had, maybe unwillingly, to their Spanish rulers. It is no coincidence that in the referendum on whether or not Italy should become a republic, held on 2 June 1946, the south voted in the majority for the monarchy and it was left to the north to provide the extra two million votes by which the House of Savoy was ousted from Italy. Politically, the south has been mainly for the Church party. When the first general election took place on 18 April 1948, the south made a great contribution to the victory of the Christian Democrats, who got 48.5 per cent of the vote against the Communists' 31 per cent. (I remember well how throughout Italy the respective slogans were displayed: a badge with the word 'Libertas' across it for the Christian Democrats, and a red star with an image of Garibaldi in its centre for the Communists.)

Similarly, it is hardly a coincidence that those who emerge best from my analysis are the northerners. That is to say, those inhabitants of that part of Italy which geographically has easy access to France, Switzerland, Austria, etc., and which is, despite the Alps, a plain where communications are easily sustained – as regards both road and river transportation. The River Po runs the whole length of northern Italy and has always provided an important communication link between one centre and the other. It is a fact that was already well known to

Shakespeare, who refers to the Po valley as 'Fruitful Lombardy, the pleasant garden of great Italy' (*The Taming of the Shrew*, Act 1, scene 1, line 4.)

If you add to that the fact that northern Italians have acquired some of the features of the Slavs, the Austrians and the Germans, overall you get a different type of personality in the north: a more disciplined one, stimulated by the pursuit of scientific research. This is not praise for its own sake of the northerner or criticism of the southerner. It is a fact of life or of history, whichever way one wishes to look at it.

Those from the centre of Italy partake of both the north and the south. But they need not feel in any sense at a disadvantage because of the ratio of the discoveries made by them *vis-à-vis* those of the north, for they can rely on Leonardo and Galileo; nor should they be too conceited towards their southern brethren, because the very culture which Florence was able to project to the whole of the civilized world during the Renaissance came from southern Italy.

THE CHURCH

I mean, of course, the Catholic Church. The effect the existence of the seat of the Catholic Church in Rome has had on the Italian nation has caused gallons of ink to flow. Between those who maintain that it was the Church that ultimately saved Italy as a nation and those who argue that Italy would have found its way much more quickly but for its existence, the shades of political and historical beliefs are so varied as to be almost incomprehensible.

In the Middle Ages, the Church was surely an asset. It preserved for us the Greek and Latin texts and the classical tradition and it represented a bulwark against the emperors. The association between the Church and Italian literature was marked in more ways than one. It cannot, for example, be mere coincidence that Dante had first admired Beatrice in church, Petrarca at the age of twenty-three fell desperately in love with Laura in church on Good Friday in 1327 and Boccaccio surrendered to the looks of Fiammetta again in church at Partenope when he, too, was aged twenty-three, but nine years later than Petrarca. There is a clear association at this time between Church and Italian literature; the influence of the Church on architecture, sculpture and painting is equally great.

On the other hand, in the seventeenth and eighteenth centuries, it stifled thought and development, thus undoing, as some have said, all the good it had done four or five centuries earlier. In the nineteenth century, it interfered with the Italians' search for freedom and for a national identity. It is too soon to determine what use it has been in the present century, though its contribution to Italian post-war politics should not be understimated.

I mentioned, earlier on, that it was thanks to the rather compact southern vote that the Christian Democrats managed to beat the Communists when the first general elections were held in Italy in 1948. To that extent, the Church performed a valuable historic function if we proceed from the premise that Communism in 1948 had to be defeated.

But these statements stem from an historical appraisal of the role of the Church in Italy and they have no significance whatsoever, in my view, when we have to deal with the psychological impact of the Church on the Italian character. In this context, what the critics of Rome say ceases to have any great significance. Let me explain. It is quite correct for those critics to say that as a result of the Church's criticism and banning of Galileo scientific progress was stultified in Italy for about two centuries. That criticism is borne out by the facts and is certainly well founded.

It is equally true to say that inasmuch as the Church is a state within a state in Italy, it has a vested interest in the Italian state never being too strong. Again, that seems to make sense.

But, to proceed from these rather easy and well-documented premises in order to criticize the Church's role in Italy in its totality, seems to me not only unwarranted but also unnecessary. It is, for example, far too easy to say that the social development of Italy has been impeded by the Catholic Church because, amongst other things, it opposes divorce. That, to me, is an irrelevancy. It is not the Church's present stance on divorce that has made any contribution of any kind whatsoever to what the Italians have or have not been able to achieve, but it is the very existence of the Church in Italy through the centuries that has left its mark on the Italians; well apart from the other consideration that the stance of the Church has not prevented a divorce law being passed in Italy in the same way that the stance of the Church in Ireland will not prevent a divorce law being passed sooner or later in Ireland.

It seems to me that there is a basic fallacy in certain of the criticisms of the Church which proceeds from the equation of divorce with progress: to me, there is no such connection whatsoever. If there has been no emancipation of the Italian woman over the past fifty years (and I do not accept that this is correct, because enormous strides have been made in that respect) it is not because there has not been a law of divorce but rather because the impact of the Church over the preceding 1,500 years has been such as to create a mentality and a psychological heritage which have delayed the emancipation of women. But to assume that progress and the emancipation of women are coincident is begging the question.

The influence of the Church has certainly ensured that woman in Italy has had a different role from that which more modern tendencies ascribe to her. But at the same time, it has had an impact on the role of man as well. This influence has been substantial and it has in the main manifested itself in four forms.

The principal form in which the Church has affected Italians, of both sexes, has resulted from its great power. This power was used for both good and evil and this is not the place to review the history of the Catholic Church. But there is little doubt that, after ancient Rome, the Catholic Church was the principal champion of things Italian. And to that extent it has permeated Italian life in many ways, some obvious, as for example in the prohibition of divorce, and some much less obvious and more subtle. What the Church has in fact done in Italy is to create a kind of benevolent freemasonry or Mafia. I mean this statement in no way disrespectfully. The body that wields possibly the greatest power on earth has always exacted gratitude and loyalty from those who have entrusted themselves to it. In Italy, particularly in the smaller towns and villages, the priest is most important. A word from him may mean the difference between finding a job and remaining unemployed. It is not merely a question of the power that the priest has exercised over the souls of his parishioners but much more a matter of the real power that he has wielded over their ordinary lives.

To that extent, until very recently, the Italian has been placed in the position where his primary loyalty, after that which he owed to his family and his children, was to the Church more than to any other organization. For these reasons, the creation of a strong state in Italy has certainly been delayed, if not impeded.

But in psychological terms, the exercise of this power by the Church has deprived the average Italian of freedom of thought because he has been constantly reminded of the debt that he owed to the Church and, through it, to his Maker. This loss of freedom of thought has been compensated by a basic, elementary religious belief (I dare not say religious fervour, for we are considerably lacking in that) which, on the other hand, has led him to a tolerant and benevolent view of life which is always a distinguishing mark of the believer. I hasten to say that I am not attacking the unbeliever; nor am I making a religious point. But I think that purely on a probabilistic principle a person who believes in any god is more likely to endorse, in his daily behaviour, certain principles of tolerance and compassion than one who does not.

All this must be viewed over, say, at least a thousand years. The constant repetition of formulae and the maintenance of certain beliefs must inevitably have affected the psychological make-up of those subjected to it. The second way in which the Church has influenced the Italians has been by its constant, determined and sometimes stubborn upholding of the principles of the Catholic faith as it has propounded them. The enforcement, successful or otherwise, of a morality which has changed little over the centuries has had a great effect on the make-up of the Italians.

Probably the best example is the Church's approach to marriage. This has been consistent since the days of the catacombs. The Church has taken the view that a marriage is made in heaven. Since, so the argument runs, it is God that in reality has joined the parties in the sacrament of matrimony, it is obvious that only death can separate them. After all, the parties got married with the intent of remaining in that state 'until death us do part'. This is certainly a point of view. In simple language, it is argued that one gets married for better or for worse.

There is also the other argument. This is put forward by more liberal-minded or more progressive people (may I repeat at this stage that I subscribe to the view that progress and civilization are not coincident) and it runs along the lines that marriage is no different from any other contract with the consequences that, as the parties enter into it, so they can get out of it at will, or indeed, at whim. I pause at this stage to remark that there is no other solution to the argument: in logic, a marriage is either indissoluble or capable of being terminated at any time by either party for whatever reason.

I find that the attitude of the Anglo-Saxon world, and the English world in particular, is highly hypocritical when it comes to marriage. Firstly, it was the Christian/Catholic approach that was adopted, namely that marriage was basically indissoluble. Then in the middle of the nineteenth century we established the concept of the matrimonial offence, to the great joy of divorce lawyers and private detectives. More recently, no doubt as a result of feminist pressures, in Britain we have adopted the concept of the breakdown of the marriage without having necessarily to attach too much significance any longer, save possibly when it comes to financial considerations, to the matrimonial offence.

The reluctance to go the whole way and be logically consistent, namely to say that once you accept that God has not joined two people in matrimony, they can get out of it at any time, I find very difficult to follow. It is almost as though there were an innate fear or shyness in the English in reaching the obvious, logical conclusion. Lest you should think that it is a poor, temperamental, misguided Latin talking who does not understand what it is all about, look at what Sir James Fitzjames Stephen has to say: 'If the parties to a contract of marriage are treated as equals, it is impossible to avoid the inference that marriage, like other partnerships, may be dissolved at pleasure. The advocates of women's rights are exceedingly shy of stating this plainly' (from *Liberty, Equality, Fraternity*, 1873). Stephen was a well-known lawyer; but he certainly was not a feminist because he proceeds from the statement I have just quoted to argue that, in such a situation, woman would be the loser. In any event, Stephen was not saying anything new.

Divorce by mutual consent had long existed in China and among the Eskimos, the ancient Welsh and the ancient Germans. After Stephen wrote the above, the principle has become established in countries of such disparate cultures and traditions as Luxembourg, Switzerland, Romania and Japan.

The logic of the argument was underlined centuries ago by Milton, and somewhat more recently by Shelley and by Montesquieu. In most other countries, Italy included, the puritanical or Catholic inheritance is causing people to sit on the fence and behave hypocritically. Leaving aside for a moment the

Catholic Church, no-one has any longer the courage to say that we either believe in the 'mystical' nature of marriage, or, if we do not, we should accept that as we embark on it, so we should be allowed to disembark from it when it suits us.

However, the Church's logic on marriage is in my view unexceptionable. Of the two solutions just mentioned, it has adopted the former. It has said repeatedly that man is quite incapable of separating what God has joined, that the spouses become a single flesh and that, accordingly, the purpose of their coming together is the procreation of children and the establishment of a family. Such an approach may be right or wrong and this is not the place to consider its merits or otherwise. But it has one major consequence which has resulted in the greatest possible impact by the Church on the Italians. The consequence is that it has strengthened the marriage bond and as a result the family as a unit. (This is not to say that Italian spouses have respected the integrity of their bond or have honoured their marriage vows in a way that other people have not. This is not the point at all. It is the principle that I am considering, not deviations from it.)

This concept of indissolubility has in turn created the kind of mentality whereby the mother has been glorified as the centre of the family, as indeed she is, and the father has accepted that his primary duties to the family prevailed over everything else, including any commitments he may have undertaken towards either the state or his mistresses. Consider how this is expressed in Italian art where woman reigns supreme. Look at all the Madonnas; the number of Italian artists who have painted them is great and the result is highly flattering to woman. Look at all the Holy Families; the glorification of the family as a unit is apparent there too. As woman reigns supreme in Italian art, I would suggest it is also a reflection of real life.

The supremacy of Italian woman has also manifested itself in the tendency of the Italians to express concepts in terms of woman. Under the heading 'Motor Car' I have already referred to the link that the Italian male makes between women and cars. This is interesting because it shows that woman is taken as a standard of either goodness or beauty or reliability or acceptability or whatever. She may be a good standard or she may be a bad standard: but she is the metre by which most things are measured. (In Tuscany, however, she may be an inferior standard, as witness the old Tuscan proverb 'Words are females, facts are males'.)

Nowhere does this emerge more clearly, in my view, than in a book written in 1625 by Cesare Ripa, under the title *Iconologia*. The book contains representations of women of different shades of colour, beauty, attire and animalistic features, which are supposed to represent different virtues, vices or situations. So you open the book and you see, for example, the title Virtue, underneath it there is represented a saintly-looking, rather coy woman and beneath that appear a few verses to explain what virtue is all about. The book is not merely about women:

it is about concepts. But in the majority of cases, the concepts are represented by women. This is a part of the glorification of woman that I am dealing with.

A further result of the strengthening of the family unit has been a clear-cut distinction, for example, between the sacred and the profane which is one of the principal features of Italian art and society and which in itself is no more than a form of realism. It is in effect a recognition of instinct and of the basic necessities of life. It is the result of a practical approach to relationships, unaffected by romantic notions.

Ultimately, it is less hypocritical than in other parts of the world and, because of this, it provides inner strength. I have always subscribed to the view that the acknowledgment and recognition of one's instincts, while usually resulting in lack of conformity and often in formal deficiency or inadequacy, gives inner conviction. On the other hand, formal correctness and apparent strength acquired at the cost of sacrificing beliefs and instincts, though at first blush impressive, derives no great strength of inner feeling and character. To that extent, northern people, who seem outwardly composed and in possession of themselves, tend to emerge inwardly weak. As Jung put it, those who ignore their instincts end up being ambuscaded by them.

The third way in which the Church has affected the life and the psychology of all Italians, whether practising Catholics or not, has resulted from its position as a state within a state. It is a peculiar kind of state, the Vatican, because whilst it has to cater for the well-being of the Italian Catholics, it has an even greater duty to other Catholics from different nations. In practice, therefore, the Church has always come to terms with the Italian government, even to the detriment of its own faithful. In practice, too, as I have already remarked, the Church has never had any great interest in strengthening the Italian state and has never provided the slightest encouragement in giving to Caesar what is Caesar's but only in taking on behalf of God that which is said to be God's.

Furthermore, to avoid problems with the state, the Church has always encouraged the faithful to do their duty by the existing, established authority. Any attempt at new or revolutionary politics has always been frowned upon by the Church. The result of this has been that Italians have developed a split view of life. In a sense, it is slightly schizophrenic. They have had to steer a middle course between what the law has decreed or allowed, and that which the Church has recommended or condemned. Never was this more clearly underlined in the political context than in the 1948 fight between the Christian Democrats and the Communists. It may have been easy for others to sit back and chuckle about the event. It was not funny in 1948 when the Russians were represented by the Church as the devil at the door of Italy.

The Italians are gradually becoming more emancipated as far as the influence of the Church goes in matters of politics. Indeed, it is probably true to say that the present-day generation attaches increasingly less importance to what the local priest has to say about that subject.

There is another sphere where the Catholic Church has had an impact, perhaps even unwittingly. It has reminded us throughout of our equality before God. You may say that other churches do the same. But, for example, in England, the identification of the Church of England with the State, resulting from the fact that the titular head of the Church is the monarch, has not had quite the same result.

I am concerned here with class consciousness. I think that it can be said that inasmuch as the local parish priest has, in theory at any rate, related to both the nobleman and the peasant, on the basis of equality (before God), coupled with extensive contacts that the Italians had as a result of travelling, banking and merchant shipping, this has resulted in dilution of the concept of class consciousness in Italy. This has not happened in England, which is still a class-ridden society. On the other hand, Italians are not at all class conscious. There is no great divide between the classes in Italy solely because of social differences. Insofar as the Italian is a snob, he is, contrary to the English, a cultural rather than a social snob.

There are reasons for this, also apart from the impact of the Church. The first of these reasons is that the Italians are very much aware of what I should term our common humanity. For this reason, we are essentially a kind people, with a great deal of understanding, if not compassion, for human foibles and frailty. That is probably the reason why, like the Chinese, the Japanese and the Greeks, we are exceptionally fond of children whom, as parents, we spoil endlessly. Indeed, it has been correctly said that Italian parents spend their lives spoiling their children when they are young and trying to put that right as they grow up.

There is no doubt that Italians on the whole are also an exceptionally tolerant people. Because they themselves have so many weaknesses and so many faults, they attach no great significance to human foibles. After all, aren't we all God's creatures and very much alike? For this reason, the Italian lacks, on the whole, the crusading spirit. It is better not to seek to convert anyone to a way of thinking nor to impose one's own views on others. If you believe (wrongly, I suspect) that the best way to enjoy life is to be drunk at the end of a party, fine, that is your choice: who am I to criticize? If you believe that your football team is the best in the world, just as fine: we shall see at the end of the championship whether you are right or wrong but, meanwhile, you are entitled to wallow in your dedication to your home town or whatever. If you believe that your party is the only one that will redeem the sins of the past and make the country great, still fine: after all, you may well be right, one political party is very much like another. Who am I to tell you that you are wrong?

But please, no airs; no arrogance; no thought, no matter how remote, that you may be better. The Italians believe that they know it all, have seen it all and have had experiences which are all embracing: no airs. If you behave, there will be no need to remind you of the fact that the Italians were there before you, a fact which is but an accident of history. I am addressing you, the reader, but I could be addressing the world at large. The approach is typical. Italians do not bother others as they have no wish to be bothered themselves. When they are, they often react disproportionately to the nature of the offence. It is almost as though the biblical saying 'Fear the wrath of the just', or whatever the correct equivalent is, takes possession of the average Italian when he is confronted with arrogance and forces him in one direction only, namely that of proving that he is better than the next man. It is quite an interesting development, for in normal circumstances the Italian does not feel any need to assert himself in an arrogant manner. True, when as usual he feels well dressed, he does have a tendency to strut about like a peacock, especially when there are women present. But it is a fairly harmless performance. Whether he is too busy enjoying his food and his women or whether he feels that by the average manifestations of a sexual nature, he has already sufficiently asserted his personality, I cannot tell: but it is true that an Italian will seldom if unprovoked go out of his way to score a point or prove himself; he will watch tolerantly as others do just that and he will not be unduly troubled. But please, no airs: we are all human beings. No airs: it is so unnecessary to put any on. No airs, or one might be tempted to cut you down to size. These reactions are especially true of southern Italians, although those from the north are equally prone to them.

It is my firm view that when an Italian has to consider someone, regardless of sex, who is said to be above him or more important or famous or worthy of respect etc., he automatically tends to visualize that person not in the social or political or professional position or location where he is to be found at work or displaying those virtues or those powers for which he is renowned, but in the privacy of his/her home performing more menial duties or obeying the laws of nature. Against that background, we are all more or less exactly the same.

It is interesting that many years ago there were on sale in Italy little terracotta ashtrays which had on them a rather charming picture of a toilet seat. The legend beneath it, as I recall, ran more or less like this (my free translation): 'Kings may be powerful and Popes may be wise, I don't know why, but when they sit here they are all exactly the same as I.'

There are other factors as well. The Italian nobleman lived in his city or town in almost medieval style, until quite recently. Certainly, in respect of the more primitive parts of Italy (I have Sicily particularly in mind) one can say that these conditions prevailed until less than a century ago. The houses of the rest of the inhabitants, the successors of the vassals of the Middle Ages, were all around. And so they remained. It was not unusual for the children of the humbler folk or the servants in these places to play with the children of the owners or the heirs to the title. Indeed, this used to happen until quite recently even in the more progressive parts of Italy like Tuscany where the farm cottages are not too far removed from the castle or principal farm house.

Ultimately, things changed because the nobility of tradition and of custom has disappeared and it has been replaced by a 'nobility' of money. The so-called self-made man, who usually should have made himself better, has a tendency to move away from the place where he was born. He does so because he is thinking of his bank account and therefore of the value of property, because he no longer wishes to be reminded of his original meagre surroundings and because he prefers to mix with people who have money. It is a fact that one tends to associate with those whose economic level is more or less the same as one's own. Hence the move away from one's roots.

None of these reasons have any significance for the true nobleman who, until recent times, looked upon his ancestral home or castle not in terms of its real property value but in historical and emotional terms as the seat of his family and the custodian of his traditions. But by the time things changed, the social levelling mentality had become established. The Catholic Church has endorsed the Italian lack of class consciousness, whilst paying lip service to the maintenance of the nobility. To this extent, at any rate, the Church has made a positive contribution to Italian society. It has ensured that Italians are realists.

My final point about the Catholic Church is that it has always taught us to accept with good spirit the evils that befall us. On the personal level, this philosophy of life has much to commend it; on the social plane, however, it has resulted in the Italians, particularly those from the south, very often adopting what I can only call a negative or resigned outlook on their social conditions. This mentality has been exploited both by those in authority and by those with what I might call greater entrepreneurial spirit; the former for the purposes of maintaining the status quo, the latter for their own private purposes or for purposes of crime. It can hardly be a coincidence that the Mafia and the Camorra have prospered in the south of Italy but not in the remainder of the peninsula. True, there were ancient traditions of honour, resistance to tyranny, reaction to injustice, need to safeguard certain basic individual requirements where the State could not assert its authority and the overlords tyrannized with their own private armies. But to some extent, the Church must bear responsibility because such organized criminal associations can only prevail where the individual, either because of his make-up or because of his attitude of resignation, is both unwilling and incapable of fighting back.

I suppose it could be said that resignation is a small price to pay for peace of mind. Certainly, one cannot blame it solely upon the Catholic Church. I seem to recall from the little philosophy I studied at school that both the Sceptics and the

Stoics preached resignation of some sort, intellectual if not emotional, or in the form of a suspension of speech and thought. Again, it will come as no surprise to learn that both these schools of philosophy had some success in the south of Italy and very little elsewhere. The impact of the climate, as I have already discussed, does have considerable bearing in this context. But, by preaching resignation over the centuries, the Catholic Church has made the social evolution and improvement of the Italians much more difficult to attain.

The above text I originally formulated in 1987 but it occurred to me on re-reading it that a different interpretation might be placed upon it from the one I intended and I should be unhappy if at this stage the reader considered the foregoing remarks as in any sense derogatory of the Catholic Church's influence on the Italians. No belief, religious or political, no structure dictatorial or democratic and no school of philosophy, thought or medicine is perfect in the absolute sense. I have mentioned some respects in which the Church's influence on Italian history and development could be viewed by some as less beneficial than it ought to have been; but I am not at all unmindful of the great benefits that it has brought and continues to bring to the humanity and stability of Italian society as a whole.

I have read the encyclicals of Pope John Paul II, published soon after his death, in their entirety. More recently, I have also been struck by the first encyclical pronouncements of Benedict XVI: I can but acknowledge, maybe even with some pride, that the Catholic Church's contribution to strengthening the family unit is its most significant and topical restatement of creed at the beginning of the twenty-first century.

□

In conclusion, allow me to summarize how the various distinctive features of the Italian people developed over the centuries, I have for many years had the opportunity of analysing Italian merits and the corresponding faults. Indeed, it is interesting to record that in the case of Italy every single character trait coin has a very clear-cut reverse side; every virtue of which we can be proud results in a vice of which we ought to be ashamed. Let us look at them one by one:

1. From the barbarians who invaded us throughout our history we have derived our sense of adventure and our desire for travel. Also from them, however, we inherited those traits that led us to the extremes of barbarity and cruelty in which we have indulged on occasions throughout our history.

2. Through our dealings with them, and our having successfully mixed our race with theirs, we have developed an instinct for diplomacy and for what is positive, as well as a certain ability to deal with people. The reverse of this is our innate ability to lie and to cheat when we consider it necessary to achieve our ends. To

this extent, we can be quite machiavellian and, where necessary, humiliatingly servile.

3. From our resistance to the invaders we have developed our resilience; the reverse of that is our utter inability to see our faults and to pull together as a nation.

4. From our constant internecine fights and struggles we have developed our political ingenuity and our machiavellism. The reverse of that is the corruption in our political, social and administrative structures.

5. From our siege mentality has come our principal asset, our resourcefulness; the reverse of that is our inability to look at ourselves as a nation and our concern with our own 'particulare', our town and our family, which are destructive of national unity.

6. From the totality of our development and history during the Renaissance we have inherited our extraordinary, unique imagination, sense of art and beauty. The reverse of this is our fondness for form rather than for substance, which leads us to superficiality and into numerous errors of judgement; and our waste of energies in allowing our imagination a free rein.

7. From the combination of the Mediterranean weather and the blue skies we have derived our joyfulness, sensuality and love of life; the reverse of that is our occasional irresponsibility and inability to be serious.

8. From the fact that our cities developed individually and independently one of the other, and indeed constantly fought against one another, we have derived our great sense of individuality and our worldliness. That has also given us our lack of discipline, of civic sense and of punctuality.

9. From the fact that we traded with everybody throughout our history, we have ultimately got our genial tolerance and total lack of class consciousness. The reverse of that, however, is our cynicism.

10. From our Roman heritage and from the fact that we were as a people both old and knowledgeable, we have inherited a firm conviction that there is nothing new under the sun, coupled with pride in our achievements in the sense that there are very few fields about which it can be said that we did not get there first. The reverse, however, is our pessimism and disillusionment with life, and our almost permanent dissatisfaction with ourselves.

Why we should be pessimistic, I do not know. It is true to say that northern Italians are on the whole less pessimistic then southerners. Indeed, some northerners are positively optimistic about life. Why people who live in Milan, which has a climate in winter which is not too dissimilar from that of Germany or England, should view life more optimistically than those who live, say, in Naples and are favoured by the sun's rays on most days of the year, is something I have never been able to explain. Perhaps their optimism is a form of despair; perhaps you must believe in your ability to mould your destiny before you can be an optimist. A fatalist, as most southerners are, can develop neither optimism nor pessimism, but only irony. Still, it is odd.

All these features go to make up a people who do not as a rule look to the future with any enthusiasm; who are ever mindful of Horace's saying 'Carpe diem', that is to say 'Grab what's available today.' The Italian on the whole adopts the stance that since he has no idea what is going to happen tomorrow he might as well be cheerful today. It is not for nothing that a very old Italian proverb says that it is much more sensible to take the egg today rather than hope to be able to eat the hen tomorrow.

A people which is ultimately tormented by its imagination because the instinctive psychological intuition with which it has been gifted makes it see the difficulties of events and the futility of long-term planning rather more than any positive side. This is, for example, one of the reasons why Italians, generally speaking, try not to enter into long-term contracts.

A people with no great sentiment for nature on its own, unless it be connected with humanity. If one looks at the history of Italian painting, there is little landscape painting for its own sake and whenever attention is dedicated to the landscape it is usually as an adjunct to the human body. And yet, we are sensitive to the style of natural beauty.

Indeed, more than one foreigner has termed the Italians children of nature. In many respects, they manifest quite primitive traits and hold equally primitive beliefs. This is not a bad thing after all: it allows them to reduce problems to their fundamentals.

For this reason, the Italians have not (at least until the deification of the profit motive came into existence with the advent of American films and Coca Cola) attached as much importance to money as they have to enjoying life and being as carefree as their more obvious responsibilities allow.

□

A people quick to criticize, yet tolerant, quick to seize on the ridiculous and to expose shams, immensely susceptible to beauty and style, refined in taste, sensuous in feeling, suspicious of mysticism, realistic, demanding, practical yet superstitious, pleasure-loving.

The generally accepted view of the Italians as subservient to the senses and to the pleasures of the flesh has a long, established history. The thought has occurred more than once to a number of writers that this slavery to the senses has consumed and destroyed the Latin race. For example, D.H. Lawrence maintained that the phallic worship of the Italians – surely, not only of the Italians, but also of the Greeks and probably of Mediterranean races generally – was a step lower than the worship of physical forces and of science. Lawrence assumed that the move from paganism and sensuality to modernism and scientific development was a necessary one in the emancipation of the Italian people, when it occurred. The creativity of the Italians would accordingly be transferred from the phallus to machinery.

It is an odd notion, which I believe to be flatly contradicted by the numerous contributions made by the Italians to science which I have already analysed. Whether phallic worship has diminished since he wrote I cannot determine.

Pleasure-loving, the Italians definitely are, but does that mean that other avenues of fulfilment must be closed to them? Herein I believe lies a misconception on the part of northern races generally. Dedication to the senses and to science are by no means mutually exclusive; dedication to science and not to the senses need not of itself produce better results. It is obviously a fact of life that the greater effort one puts into any activity, the more successful one is: hence the proverbial success in teaching by people in holy orders of one form or the other, who in theory would not be distracted by commitments to family, to the senses or to society.

But that goes to the world outside the individual: what about the world inside? Are people who dedicate the whole of their life to scientific research, to the total or almost total exclusion of the pleasure of the senses, any happier, more interesting, more fulfilled or more complete persons? I wonder.

Pleasure-loving certainly, but not romantic. I have already tried to make the point that it is a total misconception to assume that Italians are romantic. The whisperings of sweet nothings into a young girl's ear are not the fruit of romantic temperament; they are merely a natural, instinctive reaction to basic needs and to a violent demand for satisfaction of one's desires. They are means to an end and are not motivated by any particular spiritual feeling or dissatisfaction or by an over-excited sensitivity or tension of the soul. Anything but that: the hot Mediterranean sun burns the mists of romanticism and mysticism away and, in any event, the Italians are far too old and cynical even in their youth to be able ever to be truly romantic.

The reality is completely different. An Italian is incapable of considering as novel and extraordinary something as basic as the relationship with a person of the opposite sex. That somewhat exciting but essentially naive approach is left to the northerners who enjoy suffering, who tend to be physically and emotionally impotent, and ultimately ashamed of themselves and of their emotions.

The average Italian is not ashamed of being himself. Indeed, he tries on occasions so hard to be himself that he becomes a bore. And because he is who he is, it is, on the whole, of brief duration. This concept holds good for everything an Italian indulges in, simple or complicated, routine or exceptional; but it is especially true of his relationship with woman.

An Italian man cannot look at a woman for too long still thinking that she is unique. She may be unique when he first singles her out as the object of his attentions; but not after she has responded. The only Italian I can recall who could do that was Petrarca; and it is interesting to note that he was particularly successful in England; he was liked by Chaucer, admired and followed almost to distraction by Sir Philip Sydney and literally copied by Milton, Shelley and Wordsworth. But he was a very exceptional Italian. Exceptional in his style, his appreciation of woman and his patriotic fervour. Over 600 years ago, he was already moaning about the 'moral wounds that one saw so frequent in the fair body of our mother country, Italy'. His predecessor, Dante, who died in 1321 when Petrarca was seventeen, also had a similar outlook: but then, he really stared straight through Beatrice and he, too, in that respect at least, was not typically Italian, since when an Italian looks at a woman he mentally undresses her.

But let no-one with knowledge of psychiatry assume for a moment that this characteristic is a manifestation of psychical onanism. Far from it. It is merely a consequence of having a practical mind, and a concrete approach to matters sexual. There is both a spiritual and a practical value to nakedness. The spiritual one is related to beauty, the practical one to hygiene. Insofar as an Italian looks upon woman as a chattel, he wishes to inspect her in the same way as he would examine the teeth of a horse he is about to buy.

Feminists will no doubt resent this observation. But I have little doubt that if more men when choosing a wife, or women picking a husband, exercised the same care as a stockman in selecting a calf, the chances of disagreement or dissatisfaction at a later date would be greatly reduced – even more so, I would add, if prospective spouses both have a medical.

Against such background, one must reach the conclusion that the reason for all this is basic egoism, for Italians cannot as a rule ascribe outstanding attributes to any person, as that would be tantamount to admitting that there exists apart from themselves another extraordinary human being; and that, for an Italian, is impossible. That is also the reason why we consider ourselves better than the next man: as I have said, why we are not prepared to have a disc-jockey tell us what records we should listen to; why, despite our Catholic faith, we do not really love our neighbour. Individually, we all think like the boxer, Mohammed Ali: 'I'm the greatest.'

Romanticism goes with misty skies and damp climates; the former force one to hope constantly for a brighter outlook and the latter provoke a certain amount of physical impotence. Neither feature is Italian.

We are transparently Roman in culture and Mediterranean in outlook.

4
THE RENAISSANCE OF ITALY

It is taking Italy a long time to eliminate the historical differences and imbalances between north and south, which have a tendency to persist. But substantial progress is being made, and I have no hesitation in recording that a common trait of this greater unification is the new technological advance that can be seen in the ever increasing successes of Italian fashion, furniture, machinery and equipment which are being marketed throughout the world. That Italy should be at the forefront in these fields is no news: I have already remarked on the novelty of some of the ideas which have tempted people to steal from it. But what must be remembered above all is that Italian designers are today's artists. Without theorizing, without purporting to belong to any particular school or to be bound by any aesthetic code, the Italian designer proceeds with the strength of the beautiful things which he has seen all his life, by which he has been surrounded in his home town, which he has appreciated in the houses, the museums and the streets that he has frequented; he proceeds to build functional objects in a natural and spontaneous manner.

The Italian designs with the same ease as Giotto did when tending his sheep; his Cimabue, however, is not his master in the art but the manufacturer/entrepreneur who looks upon art as a means to an end rather than an end in itself. This is regrettable, but inevitable; even so, there is art in what the Italian designers create and that is why they are unique. They are to industrial design generally what the artists of the Renaissance were to architecture, painting and sculpture.

It will be clear from what I have already said that I do not accept the somewhat facile argument that is often put forward to the effect that whatever contribution the Italians may have made and whatever impact or influence they may be said to have had on the rest of the world in centuries past, there is very little left that they can give.

In the first place, it seems to me that the survival ability of the Italians is worthwhile considering and, maybe, even adapting to the new economical and social requirements in which Britain, amongst other advanced industrialized countries, finds itself. Inasmuch as Britain can no longer rest on its laurels and is forced to compete with the remainder of Europe and the world in the market place, it is developing certain traits and a certain approach to life which I for one would call typically Italian. The need for greater inventiveness, more personal initiative, a certain amount of aggressiveness and, in the business world if not in the personal one, some sailing rather close to the wind, are becoming fairly accepted manifestations of a new way of tackling the problems of modern British society. Necessity is, as usual, the mother of invention; Italians have been living under its yoke for centuries.

In the second place, one has only to walk through any of the streets in the centre of London to see how many images or echoes of Italy and things Italian are to be found everywhere and not merely in the Palladian architecture of its principal buildings.

Without mentioning names, it is only too easy to see the numerous shops that sell Italian goods, from clothes to handbags, from shoes to furniture. Some of them are already household names. And it simply will not do to argue that London is a cosmopolitan city and therefore everybody is represented here. I can think of at least one household name whose shop facias adorn buildings as far north as Edinburgh and Inverness.

But one does not even have to go as far as Scotland. Macclesfield, an English town if ever there was one, can boast of Arighi Bianchi, a furniture store which has been established there since the middle of the nineteenth century in a building of exceptional architectural interest. Antonio Arighi had come to what was then (1850) a thriving silk town from his native Lombardy, went into partnership with Antonio Bianchi and was the founder of a family dynasty in the furniture business which continues to this day.

One of the major modern suppliers of optical instruments is a firm founded by two Italians and still carrying their names. The head of the cardio-thoracic unit at Hammersmith Hospital at the time I am writing is an Italian. A Professor of the University of Turin is at the forefront in the study of cancer (experimenting with protein-thiols molecules). And another Professor at the University of Siena is an authority in the field of oncology on the biochemical damage caused to cells by another type of molecules known as free radicals. An Italian lecturer at University College London is also internationally known for her studies on protein-thiols.

In the field of entertainment, the Italian influence is exceptionally prominent. Leaving aside the sphere of more serious and classical music where the names – one thinks of Toscanini, Caruso, Gigli and Gobbi – are too numerous to record and going on to the field of more popular entertainment generally where the names are perhaps better known – at random, and in no particular order of merit because some of the following are more worthwhile than others, one can think of Semprini, Mantovani, John Bennett, Greta Scacchi, Paola Dionisotti, Katie Boyle, Tom Conti, Bobby Darren, Connie Francis, Madonna, Frankie

Vaughan, Henry Mancini, Dean Martin, Vic Damone, Frank Sinatra, Perry Como, Don Ameche – all of them Italian. One can see how the Italian ability to provide the kind of entertainment the public wants has found a fairly natural outlet in the Anglo-Saxon world. Furthermore, Margaret Thatcher's champion female entrepreneur, Anita Roddick, is also Italian.

And there are many others whose claims in the scientific field are of greater importance, albeit less well known, than those of the multifarious establishments that dispense spaghetti, pizza and other pasta dishes; these latter are by no means to be underrated since their influence has in many respects been much more profound than the superficial consumption of food may show. It has run somewhat deeper and has altered habits. Indeed, one could make a very good case for saying that the eating habits of the entire population of Britain have changed as a result of Italian influence. Habits not only in terms of the quality and type of food but of the times it which that food is taken. Eating times are no longer the same in Britain, particularly for the last meal of the day: very few people nowadays have the traditional high tea and very many have dinner at hours later than 7 pm.

And how family menus have changed as well. Dishes with Italian names that were unknown before the Second World War are now established in the kitchen vocabulary and folklore of the proverbial man on the Clapham omnibus who would be just as pleased as the next man (or woman) to enjoy a quick snack of lasagne and a glass of red wine for lunch. This would have been unthinkable say thirty years ago: beans on toast, eggs and bacon, pork pie, you name it; and lasagne? and a glass of red wine? certainly not.

I have so far been concerned primarily with England and the English as well as Britain as a whole. But the Italians are coming to the fore in other countries as well. However, before leaving England, let us not forget that an Italian now sits in the House of Lords – Lord Forte.

But elsewhere in the world the construction of chemical, petrochemical and multifarious engineering works and dams, from North Africa to Brazil, from the Middle East to India, and especially in Third World countries has, over the past twenty years, seen an increasing contribution by Italians. In America, for example, where since the beginning of the century Italian talents have been channelled all too often into criminal activities, one has witnessed in recent years a redirection of effort, almost a rehabilitation of the name of Italy by those Americans of Italian origin who are beginning to stake a claim in spheres of society and in activities somewhat higher than the humble, but necessary and pleasure-giving dispensing of food. Greater social mobility has led to increased flexibility of outlook, so that we have had a successful and fearless public prosecutor of the Mafia (Giuliani), the head of a major conglomerate (Iacocca), and a Judge of the Supreme Court (Scalia), all Italians.

At home, terrorism and organized crime are by no means defeated yet but the authority of the State has emerged strengthened from the war waged against the Red Brigades, the Mafia and the Camorra. But I believe that there is a more important and totally different way in which Italy is experiencing a new renaissance; it is a renaissance of culture of an entirely different kind. Despite the shift away from it in economic and political terms, there is no reason whatsoever why the Mediterranean should not become once more the centre of human activitiy. I believe it was E. M. Forster who wrote that 'the Mediterranean is the norm'. He meant it no doubt in the sense that the Mediterranean represented a cultural and artistic medium which served to balance out, as far as he was concerned, England and India, the East and the West, the two poles of his being.

There is today a wider meaning to Forster's words. The cradle of modern Western civilization may yet be able to show that it can also be its custodian, that it can act as a mediator between northern Europe and America on one side and the remainder of the world on the other. At least, in the political sense, if in no other, the Mediterranean may well prove capable of reconciling the differences between the ex-colonial powers and African countries. And if you look at the map of the Mediterranean, which country better than Italy can represent the focus of that activity?

What is the reality in which northern people live? They live in conditions which are hardly enjoyable, have had to adapt to totally false and artificial standards, and have to struggle with an atrocious climate.

In this climate, they have little choice but to pursue material gain and the true test of their success must be the acquisition of money. Material wealth is their primary aim. It is their bank balance and not their spiritual or physical happiness which takes priority.

But can this really be the lot of humanity? Can it be right that we should expend our energy and our vital efforts adequately to house ourselves and our families in order to keep up with the Joneses? What we do ultimately is to sacrifice our life on what is obviously the wrong altar. We may have performed our duties to our families and to our society by today's standards, but what about our duties to ourselves? Should we not be searching for happiness rather than material gain, for spiritual self-satisfaction rather than smugness? This is probably a dream, but it is a dream where the Italians still have something to say. After all, have we not reminded the world of what sweet life is all about? Taking yesterday, one has only to think of the fascination of the Grand Tour. It is easy to see why it was so necessary, and so successful. It was a combination of a release from one's background and an assault on one's senses that occurred crossing the Italian border.

The release was endorsed by the change in climate, in language and in the facial expressions of the locals. The assault was both visual and aural. It started with the beauty of the Alps, it continued with the charm of the valleys and was heightened by the abundance of villas, churches and paintings. It started as a manifestation of the beauty of nature and it ended in a glorification of the aesthetic sense of man. Wherever the visitor turned, he saw what he had come to see, and was not disappointed. The musicality of the language, ranging from the 'cantilena' type of speech along the Po valley to the more refined and yet aggressive jargon of Tuscany, to the vulgarity and solidity of the Roman dialect, and the suavity of the Neapolitan idiom, ended in the subdued, softly uttered and yet threatening Sicilian speech. This assault has continued in the twentieth century and in the Italy of today. The dialects have either mellowed or disappeared, at any rate in the major centres, but the visual impact is still far from negligible. True, the countryside has been spoilt by the erection in a haphazard and wholly inappropriate manner of advertising hoardings that litter the landscape to a degree which is a national disgrace. True, motor vehicle traffic is threatening and sometimes killing the heart of the principal cities, although that is a curse common to the whole of the modern world. But some of the displays are even more dazzling, artificial though they are, than they were one or two centuries ago, and not to be found elsewhere in Europe.

The visitor is pleasantly shocked by the elegant window displays. In any food shop that he may pass or enter, the abundance of products is truly amazing. Sometimes the arrangements are gargantuan; legs of pork, hams, on and off the bone, cheeses of all lengths, shapes, sizes, colours, stacked one on top of the other, sometimes in pyramidal form, other times at random, but always with a visual impact, an orgy of food if not of bodies. The presentation techniques in Italian food shops are unrivalled. Even if you walk in on a full stomach, you suddenly feel temptation and perhaps even pangs of hunger.

This is continued at the greengrocers'. The choice is again probably the widest in Europe but it is the way in which what is for sale is displayed that catches the eye. A box of fennel will be placed next to dark red lettuce, a bright yellow endive next to radishes, multi-coloured peppers all mixed together. The eye is tempted even where the purse is inadequate. And the displays actually walk out of the shop, almost as though they felt that they had to find more room on the pavement, almost as if the boxes of fruit wished to embrace the passer-by in a pleasurable clasp.

Even if you are in a hurry and you pop into one of the many bars (too many: are there any other countries in the world where there are as many cafes and snack bars as in Italy?); even if you walk into one of these establishments, the choice of rolls, sandwiches, the movement and vivacity of people, the gesticulating and the noise, above all the noise: they all conspire to create a picture of life that is unique in colour, sound and smells.

If you are in search of a little respite and enter one of the many churches (and how many: is there any other country in the world that has as many churches as Italy?), the peace you will find is again a voluptuous one. Gone is the coldness of the northern Gothic. Apart from the few examples of dignified Romanic style, it is the Baroque which prevails. The church is full; full of statues, pictures, votive items, candles. The representations of the saints in statues or paintings seem more human than elsewhere; they almost seem less saintly.

Clearly these are monuments to a God who is not to be found in the skies but on earth, a robust God, almost as Michelangelo painted him, a God tolerant of human foibles as no other God could be. A human God, a God, if the statement is not blasphemous, who loves a good table. A God of style and beauty.

Just as in the Renaissance we set the cultural tone and we taught the world the fashion by which they should learn to live, so I believe that we can still teach the world how to preserve its sanity amidst the chaos that so-called progress and mass-communications has brought about.

Where else can we look for guidance? Can you with any degree of conviction mention any nation in the world who can claim to have made a greater contribution to happiness than that of Italy? I am not considering either political or economic leadership, but merely feeling for life.

I do not wish to be carried away on any great wave of enthusiasm for Italy which I am only too well aware also has problems. But if I am a nationalist at all, which I doubt, I am a cultural and not a political one.

I quite see the many obstacles that Italy has to overcome: our total lack of civic sense, antiquated civil and criminal procedures, poverty, slums and backwardness let alone illiteracy in the south, our constitutional inability to pull together, our chaotic institutions, a primitive bureaucracy, a medieval outlook on political life, servilism and obsequiousness to those in authority or those who can be of use or from whom favours are expected (the modern equivalent of the kissing of hands of yesteryear), our exasperated individualism, lack of discipline, inconstancy, moodiness and envy for those with ability that forces many of our better men (musicians, artists, film directors, or whatever) to go abroad for recognition, our disrespect for those in uncorrupted authority. All these are enormous problems and we have to face them. But the Italians are not alone with problems.

I repeat, I'm only concerned with happiness. Few Italians can teach anyone civic sense, political efficiency, militarism, organization, or respect for authority. These qualities, even where they exist, may make for a comfortable life in society, but of themselves they do not contribute to happiness. They have not prevented our social order from being distinguished by violence, drug-taking, contempt for life, disregard of old age, disinterest in those worse off than ourselves, lust for money and power, sexual abuse.

I have to say, too, that generally speaking, an Italian is not easy to please; and, I know, generally speaking, he is not too happy about his lot either. He is most unhappy with his country, about which he is always complaining. He is dissatisfied with the way it is run and says it is ruined. He moans about his politicians, his bureaucrats, his diplomatic representatives, the police and everything else around him for, with some justification, he believes that he deserves better than he is being given.

He looks around himself caught in, say the Rome rush-hour traffic, considers the increased number of violent robberies, thinks of how sycophantic he has to be to preserve his employment and how subservient to those in authority if he wants to achieve anything, how long he has to wait in a queue in a government office to obtain a certificate which is said to be necessary before even the slightest administrative step can be taken. He hears with disgust the news of the poor and the weak who are being tried for petty or non-existent offences when the big and powerful get away with siphoning funds abroad in breach of exchange-control regulations and, literally, with murder. He wonders what is happening to the world when the rate of incest and child abuse is on the increase even in Italy (let alone England): and he feels totally helpless.

He then has to comfort himself and he does so in a field where nobody can interfere and where his artistic and aesthetic perceptions are allowed their full rein: he cooks and he eats. This is not to say that he himself does the cooking; he may or he may not. His mother may, or his mother-in-law or his wife, assuming that there are still any Italian wives left who are willing to cook, or his sister or his friends. It does not matter. The point is there is spontaneous comfort found in the notion that we shall all go out and have a nice meal at some restaurant, if we can, or we shall all meet at someone's home where we 'shall have ourselves a banquet'. It is in food that the Italian gets his own back over the misfortunes that he thinks are hitting him and where his true nature comes to the fore.

And quite right too. Tell me what you eat and I shall tell you what you are has become an English idiom; it is so true. And need we be reminded that Italians eat the best food in the world?

5
IN CONCLUSION

I trust that by now the reader who started out somewhat sceptical, may have come round to the view that the contributions made by the Italians in all fields of knowledge and human activity are very substantial indeed. As I indicated in the Introduction, I need to remind the reader of the inescapable fact that, from the moment we wake up until we go to bed, there is no way in which we can ignore what the Italians have contributed. The validity of my statement can be tested this way:

If your alarm clock wakes you up, it is because of the Italian development of horology. If your radio is on, then you owe it to Volta who discovered electricity and to Marconi who developed radio wavelengths.

I have already recorded the invention of the handkerchief and 'eau de Cologne', two pleasant adjuncts to good appearance and manners. Equally, I have said enough about the contribution of the Italians to the motor car. If you are using one to get to work. Stuck on a motorway or expressway somewhere? Think of the first 'Autostrada'. Similarly, if you buy a morning paper or read a paperback, Italians were there first.

When it comes to food, whether or not you accept my view that, if you eat anything worth eating, it must be Italian, and leaving on one side the ever increasing popularity of the espresso or cappuccino coffee, it is a fact that, unless you use your hands, you owe it to the Italians that a fork enables you to rise to a higher level of social behaviour.

If in your spare time you tend to your garden, or go to the theatre, ballet, bowling or to the circus, Italians were there first. If you are interested in the weather, consider that the barometer, the thermometer and the hygrometer are Italian inventions.

Apart from cricket and soccer, many of the hobbies you might indulge in, like gaming, horse-riding, mountain-climbing, or anything artistic, have been influenced by what the Italians have done. Our contributions to music and art are enormous; and matchless. Our sense of beauty and style is unique. If you are a student, then, whatever your subject, we have made a major contribution to it, be it art, economics, law, metallurgy, medicine, music, physics, or whatever.

Dropping in at the club on your way home? Do not forget Francesco Bianco, who founded White's of London, and our invention of playing cards. Using a computer? Do not forget our invention of the microprocessor. But perhaps, having reached this far, you are getting tired and bored by my reminders, and you think you ought to go to bed with, depending on your tendencies, a good book (which you may have borrowed from a Public Library – Italians established the first) or a good partner.

Quite right too. But even there you will not escape the Italians.

First of all, if you are heeding the present-day prophylactic advice, you will not have forgotten about the condom that was a seventeenth-century Italian invention. Secondly, it is now time to propound Barone's law: in bed, the Italians are supreme. Ha! There he goes again, you will be saying to yourself, adding that whatever I may have stated before which I could prove, this time I am certainly in the wrong and cannot make my point. Italian men or women cannot be better than any other. Perhaps. But *I* am not so sure. Let us take the men first.

I realize that the myth of the Latin Lover is said to be now exploded: hardened feminists have seen to that. The Latin Lover is a Gigolo who is not exciting and who expects too much. Budding Casanovas please note: all men are the same. Untrue. Generally speaking (in this particular context I am referring to men of my generation – early 50s. . .) the Italian male, especially the southern Italian, knows better than most how to make a woman feel grand. Proof, however, is a different matter.

It has always fascinated me to consider that although Italians are very well aware of their ability in this field and when talking to one another and comparing it to that of other nationalities, they need little convincing that they are justified in believing it to be great, they seem exceedingly shy of making a public point of it. Is this because of the difficulties of proof? I quite accept that any such superiority is not something that is capable of easy verification. Leaving aside mind-boggling competitions, one cannot very conveniently test ability in the bedroom with the same ease as one has, for example, a wine-tasting or a football match. But the matter goes a little further, I believe, since it is not an ability that can be determined by all and sundry: like the appreciation of a fine claret or burgundy, or a good artistic performance, it can only be left to the initiated and the experienced. Any comment passed on it by those who do not have the age and knowledge of the world to make an actual comparison, is worthless.

It seems to me that the only people who can actually decide the point I am making, apart from the Italians themselves who have already reached a conclusion about it, are experienced women in their early forties or older. The judgement of no other person has any value in this context.

Have you ever noticed how Italian men look at women? Their look is not hesitant or sly or out of the corner of an eye as though something forbidden were about to happen. It is open, direct, almost indecent in a sense, as though the man had spent the night before with the woman who is being stared at. It is, on the one hand, confident, eager, full of anticipation and expectation; or on the other, critical, disappointed, disinterested without in any way being neglectful. It says, depending on the circumstances: 'I am interested, what next?' or 'I am not interested, but it is not your fault.' Indeed, it is my firm belief that one can always recognize an Italian, in a restaurant or at a party or in any public place, by the way he looks at a woman. The process of exciting her starts early. I go further and say that Italians themselves recognize one another quite often in this particular way.

Equally significant is the manner in which an Italian will talk to a woman. For example, entertaining her across a two-seater dining table in an intimate restaurant, an Italian will normally lean slightly forward, displaying a gentle, constant, confident smile, his voice vibrating with real, or feigned interest.

Am I being too imaginative or perhaps too naïve? I do not think so. This kind of Italian look makes certain women cringe; and those who react in this way probably do not deserve to be looked at in the first place. For the real woman, however, that look has a totally different effect: it makes her feel wanted and feminine; it justifies all the trouble she has taken about her appearance and attire; it provides the inner satisfaction that is transferred to her face and to her limbs. It causes a glow to develop on her cheeks, a more jaunty step, a shrug of the head and the mane to come about. It makes her day, even if nothing else should happen; it creates well-being in her body and happiness in her soul. That male look is part of the same ability, if not destiny, of the Italians to give pleasure; it is to the heart what good food is to the stomach and beauty to the eye: it is part of the Italian tradition and of the mystique of the Mediterranean.

I admit that it is sometimes impertinent and, if used by ill-mannered or insensitive persons, rude and intrusive. But there are two sides to every coin. The patent admiration of and desire for women in turn makes woman herself more conscious of her attractions and consequently more desirable. This desirability in turn provokes desire so that a circle is established which makes both man and woman happy, at least for the time being. And on the basis that one should grasp happiness where one finds it, this is not a bad idea after all.

Such an approach to woman starts in the Italian family where the mother is queen and is developed within a society where women are neither segregated nor neglected. It is a concomitant of the fact that the stag party as an institution does not exist in Italy, any more than all-male clubs do, any more than that, after dinner, Italian women are expected to leave the room whilst the port is passed round. In a similar context, an Italian youth is just as likely to go to a football match with one or more girlfriends as he is to have an outing there with the boys.

Against this background, the presence and importance of a woman, the feeling that she radiates, is taken for granted by Italians from a very early age. They do not grow up either ignorant or terrified of her as sometimes happens in more emotionally restrained and scientifically progressive countries; and this is the reason why they are not at all concerned when, more frequently nowadays, they come across a confident woman eager to assert her newly-recognized rights and independence in social and sexual terms.

One final consideration which is of some significance. Until recently, Italian men have not had any tendency to over-indulge as far as alcohol is concerned. Northerners, on the contrary, seem to enjoy drunkenness; and that spells doom for their sexual life. To that extent, if to no other, Italians enjoy the inbuilt physical advantage of not having their sexual performance weakened by drink.

Let me conclude. It is my belief that we are witnessing a new renaissance in Italy. It is partly a technological revival and partly a spiritual and psychological one. In the first place, the country has begun to recognize that, after over forty years of democratic republicanism, it has got closer together than it ever was. It used to be said that the Calabrians (from the south) resembled the Greeks, the Romans resembled nobody, the Tuscans were like the Etrurians and the northern Italians on the whole were very much like the Austrians and the Germans. I do not think that any of these facile explanations are acceptable today and there is certainly no scientific evidence to support them.

It is a fact that until recently no real attempt has been made to unify the people of Italy. The Roman Empire ignored any kind of fusion: all it did was provide the people with a common language and a common culture.

Some traits have remained, others have been added, but it is on the whole not too easy to look at the question in historical terms. The only historical statement that can safely be made is to say that the movement of labour from the south of Italy to the north that has taken place since the early 1950s – and the intermarrriages between southerners and northerners that have been the result of this migration – are beginning to break down the centuries-old economic, cultural and psychological differences between the two halves of Italy and are becoming a major factor in a greater unification, in political and social terms, of the peninsula as a whole.

I was forgetting. We Italians are also modest. . .

A RANDOM LIST

of

Italian Words/Expressions
which have been incorporated
into the English language

(Derivatives are not given)

À battuta, abbozzo, a bene-placito, abeyance, a buon fresco, a cappella, accelerando, acqua forte, adagio, aggiornamento, agio, agiotage, agitato, alarm, alberello, al dente, al fresco, alert, alla breve, alla marcia, alla prima, allargando, allegretto, allegro, alta moda, alto, alto relievo, altruism, amaretto, ambiente, amoretto, amorino, ambassador, ambuscade, ancona, andante, andantino, ante-chamber, antic, antipasto, appoggiatura, aquatint, a quattr'occhi, arabesque, arcade, archill, argosy, aria, arietta, arioso, a rivederci, arpeggio, arricciato, arsenal, artist, a secco, a tempo, attitude, autostrada, avanti, aventurine, average, avocet, azione, bagatelle, baggage, bagnio, baguette, balcony, baldachino, baldaquin, ballerina, ballet, balloon, ballot, balustrade, bambino, bamboozle, banderolle, bandit, bankrupt, banquette, barb, barcarolle, bass, basset-horn, basso, basso all'ottava, basso continuo, bassoon, basso ostinato, basso profundo, basso relievo, bastion, beato, beccafico, bel canto, belladonna, belvedere, ben trovato, bergomas, berretta, bersagliere, bezonian, bianco-sopra-bianco, biennale, biretta, bomb, bombardon, bonaroba, bordello, bosquet, bottega, bozzetto, brave, bravo, bravura, breccia, brigade, brigand, brio, broade, brocade, brocatel, broccoli, brothel, bulletin, buffo, bumbo, buon fresco, burla, burlesque, bust, cabriolet, cadence, cadenza, calabrese, calando, calepin, cambist, cameo, campanile, campo santo, cannelloni, cantabile, cantata, cantatrice, canteen, cantilena, canto, canto fermo, canzonet, capocchia, capo d'opera, cappuccino, capriccio, caprice, capuche, carabiniere, carafe, carbine, caricature, carnival, carroza, cartel, cartellino, carton, cartoon, cartouche, casa, cascade, casemate, casino, cassone, castrato, cavalcade, cavalletti, cavaliere servente, cavatina, cavo rilievo, cedilla, cesspool, chalet, charlatan, che sara sara, chiaroscuro, chipolata, ciao, cicerone, cicisbeo, cinquecento, cipollata, cipollino, citadel, clarinet, clausura, coda, cognoscente, col legno, colonel, colonnade, coloratura, column, commedia dell'arte, commedietta, con amore, con brio, concert, concertante, concerto, concerto de chasse, concerto grosso, condottiere, confetti, con fuoco, con moto, con sordina, con spirito, contadino, continuo, contrabass, contrabassoon, contralto, contrapposto, contrapunctual, contrast, conversazione, coralline, cornice, corporeal, corridor, cortile, counterscarp, courier, courteous, courtesan, courtesy, coward, credenza, credit, crenate, crescendo, cunette, cupola, curvet, czarina, da capo, dal segno, dantesque, del credere, desco da parto, dilettante, diligente, diminuendo, diocletian, ditto, diva, divertimento, doge, dolce far niente, dolce stil nuovo, dolce vita, dome, domino, dramma per (la) musica, duce, duecento, duello, duet, duo, doumo, eppur si muove, escarp, escarpment, esplanade, espresso, extravaganza, faience, falsetto, fantasia, fantoccini, fardel, fascism, fata morgana, favourite, felucca, (de-)fenestration, ferraiuolo, festa, festa teatrale, festoon, fianchetto, fiasco, finale, finita la commedia, fioritura, flask, flauto d'eco, florin, folio, fondo d'oro, forte, forte piano, fortissimo, fracas, francolin, fresco (al), fresco secco, fritto misto, fumarola, furore, fustanella, gabbro, gaberdine, gala, galantuomo, galvanometer, gambade, gambit, gambo, gambol, gazette, gelatine, generalissimo, gesso, gesso grosso, gesso sottile, ghetto, giallo antico, girasol, glissando, gondola, gonfalon, gouache, govern, grade, gradine, graffito, grain, granite, (il) gran rifuto, gran turismo, grappa, grateful, grissini, grit, gross, grottesca, grotto, group, guache, guard, guardian, guide, guidon, guitar, gusto, harlequin, harmonica, hippogriff, hussar, illuminato, imbroglio, impassion, impaste, impasto, impost, impresario, imprest, imprimatura, improvise, inamorato/a, incarnate, incarnadine, incognito, inferno, influenza, in petto, in secco, inquest, insieme, intaglio, intarsiatura, intarsio, intermezzo, intonaco, intrigue, irredentist, isolated, istoriato, Italian irredenta, italic, jalousie, jargon, jargoon, jeans, joint, journey, lace, lagoon, lancespesade, large, larghetto, largo, lasagne, lasciate ogni speranza voi ch'entrate, latticinio, lava, lavoro di commesso, lazar, lazaretto, lazzarone, legato, leghorn, lento, lettuce, libretto, lido, lingua franca, liquorice, lira, lira organizzata, literati, loggia, lombard, lottery, luce di sotto, lumachella, macaroni, macaroon, macchia, machiavellian, madonna, madrigal, maestá, maestoso, maestrale, maestro, maestro di cappella, mafia-mafioso, magazine, magenta, magnifico, maiolica, malaria, malgre, malvasia (grape), mandolin, mandoria, manganese, manierista, manieroso, manifesto, manilla, mantua, manufacture, maraschino, marchesa, marconigram, maremma, marina, marinate, mark, maroon, martini, martini (rifle), martellato, martello, marzipan, mascherone, mask, masque, masquerade, matrimonio segreto, medal, messa di voce, mesto, mezzanine, mezza voce, mezzo relievo, mezzo soprano, millefiori, millinery, minestrone, minus, modello, monarch, monarcho, monsignore, monte di pietá, mora, morbidezza, morello (cherry), morte lenta, morticing, moto perpetuo, motoscafo, motto, moustache, muff, muslin, neapolitan, nepotism, neroantico, niche, niello, novel, novella, nunciature, nuncio, obbligato, ocarina, opera, opera buffa, opera seria, operone, oratorio, organzine, osteria, ostinato, ossobuco, ottava rima, padre, padrone, palazzo, palette, palladian, palliasse, palmetto, panache, panatella, pantalets, pantaloon, pantoffle, papabile, paparazzo, paragon, parakeet, parapet, parasol, parlante, parmesan, parmigiana, partisan, pasquinade, passacaglia, passeggiata, pasta, pastel, pasticcio, patch, patina, pedal, pedant, pedestal, pellagra, pentimento, pergola, perito, peruque, pianissimo, piano, pianoforte, piano nobile, piazza, piccola morte, piccolo, pietá, pietra commessa, pietra dura, pistol, pizza, pizzicato, poco curante, podere, podesta, polenta, policy, poltroon, porcelain, porcheria, portamento, portfolio, portico, portolano, predella, prestissimo, presto, prima ballerina, prima ballerina assoluta, primadonna, propaganda, prosciutto, proviso, punch, punctilio-lious, puntypo, putto, quadratista, quadratura, quarantine, quartette, quartetto, quarto, quattrocento, quietism, rallentando, ravelin, ravioli, recitative, recitativo secco, regatta, replica, ricercare, ridotto, rifacimento, rilievo, rima chiusa, rinzaffato, riot, ripieno, risorgimento, risotto, ritardando, ritenuto, ritornello, riviera, robusto, rochet, rosso antico, rubato, rubicon, ruffian, safflower, salami, salsify, saltarello, salto mortale, salvo, sardine, sbirro, scagliola, scaldino, scallopine, scalpellino, scampi, scarce, scarlatina, scarp, scena, scenario, scene, scenic, scherzando, scherzo, schiacciato rilievo, scirocco, scugnizzo, secco, sedia gestatoria, seicento, semolina, se non è vero è (molto) ben trovato, sempre, sentinel, sentry, sequin, seraglio, serenade, serenata, sestina, settecento, sforzando, sfumatazza, sfumato, sgraffito, siena, simpatico, sinfonia concertante, sinopia, sirocco, sistine, skat, smalto, socle, soffione, soffit, solfatara, solo, soloist, sonata, sonnet, soprano, sostenuto, sotto in su, sotto voce, spaghetti, spalliere, spolvero, spontoon, sprezzatura, squacco, squad, squadron, staccato, stance, stanza, stiletto, strega, stretto, stringendo, stucco, stucco lustro, studio, sul ponticello, sybaritic, tarantella, tardo, tarsia, tazza, telescope, tempera, tempo, tempo giusto, tempo rubato, tenor, tension, tenuto, termagant, terra cotta, terra-firma, terramare, terrazzo, terribilita, terza rima, tessitura, timpani, tirade, toccata, tombola, tondo, tontine, torso, traduttore traditore, traject, tramontano, trattoria, trecento, tre corde, triennale, trill, trio, trombone, troppo, trump, tuba, tufa, tuff, tuffa, tufo, tutti, tutti frutti, umber, umbrella, una corda, uomo universale, vaporetto, vedette, veduta, veduta ideata, vedutista, velatura, vendetta, venetian, verde antico, verismo, vermicelli, vermilion, vertu, vibrato, vogoroso, villa, villanelle, villeggiatura, villino, viola, violin, violinist, violoncello, violone, virtu, virtuoso, vista, vita nuova, vitellone, vogue, volcano, volt, volta, zabaglione, zabaione, zany, zingaro, zucchetto.

Short Bibliography

ASCHAM, Roger, *The Schoolmaster*. London: John Daye, 1570. *The Schoolmaster*. Edited by Lawrence V. Ryan 1967

ASHBY, Thomas, *Some Italian Scenes and Festivals*. London: Methuen, 1929

BARZINI, Luigi, *The Italians*. London: H. Hamilton, 1987

BOCCACCIO, giovanni, *The Decameron*. London: W.W. Norton, 1984

BOURKE, Algernon, *History of White's*. London: Waterlow & Sons, 1892

BRAND, Charles Peter, *Italy and the English Romantics*. Haarlem: Cambridge University Prsee, 1957

BRITTON, Frank, *London Delftware*. London: J. Horne, 1987

BURFORD, E.J., *Royal St. James's*. London: Hale, 1988

BUXTON, John, *Sir Philip Sidney & The English Renaissance*. London: Macmillan, 1987

BYRON, *Don Juan* London: John Murray, 1st two Cantos, 1819, 3-5, 1821, 6-14, 1823, 15 & 16, 1824 (modern edition) Penguin English Poets, 1977

CHANEY, Edward, *The Evolution of the Grand Tour*, Frank Cass, London, 1998.

COLSON, Percy, *'White's' 1693 to 1950*. London: Heinemann, 1951

DIXON-HUNT, John, *Gardens and Groves*. London: Dent, 1986

DIXON-HUNT, John, *'The Wider Sea' (A Life of Ruskin)*. London: Dent, 1982

DOUGLAS, Norman, *Old Calabria*. London: Century, 1983

GOETHE, Johan Wolfgang, *Italian Journey*. London: Penguin, 1970

GUTTERIDGE, Harold Cooke, *Nelson and The Neapolitan Jacobins*. London See Navy Records Soc. Vol. 25, 1894. Edited by H.C. Gutteridge, 1903

HALLIDAY, Frank Ernest, *Illustrated Cultural History of England*. London: Thames & Hudson, 1981

HAWTHORNE, Nathaniel, *The Marble Faun 1860* (also in The Works Vol. 4). Ohio State University Press 1986

HITCHENS, Christopher, *The Elgin Marbles*. London: Chatto & W.: The Hogarth Press, 1987

HUTTON, Edward, *Italy and the Italians*. London: William Blackwood & Sons, 1902. *In Unknown Tuscany*. London: Methuen, 1909. *Why Italian?* Firenze: Tip, Rinaldi, 1934

HUTTON, William, *History of Derby*. London: J&J Robinson, 1971

JOLLY, William, Percy, *Marconi*. London: Constable, 1972

JUCCKER, Ninetta, *Italy*. London: Thames & Hudson, 1970

LEWIS, W.S. (Edotor), *Selected Letters of Horace Walpole*. London: Folio Society, 1951

MACHIAVELLI, Niccoló, *Il Principe*. Numerous editions since 1513. Latest, London: Penguin, 1961

MAYES, Stanley, *The Great Belzoni*. London: Putnam, 1959

MONTANELLI-GERVASO, *Storia d'Italia*. Milan: Rizzoli, 1959-1987

NICCHOLLS, Peter, *Italia, Italia*. London: Macmillan, 1973

PARKS, Tim, *Italian Neighbours*. London: Heinemann, 1992

POCOCK, Tom, *Horatio Nelson*. London: Bodley Head, 1987

RIPA, Cesare, *Iconologia*. London: 'By the care of P. Tempest', 1707

RUSKIN, John, *The Works: Library Ed. (1902-'12)*. Edited by E.T. Cook & A.D.O. Wedderburn. *Mornings in Florence*. Orpington: George Allen, 1899. *Letters To His Parents*. Clarendon Press, Harold Shapiro, 1972

SALVATORELLI, Luigi, *Sommario di Storia d'Italia*. London: G. Allen & Unwin, 1940

SCOTT-FOX, David, *Mediterranean Heritage*. London: Routledge & Kegan Paul, 1978

SELLS, Lytton, *The Italian Influence in english Poetry*. London: G. Allen & Unwin, 1955

SHAPIRO, Harold (Ed.), *Ruskin in Italy*. Oxford: Clarendon Press, 1972

301

STENDHAL, *Rome, Naples & Florence en 1817*. London: Henry Colburn, 1818 or London: John Calder, 1959

STOCKER, Giglioli, *Naples in 1799*. London: John Murray, 1903

STRATHERN, Paul, *The Medici*, London Pimlico, 2005.

SYMONDS, John Addington, *Renaissance in Italy*. 7 Vols. London: Smith Elder & Co, 1875-1886

TREVELYAN, George Macauley, *English Songs of Italian Freedom*. London: Longmans, 1911.
    Englishmen and Italians: Some Aspects of Their Relations Past and Present. London: Humphrey Milford, 1919

TROLLOPE, Anthony, *Travelling Sketches*. London: Reprinted from 'Pall Mall Gazette', 1866

UKERS, William Harrison, *All About Coffee*. New York: Teas & Coffee Trade Journal, 1922

WICKS, Margaret, *The Italian Exiles in London 1816-1848*. Manchester: Manchester University Press, 1937

WILLEY, David, *The Italians*. London: BBC Books, 1984

WILSON, Timothy, *Ceramic Art of Italian Renaissance*. London: British Museum Publications, 1987

Index